HOWARD ZINN

HOWARD ZINN

A Life on the Left

Martin Duberman

THE NEW PRESS

NEW YORK
LONDON

The author and publisher gratefully acknowledge the kind permission granted to reproduce the photographs in this book, many of which were taken decades ago. Every effort has been made to trace each photographer and to obtain his or her permission. The publisher apologizes for any inadvertent errors or omissions and would appreciate being notified of any corrections that should be incorporated in future reprints or editions of this book.

Requests for permission to reproduce selections from this book should be mailed to: Permissions Department, The New Press, 38 Greene Street, New York, NY 10013.

Published in the United States by The New Press, New York, 2012
Distributed by Perseus Distribution

LIBRARY OF CONGRESS CATALOGING-IN-PUBLICATION DATA

Duberman, Martin B.
  Howard Zinn : a life on the left / Martin Duberman.
    p. cm.
  Includes bibliographical references and index.
  ISBN 978-1-59558-678-0 (hc.)
  1. Zinn, Howard, 1922–2010. 2. Historians—United States—
Biography. 3. Zinn, Howard, 1922–2010—Political and social views. I. Title.
  E175.5.Z56D83 2012
  973'.07202—dc23
  [B]
                                                              2012017592

Now in its twentieth year, The New Press publishes books that promote and enrich public discussion and understanding of the issues vital to our democracy and to a more equitable world. These books are made possible by the enthusiasm of our readers; the support of a committed group of donors, large and small; the collaboration of our many partners in the independent media and the not-for-profit sector; booksellers, who often hand-sell New Press books; librarians; and above all by our authors.

www.thenewpress.com

Composition by Westchester Book Composition
This book was set in Janson Text

Printed in the United States of America

2 4 6 8 10 9 7 5 3 1

yet again,
for Eli

Contents

Author's Note

This note isn't designed to introduce or to summarize Howard Zinn's life. I prefer that story to unfold gradually, as the book proceeds.

My intention here is to forewarn the reader on two counts. It's important, first of all, to be upfront about the fact that Howard and I knew each other to an extent (though not well) and largely shared political values, except for his comparative lack of engagement with the feminist and (especially) gay movements. In all other regards, we held common convictions on a wide range of public issues. Our views coincided about the justice of the black struggle and the injustice of the war in Vietnam. We shared admiration—our allegiance shifting back and forth—for both anarchism and socialism. We deplored the entrenched and usually unacknowledged class divisions in this country, the growing monopoly of wealth in the hands of a few, and the arrogance and destruction of U.S. foreign policy. We preferred to teach through dialogue not dictation, and we shared a skeptical view of so-called "objective" history.

Second, those familiar with my earlier biographies will know that my strong inclination is to present a rounded portrait—the private as well as the political, the interior as well as the public life of the subject at hand. This hasn't been as possible as I would have liked with Howard. In the last years of his life, he destroyed nearly everything in his own archives that might have revealed his feelings and his relationships. His clear determination was to pull the veil over the personal side of his life—his marriage, his parenting, his friendships, his affairs. If there was to be any biography, Howard obviously wanted it to be about political, not private, matters.

My own choice would have been to pay considerable attention to both. To concentrate on the public events of a given life is to run the risk of a one-dimensional portrait. And if, further, one agrees with the subject's political perspective (as I mostly do with Howard's), there's the further risk of presenting him as a candidate for sainthood rather than a fallible human being. His political commitments and activities do, of course, tell us something about his temperament and character—but much less about the quality of his relationships or his inner life. I've been able to piece together some semblance of a full portrait through interviews, research into other manuscript collections, and the reminiscences and privately held correspondence that a number of his close friends and colleagues have shared with me (see Note on Sources/Acknowledgments, page 319). But I make no claim, finally, that the personal side of the Zinn story has been captured with as much detail as the political one.

HOWARD ZINN

1

The Early Years

Jennie Rabinowitz's voice is the first to come through distinctly. In a 1973 tape that her son Howie (as family and close friends called him) encouraged her to make when in her midseventies, her heavily accented, strong, and warmly good-humored voice recounts, in jumps and starts, the poverty and oppression that marked her childhood years in the shtetl of Irkutsk, near Lake Baikal in Russia. As for Eastern European Jews, the daily struggle to survive was harsh, though in Irkutsk, most of the Jewish males were soldiers. The suffering and stubborn energy, the deeds and dreams of ordinary Jews that had once filled their individual and communal lives, have left behind few traces—a name, perhaps, mentioned in some yellowing letter, a broken headstone too weathered for the full inscription to be legible.[1]

Jennie's tape recording is far from a sustained account of her life. She starts a story, then abruptly goes back in time to begin another, itself abandoned midway. Only now and then does she pause long enough for at least a shadow outline to emerge. Her unhappy mother, Sophie Grabler, born in Ludmir, Russia, was forced at age fifteen by her own father—he slapped her hard in the face—to marry Isadore Rabinowitz, a soldier twice her age, and ultimately to bear him six children. Only later did Jennie's mother confide to her that the marriage had been miserable (Jennie herself referred to her father as a "no-goodnik"). Furthermore, she bore the disgrace of causing her family's displacement. Shtetl Jews had to register officially every year, but at one point Jennie's father fell ill and he passed the task to his wife, who somehow forgot to do it. As a result, the entire family, on forty-eight hours' notice, was put on a train and forced to leave Irkutsk. They stayed for a year in her mother's childhood shtetl near Kiev (then part of Poland), where Jennie saw trees and ate fresh fruit for the first time. Then Jennie's father and grandparents decided to leave for America, the rest of the family to follow in stages.

In 1909, it was fifteen-year-old Jennie's turn. Accompanied by a brother and sister, they went through the transatlantic ordeal of steerage, mere dots in a massive migration that in the thirty years preceding World War I saw a third of Eastern Europe's Jews leave their various homelands for the New World. The family found cheap living quarters in the back of a barbershop in Williamsburg, Brooklyn. Like so many immigrants, Jennie's father eked out a living dragging a pushcart carrying fruits and vegetables through the streets, while her mother sewed buttons in a garment shop, earning seven or eight dollars a week. Jennie herself, her education having ended in the seventh grade, went to work sewing children's coats by hand in a factory eleven hours a day, six days a week. She proudly recalls that she was "one of the fastest" workers and sometimes took home more than $20 in weekly pay—considered a gigantic sum among the poor.

Better still, she met a handsome, strongly built (Jennie herself was on the sturdy, soft side) fellow factory worker named Eddie Zinn, an immigrant from that part of the Austro-Hungarian Empire now known as the western Ukraine. Eddie, who stood five five, had only a fourth-grade education, but did, unlike Jennie, speak fluent Yiddish (Jennie soon picked it up). Both were warmhearted (though Eddie disliked blacks) and—for some undiscernible reason, given the hardship of their lives—shared a cheerful outlook. The two quickly fell, and throughout their lives remained, in love. Eddie proposed and Jennie, age nineteen, accepted; yet when he failed to curtail his habit of gambling, she broke off the engagement. Eddie got the message, gave up his "hobby," and the two were married in 1918. By then Jennie's mother was dead from TB at the early age of thirty-five, her father had remarried within six months, and, when that wife soon died as well, had remarried again.

Jennie was a quiet person but always direct and forceful when she did speak, confident and grounded; Eddie seemed content to let her rule the roost. Strong-willed—one of her sons has called her "the brains in the family"—she was also "a master of malapropisms"; she would talk of buying "monster cheese" and told a friend about the problems she was having with "very close veins." She would tell Eddie when he forgot something to "try to remember, wreck your brains."

Both had tempers, and now and then a cup would be angrily smashed, but it was understood that no hitting would ever be tolerated, short of a light smack on the behind. Only once would that rule fail. They decided to splurge on a cardboard closet that came with instructions for assembling—unintelligible to them both. Eddie nonetheless was determined to put the closet together and kept trying, with mounting frustration. Jennie kept offering suggestions, all of which failed, making Eddie still more irate. When Jennie said he should bring the damned thing back to the store, Eddie's anger broke and he hit Jennie on the head with one of the pieces of cardboard lying about. Jennie burst into tears. Eddie picked up the scattered pieces of "the closet" and left the house. Matters were soon patched up; the two really were loving soul mates.

Jennie and Eddie moved into a cold-water flat—it did have a coal stove—on Fourth Street in Brooklyn. They also took in Jennie's five siblings who were still single and needed a home (Jennie, the eldest, thought of herself as responsible for them, their primary caretaker). There was no such thing as a living room or a dining area nor, at first, even a bathroom—a washtub in the kitchen served for cleaning both clothes and people. There was a toilet but no sink, bathtub, or shower. Paying for a telephone was, of course, out of the question, but they could be called to the phone at the candy store at the end of the block. For a long time, the family didn't even own a radio—till Eddie finally found a cheap, secondhand one. A literal "ice box" served as a refrigerator: the boys would go down to the "ice dock," buy a five- or ten-cent chunk of ice, drag it home, and put it in a large basin; the melting ice would sometimes overflow during the night, rousing all hands for the wipe-up. Roaches were everywhere, and Howie never got used to them.

Sometimes they were unable to pay the electric bill, which meant that in winter months, when the sun set early, they had to feel their way in the dark. Yet Howie never remembered a time when he felt hungry; the ingenious Jennie always managed to put food on the table. Howie later wrote that the flat was "such a shithouse" that, until he was fourteen, he never brought home a single friend. In the warmer weather, he'd spend as much time as he could in the streets playing handball, softball, and stickball and making friends.

A year after their marriage, Jennie gave birth to their first child, Sonny. Though Jennie usually made the decisions in the family, Eddie firmly announced that he would not allow her to return to work (that is, to the job—unlike motherhood—that paid a salary). A deeply devoted mother, Jennie was terrified when Sonny, at age four and a half, contracted spinal meningitis. He died in Jennie's arms a week later as she was on her way with him to a hospital. A second son, Howie, was born on August 24, 1922, followed in rapid succession by three more sons, Bernie, Jerry, and Shelly. The brothers, a high-spirited, affectionate bunch, always got along well. Beginning in junior high school, Shelly—whom Howie was very fond of—became addicted to heroin, served time in prison, and died in his fifties. When Shelly was in jail, the other brothers were careful not to let Jennie know.

As a child, Howie provided the family with yet another health scare: at age two and a half, he developed rickets, a softening and weakening of the bones due to insufficient vitamin D. The doctor prescribed eating tomatoes and baking in the sun, forbade the child to talk too much or cry or fall, and told Jennie to send the boy to the country. Eddie had by then quit the factory; to make a little more money, he became a waiter (not in a restaurant but for special events, especially Jewish weddings). They rented a room upstate at $60 a summer (it took several before Howie was cured), and Eddie would visit whenever he could get time off from work.[2]

When the Great Depression came, the call for waiters sharply declined, and Eddie picked up hand-to-mouth jobs wherever he could find them, which in winter mostly meant shoveling snow and dragging a pushcart through the streets. During the first week, the pushcart brought in only $7; not wanting her husband to feel bad, Jennie cheerfully pronounced that a good start. Though Eddie loved his children dearly ("Kiss Papa" were usually his first words on arriving home, followed by a bear hug), he could also be tough on them; on one bitterly cold day, he insisted that a youthful Howie go out on the street and try to sell a crate of oranges. Hours later he'd sold all but two.

When the weather turned warmer, Eddie turned to ditch digging and window cleaning; at one point, his worn leather strap broke and he fell off a ladder onto the concrete sidewalk, hurting his back. He couldn't turn to the union for help because he hadn't been able to keep up his membership dues *and* feed his family, so despite the pain he returned to his window-cleaning job the very next day. Many of the Zinns' neighbors during the Depression were unable to meet the rent and stood by helplessly while the landlords piled up their furniture on the sidewalk.

The Zinn family was never evicted, thanks largely to the clever Jennie. It was always a struggle to stay ahead of the bill collectors, but Jennie won the battle with every landlord. She'd take up the offer some of them were being forced to make of a free apartment for a month, would pay the second month's rent, then leave and repeat the pattern. In other words, two months for one month's rent. No matter which cold-water flat they currently occupied, all four boys would share a single bed, sleeping *zu fiesens*—head to toe—to create more room. That would later serve Howard well: he'd be able to sleep anywhere under any conditions—on a hard church floor during the civil rights struggle or on a long flight to Vietnam.

Eddie once found a purse on the street that had keys and about $12 in it. He fought with his conscience for days but then heard that the purse's owner was married to a lawyer and had taken a job away from a poor working-class girl. He pocketed the money and dropped the keys in the woman's mailbox. The family was able to pay for coal and buy the kids some badly needed new shoes. Winter coats were out of range until the WPA provided them for ten or fifteen cents.

As an adult, Howard would sometimes express his anger about how hard his parents had had to work and how little they ever had to show for it; struggle and poverty remained the bookends in lives focused on survival. It taught Howard that—contrary to the foundational American myth that "everyone could, through hard work, pull themselves up by their own bootstraps"—people rarely got what they deserved. He felt he'd been born class conscious and once drew up a list, "What does it mean to be poor?" which read in part:

- bedbug stains in the sheets
- Bellevue hospital
- dental clinic
- selling blood at Lerner's
- no bank account

Jennie and Eddie didn't go to synagogue, didn't read books (but did read the newspapers, and Jennie romance magazines as well), and didn't become politically active (though they worshipped FDR). In those regards, their lives stood in contrast to many of the Eastern

European Jews who settled in large numbers, beginning in the last two decades of the nineteenth century, on Manhattan's Lower East Side. It wasn't simply that the Zinns were focused on survival—so were most Lower East Side Jews. It was more a matter, in comparatively isolated Brooklyn, of not being as exposed to the fervent intensity of Yiddishkeit culture, with its strong ties to religion and learning. The Zinns preferred listening to the radio every night: *The Lone Ranger*, *The Green Hornet*, and *The Shadow*. But early in their marriage, both Jennie and Eddie did go to night school to learn English.

Howie was the one enthusiast in the family for reading and later for politics—but never for religion. His parents noted his difference from the rest of the family and encouraged it. The first book Howie read, *Tarzan and the Jewels of Opar*, he found on the street—with ten pages ripped out. Eddie then bought his son a used copy of *The Reconstruction Period in Louisiana*. Howie eagerly devoured it even though "Reconstruction" rang only the faintest bell in his head—what mattered was that it was a book.

Why only a single member of a family becomes smitten by learning remains a mystery—except to say with certainty that the answer doesn't lie in genetics: there's no identifiable gene that accounts for bookworms. Howie made a clear distinction between learning and school, seeing them as very nearly opposites. As he wryly put it later on, "Thomas Jefferson High School wasn't much of an experience for me educationally," though the principal, a poet named Elias Lieberman, had established a creative writing program, in which Howie learned to write one-page book reviews of everything he read. He sometimes played hooky, using his lunch money to skip the boredom of the classroom and go to a movie or to a Dodgers baseball game (though he was, treasonably, a Giants fan). Even so, his grades were midlevel, his highest in history, his lowest in drawing.

One day Jennie and Eddie saw an ad in the *New York Post* that offered a full set of Dickens for ten cents a volume. They signed up—though the name Dickens meant nothing. The whole set came to twenty volumes, and Howie devoured every single one ("some of them I didn't understand, like *The Pickwick Papers*," he later said). Howard credited Dickens with stirring in him "anger at arbitrary power" and "compassion for the poor." Then, when Howie was thirteen, his parents bought him, for a precious $5, a reconditioned Underwood typewriter, which he used for a very long time. Howie's brothers weren't thrilled with the family bookworm: to gain access to the bathroom (the family now had a primitive one), they'd have to pound on the door to dislodge Howie from his reading sanctuary away from family clutter and noise. In deference to them, he shifted his refuge to a library in East New York, at the corner of Stone and Sutter. To no one's surprise, he was the only one of his brothers to graduate from high school. College never came up; "it was the furthest thing from our minds."

Howie worked after school and held summer jobs from the age of fourteen—making deliveries for a cleaner was typical. Eddie was sometimes able to get his son jobs as a waiter at holidays and weddings, work that Howie hated. To piece out his income further, he sometimes worked as a caddy, though as a result of carrying around the heavy clubs he injured his hip and ended up with one foot an inch shorter than the other. Forced to wear a body cast for six months, he kept up his spirits by listening to baseball games on the radio (he later shifted allegiance to the Boston Red Sox). And he also read a great deal, including some of Karl Marx, who early planted the seeds of his incipient radicalism.[3]

Despite his love of reading, Howie wasn't anything close to a hermit or loner. Far from isolating himself from the life around him, he liked most people and liked being with them. When younger and mostly at home, he loved playing stickball in the streets, tending to hang out with a politically minded group of teenagers several years older than he. By age seventeen, he'd begun to immerse himself in books about fascism, and they led to tentative beginnings as an activist, leafleting laundry workers to encourage them to organize a union.

A few of his friends on the street had already committed themselves to Communism and were fiercely opposed to fascist regimes; one of them left for Spain to fight against Franco. They distributed Marxist literature and discussed politics far into the night. Howie was interested but not committed. When the Soviets invaded Finland, his friends insisted the move had been necessary in order for Russia to protect itself from future attack. But to Howie, "it was a brutal act of aggression." On most other matters, he agreed with his radical friends, sharing their indignation about the gap between poverty and wealth in the United States.

One summer day in 1939, they invited Howie to join them for a demonstration in Times Square. He agreed—after all, he'd never seen Times Square. Handed a banner to carry, Howie didn't even know what was on it. The protesters were orderly and nonviolent, but suddenly, out of nowhere, mounted police charged the demonstrators with clubs. Howie was spun around and hit on the side of his head. He woke up in a doorway with a big lump on his scalp, the crowd gone. The incident made him more—not less—political. He decided that his friends on the street were to some degree right: the government wasn't on the side of the people and our much-touted freedom of speech was in practice sharply curtailed. From that point on, in Howie's own words, "I was no longer a liberal, a believer in the self-correcting character of American democracy. I was a radical, believing that something fundamental was wrong in this country . . . something rotten at the root."

Yet joining the Communist Party had no appeal for him, especially after the Nazi-Soviet pact. Some of his radical friends argued that the Western powers really weren't antifascist. After all, they'd allowed Hitler to take Czechoslovakia. In their thinking, the Soviets were acting out of self-protection in making the pact with Germany; they were really anti-Hitler and simply biding their time. Howie was unimpressed. He never, even as a teenager, believed in a commitment to any form of ideology; he thought it led to dogmatism, "an enclosed circle of ideas impermeable to doubt." He felt that some of his friends were so invested in Communist ideology that they could rationalize any policy shift in the Soviet Union as justifiable. In this, they weren't so different from most Americans, led by the nose into war whenever the government told them that its aim was to expand "liberty and democracy."

Howie was more drawn to the findings, released during the 1930s, of Senator Gerald Nye's committee. It had been appointed to investigate the background leading up to our entry into World War I. After years of diligent digging, the committee concluded—to the considerable shock of most Americans—that the U.S. had entered the war on the side of Great Britain not for moral reasons but to protect its commercial interests. The chief beneficiary was not "the people" but rather the arms industry, which pocketed huge profits.

But Howie's views were still in flux; he wasn't yet a hard-core radical, let alone an ideologue. His ongoing reading, though— Upton Sinclair's *The Jungle*, John Steinbeck's *The Grapes of Wrath*, and above all Dalton Trumbo's *Johnny Got His Gun*—did lead him initially to oppose World War II as simply a conflict among imperialist powers, and for a time he leaned toward officially becoming a pacifist (until Pearl Harbor, much of the country was isolationist and cared little about the fate of despised Jews or Gypsies).

But the more Howie learned about fascism—George Seldes's portrait of Mussolini, *Sawdust Caesar*, had a powerful impact on him—the more he felt the Axis was evil incarnate and had to be resisted. Doubtless his Jewish background explains part of his change of heart, even though he would have rejected the notion that Jewishness made up a significant portion of his identity. When Howie turned eighteen in 1940, the Depression still lingered and his family had grown desperate about staying afloat. Howie decided to take a Civil Service exam for a job in the Brooklyn Navy Yard. So did thirty thousand other young men for the four hundred jobs available. The successful candidates were those who scored a perfect 100 percent on the exam—and Howie was among them. His designated salary was $14.40 for a forty-hour week. Delighted, Howie gave the family $10 a week and used the remainder for his own expenses.

For the next three years, from eighteen to twenty-one, he served as an apprentice shipfitter, assigned to putting together the steel inner frame of the USS *Iowa*. Howard later described the work as "hard, dirty, malodorous," blazingly hot in summer, freezing in winter, surrounded by deafening noise and the awful smell from cutting galvanized steel with acetylene torches. No women were part of the laboring force, and the few blacks allowed in weren't allowed to join the craft union and as chippers and riveters held down the most physically demanding and exhausting jobs. The work was dangerous, and Howie saw many a worker injured grievously; a good number, moreover, died of cancer while still comparatively young.

No apprentices were allowed to join the craft union, but Howard formed friendships with some of the radical young workers, and together they succeeded in organizing an apprentices' association. Howard was elected to serve as one of the union's four officers. They became close friends and tended to meet one evening a week "to read books on politics and economics and socialism" and discuss them (he found *Das Kapital* particularly tough going). They also formed the nucleus of a basketball team and took great satisfaction from beating the craft union team (who'd belittled them as "apprentice boys") for the championship.

Howard finally decided to enlist in the army air force after a friend had made it sound "glamorous," though he was hardly a natural candidate: at the recruitment center, he couldn't identify a single one of the photos of airplanes shown him and was rejected. But on the spot, Howie gave the colonel in charge a plea about his need to fight fascism that was so impassioned, the colonel gave in and accepted him as a candidate. Two of Howie's brothers also served in the war. Bernie was injured in the invasion of Sicily and, after being released from the hospital, re-enlisted in the Merchant

Marine. But it was Jerry who probably had the worst time of it: his job was to detonate mines in the Philippines.

Shortly before going off to war, Howard had agreed to deliver a shy friend's flight insignia to a girl he was pursuing and thus accidentally Howie met Roslyn (Roz) Shechter, a lushly beautiful young woman blessed also with keen intelligence and an astute political awareness. The two took to each other immediately, went for a walk together that very first day, and thereafter began to date. But then came the night when Howard took her on a moonlight sail and didn't bring her home until four in the morning. Her father was furious and made it clear that he didn't think his daughter's admirer was a suitable boyfriend.

Roz and Howard had remarkably similar backgrounds. Her father, Jacob, had left the Ukrainian shtetl Kamen Kashirskiy (where they sometimes had to hide in the woods to escape pogroms), deciding at age thirty to immigrate to the United States, soon followed by his wife, Ruchel, and their two daughters. Roz also had three brothers, subsequently born in this country. Of the six siblings, she became the family favorite, the first to have a bath (the others later using the same water), the first to be given cream that Ruchel would skim off the unhomogenized milk.

Yiddish was the language spoken in the Shechter household (Howard's parents spoke somewhat mangled English to their children). And whereas the Zinns weren't religious, the Shechters kept a kosher household, and were more emotionally outgoing, at times boisterously so. Unlike their brothers, who went to Hebrew school and were given Bar Mizvahs, the Shechter girls received no formal Jewish education. As had been the case with their mother, the goal put before them was to become "good Jewish wives." For Ruchel, just as for Howard's mother, Jennie, a woman's life centered on her children. And for Jacob, like Eddie, low-paying jobs were all that was available. Jacob sold potatoes off the back of a truck (one step up from a pushcart) and carried heavy cases of seltzer water up and down tenement stairs. But unlike Eddie, Jacob managed eventually to improve his lot somewhat; he got training at a technical school and, along with his sons, eventually bought a gas station and repaired cars. They never became well off but were better off than the Zinns. As for Roz, she took classes in shorthand and typing in high school—the vocational track expected of women—and after graduating worked (for $7 a week) at a Wall Street law firm, using her limited free time to get involved with progressive causes.

Howard's work building battleships in the Brooklyn Navy Yard exempted him from the draft. But though he and Roz didn't yet know each other well, he found it difficult to leave her when, in 1943, he decided to enlist in the air force. He'd been eager for some time to join up, convinced that, unlike other wars, this one wasn't for profit or empire but solely for the destruction of fascism (later, he'd see the war quite differently). Before he could become an aviation cadet, Howard had to go through the usual four-month basic training as an infantryman at Jefferson Barracks, Missouri. Then sent to an airfield outside of Burlington, Vermont, he learned to fly a Piper Cub; from there, it was on to Nashville for a battery of tests that determined he was best fitted to become a bombardier. That settled, he was put on a troop train for Santa Ana, California, for preflight training. After completing it, he spent six more weeks at a gunnery school outside of Las Vegas, where he learned to strip and reassemble a .50-caliber machine gun blindfolded. The final step was four months in the desert outside Deming, New Mexico, to become familiar with the latest miracle weapon, the Norden bombsight. Howard did well at all stages of training and graduated as a second lieutenant.

He was then given leave and could finally reunite with Roz. They'd corresponded regularly but hadn't seen each other in more than a year. Laying eyes on her again, Howard thought Roz was just as beautiful as he'd remembered. They spent a few days in the country getting to know each other better. Both, it turned out, were devout readers and shared the same left-wing politics as well. Though Roz was the more spontaneously affectionate of the two, it was clear by the time they returned to the city that the bond between them had deepened considerably.

Roz assured Howie that her father would come around, as he did, and the couple soon began to talk about marrying. Midway into Howie's furlough, they hastily rounded up their two families and, in October 1944, a redheaded rabbi married them in his home. They spent their wedding night in a cheap Manhattan hotel, then soon afterward Howie was off to Rapid City, South Dakota, to meet his aircrew and to work together on learning how to fly the B-17 Flying Fortress that they'd be using in combat. Roz took a train out to Rapid City to join him, and that became their real honeymoon. But before long it was again time to say good-bye. The wives and sweethearts returned home, and the men shipped out for England, packed into the *Queen Mary* along with thousands of other troops.

Howard was put in charge of a mess hall that served more than fifteen thousand men twice a day in four shifts. The armed forces were still segregated at the time, and black soldiers were confined to the fourth shift. A few days out, some sort of "mix-up"—which the blacks may have deliberately planned—occurred: while white soldiers on the third shift were still eating, black troops poured into the dining room and sat down in whatever empty seats were available. A white sergeant with a Southern accent pointed to the black soldier seated next to him and called out to Howard: "Lieutenant, will you ask this soldier to move from this table?" Momentarily flustered, Howard quickly collected himself: "You fellows are going overseas in the same war. Seems to me you shouldn't mind eating together. Sergeant, you'll have to sit there or just pass up this meal. I won't move either of you." Torn between hunger and prejudice, the sergeant hesitated—then picked up his fork and started eating.[4]

After they docked, Howard's nine-man crew was transported to a Quonset hut, and they settled into the treadmill of military-base life. Even their bombing missions became routine. During his time in the air force, Howard went on a large number of raids across the

European continent—the B-17s flying so high that they were able to remain oblivious to the destruction their bombs were causing below. Howard was thereby spared any close-up of the war's horrors, of the screams and atrocities, of the dead children, the torn bodies, the glazed survivors wandering in search of family members.

None of that was accessible to the bombers. The one mission when their view of the ground was unimpaired—a food drop over Holland, for which they flew much lower—they were able to look back and see, spelled out in tulips, THANK YOU. But that was only once; the missions of destruction were multiple. Howard still believed at that point—and even today most Americans would agree—that World War II was "The Good War," the necessary war, and that those who fought in it were "The Greatest Generation." Few (except blacks, Jews, and Japanese Americans) seem to care, then or now, that U.S. policies were riddled with racism—that our military was segregated, that 120,000 Japanese Americans, most of them born here, were rounded up and put into concentration camps, and that the Roosevelt administration failed again and again to heed the many reports that Hitler was determined to annihilate the Jews.

Two weeks before the European war came to a close—which everyone knew was imminent—Howard's squadron was ordered to bomb Royan, a beautiful French resort town (one of Picasso's favorite spots) far from the front, where several thousand German soldiers were encamped, awaiting surrender. Howard and the other crew members were offhandedly told that they wouldn't be carrying their usual load of 2,500-pound demolition bombs but instead thirty 100-pound canisters of "jellied gasoline." Howard realized only long after the war that the canisters were in fact napalm. It killed or maimed most of the German soldiers, caused severe damage to the town, and wiped out more than a thousand civilians. The Allied brass was delighted that it had managed to test its latest weapon before a peace treaty could inconveniently remove the opportunity.[5]

Three weeks later the war was over. No one, including Howard, questioned whether the raid on Royan had been necessary. Only fleetingly during the war did a few doubts about the "absolute rightness" of what he'd been doing enter Howard's mind. He'd become friendly with a gunner from another crew, and during one of their political talks he'd said to Howard, "You know, this is not a war against fascism. It's a war for empire. . . . It's an imperialist war. The fascists are evil. But our side is not much better." The remark startled Howard, and "I would not accept his statement," Howard later wrote. "But it stuck with me." Many, many years later, after seeing the film *Saving Private Ryan*, Howard would angrily write in the *Progressive*, "I disliked the film intensely. I was angry at it because I did not want [it] exploited in such a way as to revive . . . the 'glory' of military 'heroism.'"

The destruction of Royan and the German garrison also came to haunt him. Twenty years later, when he'd developed a very different view about the "glories" of war, he made a side trip to Royan, looked at materials in the town archives, and afterward made inquiries to the Department of the Army. The chief of Historical Services wrote back and assured Howard that the liberation of the port of Bordeaux had "required the reduction of the bridgeheads of Royan." Howard wasn't reassured. As he realized by then, the bombing had been "a deadly work of obvious uselessness."

Both sides, of course, had earlier engaged in savage air attacks— the Germans on Rotterdam, Coventry and London, the Allies, with no pretense of "precision bombing" or of focusing on military targets, killing tens of thousands of civilians in raids on Frankfurt, Essen, Cologne, and Hamburg and closer to 100,000 in the firestorm generated by the massive attack on Dresden. Then it was Japan's turn. In March 1945 three hundred B-29s dropped two thousand tons of napalm and magnesium incendiaries on Tokyo, leaving some 85,000 to 100,000 men, women, and children dead, countless others maimed, blinded, and homeless. Some people jumped in the river for safety—and were boiled alive.

When he'd first enlisted, Howard had believed in a clear distinction between "just" and "unjust" wars, with the struggle against fascism clearly just. But by the close of the war Howard's doubts had begun to surface, the seeds having been planted much earlier by *Johnny Got His Gun* and *Sawdust Caesar*. He'd come to believe that "modern warfare, being massive, indiscriminate killing of people, is a means so horrendous that no end can justify it . . . to retaliate against violence with more violence [is] to multiply the cruelties which you set out to stop." But how, he'd often be asked, could you have liberated the concentration camps without the war?

Howard went back and forth on that tough question, though he was clear about one aspect of it: the Allies had shown scant interest throughout in the fate of the European Jews (when, for example, a resolution was introduced in the U.S. Senate in 1934 asking the president to express "surprise and pain" over the Nazi treatment of the Jews, the State Department saw to it that the resolution was buried in committee). The camps, moreover, were "liberated" so late in the war that most captive Jews were already dead. Besides, the war itself had killed 66 million people—though that was an argument against *any* war. Yet unlike Howard, most Americans still believe that World War II was a contest between the moral Allies and the malevolent Axis. Fascism *was* evil, but "democracy" also had begun to prove deadly.

No one knew just how deadly until atomic bombs were dropped on Hiroshima and Nagasaki in 1945. General Curtis LeMay had put the matter bluntly: "Bomb and burn 'em till they quit." In justifying the decision, President Truman later said, "I think the sacrifice of Hiroshima and Nagasaki was urgent and necessary for the prospective welfare of both Japan and the Allies." The welfare of *Japan*! Was Truman suggesting that hundreds of thousands of mutilated bodies would somehow purify the Japanese soul? Truman also characterized the city of Hiroshima as "a military base," implying that that had been the reason it was chosen as a target.

Yet an official government committee, the United States Strategic Bombing Survey, concluded that Hiroshima and Nagasaki had
been selected because "of their concentration of activities and population." Among those incinerated were the 15 to 20 percent of the
population of the two cities who were non-Japanese, including
eleven POW American airmen. Truman's ultimate justification for
the atrocities committed hinged on the need to bring a speedy end
to the war and to avoid the terrible toll that an invasion of the Japanese mainland would have entailed. At the time, many echoed that
argument. Many still do. As late as 1996, Arthur Schlesinger Jr.
wrote in the *New York Times*, "I have problems in seeing how a
responsible President could have done otherwise."

But the reasons for doing "otherwise" are multiple. Truman had
become aware on assuming the presidency in April 1945 that the
Allies weren't considering an invasion of Japan before November,
and some felt that none might be necessary. Truman argued that
using the bomb would save "half a million" Allied lives (Churchill
put the figure at a million). Yet when the secret files were finally
opened, the historian Barton Bernstein examined the documents
carefully and put the number of likely casualties at 46,000. Still far
too many, but in fact Japan was on the verge of surrender *before* the
bombs were dropped—as Washington well knew. The war in Europe had ended in May 1945, and in June the island of Okinawa, just
five hundred miles south of mainland Japan, had been taken after a
bloody battle. That same month, the Japanese leadership, with a few
holdouts, accepted defeat. Six members of the Japanese Supreme
War Council authorized Foreign Minister Togo to approach the Soviet Union and ask if it would serve as an intermediary in terminating the war. Emperor Hirohito also told Togo to bring the war
swiftly to a close. He immediately wired the Japanese ambassador to
Moscow that "unconditional surrender is the only obstacle to peace."

Since the Japanese code had been broken early in the war, Truman knew about these developments, yet at the Potsdam Confer-

ence in July, the Allies insisted on unconditional surrender. In response the Japanese asked only that the emperor's status be left intact—terms virtually identical with those the Allies ultimately accepted. As for that minority among the Japanese leaders who remained hesitant about the peace terms being offered, a *demonstration* of the atom bomb's ferocity on some unpopulated Pacific atoll would surely have removed those doubts.

The evidence is thus strong that the use of atomic bombs was neither essential from a military point of view nor justifiable from a humane one. Neither motivation played as significant a role in the decision to drop the bombs as did the determination, however unconsciously held, to demonstrate the remarkable reach of American military power, thereby legitimizing its right to fill the shoes of the British Empire and dominate the globe. Before "having it out with Russia," Truman wanted confirmation that "laying it on Japan" would illustrate America's power. The well-known British scientist P.M.S. Blackett (an adviser to Churchill) called the dropping of the bombs "the first major operation of the cold diplomatic war with Russia."

When the postwar International Bank for Reconstruction and Development was set up, some assumed it was designed primarily to rebuild war-torn areas. Not at all. The bank unapologetically announced that its overriding purpose would be "to promote private foreign investment all over the world." Henceforth U.S. business and government would firmly link arms in an aggressive march toward a Pax Americana characterized more by war than by peace. For more than thirty years after World War II, the U.S. government classified all information about Hiroshima and Nagasaki as "top secret," making access impossible.

Finally in the late 1970s and early 1980s, radical historians and journalists such as Gar Alperovitz, Barton Bernstein, Martin Sherwin, Jonathan Schell, and John Dower were able to use the Freedom of Information Act to force the release of Pentagon records that put the lie to the official American version. The same record of censorship succeeded in keeping secret other aspects of the war. It wasn't until 2010 that a report entitled *Hitler's Shadow* emerged from an interagency group that identified and declassified enough secret information to establish that—to a far greater extent than had been known—American intelligence officials had created a safe harbor in this country after the war for Gestapo officers, SS veterans, and Nazi collaborators.

Howard would later acknowledge that on hearing news of the atomic bomb being dropped on Hiroshima, he felt grateful. That was understandable enough—with the war over, he could go back to his life with Roz. Yet by the time he'd read John Hersey's horrifying 1946 book, *Hiroshima*, Howard had come full circle: he now believed that dropping the bomb had been an atrocity and that there was no such thing as a "good" war. Echoing Albert Einstein, Howard now made a distinction between a just *cause* and a just war: "War cannot be humanized, it can only be abolished!" Yes, Howard felt, there have always been wars—and heart attacks and rape, too. Does that mean we should stop trying to prevent the former or wipe out the latter? Are such efforts "utopian"? That's what had been said about "flying machines." Then someone invented the airplane.

Howard had started his time in the service certain that the war was wholly justified, that as he later put it, "Hitler's force had to be met with force." But when it was time to pack up and return home, he found himself impulsively marking on a box that contained his air force medals and insignia, NEVER AGAIN.

Howard's parents hadn't shared in the general prosperity that the war had brought to the U.S. Earlier they'd tried to improve their lot by opening a candy store on Bushwick Avenue in Brooklyn and living in the back of it. But though they worked hard to make a go of the store, "the king of egg creams" across the street drew most of the local business, and after hanging on for three years the Zinns had to declare bankruptcy. When Howard had been working in the

Brooklyn Navy Yard, he was able to get his parents into the Fort Greene Houses—a big improvement in their lives.

The relentless poverty of his frugal, hardworking parents made Howard aware that if he was to avoid their lot, he'd have to get additional education or, to be more precise, additional degrees. With the GI Bill offering free tuition, college for the first time became a realistic possibility and soon after returning to New York Howard enrolled—at age twenty-seven—as a freshman at Washington Square College (now New York University). Along with the free education, the GI Bill provided $120 a month. With their daughter, Myla, already two years old, and with a second child, Jeff, soon to arrive, making ends *nearly* meet was difficult. Roz and Howard originally lived in "a miserable basement room," but by a stroke of luck the family was accepted for an apartment on East Sixth Street in Manhattan—the new low-rent housing project, the Lillian Wald Houses. They felt comfortable and happy there: it proved to be a real community, and they soon became friendly with the wide variety of people—African Americans, Puerto Ricans, Italians, Irish, and other Jews. Together they worked in a tenants' council and socialized over potluck dinners and dances in the building's basement.

In high school, Roz had edited the literary magazine and won the English medal. But despite her gifts she was unable, in those prefeminist days, to pursue her dreams but had to use her secretarial skills to help support the family. With both parents out of the house all day, the children were put in a low-income nursery school. They couldn't afford to pay a doctor if either child got sick and would take them instead to hospital clinics. Howard did all he could to contribute additional money: after classes he worked initially at the Lerner Shops as a part-time shipping clerk and then switched to the slightly higher paying four-to-midnight shift in a warehouse, loading eighty-pound containers onto trailer trucks. He worked there for three years; how he found time to study—or sleep—remains a mystery. But the physically strenuous work did finally take its toll: he sustained a series of back injuries that kept him disabled and out of work for months. Wearing a back brace, he then briefly returned to the warehouse, but the pain was too severe and he had to throw in the towel.[6]

To replace the warehouse job, Howard began teaching four days a week at Upsala College in New Jersey, as well as two evening courses at Brooklyn College. Part-time academic employment wasn't as commonplace back then as it now is; what remains the same is the low salary (in Howard's case, $3,000 a year) for putting in more teaching hours than a full professor, and without any real hope of gaining tenure.

Not surprisingly, it took Howard six years to earn a BA. While still in college, he'd heard a song by Woody Guthrie, "The Ludlow Massacre," which told of women and children being burned to death in an attack by the Colorado National Guard to end a 1913–1914 strike against Rockefeller-owned mines. It was the first he'd ever heard about it; he searched through his textbooks and was unable to find a single reference to the strike. It dawned on him that perhaps professional historical writing wasn't as "objective" as he'd been led to believe.

For his postgraduate degrees, Howard shifted to Columbia University and decided to write his MA thesis on Ludlow—completing it in a single year (1952). Most students would have chosen a "safer" topic, given the current McCarthyite climate. As early as 1947, President Truman had announced the so-called Truman Doctrine, designed, he claimed, to maintain the "democratic" government of Greece in power; what that came down to in practice was the U.S. propping up a military junta—thus inaugurating what would become a string of postwar interventions to bolster dictatorships. The Korean War was also still raging. President Truman had loftily declared that the invasion of Communist North Korea's armies into South Korea had necessitated U.S. entry into the war "to uphold the rule of law"— which turned out to mean American bombers producing a swath of destruction that left 2 million Koreans, North and South, dead.

*   *   *

Howard's political activity began to accelerate. He was found guilty at a formal meeting of the National Administrative Committee of publicly associating the American Veterans Committee (he was a member) with Henry Wallace's 1948 campaign for the presidency, as well as with Simon V. Gerson's run for the New York City Council on the Communist Party ticket. Howard was suspended from the AVC for one year. Also, several left-wing lawyers he knew were being denied entrance to the bar—Howard had briefly considered becoming a lawyer himself—by character committees passing on their "moral" qualifications.

And although Howard didn't know it at the time, early in 1949 the FBI opened a Security Index file on him. In their confidential memos to headquarters, the FBI agents managed to get a large number of facts wrong, including the invention of a sister ("Doris") for Howard—which perhaps made the Bureau more, not less, deadly. The agents confidently reported that Howard was a dues-paying member of the Communist Party and attended CP meetings five times a week in Brooklyn—which he wasn't and didn't (though even today the rumor occasionally resurfaces). Roz, too, was considered a security threat; she was reported to have solicited signatures for CP nominations as far back as 1946. In 1953, their residence was placed under "discreet surveillance."[7]

By then the Cold War had turned frigid and the land become rife with accusations of "traitor." Perhaps the most bizarre (but not amusing) episode contained in Howard's FBI file is an agent's detailed account of an attempt in the early 1950s to recruit him as a source of information. On November 6, 1953, two agents from the Security Informant Program waited until Howard had left the neighborhood of his apartment and then approached him. Introducing themselves, they said they had a confidential matter to discuss with him—that "he was not being contacted with the idea of intimidating or having him incriminate himself, but for the purpose of determining his attitude towards aiding the United States Government."

Despite that stated intention, the agents began by asking Howard if it was true, as had been reported, that he was a member of the Communist Party. Howard replied that neither he nor his wife were now or had ever been in the CP. He described himself as a liberal (the word hadn't yet taken on, for radicals, a derisive tone) adding that "perhaps some people would consider him to be a 'leftist.'" Howard further acknowledged that he'd attended Paul Robeson's "Peekskill Riot" concert in 1949 and was studying for a PhD in history at Columbia.

He also affirmed his periodic involvement with certain organizations—the American Labor Party for one, and the Veterans Committee Against the Mundt-Nixon Bill (which, in a later incarnation as the McCarran Act, harshly curtailed civil liberties). Some people, Howard openly acknowledged, considered such organizations "communist," but he didn't; he was proud, not ashamed, of his political affiliations. People had the right, Howard went on, "to believe, think and act according to their own ideals," though not "to violate the rights of others."

He added (at least according to the agents' account) that he himself didn't believe in the use of force or violence, either in general or specifically to overthrow the U.S. government, and purportedly further asserted that if he had knowledge of such persons, he'd notify the FBI—which seems unlikely: Howard believed in the right of all to hold whatever opinions they wished, and he would never have assisted the abhorred FBI in any way. Throughout the interview, Howard remained "courteous" and "friendly," but he refused the request to reveal the names of anyone connected to the political groups he'd been associated with—which were now being labeled "Communist-Front" organizations. The agents recommended to the Bureau that Zinn be reinterviewed.

And three months later he was. The same two FBI agents conducted the second interview and ignored Howard's opening comment that he had nothing to add or subtract from what he'd said earlier. Undeterred, the agents proceeded to ask most of the same questions they previously had, and Howard provided the same answers. He did explicitly state that "he did not consider himself or any of his friends to be a threat to the security of the country," though under its current leadership—this he didn't say—he might almost have wished otherwise. Because Howard refused to provide additional information, and doubting that he'd change his attitude, the agents considered the case closed. Yet not quite. His name was retained on the Security Index, and periodically there was "discreet surveillance" of his comings and goings. The FBI was not finished with Howard Zinn.

For his PhD thesis at Columbia, Howard chose the topic "LaGuardia in Congress." It was an ideal subject for him. Fiorello LaGuardia had served in the House of Representatives from 1917 to 1933 and was throughout his tenure a vividly outspoken champion of social justice. His views were not only a precursor to the New Deal but in some ways went beyond it. He militantly attacked immigration restrictions and racial inequality, decried the greed of the rich, and even spoke of the need for a "new economic order" that would equalize the wealth and nationalize certain industries (railroads and mines) that were outstandingly avaricious or inefficient. Howard deeply admired LaGuardia but was able to treat his career evenhandedly, not shying away from his subject's limitations—such as occasional demagoguery and lack of analytic sophistication. Howard did considerable research in primary sources for his PhD, but later some historians would attack him for *avoiding* archival research in his subsequent books and for relying mostly on secondary sources alone—as well as for his *lack* of evenhandedness, of balanced "objectivity."

However accurate the charge of lack of archival research may be for Howard's later career, for his doctoral thesis he did a great deal of it and was able as well to write up his findings with what would become characteristic clarity. He would always be something of a stylist in his writing—rarely showy, self-indulgent, or polemical, but often witty and always lucid. Historians tend to be a rather stuffy, even prudish bunch, but that wasn't the case with Howard; squeamishness doesn't explain the degree to which he avoided—more from lack of interest than prudery—discussing La-Guardia's private history (or his own). Later, even in his autobiography, he passed lightly over or entirely avoided topics relating to love and lust, friendships and feelings, viewing them as somehow irrelevant. Thus in his dissertation on LaGuardia—which by design was confined to his public career—there are only two or three references, with scant detail, to the congressman's two marriages, fatherhood, sickness and health, or relationships.

Given the many strengths of *LaGuardia in Congress*, the Cornell University Press quickly picked it up for publication. The book came out in 1959 and received Honorable Mention for the Beveridge Prize, given for the best English-language book on American history published within the year. It was unlucky for Howard that Arthur Mann's *LaGuardia: A Fighter Against His Times*, the first volume of a full-bodied two-volume biography, came out that same year. The two books were often reviewed together, and though the critical reception for both was largely positive, several important reviews gave the palm to Mann. Howard got a good deal of praise—"a model scholarly study" wrote one critic. The most common complaint about *LaGuardia in Congress* centered on what one reviewer called its "one-dimensional" focus "on the record of issues and debates" rather than on presenting (as another reviewer put it), "LaGuardia as a human being," not merely a political animal.[8]

While Howard was still at work on his thesis, a placement bureau (they no longer exist for academics due to the lack of available jobs) contacted him about meeting with Albert E. Manley, the president of Spelman College in Atlanta, probably the most prominent and respected school at the time for black women. At their meeting, Manley offered Howard—to his astonishment—the chairmanship of the history and social sciences department at a salary of $4,000 a year. That was midrange for academic salaries at the time, yet Howard boldly told Manley: "I have a wife and two kids. Could you make it $4,500?" Manley could, and the deal was set.

Before the surprise interview, Howard hadn't given the slightest thought to teaching in a black college. The civil rights conflict had barely begun, and up to that point (1956) he'd been an onlooker, not a participant, though his sympathies were decisively with the black struggle. The years at Spelman would prove to be formative and tumultuous, but Roz and Howard had no notion of that when they packed their two kids—Myla was nine; Jeff, six—and all their belongings into their ten-year-old Chevy and in August 1956 headed off to a world vastly different from the one they'd known.

2

Spelman

It was raining and hot when the Zinn family arrived in Atlanta in August 1956. It immediately struck them that this felt different from a typical New York summer evening. Though late in the season, the air was still thick with the redolent, sweet smell of the city's famed magnolias and honeysuckle. Having grown up amid cramped, urban grit and gridlocked crowds of noisy humanity, the quiet of Atlanta felt strange, even a bit unnerving. Plus it was obvious at once that this wasn't similar to the diverse mingling found in New York. Here there was black and there was white, and skin color everywhere determined location and expectations. Atlanta in 1956 was still as rigidly segregated as it had been at the turn of the century—and that included public transportation, water fountains, theaters, and libraries.[1]

Spelman College epitomized what was true of the city as a whole. Though near Atlanta's center, Spelman was an island apart. An eight-foot-high chain-link fence—topped in part with barbed wire—surrounded the campus; Howard joked that it looked like "they were trying to keep the students in rather than intruders out." The campus itself was an attractive collection of mostly nineteenth-century redbrick buildings. For the first year, the Zinns lived in a poor white district in Atlanta, then moved on campus into the first floor in the back of MacVicar Hospital, the college infirmary, their apartment overlooking the tennis courts. In 1956, the student body consisted entirely of young black women—it wouldn't be until 1960 that a trickle of white undergraduates would begin to arrive—and the faculty was about one quarter white. The school's mission officially remained what it had been since its establishment by two white New England women in 1881: to graduate carbon copies— "sedate, quiet, careful"—of a genteel finishing school for young white ladies, including the capacity to pour tea gracefully.

Most of the students' routine was lockstep: the day began with each making her bed, cleaning her room, attending breakfast neatly dressed, and going daily to chapel at 8:00 A.M. When leaving the campus, students had to sign in and out, to be accompanied by at least two other students, to wear stockings, skirts, and dresses, and to carry gloves and a purse. Young black men from Morehouse College (of which Martin Luther King Jr. was an alumnus) and graduate students from Atlanta University Center (a consortium of six colleges)—both directly across the street from Spelman—were allowed to come calling but only for one hour; Spelman women, however, could not visit male apartments. Occasionally there would be strictly chaperoned dances, but no male student was ever allowed to enter a Spelman girl's room, and she was given exactly fifteen minutes to get back to her dormitory after a dance ended. She had an unyielding curfew every night of 9:00 P.M.

Only some two hundred thousand African Americans were enrolled in college in the 1950s (there were thirty times as many whites), and about half of that number were in all-black or predominantly black schools. The black colleges essentially survived on crumbs, receiving only 2.7 percent of state money for higher education and a mere 0.66 percent of federal funds. Howard found that some of his students, coming as they did from segregated secondary schools, were ill prepared for college though hungry for knowledge. Ironically, it was some of the "worst" colleges that (according to Howard) produced "some of the finest youngsters in the country—courageous, idealistic, informed"—those who, in 1960–61, would spark the black civil rights movement.

Some of the young women chafed at the multiple restrictions imposed on them, like one of Howard's favorites, Alice Walker, who arrived in 1962 and stayed at Spelman only two years; she got involved with the third wave of sit-ins and became a lifelong friend. Yet others, like another of his gifted students, Marian Wright (later, as Marian Wright Edelman, the founder and president of the Children's Defense Fund), were grateful to be living in a space not defined and dominated by male or white expectations—which wasn't entirely true since Spelman's president, Albert Manley, had the Board of Trustees in his pocket and most definitely set the rules.

Manley came from a particular generation of black college presidents, strict and autocratic, forced to walk a tightrope between a limited endowment and white racist power. Manley was one of a handful before 1950 who'd been determined and fortunate enough to stay the course despite the legion of humiliations and obstacles that stood in their path. Manley had become the first black and first male president of Spelman in 1952. Zinn was only thirty-four when he arrived on campus, while Manley was forty-eight. He had a complicated background, which partly explains his purposeful resolve. Born in Honduras to Jamaican parents, he was schooled first in Guatemala, then Belize, and finally in the United States, where he graduated from Johnson C. Smith University in North Carolina; subsequently he earned an EdD from Stanford. Over time, Manley and Howard would become sharply, dramatically antagonistic.

The atmosphere seemed airtight to the Zinns, both on the Spelman campus and in the city of Atlanta. But in fact by the time they arrived, entrenched conventions had been challenged on several fronts. Black Atlanta in the early 1950s, unlike most Southern cities, had a significant number of black-owned businesses and organizations, run by an elite that had managed to clear a narrow footpath through the prickly brambles of segregation. Representative figures of that generation, such as the minister Martin Luther King Sr. or the attorney A.T. Walden, had built up at least minimal, behind-the-scenes contact with the white establishment.

The 1954 Supreme Court decision *Brown v. Board of Education* had declared segregation in the nation's schools unconstitutional. Hope was initially high in black communities throughout the country, but "liberal" white detachment and Southern white hostility soon dashed it. President Eisenhower publicly stated his disapproval of the Supreme Court decision and made no effort to enforce it. Nor did Congress, dominated by influential Southern Democrats, pass a single enabling law. Instead of white schools throwing open their doors posthaste to black students, white Citizens' Councils, determined that desegregation never happen at all, rapidly spread fear through the South. And their threats were not rhetorical. When the Montgomery bus boycotts began in 1955, the leaders' homes were bombed; when the brave Autherine Lucy attempted to enter the University of Alabama, she was greeted by an angry mob and three days later, on trumped-up charges, was expelled.

More surprising, perhaps, was the response of literary and political intellectuals, North and South, to the Supreme Court decision. William Faulkner, long ambivalent about segregation, announced that separate schools for blacks were acceptable as long as they were upgraded. The well-known "liberal" Southern editors Ralph McGill, Harry Ashmore, and Hodding Carter Jr. said that in the abstract they favored the "gradual" amelioration of racial injustice but said nothing in favor of desegregating the schools. In the North, *Harper's* magazine—with a disclaimer, of course—ran an article "proving" that blacks were riddled with venereal disease, prone to criminal activity, and *intrinsically* lacking in brain power. Not to be outdone, the *Atlantic Monthly* gave the well-known historian Oscar Handlin a platform from which to argue reassuringly that desegregating the schools would not lead to social mixing.

The theologian Reinhold Niebuhr famously distrusted all forms of "utopianism," so when he and Arthur Schlesinger Jr. organized Americans for Democratic Action (ADA), they defined its mission as a devotion to "pragmatic liberalism," gradual reform, and opposition to "dogmatism" of any kind (which presumably included the dogmatic notion that blacks were entitled to first-class citizenship). They urged the virtue of "patience" in regard to social reform—as if blacks hadn't been patient for centuries. The well-known critic Lionel Trilling and the sociologist David Riesman took essentially the same stance, while adding that strenuous public engagement was somehow unsuitable for intellectuals.

The novelist Robert Penn Warren and the historian C. Vann Woodward, both liberal advocates of change, also landed on the side of "gradualism." And many other intellectuals followed suit, rallying under the banner GO SLOW. Living under the cloud of McCarthyism, with its intimidating suspicion of dissent, and in a Cold War climate that equated racial advance with communism ("the Soviets are behind it"), many in the country, including most union leaders as well as the professional "thinking class," moved like lemmings toward the safe harbor of ambivalent centrism—while abstractly advocating the "eventual" goal of desegregation.

There were notable exceptions, including Carey McWilliams, editor of the *Nation*, the Mississippi historian Jim Silver, the writers Lillian Smith and Irving Howe—and the then unknown young historian Howard Zinn. Soon after he arrived in Atlanta in 1956 and began to know his students and to mingle generally in the black community, Howard recognized that surface politeness toward whites concealed strong feelings of indignation; the brutal murder of young Emmett Till by white vigilantes the year before had pushed that anger up several notches. This suppressed rage had sometimes broken through the crust in the form of individual acts of resistance, usually punished severely. The coordinated action that had produced victory in the 1955 Montgomery bus boycott, as well as the NAACP's court battles, strongly suggested that group organizing was the prerequisite for successful change.

Even before Howard's arrival, Atlanta had seen a few victories in the long struggle for desegregation: the 1940s had marked the end of the white-only primary, the hiring of black policemen (though only to patrol black neighborhoods), and the opening of the city's golf courses at certain hours to blacks. As Howard would often say, the accumulation of such small victories, usually accomplished by people who never make it into the history books, is a necessary precursor to a more widespread upheaval.

There were no white students at Spelman when Howard began to teach there. Nor had most of the students ever had a white teacher, and it was predictable that they initially greeted "Mr. Zinn" with polite shyness (and hidden mistrust). But thanks to his warmth, his down-to-earth style, and his obvious lack of racism, the students quickly realized that they had a friend in Howard. During his first year at Spelman, he became faculty adviser to the student-run Social Science Club, where issues of the day were discussed and debated.

In January 1957, a mere six months after arriving, Howard suggested that he and the students visit the Georgia state legislature to observe its workings. They were joined by a few male students from Morehouse (one of them named Julian Bond, who the Zinns would come to know well) and by their white apartment neighbors Pat and Henry West (who taught at Spelman). The group numbered about thirty, and no intentional disruption had been planned. But when they went to sit in the gallery, they were confronted by a COLORED sign designating a small section. The group conferred and decided to sit instead in the largely empty WHITE section.

That produced an immediate uproar from the floor of the legislature. Members stood in their seats and shouted up at the miscreants, while the Speaker grabbed the microphone and yelled, "You nigras get over to where you belong!" Police quickly appeared and escorted the group out into the hall, where they conferred and—

the mass upheavals of the civil rights struggle hadn't yet begun—resentfully decided to return to the COLORED section. At which point the Speaker, again using the microphone, called up to them that "the members of the Georgia state legislature would like to extend a warm welcome to the visiting delegation from Spelman College." As long as the rigid separation of the races remained unchallenged, no one could exceed white southerners in graciousness.

At the beginning of 1957, nonviolent radical activists such as Ella Baker and Bayard Rustin helped to organize the Southern Christian Leadership Conference (SCLC) led by activist ministers, including Martin Luther King Jr. Like most men at the time, the ministers held sexist views—women were meant to be subordinate helpmates; SCLC's mission was racial, not gender equality—and neither Ella Baker nor Rosa Parks was invited to join the patriarchal inner circle (though in 1958 SCLC did hire Baker as a full-time staff member in Atlanta). Nor were relations particularly cordial between SCLC and the NAACP, which tended to view the upstart new organization as unnecessarily duplicating its own civil rights work.[2]

During the year that she worked for SCLC, Baker's discontent grew. Somewhat blind to King's relative modesty in the face of so much adoration, she deplored SCLS's growing reliance on his celebrity and its concomitant emphasis on a top-down organizational strategy that had the double effect of discouraging participation among poor, grassroots blacks while encouraging the all too familiar kind of demeaning deference that already marked their relationship with whites.

After leaving SCLC, Baker increasingly turned her attention to grassroots activity. Within the year, she and Howard would meet, but before that Howard suggested to the Social Science Club early in 1959 that the group might find it interesting (in his words) "to undertake some real project involving social change." One of the students suggested trying to do something about the segregation of Atlanta's public library system. The idea was enthusiastically taken up and the target chosen was Carnegie, the main library in Atlanta.

Along with Howard, the students enlisted the help of Whitney Young, then dean of the School of Social Work at Atlanta University (in 1961 he became head of the National Urban League), and Dr. Irene Dobbs Jackson, professor of French at Spelman and the sister of Mattiwilda Dobbs, then a well-known coloratura soprano and the first black singer to be given a long-term contract at the Metropolitan Opera. (Irene Jackson's son, Maynard Jackson, would in 1974 become the first African American mayor of Atlanta).

The group carefully discussed a strategy. That it would adhere to nonviolent tactics went without saying. Beyond that, it was decided to rely on polite but persistent requests from Carnegie for books with obviously relevant content: John Stuart Mill's *On Liberty*, Tom Paine's *Common Sense*, or John Locke's *An Essay Concerning Human Understanding*. Each request got the same response: "We'll send a copy of that book to your Negro branch." (Atlanta had three libraries for blacks, all of them inadequate.) To further heighten the library's uneasiness, hints were made that a lawsuit might well follow if black students continued to be denied access to the books at Carnegie itself, with Professor Irene Jackson as one of the plaintiffs.

Howard was sitting in Whitney Young's office talking about possible next moves when a phone call informed Young that the library board had just made the decision to end segregation throughout the Atlanta library system. That substantial victory preceded by nearly two years the wave of sit-ins in 1960–61 for which Greensboro, North Carolina, became the symbol. Greensboro, in fact, wasn't the first sit-in. There were several dozen during the 1950s, yet even through the frightening struggle in 1957 at Central High in Little Rock, the underground fires of resentment and anger weren't quite at the flash point.

On February 1, 1960, four black freshmen from North Carolina Agricultural and Technical College sat down at a Woolworth's lunch counter in Greensboro, asked for service, were refused, and then stayed put at the counter until the store closed at 5:30. The follow-ing day, they returned—along with twenty-three other students—and in the next few days the protest quickly expanded, with at least eight other sit-ins that week in North Carolina alone.

Greensboro proved the turning point. The time now *was* ripe. The slower means for producing social change, such as court cases, that the earlier generation had relied on to move desegregation for-ward now seemed too slow for the new generation of college students. Far more than their elders, moreover, they were insistent on basing decision making in the movement among ground-level participants. In their intensity, the sit-in generation sometimes forgot or mini-mized the major contributions that the older black organizations had made—necessary precursors, perhaps, to the militant turn the movement was now taking. The NAACP had worked through the courts, CORE had mostly focused on producing change in the North, and SCLC had primarily operated through the most power-ful of black institutions, the church. Several leaders of the older organizations—Roy Wilkins in particular—had their doubts about the confrontational style, the "aggressiveness," of the sit-ins, fearing they'd prove counterproductive.

If some members of SCLC and the NAACP were caught by surprise and reacted with disapproval, others, including Martin Luther King Jr., welcomed the new energy that now infused the black struggle. The (partly) spontaneous and variable nature of the sit-ins did take many by surprise, including many of the historians who later wrote about them. Historians tend to be logical-minded types not comfortable with unexpected spontaneity, and thus not likely to factor it into their rational and confident "explanations" of why a given event takes place—thus missing the opportunity to underscore the messy triggers of change, the mysterious and un-premeditated elements in human behavior.

The Greensboro sit-in was widely covered in the national media, and a veritable firestorm of sit-ins followed. Within days, a group of Atlanta University Center (AUC) students went to talk with

Benjamin Mays, the most liberal of the AUC college presidents. Mays gave them his blessing, but soon after he got a phone call from Roy Wilkins, the conservative head of the NAACP, who'd somehow gotten wind of the students' plans. He told Mays, who relayed the message to the students, that they should stick to their studies and the NAACP would continue the desegregation battle through the courts.[3]

Student leaders from all six colleges of the AUC consortium decided to ignore Wilkins and to publish "An Appeal for Human Rights" in three Atlanta newspapers, including the *Atlanta Constitution*. Roslyn Pope, president of the Spelman student government and close to Howard and Roz (she was one of many students who used the Zinns' home as a combination sanctuary and planning center), wrote most of the first draft.

The reworked "Appeal for Human Rights" appeared on March 9, 1960, and was reprinted in the *Nation* on April 2. Howard thought the students had produced a "remarkable" document. It itemized black grievances in eloquent detail and asserted the determination "to use every legal and nonviolent means at our disposal" to end the widespread suffering under segregation. "The students who instigate and participate in these sit-down protests," the text read, "are dissatisfied not only with existing conditions, but with the snail-like speed at which they are being ameliorated."[4]

Ernest Vandiver, governor of Georgia, immediately branded the Appeal "anti-American," claimed it could not have been written by students (talk about a backhanded compliment), and predicted that this "left-wing statement is calculated to breed dissatisfaction, discontent, discord and evil"—apparently a reference to a line in the Appeal stating "We do not intend to wait placidly for those rights which are already legally and morally ours to be meted out to us one at a time."

Six days after Vandiver's outburst, several hundred students from AUC staged sit-in demonstrations at ten different eating places in the city—including restaurants in the State Capitol and City Hall. Howard's role was to call the city's newspapers at exactly 11:00 A.M. and read to them the list of restaurants where the students planned to sit in. Seventy-seven of the students were promptly arrested—fourteen from Spelman, nearly all from the Deep South. One of them, Marian Wright, was photographed sitting calmly in a cell reading C.S. Lewis's *The Screwtape Letters*—a photo widely reproduced. By April the sit-ins had spread throughout the upper South, and there were even a handful in the Deep South (though none of those, unlike in the border areas, were successful). That same month, students from various colleges gathered in Raleigh, North Carolina, to form the Student Nonviolent Coordinating Committee (SNCC, often pronounced "snick").

By midsummer of 1961, an estimated fifty thousand students (some of them white, like Jane Stembridge, Bill Hansen, and Bob Zellner, who became well known in the movement) had participated in sit-ins—four thousand had spent time in jail—and 110 cities had desegregated public facilities. Yet the Deep South still held firm. The arrested Spelman students were never brought to trial, but a remarkable change had come to pass. Even the school's cautious president, Albert Manley, shifted ground. At commencement that year, he spontaneously congratulated the senior class "for breaking the 'docile generation' label" with their demonstrations. At roughly that same time, the first white students arrived at Spelman as part of an exchange program, and several liberal whites joined the faculty. Simultaneously, the amount of contact with white students from other Atlanta colleges (like Emory) escalated.[5]

This shift in climate meant that a significant number of Spelman students would become or remain active in the series of protests that soon followed. The next target chosen was Rich's Department Store, Atlanta's largest. Again, Howard and Roz played significant roles. Entering Rich's, they bought coffee and sandwiches at the counter and then sat down at one of the tables. By prearrangement, two black students then joined them. Another group of four followed (including, again, Pat and Henry West) using the same strategy. Instead of calling the police, Rich's simply turned off the lights and shut down the lunch counter. A few more black students also showed up, and in the semidarkness they talked contentedly among themselves until closing hour. By fall 1961 Rich's ended its policy of segregation, and nearly two hundred other Atlanta restaurants followed suit.

The success of the sit-ins, and the subsequent Freedom Rides, was frequently accompanied by violence. From Anniston to Montgomery, from Jackson to Tallahassee, those brave enough to challenge restaurants, libraries, bus and railroad terminals were often greeted by gangs of toughs, police dogs and tear gas, ammonia and acid, bats, knives, clubs and fists. Severe beatings and occasional deaths took place throughout the South. The *Richmond News Leader* described one such reception: ". . . a gang of white boys come to heckle, a ragtail rabble . . . grinning fit to kill . . . and some of them, God save the mark, were waving the proud and honored flag of the Southern States in the last war fought by gentlemen." The reaction in Richmond was gentle compared to the response in Houston, Texas: "Another Negro flogged with chain by three whites, symbol KKK carved on his chest and stomach, hung by knees from oak tree."

When discussing strategy or planning an action, Spelman students often used the Zinn apartment, which meant that to do homework young Myla and Jeff had to retreat to their bedrooms. Howard and Roz were careful not to push their own political views on their children; Myla, for one, has no memory "of my parents talking to us about 'politics' or 'social justice'"—though Jeff, to the contrary, recalls "an atmosphere of politics 24/7." She and Jeff were, after all, youngsters, facing enough challenges of their own in moving from the warm community of the Lillian Wald housing project in New York to the strange new world of Atlanta. Yet before long, Jeff was bringing white classmates to the campus to meet and play with black youngsters.[6]

Myla entered the Lee Street School in the third grade; it was within walking distance of the Spelman campus, located in a poor white section of Atlanta (some of her classmates were so poor they walked to school barefoot). Everyone in the family had to make adjustments, but Myla's was perhaps the most difficult. Fortunately Roz and both children got involved in some of the campus theatrical productions. A true highlight—for the Zinns and for the community—was when Roz dazzlingly played the role of Anna opposite Johnny Popwell, a powerfully built Morehouse football player, in a production of *The King and I*, with both Jeff and Myla among the king's children. For Jeff, theater would become a lifetime passion, and for Myla it became a considerable respite from the isolation and alienation she experienced when the time for high school came around. She entered the recently desegregated Joe E. Brown High School and tried her best—unlike most of the white students—to be friendly to the small group of black students, and to one girl in particular. But perhaps frightened by the predominantly white atmosphere, the black students chose to hang out and eat together.

As a northerner (and perhaps perceived as a Jew), Myla was generally treated as "different" by most of the students, white and black, and felt "pretty alone" throughout those years. Once again she turned for comfort to theater. She became a member of the Actor's Lab led by the dynamic Kay Hocking (who'd been a part of FDR's WPA Theater Project and was married to a professor of philosophy at Emory University). When she was fifteen, Myla tried out for the role of Anne Frank in a production at Atlanta's main professional theater, Theater Atlanta. She remembers walking into the auditions surrounded by girls with beehive hairstyles, and, as she puts it, "for the first time in my life, I was exactly the right person in the right place!" She got the part.

Howard, along with several other Spelman faculty members, worked out a plan for Non-Western Studies at the Atlanta University Center. What followed for Howard was a Ford Foundation fellowship for East Asian studies at Harvard. The family spent two academic terms in 1960–61 living in Boston in a one-bedroom third-floor walk-up on Newbury Street. Everyone in the family enjoyed the change of scene. For Myla it was closer to a parole—she liked the Commonwealth School she went to, sailed on the Charles River, swam at Crane's Beach, went to Joan Baez and Pete Seeger concerts, and made new friends. In Cambridge, Howard and Roz met the historian Marilyn Young for the first time, who quickly became, and remained, one of their closest friends.

When the Zinns returned to Spelman, Howard became the director of the Non-Western Studies program and taught an undergraduate course on China. Soon after, in late summer of 1961, Alice and Staughton Lynd and their two children arrived at Spelman. Staughton's parents, Robert and Helen Lynd, both professors (he at Columbia, she at Sarah Lawrence), had together written *Middletown*, among the handful of classic works in sociology. Staughton had been an undergraduate at Harvard and Alice at Radcliffe; they met and married when still quite young and shared a radical political perspective—Staughton had declared himself a socialist (of the decentralized-decision-making kind) at age seventeen, and that was not a fly-by-night decision subsequently abandoned.[7]

Staughton and Howard had initially met in 1960, at the Columbia "smoker" held during the annual American Historical Association meeting in New York City. Howard was officially chair of the tiny history department at Spelman, and Staughton, having completed his doctorate at Columbia, was looking for a job—but *only* a job teaching at a black college: he and Alice both wanted to be a part of the burgeoning struggle for black rights. That was all Howard had to hear; he hired Staughton on the spot. To get to know each other better, Staughton, Howard, and their children (Myla was then thirteen; Jeff, eleven) went on a climbing expedition in New Hampshire during that summer. Howard and Staughton discovered still further political affinities—especially those revolving around race, class, and nonviolence—though the two men couldn't have been more different in their backgrounds, Staughton the privileged son of famous parents, Howard the offspring of poor Jewish immigrants.

As the Lynds arrived at Spelman, Pat and Henry West were leaving so that Henry could pursue graduate work at Harvard, and the Lynds were given their apartment in the same building on the college campus where the Zinns lived. Howard and Staughton soon began to share notes on nontraditional teaching and began to play tennis together regularly. Before long they became, and would remain, close and loyal friends. The Zinns also eased the social adjustment for the Lynds, introducing them to close friends like the poet Esta Seaton, who taught English literature at Spelman, and her husband, Danny.

Staughton and Alice held no brief for the fatuous view still held by many Southern whites (and plenty of Northern ones, too) that most blacks were content with the system of segregation and that the recent spate of sit-ins and marches was the work of outside agitators. The Lynds were also sympathetic to SNCC's view that further progress hinged on the increased use of civil disobedience, on exerting direct pressure. This was decidedly *not* the preferred tactic of the older black leaders and organizations.

A number of more conservative ministers in one of those organizations, the SCLC, expressed concern about the way SNCC had been "breaking the law." SCLC's president, Martin Luther King Jr., though well disposed toward the young militants, spoke eloquently at an Atlanta mass meeting in October 1961 in favor of "calm reasonableness." But to the young militants, that phrase was an echo from an earlier time and generation and was no longer applicable to the current situation. Unlike the older black leadership, SNCC viewed the glass not as wondrously half full but as lamentably half empty. Yet Howard, for one, didn't believe the generational divide was as distinct as others did. In a 1962 letter, he argued that "just behind the thin hard membrane of Southern Negro conservatism . . . is a deep reservoir of anti–status quo feeling." This may have been part of the reason Henry West described Howard as "the wisest commentator on public affairs that I have ever known or read."

The presidents of Atlanta's black colleges gave abstract support to the ultimate goal of complete desegregation, but even Benjamin Mays of Morehouse advised against direct action. The AUC presidents continued to focus instead on the prime importance of cooperation with liberal Southern whites, of employing a soft tone and placing emphasis on black voter registration. Some black colleges, preeminently Fisk University, supported their students unequivocally, but others, such as Southern University in Baton Rouge (the largest black college in the United States), expelled leaders of the sit-ins; some two hundred students withdrew in protest and several faculty members resigned.

More than political strategy was involved in the generational split. Differences in personal style and behavior added to the discord. The older generation, mostly middle class, modeled its comportment on conventional white behavior, whereas the younger radicals preferred the blue jeans, T-shirts, and overalls of the ordinary worker. And they also challenged the divine right of males to lead; there was no more powerful figure in SNCC than Ella Baker, and a significant number of other women took on leadership roles as well.[8]

As the movement hurtled forward, both sides gave way *somewhat* to the other's perspective. By the summer of 1961, SNCC added voter registration to direct action as a leading tactic. And some of the older generation (CORE, after all, became a prime instigator of the Freedom Rides) began to lean more toward militancy, no one more so than Martin Luther King Jr., himself comparatively young. He spoke out admiringly of the way SNCC militants continued to hold to nonviolence even as the group broadened its goal to include economic rights and the empowerment of "ordinary" people.

By 1961, Atlanta and Nashville had become centers for SNCC, its Atlanta office staffed by two full-time people. By then Ella Baker and Howard had been invited to serve as senior advisers to SNCC, a measure of the high regard the radical generation of young black students had for them. The spring and summer of 1961 saw a new development—the Freedom Rides. Designed to put an end to segregated interstate travel, they were no sooner inaugurated than they were met with savage beatings, firebombs, arrests, and jailings. In Anniston, Alabama, the melee was so bloody that several Freedom Riders had to be hospitalized.

The federal government tut-tutted over the violence but continued to do nothing to stop it, though Howard and others strenuously pointed out the several sections in the Constitution that allowed for, even mandated, intervention by President John Kennedy and Attorney General Robert Kennedy. But if they had the justification for acting forcefully, the Kennedys lacked the will. When the Freedom Riders were beaten with clubs in Birmingham and their buses burned, Robert Kennedy did nothing, though the Fourteenth Amendment to the Constitution gave him the right, even the obligation, to overrule the states and to use the power of the federal government to protect citizens against racial discrimination.

Then in 1961 the Justice Department sent a shock wave across the country. It initiated a large-scale prosecution—not against those who'd been beating and jailing nonviolent protesters but against eight black leaders of the so-called Albany Movement (plus one white sympathizer). Whose side was the federal government on? Its answer, of course, was all at once to deny there were sides—and to claim neutrality.

While the administration, reliant on Southern white votes, continued to dither, the Interstate Commerce Commission ruled (and here the Kennedys *did* exert some pressure) that interstate bus and train travel must henceforth be completely desegregated. Still, an abstract pronouncement from on high hardly guaranteed local compliance, especially not in the Deep South. That became all too clear when Charles Sherrod and Cordell Reagon, both veterans of the Freedom Rides, decided—with a courage unimaginable to most—to test the ICC ruling in Albany, Georgia. They set up workshops to train volunteers in nonviolent action and picked up a dozen or so recruits for the tryout run. The plan was to sit at the lunch counter in the Albany bus terminal and try to get served.

But FBI agents had in advance alerted Albany's notoriously racist sheriff, Laurie Pritchett, and he planned a painful reception for the protesters. Cleverly circumventing the ICC ruling, he arrested the students for "failing to obey the orders of an officer" and had them jailed. This in itself didn't overly alarm those arrested, since "fill the jails" had already become one of SNCC's key tactics. But SNCC did notify the Department of Justice about the jailings. Nothing happened. SNCC decided to try again, this time targeting railroad travel. Once again Pritchett had them arrested, shifting the rationale to "disorderly conduct."

Within Albany's black community, word of SNCC's ongoing defiance spread quickly. Grassroots black support for the students became so decisive that much of the community's middle-class leadership fell into line—which hadn't usually been the case elsewhere. Three weeks later, Martin Luther King Jr. arrived in Albany to join the protest. Mass meetings and marches followed, along with many arrests (the total at one point reached 737). This time the ever inventive Pritchett cited the offense of "parading without a permit" and—somehow—he also got the city attorney to obtain a *federal* court order banning further demonstrations.[9]

At the height of the ongoing struggle Howard, who'd been in and out of Albany since December 1960, got a phone call from the Southern Regional Council, an organization in Atlanta that specialized in gathering data on race relations; the SRC asked him to go again to Albany and do a formal report on what was going on there. Howard immediately accepted the assignment. A number of SNCC organizers were already at work there, and several of his students had been jailed; he hoped it would be possible to visit them, but as it turned out the authorities denied him access. Refused the right to see them, he stood outside the jail, a stone building topped with barbed wire, and shouted up to students and friends who'd been arrested.

The day after Howard arrived, local officials and the Albany Movement reached a verbal agreement, but in fact it made few concessions to the black community and soon fell apart. Martin Luther King Jr. and his close associate in SCLC Ralph Abernathy were called back to Albany from Atlanta to stand trial for leading an earlier demonstration; they were found guilty on July 10, 1962, and sentenced to forty-five days in jail or the payment of a $178 fine. They chose jail.

The trial produced a sensation, even leading Burke Marshall, head of the Civil Rights Division of the Justice Department and previously resistant to intervention, to put in a number of strategic phone calls to Albany officials. As a result, King and Abernathy were released the following morning. Soon after, a number of high-powered lawyers, including William Kunstler of the American Civil Liberties Union, started to put together a series of court cases to challenge Albany's unbending defense of segregation.

Further marches, prayer meetings, and demonstrations—along with arrests and bloody beatings—followed. The Justice Department, besieged by delegations, letters, and telegrams, in August 1962 finally filed a friend-of-the-court brief in support of the Albany Movement. Up to then the department and its head, Attorney General Robert Kennedy, had, through their inaction, essentially been collaborators with the segregationists.

Howard continued to go back and forth between Albany and Atlanta, and in December 1961 the FBI, which had let his file go dormant since the mid-1950s, picked up his trail again. Still referring to him as a "Communist," one agent reported to J. Edgar Hoover that Zinn had been critical of Attorney General Robert Kennedy "for his failure to prosecute civil rights violations and to protect the negro against white violence."

From the Bureau's point of view, the foremost grievance against Howard was that he'd been denouncing the FBI itself for standing by and not protecting blacks when they were physically attacked. Going still further, Howard pointed out that one of the great problems the Albany Movement faced in getting FBI agents to take action on its behalf was that most of them were southerners in origin and had been deeply influenced by the mores of their communities of origin. Whatever the reason, the FBI was no friend of the civil rights movement (there were no black agents). "Every time I saw FBI men in Albany," Howard claimed, "they were with the local police force."

In the presence of beatings and mistreatment in general, the FBI had the constitutional right to intervene, yet seemingly indifferent, its agents at most wrote down complaints in a notebook—and then did nothing further about them. "Can you imagine," Howard later said, "the FBI watching a bank robbery and taking notes?"

One day in Selma, Alabama, the novelist James Baldwin was on the scene when two young black men stood on the steps of the Federal Building peaceably carrying signs that said REGISTER TO VOTE. The notorious sheriff Jim Clark grabbed the men, threw them into a police van, and took them to jail—their fate all too predictable. Baldwin, accompanied by Howard, went straight into the FBI's office in the Federal Building and directly asked the head of the unit why Sheriff Clark hadn't been arrested for violating the constitutional rights of the two men. "Oh, we don't have the power to make arrests," the FBI man calmly responded. But he was either ignorant or lying, for not only the Fourteenth Amendment but also Section 242 of Title 18 of the U.S. Code provided clear legitimacy for making the arrest. Howard thought that one possible solution to the FBI's hostile indifference was to create a special corps of several hundred plainclothes federal marshals—similar to the T-men used by the Treasury Department—"for the sole purpose of enforcing federally guaranteed constitutional rights in many parts of the country where they are consistently violated." But the suggestion amounted to whistling Dixie. In a mid-1960s poll, 85 percent of Americans expressed "strong admiration" for the FBI.

In February 1963, Judge J. Robert Elliott announced his ruling in Albany against the movement's appeal for desegregation. After the hearing, as if to atone for it, Howard drove out to Lee County, where the previous night a number of black homes had been shot into from passing automobiles, and commiserated with the families involved. The Albany struggle sputtered on throughout 1963. Pritchett's police became increasingly violent, and the federal government continued to do little about it. In an article in the *Nation*, Howard put the blame squarely on the Kennedy administration and its timid Department of Justice. "The national government," he wrote, has "failed again and again to defend the constitutional liberties of Negroes. . . . By restricting its activity to a few ineffective court appearances the Department of Justice left the rights of Albany citizens in the hands of Police Chief Pritchett, who crushed them time after time."[10]

Without giving up its determination to desegregate interstate facilities, SNCC, in coordination with CORE and the NAACP, added an additional goal to its agenda—voter registration—with the state of Mississippi a primary target and with the already legendary Bob Moses as its lead organizer. But the decision wasn't unanimous. Andy Young, then working with SCLC, was among those who argued that taking on Mississippi was a mistake—the odds were simply too great. But Ella Baker took the opposite view, arguing that white supremacy was at its worst precisely in the rural areas of Mississippi, and if it could be toppled there, the rest of the Deep South might follow. Given her long experience working in the state, Baker's position won out.

Greenwood became the initial hot spot, and Howard and Roz were there during the height of the turmoil; he described SNCC headquarters as having "the eerie quality of a field hospital after a battle." At first the NAACP leader Aaron Henry became the racists' victim of choice: an explosive device was thrown into his home,

49

another ripped off part of his drugstore's roof, and bullets were shot directly into his house. Then on February 28, 1963, twenty-year-old James Travis, a native Mississippian and a SNCC field secretary, was driving along U.S. 82 about seven miles from Green-wood, along with Bob Moses and Randolph Blackwell (a field direc-tor of the Atlanta-based Voter Education Project), when three unidentified white men in a car without a license plate pulled up alongside of them and let go with a blast of gunfire. Moses and Blackwell were unhurt, but Travis was hit in his shoulder and neck, where the bullet lodged behind his spine. The doctor who patched him up said that Travis would have died instantly if the bullet had entered his body with slightly more force.[11]

The episode was part of a reign of terror. That same month, an-other drive-by shooting shattered the car's glass but left no one hurt. Eleven voter registration workers, including SNCC's execu-tive secretary, James Forman, were arrested, charged with "inciting to riot," and sentenced to four months in jail. The Greenwood po-lice turned a dog loose on a group of blacks attempting to register. The SNCC office in Greenwood was set on fire, the phones ripped out of the walls, and all office equipment destroyed; the Green-wood police said they could find no evidence of arson. Four black-owned businesses were burned to the ground, just a block away from the SNCC office. And so it went: shootings, beatings, harassment, and burnings became commonplace. The climax came on June 12 with the murder of Medgar Evers in the driveway of his home.

Instead of being intimidated, remarkably, still more volunteers arrived—many from NAACP and CORE—to supplement the SNCC workers already on the ground. And Mississippi's own black citi-zens, long subjected to white violence and humiliation, slowly began to join the activists—among them the sharecropper Fannie Lou Hamer (who Howard and Roz grew to greatly admire). After trying to register to vote, Hamer was fired from her job, lost her home, and had to take refuge in a friend's bedroom—into which someone pumped sixteen bullets. Undaunted, Hamer next tried sitting down in a white waiting room at the bus terminal; she was thrown into jail, where she was beaten all over her body with a blackjack.

When released, Hamer decided never to return to the life of a sharecropper. She became a field secretary for SNCC, joining a number of women in leadership positions, thus also affronting the gender norms of the day. In that, and in stressing maximum input from local black communities (what was beginning to be called "participatory democracy"), SNCC was proving itself a provocative alternate social structure to the traditional one of middle- and upper-class white men monopolizing power and governing through top-down decisions.

When someone later praised Howard (they should have added Roz) for the courage he'd shown in putting himself on the front lines time after time, he responded "it's not courage to me . . . I'm not going to be executed. I'm not even going to be given a long jail sentence. I may be thrown into jail for a day or two, and that has happened to me eight to nine times. I may be fired, I may get a salary decrease, but these are pitiful things compared to what happens to people in the world."

Howard felt that newspaper accounts of what conditions were like in Black Belt jails insufficiently conveyed their horror. He decided to tape-record several of the young activists, including Willie Rogers, who'd been recently released: "We stayed in the hot box two nights. It's a cell about six foot square. . . . Long as they don't turn the heat on—with three in there—you can make it. There's no openings for light or air . . . they had a little round hole in the floor which was a commode. . . ."

One day, Howard and Roz drove with Bob Moses, Stokely Carmichael, a veteran of the sit-ins and Freedom Rides, and others to another dangerous spot, Itta Bena. "People came out of the cotton fields to meet in a dilapidated little church," Howard wrote, "singing freedom songs with an overpowering spirit." One of them was a fragile, tiny, seventy-five-year-old woman who'd just spent two months on the county prison farm for trying to register to vote.

SNCC, denied the ballot in the election for governor, decided to run its own Freedom ticket, with Aaron Henry for governor and Edwin King, the twenty-seven-year-old white chaplain at Touga-loo College, for lieutenant governor. Ballot boxes were placed in black meeting places and churches throughout Mississippi, and hundreds of volunteers canvassed every corner of the state. In the upshot, some eighty thousand black voters cast their ballots for the Henry-King ticket. They won no office but did affirm the dignity and determination of African Americans throughout the state.

Dramatic events like the Freedom election drew much more media attention than did the daily hard work, discomforts, and dangers faced by SNCC's band of volunteers. The conditions under which blacks lived in rural Mississippi—the grinding poverty and grisly brutality—could hardly be imagined by outsiders. Terrell County typified those conditions. Blacks were a majority of the population in Terrell in 1960, but only 51 out of 8,209 were registered voters. In thirteen Mississippi counties, no blacks at all were registered to vote. Nothing had changed by 1963, yet forty people of astonishing courage turned up for a voter registration meeting in a local Baptist Church. Though several were arrested and a nearby black church burned to the ground, the county's Judge Elliott refused to grant an injunction to prevent further intimidation of prospective voters, giving as his opinion that there was no evidence of any danger to those attempting to register.

It had become increasingly clear by 1963 that litigation alone would not solve the voting issue as long as segregationist judges like Elliott presided over it. Given the frustrating lack of change, some members of SNCC began to question the tactics of nonviolence. They were tired of passively enduring white violence and of being accused by such "moderate" voices as the *Atlanta Constitution* as being "lawbreakers" for engaging in sit-ins, thereby "forcing" the police to make arrests. When President Kennedy finally got around to proposing his modest civil rights bill in 1963, a number of prominent Southern white "liberals" resisted some of its provisions. Ralph

McGill opposed the public accommodations provision as a violation of white property rights—as did the *Atlanta Constitution*, and on the same grounds. Even a few African American leaders expressed their ambivalence—their caution outraging those in SNCC.

At SNCC's annual conference, April 12 to 14, 1963, in Atlanta, three hundred young people (one third of them white) gathered to plan for the future. Howard appeared as one of the principal speakers. As if to bolster everyone's spirits in the face of an essentially stalled voter registration drive in the Deep South, Howard—whose optimism was nearly always on call, as intrinsic to his person as his warmth—put the best face on it. After all, he declared, the ongoing problems of discrimination can't be solved by the ballot anyway: "People voting are coming into a basically undemocratic political structure. When Negroes vote, they will achieve as much power thereby as the rest of us have—which is very little." The best hope of a solution was to create "centers of power," such as SNCC itself, outside the formal federal structures and to use those centers as channels for exerting pressure on both local and national governments. There was no guarantee of success, of course, not as long as the present administration remained in power; the president had done just enough, Howard felt, "to keep his image from collapsing in the eyes of twenty million Negroes." But no more than that.[12]

A sort of underground debate ran throughout the conference about the continuing viability of nonviolence, along with complaints voiced about the advisability of continuing to allow whites to participate in the black struggle. By 1963 many young white radicals on the country's campuses were getting involved in the burgeoning Students for a Democratic Society (SDS). The new organization was deeply concerned with the ongoing black struggle but was also invested in a general restructuring of society, the economy included, and would soon be in the forefront of protests against the escalating war in Vietnam. Not that radical young whites were alone in urging the need for a large-scale social renovation. Julian Bond, for one, told Howard that "integration into *existing* white society [is] not enough; [we] need to change this society."

Howard also expressed a muted but favorable view of Malcolm X and the developing Black Muslim movement; they "served as gadfly to both whites & Negroes," he said, and besides, they "say things other Negroes want to say" about the "white devil," but haven't yet dared. Howard also thought Malcolm "an important counter, you might say, to whatever tendencies there were in the civil rights movement to naivete. Malcolm was not going to be taken in by the black establishment or the white establishment. He analyzed the March on Washington" (as did John Lewis, who spoke out vividly and negatively during the event itself) "as an example of a controlled movement, a movement controlled by the powers that be." Malcolm was a scary voice to most white people because he talked about the necessity of self-defense, yet he never sanctioned deliberate incitement to violence.

During the April 1963 conference, the emerging voice of Black Power remained only an undercurrent, and most of the SNCC leadership spoke out in favor of continuing white participation. According to Howard's notes on that conference and on the November 1963 meeting that followed, the well-regarded Lawrence Guyot insisted that "the criterion should be who can do a good job—& if he's green or yellow or red" is irrelevant. Bob Moses agreed: "the *type* of person you have is much more important than whether he's white or not . . . otherwise we'll have a racist movement . . . I'll gladly leave if that's the kind of organization you want." To which Fannie Lou Hamer added, "If we're trying to break down this barrier of segregation, we can't segregate ourselves."

But not everybody agreed. One man spoke about the fact that despite the rhetoric of brotherhood, there were many in the black community who felt apprehension and anger toward whites. "Yes of course they do," Howard responded, "and we need to recognize those feelings—but not give in to them. It was ironic, and even a bit saddening," he continued, that SNCC, "the most advanced group in American society on race relations, is still caught by the mystique of race"—it showed "how tough it is to overcome." In rebuttal, someone else recounted a discussion he'd earlier had with a fellow SNCC worker who'd said he was joining the Black Muslims because "'whites are taking over the movement.' I had this feeling inside," he went on, "that the things he was saying were true." Then he added—presciently, it would turn out—that he'd "feel better if the whites worked in the white community."

Another prominent black leader, Ivanhoe Donaldson, strongly seconded the feeling that whites were taking over the movement: "We're losing the one thing where the Negro can stand first." That again brought Howard to his feet. He insisted that a solution to such feelings did exist: it was *contact*, which separation into white and black movements would prevent. James Baldwin was at one of the two meetings and seconded what Howard said: "Whites coming into the movement must forget they're white. We, too, must forget we're Negro . . . this is the way to create a new world—out of a commonness of purpose and decent respect for all the people who contribute to it."

After the SNCC conference, the novelist Clancy Sigal (*Weekend in Dinlock*; *Going Away*) approached Howard and asked if they could talk. Howard and Roz had dinner with him—for four hours—a few days later. Sigal had been living in England for seven years and, as a "traveling radical," had returned to the States to assess current developments. He'd found the country "qualitatively worse. Except for Negroes in South, finds country in decay," Howard wrote, abbreviating the conversation in his diary. He and Roz both liked Sigal and found him "very intelligent and articulate." But when Sigal asserted that "Negroes *are* different," Howard argued the point with him, willing to acknowledge that an afflicted history had made certain features of black culture distinctive—especially its greater empathy toward suffering—but refusing to accept any biological differences; blacks were simply human beings, with the same needs, capacities, and aspirations as anyone else. Howard later generalized that belief: "groups do have different characteristics," he wrote in his diary in 1963, "[as the result of] historical experience, but [there's] no innate special mystical quality to a group which is independent of experience."

That year, Beacon Press in Boston approached Howard about writing a book about the NAACP; he suggested that instead he do one about SNCC—an on-the-spot work of reportage rather than a comprehensive scholarly account. Beacon immediately accepted the substitution, and Howard set to work. He usually wrote quickly, and this time was no exception. But because of his teaching responsibilities, about which he was scrupulous, and his commitment to SNCC, which kept him constantly moving back and forth between Atlanta and the shifting crisis points in the ongoing black struggle, his schedule was hectic. Even so, he was able to finish his relatively short book on SNCC quickly, for it was based not on archival research but rather on his own experiences, as well as on tapes he'd made with various members of SNCC.

SNCC: The New Abolitionists was published in 1964 to a largely favorable reception. The book remains one of Howard's strongest—passionately argued, intense, and persuasive, though it has a few peripheral problems. The text isn't always easy to follow chronologically, because Howard sometimes jumps back and forth in time, making it difficult at certain points to know which events are taking place in what year. Also, he quotes freely from various SNCC workers but usually without letting the reader know whether a given quote is verbatim (tape recorded) or from his own memory. Even so, nearly sixty years later, *SNCC* remains memorably alive.[13]

Given the real-world roles that a number of Spelman undergraduates had been playing in civil rights struggles—with Ruby Doris Smith (who spent two months in a Hinds County prison), Herschelle Sullivan, Bernice Johnson (Reagon), Leonore Taitt, and others in leadership roles—the fantasy land of a finishing school atmosphere seemed more and more anachronistic to them. When the administration insultingly announced that it intended to start a new project "to improve students' table manners," a wave of exasperation swept the campus. Soon after, Betty Stevens, one of the activists and a student particularly close to Howard, received a reprimand from Spelman's Board of Review. An assistant dean publicly criticized her for not having gone to the Blue & White Banquet that year and reminded her that "students didn't pay enough [tuition] at Spelman to warrant their assuming so much prerogative."

That would prove the opening round in what would rapidly become a series of angry outbursts and recriminations, with the stunning climax putting the Zinns in the direct line of fire. Howard was well aware of the spiraling cycle of distrust between him and President Manley. In an effort to halt the deterioration in their relationship, he asked for and was given a private meeting. During it, Howard told Manley that given the many differences of opinion between them, some conflict couldn't be avoided, but he hoped that the atmosphere could become less strained. Manley's response was that the students' incendiary talk of being engaged in a "revolution"—Manley meant on the Spelman campus, not in Southern race relations—angered him.[14]

Manley wondered "if they got that in their classes." Probably so, Howard responded, already aware that Manley was uninterested in reducing the amount of strain between them. After all, Howard continued, they do a lot of reading for their classes and doubtless had "encountered revolution." Manley shifted to another grievance: some faculty members had told him that other faculty had been helping students to prepare their various petitions protesting conditions on campus. Howard assured him that was false information, that the petitions arose from the "intense student feeling and he should recognize this."

Manley insisted that certain faculty members (guess who?) *had* been supporting the student rebels. Howard refused to deny it: certainly *he* had, he told Manley, "and would support them in matters where I thought they were right." Manley suggested that in the future Howard go through appropriate faculty channels. Howard rejected the suggestion, telling Manley that "if the students thought petition was necessary, that was up to them," and in his opinion "they had a perfect right." Manley didn't give an inch (nor for that matter did Howard, who could be stubborn on matters of principle).

The proper role for faculty, Manley went on, was scholarship, to which Howard replied that he, for one, couldn't create an artificial wall between his roles as a teacher/scholar and his "concern for student rights." After all, he added, the subject matter he taught related to matters of democracy, "and it would be meaningless to teach it in theory and ignore it right around us in practice." Manley then accused Howard and his allies of wanting "to overturn the school." No, Howard said, he'd never advocated disobeying the school's rules, but instead had supported those who wanted to change them.

Manley responded that Spelman is "a small, private Christian college . . . and had to stick to its basic character" (Howard thought he detected a needless stress on *Christian* but realized he might be "too sensitive"). Howard agreed with Manley's description of Spelman but didn't see why it couldn't become a more *liberal* small college. Toward the end of their meeting, the tone improved somewhat, and "all in all," Howard characterized the discussion as "friendly"—an instance of his optimism clouding his judgment.

In any case, nothing quieted down on campus. Students kept checking in with Howard to report a variety of their grievances: Betty Stevens, with tears in her eyes, told him that the "unending pressure" on her as president of the student body was causing her to feel depressed. Another young woman complained of feeling "cramped." Another felt that the school was trying to take away whatever individuality she had, and yet another asked Howard how anyone could grow in an atmosphere so "warped." One young woman from Africa told him that "Spelman is like a coffin; you have to fit it exactly either by stretching or shrinking . . . says she feels her years here have been wasted." "We go in this whole stupid Spelman struggle," Howard wrote in his diary, "from days of hopelessness to days when we think Manley may begin to recognize reality."

Several of Howard's most promising students, fed up at the restrictions and pressures, began to resign, and editorials in the undergraduate paper grew ever angrier. One issue printed a letter from a junior who described herself as "disgusted, sickened and revolted by the hypocrisy, the under-handed dealings, the evasive answers and lies, the deceit, the glaring discrepancies, the treachery . . ." Another letter denounced the "silly rules" that kept "little girls behind a prison fence . . . we are mature young ladies with minds and ideas of our own." Howard wholly sympathized when the young husband of a Spelman student spoke bitterly to him about how in general "Negro colleges [are] worse than segregationists in [their] lack of faith in young Negroes," in how they "mistake lack of literacy for lack of intelligence" and fail to understand that "college is [the] *last* chance for young Negroes" to have the "freedom to learn and act before going out in [the] world."

Howard agreed. He felt that most of his students—not to be confused with most of the student body—reacted best not to "Christian platitudes" but to someone who "speaks to them sharply about something meaningful and expresses a radical viewpoint; they find it terrifically stimulating." In his teaching, Howard always made it clear at the start of each course that he held certain political views yet welcomed dissent and discussion. Those views included his detestation of war and militarism and his belief in a democratic socialism that would more justly distribute the world's wealth.

When the Social Science Club scheduled a meeting "On Liberty—at Spelman," the room was jam-packed with some 150 students (20 to 30 was the usual number attending), plus a number of Howard's close friends on the faculty, including the poet Esta Seaton and Staughton Lynd. Manley had been invited to attend but said he had a previous engagement. Dozens of students spoke (in

Howard's opinion, "boldly, movingly"), offering new details of the oppressive conditions on campus: Students who didn't attend Sunday concerts weren't allowed to sit on the porch or to leave their rooms. The door to the game room was kept locked because there was new furniture in it. Students had to leave the movies early in order to get back to campus before curfew. Howard also spoke up: "In our commencement orations we tell students to have the courage to dissent, but when one does we chop her head off." Students kept crowding into the room until it felt as if every undergraduate on campus was there—to Howard, "total, unanimous, crushing evidence of discontent." The question now was whether anything would come of it.

Howard had taped the Social Science Club event and at the next faculty meeting suggested that he play it. President Manley said he didn't have the time, even after Howard offered to cut down the tape's length. But Manley did have time to express himself fully. He challenged the need and right of the Social Science Club to have sponsored the "On Liberty" session, when regular student government channels already existed. It was always possible, he said, "to assemble a large number of students for a gripe session," but "the proper channels" should have been used in this and all future cases. By "proper" Manley clearly meant "traditional."

Howard then spoke at some length, and somewhat combatively, about the need to always provide opportunities for "free, honest discussion" of student grievances. Democracy required "going outside regular channels when those channels no longer allow [the] free flow of ideas and action." At that point, several faculty members expressed disagreement with him. One said that "Mr. Zinn" always spoke at too great a length—"it's one of his techniques." Another characterized the Social Science Club as "dangerous." A third insisted that dissident faculty would not raise such a "fuss" at Emory or Agnes Scott (though why not was left unexplained). Both Staughton and another ally of Howard's had their hands up to rebut such comments but instead of calling on them Manley spoke again himself. He reiterated his refusal to listen to the tape or to any complaint that didn't come through regular channels. He then declared the meeting at an end and got up to leave, even as Howard was still calling out, "Dr. Manley . . . Dr. Manley . . ."

The faculty as a whole had rather obediently deferred to Manley; Howard, though not a cynic, thought its compliance might have been related to its being that time of the year when Manley determined the pay scale for each faculty member (a power at many colleges wielded by academic departments). After the meeting was adjourned, Howard stood outside for a while discussing the evening with a few friends, including Esta and Staughton. Howard told them that he felt "very depressed"—for him, a most atypical state.

He thought the faculty might fight for themselves on certain matters but not on behalf of students; it was now up to the students themselves to produce change. As if alarmed at having caught himself in a pessimistic mood, Howard quickly went into reverse, telling the others that he *was* "still optimistic." After all, he said, "all social change involves tension, temporary defeat, disappointment, conflict before surrender." Staughton walked Howard home, and the two talked together a little longer. There was no reason, Howard told Staughton, that Spelman *had* to change. It could indefinitely remain a "petty and mediocre" place. And yet, taking everything into account, he continued to feel that "it is close to change."

A few days later, Howard talked over what had happened with Esta Seaton. They agreed that the biggest problem hadn't been their "rashness" but rather their tendency to become too immersed "in the idiocy" around them and to lose perspective—though they also agreed that it was important to "say things that seem outlandish to the lunatics in this set-up." And the "set-up," in their view, included the entire Negro college system; recently Howard had heard a complaint about Benjamin Mays's "pettiness [and] dictatorship at Morehouse"—and Mays was purportedly the most open-minded of the local college presidents.

Howard continued to get reports, mostly from students, about Manley's unchanged behavior. He'd said yet again that student dissidents were being manipulated by others, implying that a few faculty members were responsible for the ongoing turmoil. ("Isn't it interesting," one student was reported as saying, "that it's the *white* faculty supporting us.") Manley maintained the conviction that "all that really interested Spelman students was 'social activities.'" Yet they chose to dedicate the yearbook to someone who wasn't a Manley favorite, which resulted in the administration pressuring them through reductions in scholarship money and the like to retreat to an alternate name.

One faculty member friendly to Howard told him directly that he was "pushing too hard for [the] students. Wrong tactics. Need to go easy. Antagonizing faculty." Howard wasn't convinced. He told a friend that if Manley continued to ignore the extent of student discontent, then protest against his policies would have to continue, regardless of the animosity and recriminations it produced. His temperamental optimism reasserting itself, Howard predicted an ultimate victory, after which the bad feelings would dissipate, and then the pro-Manley forces would claim that this was what they'd wanted all along.

Howard's closest friends remained utterly loyal to him. But some Southern white liberals felt much more ambivalent. Leslie Dunbar, head of the Southern Regional Council (SRC) and a staunch defender of black rights, was a case in point. "Les" was known to defend Howard openly against the occasional charge that he was a Communist, yet the two men discovered over lunch one day that they weren't on the same page on the issue of allowing alleged communists to belong to civil rights organizations. "I don't want them," Les said tersely. "That's a very slippery business," Howard responded, since the communist label was likely to have come from the FBI or HUAC (as was the case with Howard himself) and not from a reliable source. One of Les's colleagues at SRC told Howard that just minutes before that lunch, Les had looked over a list of potential teachers for an SRC summer civil rights project and when he found

Howard's and Staughton's names on it had commented, "These are good men" but added that they'd make the list a "loaded" one.[15]

Despite his ongoing involvement with SNCC, the time-consuming struggle at Spelman, and participation in a new outburst of sit-ins at Atlanta's recalcitrant restaurants, Howard managed to snatch away enough time to piece together a new book, *The Southern Mystique*. It was handled by the prestigious Sterling Lord Agency in New York and published in 1964 by the eminent publishing house Knopf. Such auspices were signposts of Howard's growing emergence as a public figure. Moreover, the book was widely reviewed by a distinguished group of critics, including C. Vann Woodward, Lillian Smith, Pat Watters, and Ralph Ellison (whose piece ran on the cover of the *Herald-Tribune*'s Sunday *Book Week*). All four of them gave the book serious consideration, carefully marking its strengths and weaknesses.[16]

Only about fifty pages of *The Southern Mystique* were entirely new; the rest of the roughly 270-page book had previously been printed in various publications. "The South is still the most terrible place in America," Howard wrote in his introduction to the book. Yet by mid-1963 it had become *somewhat* less awful. He offered Atlanta by way of proof: the libraries, buses and transportation terminals, some theaters, hotels and restaurants, the public tennis courts, golf courses, and swimming pools had all been desegregated. Yet the mind-set of most of white Atlanta, Howard believed, hadn't much changed: most continued to regard blacks as their *biological* inferiors and still preferred a segregated society.

Howard also acknowledged in the book that such changes as had taken place weren't in themselves remotely sufficient. In a few cities, such as Atlanta or Nashville, segregation in public accommodations had begun to break down. But nearly a decade after the Supreme Court announced its antisegregation *Brown v. Board* decision, less than 1 percent of black students were attending classes with whites in the public schools of the eleven states that had once made up the Confederacy. Howard emphasized the few bright spots that had begun to appear—they did at least show that change was possible. How much change? To answer that crucial question, present-minded Howard utilized not history but current "situational psychology." Whereas Freud had stressed the primary importance of instinct and early childhood experience in determining lifelong patterns of behavior—the past, in other words, significantly influences the present—in the 1960s the (*very* American) emphasis among leading psychological theorists (Kurt Lewin, Gardner Murphy, Gordon Allport, Dorwin Cartwright, and Harry Stack Sullivan) argued that people are far more malleable in their behavior, more "amenable to sweeping change," than the "pessimistic" Freud had suggested.

Or in Howard's words: "Our overly heavy sense of history has left us unprepared for the possibilities of swift change in the white South . . . the past is elephantine only if we view ourselves as pygmies." Howard's rock-bottom positions were: we "can make what we want of our lives" and "we are fundamentally designed to do good." Such sanguine hypotheses are the needed ingredients for sustaining any active commitment to social justice issues. Whether or not these beliefs are in any ascertainable sense "true" has been much argued—but without resolution. (Recently the pendulum seems to have again swung away from Freud and back into the "situational" camp[17].) In any case, focusing on Atlanta and Nashville to demonstrate that the white southerner had "no special encumbrances that cannot be thrust aside" didn't prove that the same could be said for whites in Plaquemines or Sunflower counties as well. In such places devotion to segregation was so intransigent that in 1964 there was considerable reason for believing that it did take precedence over all other values.

Howard was probably well aware of the bitter inflexibility of such areas but underplayed that side of the picture for the purpose of encouraging antisegregationists to act. Much had been said about the difficulty of producing change in the South and not enough about its feasibility. Temperamentally, Howard would always be inclined to stress possibilities over intractability, especially since he felt that the latter had for too long served as a rationale for pessimism and apathy. As an activist and optimist, it was inevitable that Howard would downplay the obstacles to change and emphasize instead those aspects of social reality best calibrated to encourage and sustain involvement.

Howard questioned yet another truism: the notion that North and South were unbridgeably different from each other in how they viewed blacks. In Howard's view, the South was simply the North writ large: arguably the North was somewhat less prejudiced, but in 1963 it remained overwhelmingly racist—as, to a significant extent, it still is today, though the age cohort eighteen to twenty-five has more progressive attitudes than its predecessors, one of the few grounds for being hopeful about the future. Still, in a highly regarded survey done in 1990, a full 57 percent of nonblacks rated blacks as "less intelligent than whites." Still later, in 2009, the Pew Research Center put median household net worth for blacks at $5,677, for Hispanics at $6,325, and for whites at $113,149—an astonishing racial divide.

Residential segregation in the North and West, moreover, remains as powerful as ever, except in metropolitan areas with small black populations, like Tucson. Three quarters of Americans live under highly segregated conditions. Moreover, if a neighborhood becomes as much as one third black, 57 percent of whites polled feel "uncomfortable" and 40 percent say they'd immediately move out. Similarly, American public schools are becoming steadily *re*segregated, and three quarters of all African Americans are still housed in highly segregated neighborhoods, leading to segregated schools. As well, in a notoriously unequal criminal justice system, blacks, roughly 13 percent of the population, account for nearly 50 percent of prison inmates. Nor has our electoral process seen any marked changes. As of 2012, only two blacks have ever been elected governors of their states, and in the current Congress not a single

senator is black. Yet liberal gradualists continue to argue that electoral politics is the best avenue to social change—even though it's
nearly impossible for blacks to win a majority of white votes (in
2008, Obama won with only 43 percent of the white electorate supporting him).

In *The Southern Mystique*, now nearly fifty years old, Howard
ignored the still flourishing debate about whether purported differences between the races were genetically, environmentally, or cul-
turally produced. He refused even to acknowledge the question,
dismissing it as unanswerable, along with the related question of
the origins of prejudice. Howard's interest was in changing the
social order, not in "metaphysical conundrums" embedded in the
problematics of causality. He instead asserted that "for race prejudice the operable cause . . . is separation on the basis of inequality."
It followed, in his view, that *contact* between blacks and whites
would prove a "universal detergent" for racial dislike.

But "contact," Howard further argued, "must be massive, unlike
those 'integrated' situations in the North." Surely he was right in
his general insistence that contact often does dissolve racial antipa-
thy. The problem is how to achieve it, let alone on a massive scale.
Even in 2012, the opportunities for engagement beyond the workplace are infrequent, probably because most whites don't *want*
additional contact, and even if they do, segregated residential areas
and public schools would prevent it from happening on a widespread basis.

In the civil rights era, Howard was able to argue that in the
white southerners' hierarchy of values, the wish to maintain segregation was not all-important. The profit motive and the desire to
stay out of trouble with the law were among the values held more
strongly than segregation. The white southerner, Howard felt, had
"no special encumbrances that cannot be thrust aside in this moment of history." Yet surely Howard would never have claimed—
his own family being but one generation removed from the shtetl

and poverty—that Jews and Christians had no historical differences that couldn't be readily "thrust aside." Howard could hold that view in regard to black-white relations only by ignoring the South's special history with slavery and the failed Confederacy, along with all the arguments that had been used to justify them—preeminently the belief that blacks were innately inferior, thus making their reduction to second-rate status necessary—arguments that are still used today, though less openly, as justification for ongoing separation in housing and schools.

It was this sort of analysis that most bothered Howard's critics. Lillian Smith was the most dismissive of *The Southern Mystique*, though she did at least credit Howard with being "a courageous, decent, intelligent man whom the reader cannot fail to respect and want to listen to." And that was about all she gave him. As a writer who'd spent much of her life thinking about the complexities of the South, Smith found Howard's generalizations "shallow." She felt they weren't grounded in "a sufficient variety of facts" to warrant his large claims, and she thought his effort "to push away the past almost completely greatly mistaken . . . the problems of the South are not made easier by oversimplifying them, by overstressing the present." He also failed to see, Smith argued, that the South wasn't simply the North "writ large." Northern prejudice—a severe neurosis—wasn't the same as the South's racism—a *psychosis* that involves "terrifying splits, loss of the realities of a democratic government based on law, a regression to primitive thinking and acting."[18]

C. Vann Woodward wrote a lengthy piece on *The Southern Mystique* that was more intricate and subtle but finally no less an attack than Smith's. Like her, Woodward started with a compliment: the South had never had "so genial and disarming a critic." That suave opening soon devolved into an elegant dissection. Like Smith, Woodward expressed dismay over Howard's omission of any significant discussion of the South's special historical experience—slavery, secession, and Reconstruction. The omission, Woodward felt, overemphasized the similarities between the North and South and thereby missed the fact that the South had a highly distinctive heritage and culture. Woodward also found Howard's view that we have "an overly heavy sense of history" odd coming from a historian, doubly odd given this country's entrenched ignorance of the past and its careless lack of interest in it. No less irritating to Woodward was Howard's blithe dismissal of Freudian psychology. Woodward did express agreement with Howard's view that Southern folkways were neither immutable nor impervious "to rational appeal and legislative action." The South, Woodward acknowledged, *had* changed to a degree over the past few years.

But he did not agree with Howard's recipe for still greater change—namely, as Woodward put it, "some sort of prefrontal lobotomy on society that blocks off the past irretrievably from the present." If, as Howard seemed to claim, people can shift away from their allegiance to segregation quickly and fully, then Woodward believed "the stability of the new order is somewhat in doubt." As for Howard's panacea of massive contact between blacks and whites, Woodward thought there was scant evidence to encourage belief in its possibility. If contact ever *could* be made massive and sustained, that would mean that race prejudice no longer existed.

Woodward's was a tough assessment—he might at least have mentioned Howard's felicitous style—but it was straightforward as compared with Ralph Ellison's elliptical treatment of the book. At the start of his review, Ellison precisely located Howard's "passion to discover a rationale for hope and a theoretical basis for constructive action." And at the review's close, Ellison made some very admiring comments on the man and the book: "One needn't agree with Zinn, but one cannot afford not to hear him out . . . we must read him with the finest of our attention." But between his opening and closing compliments, Ellison itemized a number of criticisms.

Essentially, he sounded many of the same complaints that Smith and Woodward had, though more circuitously and with less severity. He thought Howard's omission of any discussion of "causation" a mistake, because it amounted to ignoring the ongoing weight of history: "Not only does it blithely put aside the intractable fact that human beings are creatures of memory and spirit, as well as of conscious motivation, but it makes too much mystery of what, in its political aspects, is really a struggle for power." In "shrugging off the encumbrances of the past," Ellison felt Howard had "failed to observe them . . . in sufficient detail."

Furthermore, he wondered whether Howard hadn't latched on to post-Freudian theory because it was tailor-made to his own optimistic disposition and could be used generally to inspire activism. As for Howard's argument that "the most vicious thing about segregation" is "its perpetuation of the mystery of racial differences," Ellison felt that what was worse was segregation's impact "upon individual and group alike." Most blacks, he argued, know from their own experience the lack of evidence in support of white supremacy; "they also know that they haven't lived all these years as servants to a race of gods." He also disliked what he called "an overtone of individual salvation" that he felt was sounded throughout the book—though the complaint seems idiosyncratic. In sum, Ellison felt that "in concentrating on the mystery of race," Howard had overlooked "the more intriguing mystery of culture."

Howard, in general, took criticism in stride, knowing it reflected the individual's own values more often than the merits of the work at hand. And it helped that a number of shorter reviews by lesser-known figures were mostly positive ("a reasonable and moderate analysis"). But surely, like any writer, to be criticized by three of the country's best-known intellectuals had to have been unpleasant for him—and for Sterling Lord and Knopf, as well, who never again represented and published his work.

3

The Black Struggle I

Thanks to his dynamic drive and a hectic set of commitments, Howard was soon on the go again. His daughter, Myla, later said of him, "I never (ever!) heard him say he was tired. Or even act as if he was tired. But he also never did things in a high energy way. He did whatever he did . . . in the same deliberate, relaxed manner." Along with his teaching, his deep involvement with Spelman politics, and his work for SNCC, Howard began to do more and more public speaking. He had a magnetic flair for the theatrical (later in life he'd try his hand at writing plays) and always felt thoroughly at home on a platform, enjoying the experience without being narcissistic about it—oh, a little vanity now and then about his invariably enthusiastic receptions but not any significant egoism. Howard had no nerves before a speech and usually spoke conversationally, without notes, never patronizing an audience, never playing the self-regarding expert, always encouraging an audience to participate in dialogue and debate with him. He and his listeners would become a "team," together exploring an issue, trying to resolve it in a satisfying way. He had something of real genius at

engaging an audience, establishing an almost magical rapport—
and it's no surprise that invitations to speak began to mount.[1]

At the same time, Howard remained committed to the black
struggle and active in it. When negotiations with those Atlanta
restaurant owners who still refused to desegregate heated up again
in the early spring of 1963, he participated in a number of sit-ins.
Leb's, which specialized in Jewish food, became a particular target.
One evening Howard and three other men—two of them white, two
black—scouted Leb's to make sure there were empty tables. Howard entered alone, and then all four of them walked briskly through
a roped entrance, past the cashier, and sat down at one of the tables.
The manager immediately came over. Jewish and friendly, he told
them that his own thoughts might be otherwise, but the restaurant
had a policy of segregation; he had a wife and kids—and therefore
couldn't serve them. They chatted and joked with the manager
about how desperately they hungered for Leb's famous hot pastrami. He said he'd gladly "wrap up some beautiful pastrami sandwiches for them to take out" but had to follow orders and couldn't
serve them in the restaurant. Not wanting to give the pleasant guy
too hard a time, the four decided to leave.

But then they spotted Charlie Leb himself, along with two
plainclothesmen, and changed their minds. A black busboy put four
glasses of water on the table and said, "Wish I could do more," and
went away. Leb swept the glasses off, shouting, "These are mine!"
To which Howard said, "That's the Passover spirit!" By now the
place was getting crowded, and at eight—they'd been there two
hours—they decided to leave. They called Leb and told him that
they'd be back. He apologized over the phone for having yelled at
them and invited them to his office, where he offered them drinks
(they declined). Though everyone in town knew that Charlie Leb
was a millionaire (he owned four restaurants), he told them that he
had no money and therefore couldn't afford to take the risk of desegregating. They suggested he think it over, that the risk of inte-
grating was small compared to the likely turbulence after more

sit-ins. Within a few weeks, restaurant sit-ins rose to a crescendo in Atlanta—forty people were arrested in one day—and the ongoing struggle would continue for some time longer.

Howard had to leave town briefly to participate in a Capitol Press Club panel in Washington, D.C., entitled "What Is the Future of the Negro." He was joined on the panel by Lerone Bennett, the editor of *Ebony*, Berl Bernhardt, staff director of the Civil Rights Commission, and the cartoonist Herbert Block (Herblock), who Howard found "very pleasant." It wasn't a run-of-the-mill discussion and went on for a full three hours. Lerone Bennett, who was far more militant than the magazine he edited, predicted that "eyeball-to-eyeball confrontations" would soon be the order of the day in the South. Howard forecast "tremendous Negro energy going into the wide end of the funnel [with] a tiny bit of national action coming out the other end." He portrayed President Kennedy as "hesitant," Attorney General Robert Kennedy as "callous"—an overstatement—Vice President Lyndon Johnson as "diffident," and the FBI as "incompetent in the area of civil rights." Herblock leaned over to Howard and whispered that he was glad he'd socked it to Johnson—"he deserved it."

Howard had been eager to get in his criticism of Johnson because the Press Club was planning a dinner that same night to honor the vice president. But Berl Bernhardt (named as one of the ten young "men of the year" by the Junior Chamber of Commerce) took umbrage at Howard's criticism of the federal government: President Kennedy, he insisted, "*had* taken a moral stand" (and in recent months, in truth, he had at least moved in that direction). Bernhardt also claimed that the FBI had been producing "many good reports" on civil rights. Howard doubted that such "good" (pro-black) reports existed, and even if they did, the FBI had done nothing to implement them. Howard ended by predicting that blacks were in danger of becoming part of "miserable white society" and urged them to use their present-day militancy "to overturn this society, non-violently . . . to bring revolution in the national political structure, the economy, the social structure." This was as all-encompassing an indictment of the white world as Howard had yet ventured, and a mark of his ever deepening radicalism.

Back home, the Zinn family went out to celebrate Myla's birthday with dinner at Stouffers, one of the Atlanta restaurants to have desegregated. From there, they went on to a Joan Baez benefit concert for SNCC and the militant Emergency Civil Liberties Committee, where the crowd of mostly white Emory students sang "We Shall Overcome" with a decent amount of fervor, in Howard's opinion, even if no match for a black group. Afterward, through prearrangement with the folksinger Guy Carawan (who Howard had known for some time), Baez came back to the Zinns' place. They'd earlier invited a few people from Spelman, SNCC, and Emory, but as they got closer to home, they found the road blocked with people and cars, the house jammed, and the sidewalk filled with those trying to get in.[2]

It was a beautiful night, so Howard sent most of the people to the grassy backyard of the building, promising that Joan would soon join them. She ate a banana in the kitchen and then promptly went out back and sang far into the night. Spelman girls in a nearby dorm hung out of their windows, in pajamas, to listen, though at midnight various housemothers began to phone, reminding their "charges" of curfew; some of the young women left, others said they'd take their chances. Myla cut her birthday cake, and then, around two A.M., Joan left. Or tried to. A group followed her along the road, then formed a circle around her and sang verse after verse of "We Shall Overcome" before finally letting her go. Howard thought the scene "eerie and thrilling."

The next day, he looked out of the back window—and there was Joan Baez, lying on the grass alone. The Zinns all went out to her and talked. Howard thought her "very intelligent and articulate . . . very impressive." But the intimacy was soon interrupted by some newsmen and photographers who'd somehow managed to find out where she was and plied her with questions. She told them that the most important quality in a person was not their skill at singing but rather what kind of human being they were. Which to her meant that Pete Seeger was at the top of the list. She also said, in regard to the escalating war in Vietnam, that if she were a man, she'd be a conscientious objector.

The day after the magical experience with Baez, Howard joined a handful of others in again picketing Leb's restaurant. Leb himself came out and, according to Howard, was "foul-mouthed, nasty [and] nervous" and tried to get a cop to arrest Howard for handing out leaflets (there was uncertainty all around about whether a city ordinance required a permit for that). Pedestrians passed by the pickets, calling out the standard epithets: "Nigger lover!" "Commie!" "White nigras!" One said to Howard with a somewhat confused anger, "You look Italian. Why don't you go back to Khrushchev?" But several other passersby made encouraging remarks, and one man stopped to give his card and to say they should "call him for help." The pickets stayed for about three and a half hours—and went back again two days later, this time with an all-white picket line, newsreel cameras grinding away, and hundreds of viewers standing around. Leb responded with signs in the window reading "I SERVE WHO I PLEASE" and "I MUST PROTECT MY INVESTMENT."

The following day, Roz joined a small interracial group of pickets at Leb's (other groups were simultaneously picketing various other segregated restaurants in the city). One tough-looking young guy stopped to talk to her for a long time, then went away, then came back again to tell her, "You're right. I just don't have the courage to do what you're doing." Howard, too, got animated approval, but he also had to face down a young man who stood two feet away from him "and just stared, with hate in his eyes." A week later, the Atlanta Chamber of Commerce unanimously passed a resolution calling on the business community to desegregate, without explicitly including restaurants. But city policy soon clarified: when two black Morehouse students picketed Leb's the next day, one of them was arrested and sentenced to thirty days on a work gang.

The spring of 1963 saw mounting protest among Spelman students against the Manley administration. The previous spring, they'd organized a petition to the administration asking, in essence, that the college's rigid rules be liberalized, with over half the student body signing it. The petition infuriated Manley. He called in a number of student leaders, including the new president of the senior class, Lana Taylor, and reminded them that if they didn't like conditions at Spelman, they could always go elsewhere. Lana Taylor herself was subsequently refused a scholarship on the grounds of "poor citizenship."

The students weren't cowed; by then as many as eighty of Spelman's undergraduates had spent time in jail for participating in an assortment of civil rights demonstrations, and they'd learned how to control their fear in the face of bullying. Their next response to the intransigent Manley was from the Social Science Club (Howard was still its adviser), which called a meeting to air student grievances against the administration. More than two hundred students (out of a total enrollment of some five hundred) and a dozen faculty members, including Howard, showed up, and one by one the students angrily recounted tales of antiquated rules and personal humiliations. Yet Howard felt that "it was becoming clear that Manley saw me as an instigator rather than simply a supporter of the protest."

In April, he again initiated a meeting with Manley "to generate," in Howard's words, "some cordiality." The meeting failed, "with absolutely no agreement on anything." Manley insisted that Howard should have cleared the Social Science meeting with him first. To which Howard said, "that was intolerable—that on a democratic campus any group should be able to meet any time on any subject without clearing it with anyone." Manley reacted with his usual mantra: "That's where we disagree."

By early June, classes were over, and the Zinns were preparing to head north to spend the summer in a cooler climate. Then came a phone call from Grady Hospital informing them that Alice and Staughton Lynd's five-year-old son, Lee, had fallen down a stair-well and been "badly hurt." Rushing to the hospital, Howard and Roz learned that Lee had suffered a serious skull fracture and had internal bleeding. The neurosurgeon at Grady decided to operate, and it was a timely decision: he repaired a severed artery and vein and removed a blood clot from Lee's brain that would almost surely have killed him. In the short run, he had psychotic seizures—even to the point of physically attacking Alice—but he eventually made a full recovery.[3]

With that crisis on its way to being resolved, the Zinns reacti-vated their plan to head north. Packing up their old Chevy, the family climbed into the car, ready to leave. Howard asked them to wait for a moment while he checked the mailbox one last time, hoping for an overdue salary check. Instead he found a letter dated June 1, 1963, from the Office of the President. It read, in part: ". . . you are relieved of all duties with the College after June 30, 1963. The College's check [$7,000—one year's salary] for your ter-mination pay is enclosed."

Howard was stunned. Antagonism between him and Manley had long been apparent, but despite all the warning signs, Howard had never expected their hostility to end this way. He firmly be-lieved that after seven years at Spelman, having been promoted to a full professorship, he did in fact have permanent tenure and could disagree with the president without fear of consequences. Of course, he would have anyway. Howard broke the news to Roz, Myla, and Jeff. It hit Roz hard, but the children reacted differently. Myla had been campaigning for them to leave Atlanta for years, but her father's abrupt dismissal made her indignant ("We won't go! We'll refuse to go!"). Jeff, on the other hand, took the news "easily, humorously"—just as (in Howard's opinion) he usually took every-thing.

Howard then left for his office to check out the college's employment regulations. He discovered that his own case was a bit blurred: he either had permanent tenure or, if he was currently on a five-year contract, the following year would only be his fourth.

Word that Howard had been fired spread quickly. Staughton, despite his son's accident, immediately got on the phone to solicit advice and ask for help. Howard wanted to fight the dismissal and felt he had solid legal grounds for doing so—especially after he contacted the AAUP (Association of American University Professors) and was told that in its opinion, he did have tenure and would have a strong case to that effect if he chose to go to court. The AAUP set up a committee to investigate the firing.

Though the students were scattered for the summer, a number of them heard the news and contacted Howard and Roz. Betty Stevens, who'd earlier been the student body president, wrote directly to Manley: "Zinn is admired, respected, and loved by all the Spelman students . . . this man is not just a teacher, he is a friend to the students . . ." Alice Walker, who Howard considered his most gifted student, wrote to tell him that the news had so upset her, she'd been unable to complete her first letter to him: "You know how much you mean to us. Whatever I can do to help, please, *please* let me know." At the end of the fall semester, Alice transferred from Spelman to Sarah Lawrence.[4]

The historian Harry Carman, who'd been one of Howard's professors during his graduate student days at Columbia, knew several members of the Spelman Board of Trustees—a decidedly conservative group—and got in touch with the more centrist ones (preeminently Charles Merrill, who sponsored fellowships for Spelman students to study abroad). But Carman doubted that the board would do anything to counter Manley's decision, a prediction that proved accurate. He also spoke with Benjamin Mays, the president of Morehouse College, who told him that in every controversy between the administration and the students, Zinn had sided with the students; Mays ambivalently added that "it was terrible that this had to happen but . . ." Carman told Howard that he'd heard of openings for a deanship or an appointment as head of the social science department at C.W. Post College on Long Island and asked if he'd be interested. The salary for either job would be around $10,000—a large jump in income for the Zinns. But Howard turned down both prospects out of hand; he "needed to find a job that closely suited my interests."[5]

Howard's dismissal created a considerable uproar. Jim Forman, a prominent member of SNCC, wrote to Manley urging that Howard be reinstated "both for the good of Spelman College and for the good of the movement for human dignity in Atlanta and in the South." Vincent Harding, the African American historian and minister, who Howard considered "a remarkable guy" and longtime friend (and who sometimes wrote Martin Luther King Jr.'s speeches, later becoming the first director of the Martin Luther King Jr. Memorial Center), immediately spoke to both Coretta and Martin Luther King Jr. about getting involved in the protest. (Howard had met them but didn't know them well; he thought Martin Luther King Jr. "very quiet and very modest, very low key, thoughtful, measured.") Over two hundred Spelman students, moreover, signed "An Expression of Student Concern," referring to Howard as "a great professor and . . . wonderful friend."

Howard himself went to work on what would become a comprehensive thirty-five-page summary, which he sent to the Board of Trustees (and others), recounting his years at Spelman and the problems he'd encountered there. It began with the forthright statement that he intended "to speak frankly," though not, he hoped, harshly. Yet Howard's anger was transparent throughout, a justifiable anger that made it easy for those who disagreed with his position to misjudge the document as needlessly severe, giving them an excuse for dismissing without evaluation the fraught circumstances he recounted. For Howard, though, it was impossible to tell the full truth while at the same time keeping his tone entirely neutral.[6]

At the beginning of the report, Howard sounded detached enough. His hope, he wrote, was to throw light not only on conditions at Spelman "but on contemporary problems of higher education in general." Spelman, he felt, was not "uniquely undemocratic," though it did have "a particularly damaging concentration of these disabilities, and its students, who have faced enough injustice in society, can least afford them." Howard made no effort to disguise his long-standing and cumulative disagreements with Manley and acknowledged that, in the last year in particular, he'd been a sharp critic of administrative policies. This, he argued, was all to the good: "The free interplay of opinion was beneficial to everyone," though Manley, apparently, "did not share these assumptions." He had tried to silence students and faculty alike and, if that failed, had invoked punitive action against his critics.

According to Howard, the basic problem was that Spelman was failing to move with the times, had not kept pace with the rising "revolution of expectations" that had taken root among black people everywhere. Instead, Manley had been "rigid and dogmatic." He'd acted "like a colonial administrator in a country burning with nationalistic fervor"—perhaps *the* most damning analogy Howard could have chosen. Manley, Howard further wrote, "has been cold, unsympathetic, and at times brutal to faculty and students" (Howard was only on page two of his thirty-five-page report, but his passion had already taken over).

In regard to his own dismissal, it had been done with "no warning, no reason given, no explanation"—which was entirely accurate. In his reading of Spelman's "Policies and Rules," Howard felt it was clear that a promotion to the rank of full professor (which he'd received in 1959) carried with it permanent tenure, "provided the faculty member has served the institution at least six years." Where the rules became clouded was in the omission of any description of the tenure status of someone who was promoted to a full professorship *before* six years of service (Howard's promotion had come after three years). By 1963 he'd completed a total of seven years on the faculty, but his promotion had been uniquely early. Manley would later claim that after being granted a full professorship in 1959, Howard had then been given a five-year contract (for which there was no such provision in the rules), 1963 being its fourth year and a terminating check providing for his fifth and final year. Howard's counterargument was that the AAUP had already told him that his interpretation of tenure was "reasonable." He then proceeded in his report to list his own multiple contributions to the college, to the larger community of Atlanta, to the civil rights struggle, and to scholarship. He felt it "embarrassing" to do so, but there was no other way to demonstrate that his dismissal had no basis other than personal animus—it had been a deliberate attack on academic freedom. The list of his contributions was long, impressive—and unpadded.

Howard proceeded to detail the lack of democracy at Spelman: the demeaning, infantilizing treatment of students, the authoritarian attitude toward faculty, the suppression of dissent, and the lack of democratic channels for governance. In regard to students, Howard's deep affection for them and his staunch defense of their liberties were transparent and touching. He provided moving instances of how Manley had reprimanded student after student for expressing any disagreement with established campus procedures—and noted that the complaints had come from the best students, the ones most determined to find their individual paths and to resist autocratic attempts to reign them in.

Manley had let their letters of protest or their requests to speak with him go unanswered or had handled them dismissively. When a group of students asked to attend monthly interracial meetings of undergraduates from various colleges in the Atlanta area, Manley issued a blunt denial on the grounds that such meetings would interfere with Sunday vespers. When he received a petition signed by more than half the student body that included specific suggestions on curriculum revision and on the expansion of social freedom—like being allowed to go into Atlanta more often—he scornfully rejected it and called in two dozen student leaders to berate them angrily for failing to go through "regular channels" and to reiterate his standard response to protest: "If you don't like it at Spelman, you can always leave."

Sometimes Manley had taken that action into his own hands by denying renewal requests for a scholarship on the grounds of "poor citizenship"—thereby denying limited-income students the ability to attend college. Howard thought such actions "crass and brutal." He pointed out that the greatest complaints made against the current cohort of college students were its apathy and conformity. Now that they were coming out of a generational coma, asserting their independence and involving themselves in public affairs, "they were being treated like misbehaving children and told that 'father knows best.'"

Here and there, Howard included in his report a few complimentary lines to soften his indictment of Manley: "I appreciate very deeply the fact that in your administration some extremely welcome changes have taken place. . . . I am only suggesting that the rate of change be speeded up in view of the rapidity with which changes are taking place in the nation." But there weren't many such attempts in the report at appeasement or conciliation. Instead, it was overwhelmingly, formidably tough-minded and unsparing. If Howard was interested, and he claimed he was, in some form of reconciliation—highly unlikely in any case—he went fishing with the wrong pole. Though he was known for being generous and kind in interpersonal relations, when Howard felt any vital principle at stake he refused to give ground.

He mocked Manley's constant assertion that one should go through "proper channels" for grievances. As Howard (accurately) pointed out, faculty meetings were run undemocratically, and faculty committees were "hand-picked and powerless"—in short, the "proper channels" that faculty and students alike were told to use "turn out to be either dead ends or wandering mazes." When faculty meetings were held, Manley treated its members, Howard wrote, like "errant children," and deliberately crowded the agenda with routine items that left no time for raising questions of import.

Howard next took on a linked set of issues inflammable in a South that prided itself on Christian devotion. He attacked many of the religious observances at the college—"the air of piety, the ceremonial occasions, the compulsory chapel attendance"—as "pompous and empty ritual." By way of proof, he pointed to the college's treatment of its employees, which lacked any spirit of generosity. Maids were paid 55¢ to 65¢ an hour, laundry workers $20 a week, night watchmen (who worked twelve hours a night, six days a week) $1.15 an hour. None of them was given help with paying medical bills, and whereas workers in academia usually got one to three months vacation, at Spelman they got one week. The college was teaching its students "that Christianity is rhetoric and ritual rather than human sympathy," and that "democracy is something to be talked about but not practiced."

Howard saved his most striking indictment for last. He drew a direct analogy between the Spelman administration's rigid attitudes and the arguments for maintaining segregation, linking Manley's authoritarianism and that of white segregationists: both frequently justified themselves by speaking of "tradition" and "our way of life," and by asserting "how much progress we've made under the old system." Both would claim that "these people" (students/blacks) are content with the way things are; "agitators are stirring them up" and they "aren't ready for freedom." Both poohpoohed signs of dissatisfaction as "just ordinary griping," refusing to recognize any serious discontent. All of which was tantamount to yanking the tail of an already enraged bull. Not that the analogy wasn't cogent—but that made it less, not more, palatable.

Howard's analogy would have infuriated the most composed and imperturbable of human beings, which Manley was not. It was about as politic as calling a Jew a minion of Hitler. Besides, Howard might have shown a drop of sympathy for Manley, a product of different times, forced to maintain a line between the still-dominant pattern of segregation and a growing militancy among the younger generation of blacks. Isobel Cerney, the wife of Ed Cerney, one of Howard's faculty allies, felt strongly that Howard was "too aggressive" with Manley.

Neither Howard's report nor the many letters, mostly temperate, that individual students, faculty members, and prominent civil rights figures sent to Manley received a hearing, an invitation to further discussion, or even, in most cases, a reply. When Howard himself wrote to the president in mid-June asking for an explanation for his dismissal, Manley did respond—but only to say that "it is not necessary for the college to give reasons when it is decided not to renew the contract of a teacher."[7]

When Leslie Dunbar and Vincent Harding made the same request for an explanation directly to Manley, they got a comparable response: in some thirty years as an administrator, Manley told them, he'd "never made it a practice to discuss internal matters with those who were outside of the immediate situation"—or, he might have added, *inside* the situation either. Not even *Jet* magazine could get in touch with him; every time they called, they got the same response: "He's in conference."

Nearly everyone already knew—or thought they knew—why Howard had been dismissed: over the years, he'd repeatedly challenged Manley's authority and, following his conscience, staunchly supported student struggles for more freedom on campus and "democratic liberties" off campus. That wasn't, of course, Manley's explanation. According to him, if Howard had refrained from going to the AAUP and asking for an investigation into his firing, Manley wouldn't have been averse to some sort of compromise (or so he told Staughton Lynd). But that argument wasn't persuasive, because up to that point Manley had firmly resisted every suggestion of an accommodation—even any discussion that might have produced one.

Manley now complained that if Howard had a grievance, he should have gone to the appropriate administrative officer on campus—as if there was the slightest chance he would have been met with anything but hostility. The opening gun in Manley's resistance to an AAUP inquiry was an insistence that no "dismissal" had been involved; he'd simply made the decision not to renew the contract of an untenured professor. The AAUP saw the matter differently. It notified both Manley and Howard that, according to Spelman's own regulations, Howard's promotion to a full professorship in 1959 had automatically carried with it the presumption of tenure. The AAUP also mentioned Howard's "national reputation as a teacher and a scholar."[8]

Manley's retort was a bit snappy. He made a point of informing the AAUP that during the previous year Howard had been turned down for both Guggenheim and Fulbright fellowships (but failed to mention that Howard had received a Ford Foundation fellowship in 1957 and had been a postdoctoral fellow at Harvard in 1960–61). Manley then added that he knew "of no outstanding book in history that [Zinn] has written or articles of great significance in the history journals." Manley was being disingenuous. It seems unlikely (though possible) that he didn't know that Howard's *LaGuardia* had been a finalist for a major prize and that he was about to publish two books (*SNCC* and *The Southern Mystique*); he'd also had pieces in such prestigious national journals as *Harper's* and (several times) the *Nation*. The meticulous Manley had specified "history journals," but Howard's lack of appearance in those was partial testimony to his *national* prominence.

Given the seeming impasse, Howard and Roz (the children were in summer camps up north) spent most of July 1963 in Greenwood, Mississippi, where Howard completed his interviews with SNCC people for his book on the organization. During their stay, Howard heard and tape-recorded many new stories from Bob Moses, Charles Sherrod, Stokely Carmichael, and others about the ongoing dangers and brutality that were daily companions of the black struggle. He learned about the killing of the farmer Herbert Lee, father of nine, and the subsequent acquittal of the killer on the grounds of "self-defense." He learned about the fourteen-year-old boy, falsely accused of burglary, who the police stripped, threw on a concrete floor, and bullwhipped. Bob Moses himself had been attacked by a police dog and had been in a car with another SNCC worker when thirteen .45-caliber bullets riddled it, wounding the second man in the shoulder and neck, very nearly causing his death.

In late summer, the Zinns moved to Boston, where they'd earlier spent nearly a year at Harvard, a time they'd thoroughly enjoyed. In October, Howard returned briefly to Atlanta to ship the family's belongings north and to see his friends. When he stopped off at the SNCC office, he found it jammed with more than 130 students who'd come to say good-bye and to express their support. It was, as Howard put it, "an emotional reunion." It left him feeling that the years at Spelman, despite all the turbulence, had been "a loving, wonderful time." Watching the students over the years change their attitudes and challenge authority, both on and off the campus, reminded him of "the extraordinary possibilities in all human beings, of any race, in any time."

By that point, Manley's attempt to discredit Howard had headed in a new direction, and the dispute heated up all over again. In an oblique letter to Robert Van Waes, the AAUP staff member handling Howard's case, Manley expressed "regret" that Howard had decided "to make a *cause celebre*" of his dismissal, "for the College has gone to rather special pains in an effort to spare Dr. Zinn unnecessary embarrassment and to give him an opportunity to 'save face.'" He'd been unwilling to talk about the matter directly to Zinn, Manley claimed, because he didn't want to run the risk that Zinn's wife might somehow get wind "of these disclosures." A few weeks later, Manley went up to the AAUP Washington office for an "off the record" meeting with Van Waes to lay out the particulars of his new indictment.

It turned out that Manley's cryptic remarks related to a morals charge dating back to 1959, one that had long since become fairly common gossip on campus. As one anonymous student had put it, "Howie tried to 'lay a dame.'" Mrs. Benjamin Mays told a more elevated version to Staughton (and others), referring simply to the so-called incident with a student—who, it turned out, had been the winner of a much-coveted Merrill scholarship to study abroad.

What the "incident" actually consisted of depended on who told you what and who you believed—close kin, in other words, to a tale like *Rashomon*. Howard referred to it in *The Southern Mystique*, but earlier, in the first draft of the book, he'd written a longer account in which he later made several changes. According to his draft version, Howard was driving off the Spelman campus on a cold, dark night in December 1959 when he spotted a student he knew and offered her a lift: "We talked, rode on. I parked the car at her destination [a faculty member's house] and we were still chatting when powerful headlights swept through the car." They came from a patrol car. Two white policemen ordered them out of Howard's vehicle and into the back seat of theirs.

According to Howard's draft version, he said, "If you're arresting us, what is the charge?" The older of the two policemen turned from the front seat to face them. "You settin' in a car with a nigger gal an' wantin' to know what's the charge!" They were taken down to the police station, formally booked for "disorderly conduct," put in separate cells, and then soon released on bond, the case dismissed.

Neither Howard's draft nor his printed version of the episode carries any sexual overtones. But President Manley's letters to the AAUP, and his "off the record" meeting with Van Waes, most definitely do. In an effort to resolve the discrepancy, Van Waes asked Howard for more details about the incident and told Manley, quite sternly, that since the AAUP "has been reliably informed that it is a common campus rumor that Professor Zinn was dismissed, in part, because of the student incident," it was "invidious and highly damaging" both to Zinn and to Spelman that "the basis for the dismissal action has never been formally stated, and no hearing has been held to test its truth or falsity." He urged that Manley at once inform Howard that the basis of his firing had been, at least in part, a question of morality.

Manley complied, but in his characteristically oblique way. He wrote Howard that if the AAUP decided to investigate, "there are certain documented facts concerning your personal and private relationships with a student, which are extremely relevant to your fitness to serve as a faculty member in this or any other institution, which would necessarily be brought to public light, along with the fact that you have not been truthful with the College on this matter." The letter sent, Manley wrote confidently to Van Waes, "I trust that Dr. Zinn will see fit to withdraw his demand for an investigation; if he does not, then I am genuinely sorry for him."

Howard, too, met Van Waes's request for more details. He pointed out that although the arrest had taken place nearly four years previously, nothing had ever been said to him about it. Instead he was regularly given salary raises during the years that followed, recommended for a postdoctoral fellowship, and appointed director of the Non-Western Program of the Atlanta University Center.

Howard added that on the evening of his dismissal, Manley had had a conversation with Roz and had told her that until the spring of 1963, "everything was just fine." Howard had also heard, from three separate sources, that Manley had told President Benjamin Mays of Morehouse that "the reason for the dismissal was my [Howard's] support of the student protest," the key episode being the Social Science Club meeting where students had loudly voiced their criticisms of the administration. Howard felt, therefore, that (as he wrote Van Waes) "the evidence of why I was dismissed is so clear that it would be ridiculous for me (or the AAUP) to get involved in answering rumors and innuendos which stray from the real issues . . . no-one can look for *personal* reasons in my case with any real justification."

Howard's reply didn't satisfy Van Waes. He asked him early in 1964 to come to the AAUP's office in D.C. for a personal meeting. Howard complied, and Van Waes subsequently wrote up a lengthy report on their "very frank" exchange. According to Van Waes, he began by asking Howard for more details about the incident. Howard essentially repeated what he'd said earlier, but this time added that the student was so "agitated" about problems she was having with her boyfriend that the conversation had become "involved and protracted," leading him to park the car "in a residential neighborhood some distance beyond the campus and her original destination. Seeing the parked car, some neighbor called the police."

What Howard didn't mention to Van Waes was that he'd parked on a dead-end street. But he did tell him that he hadn't previously stated the location of the arrest in order "to protect the girl, who would have been punished for violating her 'sign-out' statement (required by the college) concerning her destination." After they were released on bond, Howard went on, he and the student went straight to President Manley's house. He wasn't home, but they did tell his wife about the arrest—thus giving the lie to Manley's subsequent claim that he'd found out about the incident only recently (it remains conceivable, if barely, that for whatever reasons of her own, Manley's wife never told him the story).

If any attempt was made by Manley "to ruin him" (the student was a minor) by making the disputed evidence public, Howard told Van Waes, he would immediately institute a suit of libel for defamation of character. Howard added that though "his wife is ailing and he does not want her to be affected by a controversy of this kind," he was aware that even if he won the lawsuit, the airing of it was bound to have "nasty" consequences and put his career in serious jeopardy. Van Waes agreed and asked Howard—who'd earlier expressed no interest in a "mutual accommodation"—whether he'd be open to explore some basis for a possible settlement. Specifically, Van Waes mentioned an additional year's salary, withdrawal of the letter of dismissal, and an opportunity to resign instead. Howard expressed a "cautious willingness" to proceed along those lines. Manley, it turned out, was also willing to explore a settlement. A public controversy, after all, would mean an investigation into how he ran Spelman and reveal the many objections to his authoritarian style.

In the meantime, Howard contracted pneumonia and for a time was hospitalized. When released, he wrote Manley that "there is something about lying in a hospital bed, very sick, with time to think, that clears the moral passages." He then went on, in a letter that was pungent and unsparing, to make it clear that any prospect of "reconciliation" had passed. Among much else, he told Manley that his "sexual imagination has been working overtime in order to manufacture some tidbit of gossip about me which might be useful to you." Though he'd branded Howard "unfit" to serve on a faculty, Manley had never dared to "challenge my fitness in an open hearing before you dismissed me."

He could not even detect, Howard wrote, "the sincere moralizing of the true Puritan." After all, Manley knew perfectly well "that homosexuality and alcoholism have been openly existent on the faculty for years." (In 1964, it should be added, the cultural climate equated homosexuality with pathology, and no gay rights movement existed to deconstruct the equation; nor, oppositely, had alcoholism been elevated to the certified status of a disease.) Even so, Howard (unlike most contemporaries) expressed regret at having to call attention to "such people"—"I happen to believe they have a right to lead their lives as they see fit"—but did so only to point out that Manley had never taken action in regard to "open, aberrant behavior." Furthermore, Howard underscored the fact that only "when faced with investigation by the AAUP and possible censure of the college for a brazen violation of both its own tenure rules and the principles of academic freedom" did Manley "suddenly come up with a new reason" for firing him.

Despite Howard's evident willingness to proceed with an AAUP investigation, Manley refused to give ground on a single point. He continued to insist to Van Waes that Howard was morally unfit "to serve as a faculty member at a Christian college for young ladies." Manley also continued to insist that the college had terminated Howard in the manner it did "solely for the purpose of sparing him and his family and other persons from the considerable embarrassment and disgrace which would have been caused if the college had made formal charges against Dr. Zinn and held hearings." Manley was being entirely disingenuous. He knew perfectly well that standard academic procedure for terminating a faculty member with tenure, disputed or not, included an explanation and, if asked for, a hearing.

The round robin of letters, accusations, and recriminations continued for another six months, but little new was added—unless it be Manley's description of Howard as having a "unique penchant for controversy" (quite true when faced with injustice) "and notoriety." (So little true that one historian has insisted that when Howard, in his later writings, described his role in the black struggle, he was downright "self-effacing . . . he showed no inclination toward celebrity.")[9]

At one point Manley threatened to publish an "official" report on Howard's dismissal, highlighting the issue of "moral turpitude." He claimed to have affidavits from the two policemen who'd arrested Howard and the student, along with "statements from others that tended to corroborate these affidavits." He also informed the AAUP that he "had statements from neighbors that, to their irritation, a car like Zinn's was parked there frequently." The AAUP warned Howard that regardless of the accuracy of Manley's claims—and it had no knowledge of their truth or falsehood—their release would have a devastating effect "upon your future personal life and professional career."

Howard refused to blink. "It disturbs me," he wrote the AAUP, "that you think I should hesitate before calling for an investigation of Spelman College under Manley's administration," and he did formally request that such an investigation begin. But by the end of the year, Manley had instructed Spelman's lawyer not to respond further to any communication from the AAUP. Despite considerable sentiment within the AAUP that an investigation should be authorized, the general secretary ultimately decided against it: "I just don't see what more we can do in his [Zinn's] case. I take it that it is clear . . . that this is exactly what he himself feels." And thus it was that early in 1965, Van Waes informed Howard that "this office has decided not to pursue the matter any further" and that he believed "this decision is in accordance with your own wishes."

By then, Boston University had offered Howard an associate professorship in the Department of Government, and he'd accepted it. As he wrote Van Waes, he'd had, by late 1964, "several opportunities to write about my Spelman experience" and felt the time had come "to forget about the whole thing and call off an investigation." The only reason he gave for the turnabout wasn't entirely compelling: that an interview had been published in *Book Week* in tandem with Ralph Ellison's review of *The Southern Mystique* that ascribed to Howard the kind of statements about Manley that, even in his angriest moments, he'd never made. It could be argued that an AAUP investigation would have provided the opportunity to set the record straight and, further, that airing the truth about conditions at Spelman might have changed them for the better—which Howard had long fought for.

Perhaps he was simply sick of the extended and draining controversy. The new life that awaited the family in Boston promised to open up an entirely different set of prospects and experiences for the Zinns. They did maintain some of their ties in Atlanta, though three close friends, Staughton, Esta Seaton, and Renate Wolf, resigned in stages; Wolf, a novelist and refugee from Germany and a single parent, resigned immediately after Howard's dismissal, despite having no academic appointment in hand.

Both Howard and Roz retained their devotion to the black struggle, and Howard frequently returned to the South for SNCC meetings. They'd left Atlanta convinced that both the democratization of Spelman and improved circumstances for blacks would continue. Nearly fifty years later, conditions at Spelman *have* changed drastically, but it's debatable whether racism, despite marked external shifts, has become substantively different for blacks. Howard, for one, would continue optimistically to forecast additional advances in the future—for that was Howard.

4

The Black Struggle II

The family's return to the North was hectic. A pleasant (yet affordable) place to live had to be found—eventually the second floor of a house in Newton would provide the solution—new schools for Myla, sixteen, and Jeff, fourteen, located, and adjustments of every sort made to an unfamiliar neighborhood and neighbors. Howard's severance check from Spelman allowed him to stave off the need to start teaching again immediately. That allowed for some breathing room, and by fall something like normality had returned. In October Howard was able to travel to Selma, Alabama, the latest hot spot in the ongoing struggle to register voters. Selma's foul reputation as a racist swamp was well deserved: located in Dallas County, it was 57 percent black in 1963, though only 1 percent of this population had ever been allowed to cast a ballot. SNCC declared October 7 Freedom Day and confidently announced plans to register hundreds of black people. Jim Forman came in from Atlanta and James Baldwin from Birmingham. (*The Fire Next Time* had recently come out in book form to a storm of discussion and praise.) Howard was part of the small group that greeted Baldwin on his arrival.

The next morning, blazingly hot, saw the swift assemblage of hundreds of black people on line at the county courthouse, preparing (they hoped) to register to vote. Surrounding them were the notorious Sheriff Jim Clark's posses of deputies, helmeted, with clubs and guns dangling from their sides. Before much time had passed, Clark arrested three SNCC workers peacefully carrying placards. That infuriated Howard. He'd taught constitutional law for several semesters at Spelman and felt that the arrests were clear-cut violations of both the 1957 Civil Rights Act (which prohibited interference with the right to vote) and the First Amendment's guarantee of free speech.[1]

The next indignity arrived in the form of an announcement that during the lunch break—its duration not specified—there would be no further registration (there had barely been any during the entire morning). That raised the question of how to get food and water to the multitude of people who remained patiently on line in the hot sun. Howard protested this inhumane treatment directly to the senior Justice Department attorney present. His response was, "I believe they do have the right to receive food and water. But I won't do it. It's no use. Washington won't stand by me."

Two SNCC field secretaries, Avery Williams and Chico Neblett, decided to do something about the obvious suffering of those still waiting on line. Their arms filled with food, they crossed over to the would-be voters. Or tried to. Halfway, the troopers pounced, threw them to the ground, used their cattle prods freely, and then dumped the two in a police van. Howard and James Baldwin went straight into the FBI office in the federal building directly across the street from the courthouse to protest the failure of the FBI agents to intervene, and Howard cited to them the relevant sections of the Constitution and the U.S. Code that not only justified but *mandated* FBI action. The Bureau's section chief all but literally waved them away.

They sat outside on the steps of the federal building with the young black lawyer John Conyers—later elected to Congress—and talked about the unmistakable contempt for the law shown by those with the responsibility to uphold it. After the leisurely Southern lunch finally ended, the county courthouse was briefly opened, though scant registration was done. When the courthouse closed its doors for the day at 4:30, the line of would-be voters, visibly disappointed, gradually broke up. Three hundred fifty people had stood on line from early morning to late afternoon without food or water. "Those people should be given medals," Conyers said. As Howard later wrote, he was beginning to understand that history rarely recorded the contributions of so-called ordinary people to the unfolding of events. This new understanding would profoundly affect how he would henceforth write history.

At a packed church meeting that same evening, Baldwin addressed the gathering: "The sheriff and his deputies . . . were created by the good white people on the hill—and in Washington—and they've created a monster they can't control." Howard would return to Selma in 1965, when an attempted march across the Pettus Bridge would lead to a bloody police assault.

In December 1963, the SNCC staff met in Atlanta for five days. A number of important items were on the agenda, and most of SNCC's best-known leaders were in attendance: Bob Moses, Ella Baker, Charles Sherrod, John Lewis, Stokely Carmichael, and Jim Forman among them. After consulting with Ella Baker, and speaking for both of them, Howard gave the opening presentation. In essence, he asked the gathering to reconsider its ultimate goals and to expand its priorities. Attacking the current emphasis on the profit motive as the basis for a humane social structure, he strongly suggested that it might be time to enlarge the struggle against racism to include broad economic issues.[2]

The Zinn/Baker strategy was received with enthusiasm, a mark of the radicalization of the struggle since its early days when desegregation was the primary, even sole, consideration. Howard believed that intense study and careful discussion were required before settling on reconfigured goals, on determining the desirable future scope of SNCC and whether nonviolence any longer met the demands of the new militancy. Ella Baker strongly supported Howard's suggestion that SNCC undergo a process of internal scrutiny that would inform future activism. Howard himself envisioned the SNCC staff taking turns every three months or so in groups of, say, twenty-five, to attend a five-to-six-day "intensive"—a "refueling" session in the social sciences and humanities, conducted away from current areas of struggle, which would combine lectures, reading, and discussion in "a kind of rest-recreation period." On February 9–10, Howard met with four others (including Ella Baker) in Washington, D.C., to iron out details for these sessions.

He then set to work drawing up a memorandum that outlined a proposed educational program for full-time civil rights workers in the South, which had been endorsed at the December 1963 meeting of the SNCC staff. Many of those workers had dropped out of college (or had never spent much time there) in order to devote their energies to SNCC. Howard envisioned setting up an educational system that would allow the approximately two hundred field workers to continue their civil rights work and at the same time proceed with their education; his memo suggested a curriculum that ranged from novels to books about "major currents in 20 century world history"—especially fascism, communism, and anticolonial movements.

Howard continued to go from Boston to an assortment of meetings. In late January 1964, he was in Hattiesburg, Mississippi, as part of SNCC's voter registration drive. The local newspaper, the *Hattiesburg American*, decried the presence of "outside agitators" and advised the black population "to ignore whatever goes on, and interfere in no way . . ." At a mass meeting, Ella Baker emphasized, as did Howard, the risks that would attend their efforts—probably no reminder was needed, given the murder of Medgar Evers six months earlier—as well as underlining the importance of advancing a movement that was becoming concerned about class as well as racial inequalities.

Despite a drenching rain, a significant number of people showed up to register the next day, but although they remained patiently on line for many hours only a handful succeeded. But yet another SNCC worker underwent a bloody beating after being thrown into Hattiesburg's jail, and a furious Howard wrote that the executive branch of the federal government was failing to protect U.S. citizens "against local lawlessness." Nor, after John F. Kennedy's assassination, did any such intervention arrive from the new Lyndon Johnson administration, despite the huge March on Washington the year before.[3]

Two months later, Howard attended a weekend conference in New York to help develop a curriculum for what was being billed as "Freedom Summer" in Mississippi, a far-reaching project that Charlie Cobb had pushed for; as part of it, Staughton Lynd would play a key role in organizing Freedom Schools. As plans for Freedom Summer began to take shape, Howard suggested that the arrival of an expected one thousand students from the North might well lead to violence and killings. He suggested that in advance of such a likelihood, protection be sought from Mississippi's governor and from President Johnson. Howard further suggested that a committee of civil rights leaders call on President Johnson to argue in person for securing the safety of local protesters.

Bob Moses agreed with Howard, but Staughton was less convinced. He believed that inviting federal intervention was "a sound tactical demand," but thought "it would be a tragic mistake for the movement to look to the Federal government for ultimate, strategic effectiveness" instead of focusing on building a strong grassroots movement within Mississippi. Nonetheless, Howard and others organized a petition, signed by some fifty prominent citizens, and sent it directly to President Johnson, urging him to station a sufficient number of federal marshals in Mississippi to prevent or immediately suppress any actions aimed at depriving American citizens of their rights.[4]

Thanks largely to the persistence of SNCC field worker [Ekwueme] Michael Thelwell, later a writer and professor of Afro-American Studies, some twenty people from Mississippi gathered on June 9, 1964, at the National Theatre in Washington, along with a distinguished "jury"—including former Sarah Lawrence president Harold Taylor, writers Paul Goodman and Joseph Heller, *New Republic* editor Murray Kempton, and psychiatrist Robert Coles—to provide evidence about the need for a federal presence in Mississippi *before* the onset of Freedom Summer.[5]

The event, and especially the testimony given by the Mississippians in regard to the endemic violence in their state, profoundly moved those in attendance. Joseph Heller summed up the prevailing feeling: "I was very frightened, very depressed, by what I heard today. . . . It seems bizarre to me to have troops in Asia to protect Vietnam from communism, when we have tyranny in Mississippi just as bad." When the hearings were over, the people from Mississippi got back on their chartered bus and started the thousand-mile trip back home. Those who had heard the words spoken in the National Theatre that day may have been deeply stirred, but the media largely ignored the event, and no response came from either the White House or the Justice Department.

But that didn't deter SNCC and CORE workers. The voter registration drive in Mississippi proceeded under an umbrella coalition—the Council of Federated Organizations (COFO)—with SNCC and CORE providing most of the workers and leaders and the less enthusiastic SCLC and the NAACP also participating to a degree. The SNCC and CORE workers continued to travel the state, consulting with local leaders, speaking at mass meetings, dispensing information about upcoming Freedom Summer events, and recruiting students to attend the Freedom Schools. Most of the victories that had accompanied earlier sit-ins, Freedom Rides, nonviolent marches, and protests had been pretty much confined to upper-South cities, where some flexibility existed around the edges.

There, the Justice Department had now and then filed suits and gone to court, producing at least some worthwhile outcomes.

The Deep South was another story entirely, with Mississippi, Alabama, and southwest Georgia the standouts for widespread violence, police terrorism, and unyielding resistance among the white population. Limited legal action would do nothing, would be about as effective as playing tennis with squash balls. What was needed was on-the-spot enforcement of the constitutional rights of black people, and that in turn meant on-the-spot enforcers. FBI agents stationed in the Deep South had thus far proved useless—they'd been far more sympathetic to the local police than to black rights. It was for that reason Howard had suggested the appointment of a special federal force of civil rights agents empowered to do the job and to make immediate arrests, the statutory basis for such action having been clearly established in Section 242 of Title 18 of the U.S. Code. Howard's suggestion had been ignored.[6]

On June 20, just as volunteers for Freedom Summer were beginning to arrive in Mississippi, a deputy sheriff arrested three young CORE workers, James Chaney, Andrew Goodman, and Michael Schwerner, on charges of a "traffic violation" and put them in jail in Neshoba County. Released that evening, they were on their way home when two carloads of KKK members stopped them on a remote rural road. The three were never heard from again—it was as if they'd disappeared into thin air. There was no further word on their fate throughout Freedom Summer, though many accurately guessed at it. Two months later their bodies were discovered. All three had been murdered, and Chaney, the one black, had been chain-whipped and mutilated as well. It wasn't until 2005 that Mississippi gave anyone a significant sentence for the crime—and that was one man only, Edgar Ray Killen.

Howard, along with many other SNCC workers, attended the memorial service for the three. Standing on a pile of rubble—all that remained of the burned-out Mount Zion Baptist Church, which Chaney, Goodman, and Schwerner had gone to investigate—Bob Moses surprised the crowd by reading a headline from the morning paper: PRESIDENT JOHNSON SAYS "SHOOT TO KILL" IN GULF OF TONKIN. Then he added, "This is what we're trying to do away with—the idea that whoever disagrees with us must be killed."

Most of the arriving volunteers for Freedom Summer were Northern whites, and their presence resurrected a long-simmering debate in the movement. A handful of whites—people like Bob and Dorothy Zellner, Jane Stembridge, and Casey Hayden, not to mention Howard Zinn—had participated in earlier sit-ins and protests. But at least as far back as the five-day SNCC conference in December 1963, discomfort had surfaced about the appropriate role for whites in the black struggle. Freedom Summer intensified that feeling. The sudden arrival of hundreds and hundreds of scrubbed, untrained young white people felt to some like an invasion. Only a few denounced the well-intentioned young as superficial do-gooders who in two months would shrug off their experiences in Mississippi and go back to their comfortable lives. But many more did feel that the summertime white soldiers had little awareness of the potential consequences of their arrival.[7]

Howard took handwritten notes on one of the more controversial discussions within SNCC that took place over the issue. One seasoned and highly regarded black Mississippi field worker remarked that the white volunteers could "do as much in their own city as here. They come here, then go back & say, 'Ah, I have been liberal for a week' . . . the basic emphasis should be on the people of Miss[issippi] . . . they should remove their own shackles." Another prominent SNCC worker thought the whole idea of having all these white volunteers come to Mississippi was to get them arrested—and get Freedom Summer some needed publicity. No, Bob Moses coolly responded, that wasn't it at all: we "wanted them to get out the vote."

The group then discussed a set of propositions that had come up earlier: that a white person shouldn't direct a project but should work in the field, preferably in the white community. In other words, Bob Moses chimed in, we should "get rid of whites." "Noise and commotion" then followed, along with some shouts of "No!" When things quieted down, someone said that what was meant was "no whites in certain leadership positions, they did not say no whites at all." But then someone else broadened the objection: "Any time you have whites in the office they're going to take over . . . they tend to perpetuate the idea of white superiority," not to mention the awful prospect of reinforcing a deferential "slave mentality."

Bob Moses pointed out that there had already been objections to whites working even in the field, because some felt they were more articulate and "they're going to do the talking," while the "Negro person" stands quietly on the side. "Which perpetuates the idea of inferiority," somebody else added. But Charlie Cobb—who many credit with the original idea for Freedom Summer—disagreed, recounting his own experience of canvassing with whites: "I being a Negro could articulate it better than the whites." Since the conversation had begun to repeat itself, Bob Moses summarized: "The tone I get is—the white people came in & took over & now we're gonna put them in their place." But in his view, whites hadn't taken over, and much of the unexpressed fear that they would centered on past experience with racist whites who thought of blacks as inferiors and treated them accordingly.

Doubts were also rising about nonviolence as a moral guide, let alone as a useful tactic. Local blacks, under constant threat of physical assault, had always believed in the right to self-defense. In practice that meant having firearms and using them when attacked. Even Ella Baker felt she might retaliate if confronted with force, though she respected those who could resist. Black Power and the exaltation of self-defense were about to move center stage.

The Zinns were essentially still living on Howard's severance pay from Spelman, though his writing did bring in a little extra money. He probably would have gone to Mississippi for the summer anyway, but it certainly helped when the Eleanor Roosevelt Foundation gave him a grant of $800 to develop "educational programs for students in the South." On July 7, the Freedom Schools opened their doors. At that point, twenty-five schools were in operation, with a total enrollment of more than 1,500 students. As well, an acting company was being developed to tour the state, performing the documentary play *In White America*, along with a presentation of four films from the AFL-CIO film library. Interschool baseball games were also organized, and volunteers were trying to raise money to make a film about the Freedom Schools.[8]

Predictably, Senator James O. Eastland of Mississippi raised the cry of a Communist-backed "conspiracy to thrust violence" into the state—the implication being that it had previously been unknown there. Staughton Lynd, who'd done yeoman work as director of the schools, had long been worried about local, homegrown violence from racist whites. No clear sense had developed, despite numerous meetings on the subject, as to whether the purpose of the summer project was to provoke federal intervention or to build up the grassroots movement in Mississippi. If the chief purpose was to bring about intervention, then whites—for whom the national government held a unique fondness—should be sent into all areas, regardless of danger. But if the main purpose was to register voters or conduct Freedom Schools, whites should be somewhat confined.

Roz accompanied Howard to Mississippi and helped out in the Jackson office during Freedom Summer. Howard worked primarily with the Pratt M.E. school in West Jackson, an area that ranged socioeconomically from the middle class to the destitute. The Freedom Schools in Jackson faced less harassment than did those in other areas of the state, allowing Howard to spend some of his time planning for three follow-up institutes (November 1964, February and May 1965) for civil rights workers who'd dropped out of formal education. Each institute would last a month, and the broad aim would be to provide those who'd left school in order to work in the

South, a chance to immerse themselves in reading and discussion about broad questions of economics, philosophy, and history.

Though estimates differ, by late July the number of functioning schools throughout the state had risen to about 40 (and then to 50)— twice the figure originally projected—with some 200 volunteers teaching some 2,000 students, in classes with enrollments of 25 and up. The schools were mostly located in church basements; as a result, several of the churches were bombed and destroyed. Typically the school morning would start with black history, followed by special courses (French and typing were particularly popular) or projects like theater or the school newspaper. In the evening, classes were held for teenagers or adults who worked during the day.

In rural areas, where recreation facilities were mostly unknown, the Freedom School often became the center for teenage social activities. In Carthage, to give one example, the entire black community assembled at the local church to greet the Freedom School staff, and when two days later the staff was evicted, the community arrived with pickup trucks, moved all the books to a new site, and began construction on a hitherto unthinkable "community center."

Students were also attracted to the informal and questioning spirit of the Freedom Schools, with their special emphasis on connecting education to the student's own lived experience. This kind of radical pedagogy, via Paulo Freire and Myles Horton of the Highlander school in Tennessee, was quite unlike the top-down authoritarianism they'd previously known. Indeed, Freedom School students were *encouraged* to question authority. The success of the schools led to considerable anxiety about what would happen after Freedom Summer came to a close. Staughton Lynd worried about it, too. He hoped that the schools would combine with community centers—as some already had— to offer educational programs. He hoped, too, that some of the volunteers would stay on (half of the coordinators were black); when polled, one in four volunteers said they intended to remain, but if even only one in five did, that would mean fifty radical teachers. Other teachers might be drawn from the adult black community. Furthermore, every summer volunteer was asked to find and train a local resident to take his or her place when the season ended.[9]

Yet the Freedom Schools gradually dissipated, and in 1965 no Freedom Summer took place. There was a good deal of discussion at the end about setting up a comprehensive alternate school system, but lack of resources stood in the way. In Staughton's opinion, any attempt at a set of parallel institutions would almost certainly have collapsed, leaving the students "to face the world without even a high school diploma."

Did the Freedom Schools accomplish anything? They certainly did not bring about the "crisis of conscience" in the white South that the more optimistic had hoped for. Local white resistance, which included bombings, prompted for many blacks a conversion from direct-action nonviolence to the conviction that hard-core white racism could be dislodged only by force. And that would have to come from the federal government. Even in the unlikely event that the majority of blacks would prove willing to resort to violence in Mississippi, it would almost certainly lead to widespread retaliation, firings, and jailings, which black breadwinners could ill afford: in 1964, two thirds of Mississippi's black families had an annual income of less than $2,000.

The benefits of Freedom Summer were more indirect—less tangible but very real. It had opened up to several thousand black teenagers the awareness that true schools weren't focused on rote learning but on using academic information to explore and measure one's own experience. Howard, in typical fashion, posed the purpose of schools as a question: "Can we solve the old educational problem of teaching children crucial values, while avoiding a blanket imposition of the teacher's ideas?" The students had learned, too, that economic deprivation wasn't an immutable fact of life for blacks, but rather the by-product of a system that unequally and unfairly siphoned most of the wealth to a tiny segment of society.

Many of those students had also learned not to automatically defer to authority but always to raise questions and not to feel intimidated by white teachers. Old habits would die hard, but once termites had been inserted into the woodwork, the long-standing structures would begin to crumble. Many a youngster began to show up at mass rallies and to help canvass for voter registration.

The students themselves put the benefits of the Freedom Schools best. In their prose and poetry, they made clear that for them the summer had been a triumph. One of them, Naomi Long Nadget, captured the feeling of many:

I've seen daylight breaking high above the bough,
I've found my destination and I've made my vow;
So whether you abhor me or deride me or ignore me,
Mighty mountains loom before me and I won't stop now.

The effect on those directly involved with Freedom Summer may have been large, but ten years after the Supreme Court's *Brown v. Board* decision, the states of the old Confederacy had enrolled a mere 2 percent of black students in white schools. The Civil Rights Act that passed in July of that summer, along with the Voting Rights Act of 1965, was touted by liberals as some sort of wondrous culmination, thereby enabling them to regard the civil rights issue as resolved ("Now it's up to *them*"). In fact to date little more than tokenism had been achieved, with no fundamental change in school segregation or voting rights.

Inspired in part by the growing number of African nations declaring their independence from colonial rule, and even more by the patch of ground, whether viewed as small or large, thus far gained through protest, the spring of 1964 saw the investment of considerable energy into forming the Mississippi Freedom Democratic Party (MFDP). It was designed to challenge the all-white Mississippi Democratic Party, which had barred blacks from participation in the precinct-level elections that chose delegates to the party's national convention. MFDP was implicitly meant as an in-your-face challenge to a Johnson administration centered on partial concessions and ambiguous directives, as well as to purported white allies in the North to "get off the pot" and wholeheartedly join in remaking mainstream politics so that it could come closer to meeting the needs of the people.

When the National Democratic Convention opened in Atlantic City in August 1964, there was considerable optimism that the MFDP delegation would be seated. In advance of the convention, many left-leaning white liberals had signaled their support for the MFDP challenge—including the influential Joseph Rauh, lawyer for both the United Auto Workers and Americans for Democratic Action (ADA). Rauh agreed to serve as the MFDP's legal counsel, along with Bill Higgs of the Institute for Policy Studies, a think tank to the left of Rauh and the ADA. The MFDP's confidence was further bolstered by the thousands of affidavits it brought to Atlantic City documenting the brutality that had previously greeted blacks attempting to register and vote.

But the MFDP hadn't counted on the strong pull of traditional politics. Lyndon Johnson wanted to be elected president in his own right, and he knew that the one-party South would remain Democratic only if its conservative white values went basically unchallenged. He and his aides went to work on those convention delegates—including blacks from other states—who'd expressed sympathy for the MFDP and wore them down by a combination of threats and dangled promises. And thus it was that instead of its sixty-eight delegates being seated in place of Mississippi's official racist slate, the MFDP ended up being offered two "at-large" seats, turning its preconvention optimism about empowerment to angry disillusion.

The MFDP turned down the two-seat "compromise" against the advice of Martin Luther King Jr., Bayard Rustin, Joe Rauh, and others, and despite widespread accusations in the national media that the "morally absolutist" rebels were being "naive" about how the democratic political process actually worked. No, they now understood that process well—and the profound cynicism that underlay it. The consequences would be historic, changing the shape of the struggle, illuminating the top-down nature of "democratic" politics, shriveling up the country's heart. Lyndon Johnson, however, couldn't have been happier: two months later, he won the presidency with a landslide victory over Barry Goldwater.[10]

All movements for social change are incremental, involving shifts over time in attitude and program that reflect the accumulated experience of those involved as well as changes in the political climate. The treatment of the MFDP during the Democratic National Convention embittered many; the offer of two "at-large" seats was viewed as a patronizing dismissal of the ability of ordinary people to make competent judgments. The fact that a number of leading black figures—including Martin Luther King Jr., Bayard Rustin, and Roy Wilkins (head of the NAACP)—had encouraged the MFDP to accept the compromise deepened the distrust between the older civil rights organizations and the newer ones, like SNCC and CORE. At the same time, it moved the younger workers into a sympathetic alliance with the largely white SDS (Students for a Democratic Society) national protest movement and its emphasis on the guiding principle of participatory democracy.

Howard returned to the South in 1965 for the last half of the march from Selma to Montgomery. The group of some three hundred people, mostly black, slept in a field near the main highway. It was a sea of mud "so deep one's shoes went into it to the ankles, and to pull out after each step was an effort." They put up two large tents, one for men, the other for women, but they soon filled up, and a number of people had to sleep in the open air near the road, patrolled by soldiers in full battle dress—at last called out, by presidential order, after the mayhem that had greeted the first attempt to cross Selma's Pettus Bridge. Protection for civil rights protesters was, in Howard's opinion, long, long overdue. The rest of the world, he felt, hadn't been able to understand why the most powerful government on earth had previously denied its ability to defend blacks against beatings and murder. Up to now, the government's argument had been that our unique "federal system" prevented the national government from encroaching on local authority, an argument that had become increasingly bizarre as the atrocities and bodies piled up.

For the last stretch, several thousand people joined the march. As they set out again at 7:00 A.M., Howard and a young SNCC worker struck up a conversation. "You know," the black worker said, "I saw one of those Vietcong guerrillas on TV the other day. He was ragged, angry, dark-skinned, and poor. I swear he looked just like one of us!" Howard's take on the comment was that "the revolution of the hungry is rising on all sides," in Asia, Africa, and Latin America, and he thought it "awesome [and] inexorable." He thought, too, that the "revolution's only representatives in the United States are young Negroes and whites offering their bodies in the deep South."

Many older white moderates and liberals began to express doubts about SNCC's shift in direction and its rising militancy. The columnists Rowland Evans and Robert Novak—if they could even be called moderates—raised the specter that SNCC had been "substantially infiltrated" by Communists. And the *New York Post*'s James Wechsler, whose liberal credentials were more authentic, expressed similar fears, except that his Communists were Chinese rather than Russian. There was also disapproval of the growing alienation among SNCC workers from the old-line black leadership. Reports reached Northern white liberals that some SNCC workers took a dim view of Martin Luther King Jr.'s "Baptist rhetoric" and the way his organization, SCLC, told people what to do. SNCC's countermodel was to help local blacks organize their own grassroots movement, and then leave.

SNCC, and to a lesser degree SDS, had in fact become more anarchistic—not in the conventional and mistaken sense of bomb

throwing and nihilism, but rather in its distrust of authority, especially when centralized, and its rejection of all forms of ruling over
others in favor of voluntary association and communities of the
like-minded, that is, the nonconformists. Anarchists emphasized
the entitlement of all individuals to their specialness. A more concrete affinity between philosophical anarchism and SNCC (or even
the New Left in general) was the emphasis on simplicity and the
minimal accumulation of goods. Finally, there's a comparable association of the basic virtues with "the people," especially with the
poor and downtrodden.[11]

By 1965 the mounting war in Vietnam added another matter of
grave concern to the political agenda. Even before the escalations,
Bob Moses had spoken out against the war, angrily questioning
why the government was willing to send troops halfway around the
world for uncertain goals but was still unable to send marshals into
Mississippi to protect blacks against racist violence. Back in 1945,
Vietnam, under the leadership of Ho Chi Minh, had declared its
independence from French colonial rule. But over the next decade,
the U.S. contributed nearly $3 billion to try and help the French
reclaim the country. Thanks to Ho's brilliant leadership, the French
accepted defeat in 1954 and signed (though the U.S. did not) the
Geneva Accords.[12]

The elevation of Ngo Dinh Diem, who'd been living in the
States, to power in South Vietnam, was supported by the U.S. government. Free elections were supposed to follow both in South
Vietnam and North Vietnam, but because it was commonly assumed that Ho Chi Minh would win both, Diem refused to hold
elections in the South. The increasing corruption of his government and his repression of the Buddhists persuaded the National
Front for the Liberation of South Vietnam (NLF), a coalition
group, to build up its insurgency.

Lyndon Johnson had declared as early as 1963 that he refused
to go down in history as the president who'd "lost" Vietnam (the

implication being that he owned it). Even before the extension of the war early in 1965, many influential voices were raised against it. According to polls taken at the time, a large majority of Americans registered dissatisfaction with the prospect of escalation and preferred negotiations. Skepticism was also pronounced within the intelligence community, the press, and among many leading figures in Congress—including Mike Mansfield, Richard Russell, J. William Fulbright, and vice president–elect Hubert Humphrey. In short, the prospect of a heightened U.S. involvement in Vietnam was not particularly popular and certainly not foreordained.

It was the enigmatic Lyndon Johnson who ultimately made the decision to "Americanize" the war in Vietnam and who set about gathering support for it. A vast army of historians has scrutinized Johnson's motives, yet consensus remains elusive. Even in retrospect, it would be difficult to argue that Vietnam held any vital threat to our security or that the leadership in South Vietnam wasn't characterized by corruption and in-fighting, or that the general population wasn't both war-weary and anti-American. Yet Johnson went ahead anyway, not even bothering (the same had been true of recent presidents generally) to consult with Congress, as the Constitution required, for a declaration of war.

Johnson's decision to escalate was no break with presidential tradition as far back as the antics of presidents McKinley, Teddy Roosevelt, and Woodrow Wilson, and throughout the 1950s and early 1960s, the United States had staged a series of interventions in the internal affairs of other countries, especially those in danger of falling into "Communist" hands. In the preceding fifteen years alone, the U.S. had supported the racist regime in South Africa and the brutal Duvalier government in Haiti, and it had overthrown the leftist regimes of Jacobo Arbenz in Guatemala and Juan Bosch in the Dominican Republic.

Yet this is not to say that Johnson's declared intention (like so many of his predecessors) to "make the world safe for democracy" was mere hypocrisy, designed to cover his real motive of extending

American power and opportunities for its business leaders. What must also be taken into account is the likelihood that Johnson *did* believe in his own anticommunist rhetoric, *did* believe in the country's mission to spread Christianity and "democracy." Johnson may well have been taken in by his own rhetoric, however self-deceiving and misguided it may appear. In any case, the decisive months of late 1964 and early 1965 set the country on a path that would cause widespread death and destruction, bringing infinite grief in their wake. The main responsibility lies with President Johnson, but the Congress and the American people surely bear part of the blame.

Those influential members of Congress who'd earlier opposed escalation now turned deferential and not only fell in line with the administration but passed the so-called Tonkin Gulf resolution (named for the 1964 incident—subsequently revealed as fake—of North Vietnamese torpedo boats purportedly attacking American destroyers). The resolution gave the president, in advance, approval for whatever wartime measures he felt necessary. As for the country itself, an ill-informed and dutiful public initially fell into a kind of bewildered trance from which it was soon roused through the standard device of flag-waving jingoism.

But not everyone was smitten by notions of pride and glory. Howard had no illusions about communist rule in Vietnam, but when the United States began its deliberate, large-scale bombing of civilians, he became one of the earliest critics of the war. Nor did he feel that protest would detract from the black struggle—he thought the two intricately linked. Civil rights workers in the South had long ago learned to distrust the government, local and federal, and they were among the first to resist the draft.

The older, more conservative black organizations—especially the Urban League, the NAACP, and SCLC—initially tabled all resolutions that condemned American policy in Vietnam. But increasing numbers of young blacks were scornful of those organizations and were outspoken against the war. In 1965, it remained unclear whether the civil rights movement and the protest against the war in Vietnam would become mutually supporting issues or divisive ones.

In the fall of 1964, Howard had begun to teach at his new academic home, Boston University. He was as conscientious and as devoted to his students as he'd earlier been at Spelman—and no less conscientious about what he viewed as his public obligations. In the spring of 1965, he and Herbert Marcuse were the principal speakers at an antiwar protest on the Boston Common. It drew a disappointingly small crowd of about one hundred people. Still more discouraging, at Howard's own university, it was possible to get six thousand signatures on a petition that pledged support for Johnson's Vietnam policy.

In a Gallup poll, only 4 percent of Americans believed there was no Communist influence in the antiwar protests, against a full 78 percent convinced that there was "some" or "a lot." At the same time, Johnson began the bombing of North Vietnam and by the end of 1965 had sent 185,000 troops to South Vietnam. It was a difficult, even dangerous, time for those openly declaring themselves against the war.[13]

That didn't stop the War Resisters League (WRL) from issuing as early as July 1964 a memo calling for the unconditional and immediate withdrawal of all American troops from Vietnam. That same summer, WRL also cosponsored a protest outside the Democratic convention—which drew, alas, a mere four hundred people. Undeterred, David McReynolds, a longtime WRL staff member, coordinated the very first nationwide demonstration against the war, this time drawing a much larger crowd.[14]

The continuing apathy among most middle- and upper-class whites about the war reflected the fact that among them fewer than 10 percent of the able-bodied of draft age would actually end up in the military. This was in stark contrast to World War II, when fully 70 percent of the draft-age population served. Who took up the slack? The working-class poor, of course, along with a disproportionate number of minorities. Among privileged whites, even fewer were drafted, thanks to a deferment system favoring those enrolled in higher education. Class, not race, marks the most striking differential between those who did and did not serve. Whether class is defined by income, job status, or educational level, the least favored in the country bore the yeoman's share of the war. A statistically tiny percent of the wealthy served in Vietnam, while a full 80 percent of the armed forces had no more than a high school education.

In August 1965 Howard wrote an article in the *Village Voice* in which he advocated a discussion within SNCC on the question of whether civil rights workers should take a stand on the war in Vietnam. He gave as his own opinion that they should. How would they feel, he asked, if the various peace organizations refused to take a stand on black civil rights on the grounds that it might drain time and energy from protesting the war? Furthermore, Howard likened the National Liberation Front—originally a small armed force consisting of various ideologies, with Communist Party cadre at its core committed to land reform, which the autocratic Diem government had labeled Commie—to civil rights workers in the American Deep South, characterizing both as "homemade uprisings against an oppressive system." In 1965 the NLF had no power in South Vietnam, though Howard somewhat minimized Communist influence in its ranks.

A number of black civil rights workers had been active in the antiwar movement from its onset, and some of the leading figures in SNCC—including Bob Moses and Fannie Lou Hamer—had already spoken out against the war. As early as 1964, Moses had declared his solidarity with the Vietnamese people, and the following year a number of SNCC workers refused to serve in the military. Fannie Lou Hamer vigorously denounced the war as emblematic of how the U.S. treated people of color. And SNCC as an organization came out in opposition to the draft fully a year before SDS did. SNCC was far ahead of the general population in criticizing American policy in Southeast Asia, pointing to the hypocrisy of sending troops to "fight for democracy" abroad while refusing to send marshals to secure black voting rights in the Deep South.

Yet there wasn't unanimity in SNCC in favor of taking a public stand against the war. Some members foresaw that Vietnam could shift the national focus away from the issue of black civil rights and make it impossible to give any substance to Johnson's proposed plan for a "Great Society." To help forestall such an outcome, some argued, too vociferous a stand against the war should be avoided: it could compromise fund-raising efforts and also, as one of them said, "hand our enemies the means of effectively red-baiting us. And we can be hurt by such red-baiting." And although cooperation from the government had thus far been starkly inadequate—under both Kennedy and Johnson—arguing against the war could jeopardize the chance that federal help in the future would become more pronounced.

To some extent Howard himself exemplified the shift in focus from the black struggle to the antiwar movement, though he tried hard to resist the pull. When a memo arrived from a SNCC worker addressed to "defunct executive committee members," Howard felt wounded and promptly replied. He'd done his best, he argued, to continue attending the executive committee meetings, but teaching prevented him from "getting away as often as I would like." He went on to describe himself as "not really a working member of the Executive Committee in the way that others are"—a statement, or even a feeling, he'd never entertained earlier. He now defined his work for SNCC as "writing about the Movement, speaking in various parts of the country about it—performing, in other words, a secondary and supporting role rather than the primary work that is being done by staff people" (and, earlier, by him as well). He arguably characterized his work for SNCC, past and present, not as part of the decision-making process but as "educational," and he suggested setting aside a few Executive Committee meetings—which he could attend—that would not discuss matters like personnel or finances but would be strictly devoted to substantive issues like "economics and politics."

There can hardly be any question about Howard's ongoing and passionate concern for the civil rights cause; it was a case of juggling too many balls rather than letting one simply drop to the floor. He did continue to write about the black struggle, sometimes in conjunction with the war in Vietnam. Early in 1966, for example, he solicited both *Commonweal* and the *Saturday Review* for commissions to write about why civil rights workers, and especially "the militant and younger elements," were "so unsympathetic, even hostile, to the administration's foreign policy." He characterized his main theme as the contrast between the way many liberals saw the administration's foreign policy "as a reversal of its progressive domestic moves" and the way civil rights militants "see a connection between the administration's coldness to revolutionary movements abroad, and its coldness to the bolder demands of the Movement."[15]

When the Johnson administration, perhaps in an attempt to reclaim its tarnished reputation, announced a June 1–2, 1966, White House Conference on Civil Rights, SNCC cut the ground out from under it. John Lewis and Stokely Carmichael (SNCC's new chairperson) cosigned a statement to the effect that Johnson couldn't be serious, given how little he'd done about the beating and murder of civil rights workers. The conference was being called, they said, because the country's prestige was suffering internationally due to its interventions in the affairs of nonwhite nations—not only Vietnam but the Dominican Republic, the Congo, and South Africa. "Our organization is opposed to the war in Vietnam," the statement continued, "and we cannot in good conscience meet with the chief policymaker of the Vietnam War to discuss human rights in this country . . ."

Soon after, Carmichael and SNCC's New York office issued a lengthy "special bulletin" to counteract what it called the "vastly distorted reports and outright lies" that had been appearing in the press about the organization's recent annual conference near Nashville, where Carmichael had been voted in as chair over John Lewis, who'd served in that capacity since 1963. The bulletin recounted the recent efforts in May 1966 in Lowndes County, Alabama, which was 80 percent black but contained not a single black registered to vote, while white registration had reached 118 percent of those eligible. Most blacks in Lowndes were functional illiterates living in squalor and hopelessness. To change all that, it made no sense to try to influence the local Democratic Party (as Carmichael said, it would have been "like asking the Jews to reform the Nazi party") because no white moderates existed in Lowndes. Instead SNCC, with the cooperation of CORE, encouraged local black people not to participate in the Democratic primary and to form instead an independent party, the Black Panthers. After working for months to register black voters, SNCC hoped for an electoral victory over the Democrats. But it was not to be. A combination of black fear and white intimidation kept enough blacks from the polls to allow the Democratic Party to maintain control.

Besides, black majorities existed in only eleven of Alabama's sixty-seven counties. Many of the ills from which African Americans suffered—limited education, few job opportunities, lack of decent housing—required national resources to repair. Such an effort required a clear-cut national will to accomplish change, and that was less likely than ever now that the war in Vietnam had moved center stage. True, the 1964 Civil Rights Act and the 1965 Voting Rights Act had been passed, but their implementation had been feeble. Nearly 95 percent of black children still sat in segregated classrooms, and a mere forty federal registrars had been sent into the South, even though a large number of areas still had less than the 50 percent black registration that, according to the 1965 Voting Rights Act, should have warranted intervention.

The liberal coalition that had produced the toothless federal legislation seemed satisfied with it, especially in combination with the distraction of Vietnam and the rise of Black Power, with its intimations of violence (more in the white imagination than the black intention). When SNCC decided to exclude whites, advising them to organize their own communities, liberals tut-tutted about "ingratitude," pointed the finger at "reverse racism," and felt confirmed in their decision to abandon the struggle. SNCC denied the charge of reverse racism, insisting that they advocated black consciousness and pride: "We seek to overcome the Negro's sense of shame about such things as 'Negroid' physical characteristics, and to encourage the sense of dignity which enables a people to free themselves internally and externally."

Not surprisingly, SNCC turned its energy to the acquisition of political power on the local level. The belief was that if successful community power bases could be formed—and SNCC hoped that a poor white base would emerge with which they could combine—it would then be possible to apply pressure on the state and federal levels to legislate change. Among many whites, cries of "black nationalism!" arose, along with the accusation that SNCC now considered integration "irrelevant." (What Carmichael had actually said was, "integration is irrelevant when initiated by blacks").

The then left-wing *New Republic* editorialized that "SNCC, after all, is not declaring war on whites; it is asking blacks to unite in their self-interest." But the magazine also favorably quoted Bayard Rustin, who'd said that "the future of the Negro struggle depends on whether the contradictions of this society can be resolved by a coalition of progressive forces which become the effective political majority in the United states." Ah, yes! Carmichael might justifiably have replied, "that coalition of progressive forces—whatever happened to it?" Both Staughton Lynd and Howard maintained a "good feeling about SNCC," with Staughton suggesting to Howard that "black power" was "really your old suggestion about centers of power."

The black community in general didn't share that "good feeling." Though the CORE convention voted its approval of the turn to Black Power, Whitney Young of the Urban League and Martin

Luther King Sr. expressed the feeling of many when they publicly chastised Carmichael as a "separatist." At NAACP's convention in early July 1966, Roy Wilkins went so far as to characterize Black Power as "Black Death." Even John Lewis resigned from SNCC. And then in mid-August, dynamite was purportedly found in SNCC's Philadelphia office. That rumored "discovery" fired up the largely condemnatory white media still further. Columnist Pete Hamill wrote a series of denunciatory articles in the *New York Post* in which, with little evidence except for the distorted kind, he excoriated SNCC as "anti-white" and condemned its new turn as an impractical go-it-alone policy.

SNCC fought back. Speaking at Howard University on October 14, 1966, Carmichael characterized Black Power as "a positive and redemptive force in a society degenerating into a form of totalitarianism," and he denounced the widespread misuse of the catchphrase in the national media. To say, as many whites did, that SNCC had abandoned the goal of integration was tantamount to saying "that there was nothing of value in the Negro community" (Carmichael), "so the thing to do was to siphon off the 'acceptable' Negroes into the surrounding middle-class white community." But it was "hardly a concern of the Negro sharecropper, or dishwasher or welfare recipient, whether a certain fifteen dollar a day motel offers accommodations to Negroes"—integration "speaks not at all to the problem of poverty, only to the problem of blackness." Those who held out the goal of integration, Carmichael insisted, "would not develop the black community as a functional and honorable segment of the total society, with its own cultural identity, life patterns and institutions, but would abolish it."

Carmichael was arguing against assimilation on white terms, and insisted that the black community "must win its freedom while preserving its cultural integrity." In the interim period, until the constituent communities proved willing to accept the mosaic as a model, each part essential to the whole even as each retained its specialness, institutionalized racism and its by-products had to be resisted. Carmichael pointed out that in the last twenty years of the struggle for "integration," the gap between white income and black income had doubled, housing conditions in the ever more segregated large urban ghettos had worsened, and infant mortality rates had declined for whites and steadily risen for blacks. "No one is talking about taking over the country," Carmichael said, but rather "taking control over our own communities," and replacing machine politics, which gave a few political offices to reliable, selected blacks, with genuine community control.

In the summer of 1966, Makoto Oda, the well-known writer and chair of the Japanese Peace for Vietnam Committee (Beheiren), invited three Americans, Howard, Roz, and the young black SNCC worker Ralph Featherstone, to spend several weeks in Japan, all expenses paid, to speak to a variety of groups about the war. Howard immediately said yes; he loved both travel and talk—even if the FBI had labeled Beheiren "Communist-dominated." Roz was much less in love with travel and talk but, once there, became no less thrilled with Japan than Howard. She wrote their old friends Pat and Henry West that Oda was "incredible . . . very interesting, very sensitive, yet ribald—a real Balzacian person."

Howard's own enthusiastic letters home talked about their "fantastic companions," their happily frantic schedule (two or three large meetings every day), their travels up and down the country (twelve different cities in thirteen days), and the generosity of their welcome everywhere. All the meetings with students were oversubscribed, and the more formal lectures, usually lasting four hours, were delivered to packed houses—often a thousand or more people. The Japanese, Howard soon learned, were all but unanimously against the war, and he and Featherstone were put in the front of a large Stop the War in Vietnam march (in the rain).

Howard considered the visit to Japan "the most intense fifteen days" of his life, "physically exhausting, emotionally revivifying." He contrasted the "morally thick" attitude of his fellow academics in the

United States toward the war in Vietnam with that of the Japanese: "Among those we spoke to and with in Japan, the opposition to American policy was a hairbreadth from unanimous." He thought the explanation for the Japanese opposition to American intervention in Vietnam lay in the Japanese people's "piercing consciousness" of their own recent history. At meetings he would hear someone say, again and again, "You're behaving in Asia as we once did."[16]

It was only Edwin Reischauer, the distinguished American scholar of Asia and then ambassador to Japan, who Howard found less than politically thrilling, though charming personally. He felt Reischauer was living in "a comfortable bubble," either unaware or unimpressed with Japanese opposition to the war. Howard spent his last hour in Tokyo in "rapid-fire dialogue" with Reischauer, "trying to penetrate that bubble," but with no success: "It was like listening to an LBJ press conference, or a McNamara briefing."

Once back home, Howard started to get a mounting number of requests to talk about the war at this rally or that teach-in. If the date on his calendar was open, he nearly always said yes. He did so primarily out of a sense of moral obligation rather than personal egotism, though being human he did enjoy the crowds, the give-and-take, and the admiration. In 1966, the peace movement in the U.S. still wasn't very strong, consisting of roughly 10–15 percent of the population; the first large-scale protest march wouldn't take place until the spring of the following year.

In a piece for the *Nation*, Howard argued that our military action in Vietnam could be justified only if it was "helping a determined people to defend itself against an outside attacker." The administration liked to argue that it was acting only to counteract the "aggression" of Communist North Vietnam against the South. But in fact guerrilla insurrection in the South was a grassroots reaction against the Diem regime's policy of herding villagers into concentration camps called "strategic hamlets" and consistently using torture; the insurgency did not originate in Hanoi, and it preceded the Communist decision to take part in it. When the first battalion of some five hundred North Vietnamese—and this is according to U.S. intelligence reports—arrived in South Vietnam in late 1964 or early 1965, the U.S. already had forty thousand troops there and had flown thousands of bombing missions. The first foreign invader of South Vietnam had been the United States.

Unlike many who protested the U.S. bombing assault on North Vietnam, Howard was not ideologically committed to nonviolence. He believed that nonviolence should always be the starting point but at the same time believed that it was "logically indefensible" to hold to an unwavering commitment to nonviolence. He would himself be willing to use or approve violent tactics in at least two instances: "Self-defense against outside attackers or a counter-revolutionary force within" (picking up arms, say, for the defense of the Loyalist government in Spain in the 1930s against Franco's fascist attack) or "for the purpose of overthrowing a deeply entrenched oppressive regime, unshakable by other means." But when and how does one know that with any certainty?

Howard was clear that there could never be justification "for visiting violence on the innocent"—a standard that in his view should have ruled out the strategic bombing of German cities in World War II. Yet how could one avoid such a risk when deciding to fight against Hitler? And could he have been stopped without a limited (unlike the limitless attack on Dresden) strike against selected cities? For that question, Howard had an answer that satisfied him but would not have persuaded, say, the War Resisters League: if the violence becomes too intense or prolonged, no victory would be worth the cost—but Howard didn't have any persuasive definition of "too intense" or "too prolonged." The War Resisters League would have avoided such conundrums by refusing to countenance violence in any circumstances.

In September 1966, in a lengthy *New York Times* essay, Arthur Schlesinger Jr. argued—to the deep satisfaction of many liberals—that having chosen to enter the Vietnamese war, "we cannot lightly abandon it. . . . Our precipitate withdrawal now would have ominous reverberations throughout Asia. . . . No thoughtful American can withhold sympathy as President Johnson ponders the gloomy choices which lie ahead." Howard was both thoughtful and American, though unlike Schlesinger he had no wish to be part of the political establishment.

Yet Schlesinger *was* a liberal, and in his essay he did argue against several of the administration's assumptions. He didn't agree that the war was a clear-cut case of aggression originating out of Hanoi, nor did he agree that we could somehow pull out a military victory. But Schlesinger didn't agree with the two salient points Howard had made:

- That war is a monstrously wasteful way of achieving a social objective, always involving indiscriminate mass slaughter unconnected with that objective.
- That there is no necessary relationship between liberalism in domestic policy and humaneness in foreign policy.

Yet Howard *had* sanctioned violence in some cases, even while predicting that once used it would likely escalate.

It's worth noting that when Howard spelled out his radical views, he didn't cite as contributory any of his youthful experiences. Yet surely a poverty-stricken youth had some effect on the way he viewed the powerful (others with his background, of course, have grown up coveting wealth and power). The experience of Howard's father, a hardworking and honest man who'd never been able to earn much money or live comfortably, may also have been formative, instilling in Howard empathy for those who lacked the leverage to shape their own lives.

Such examples of influences could be multiplied many times over. The point is that the subject didn't much interest him—and that was related to his attitude toward introspection about the inner life. The personal psychology that most of us find fascinating, Howard regarded as somewhat trivial and self-indulgent when compared with the great public issues at hand. He almost never gossiped about others or analyzed and revealed much about himself. According to his grandson Will—who, except for Roz, was probably closer to Howard than anyone else—he was "uncomfortable with 'messy' feelings and avoided conflict." Passionate in his public life, some found him slightly reserved in his private one. To quote Myla, "He didn't talk about his personal feelings and prided himself on being rational and reasonable." His was an even-tempered, easygoing personality, engaged and approachable, and his amiability was real, not a mask. But angst wasn't Howard's style. He'd prefer that you not tell him your troubles, but if you persisted, he'd listen sympathetically even while hoping you wouldn't linger on them too long. Gentle, funny, and warm, he was liked by almost everyone, but that didn't necessarily make him, as he would learn from Roz, an ideal companion for the exchange of intimate revelations. Roz "did the emotion in the family," according to one close friend.

Central to the argument of Howard's pathbreaking 1967 book, *Vietnam: The Logic of Withdrawal,* was the falsity of the Johnson administration's claim that the conflict was due primarily to aggression from the North. It's unlikely that the government truly believed in its own argument (it knew that if any cause was "primary," it was the wish to thwart China's domination in Asia); besides Johnson had failed to prove his case against North Vietnam. The National Liberation Front (NLF) had inaugurated a civil war in the South as a local rebellion against its own malign government; only several years later, after the United States had entered the war in force, did substantial aid from the North begin to flow (as late as January 1966, when there already were 170,000 American troops in Vietnam, a senatorial committee under Mike Mansfield visited the country and reported to the Committee on Foreign Relations that there were still only about 14,000 North Vietnamese troops in the South—some 6 percent of the NLF's total strength of 230,000.[17]

The NLF did represent a nationalist-Communist revolt against Diem's and, later, General Ky's brutal puppet administrations, and that alone, given the U.S. attitude toward Communism (still phobic, though Senator McCarthy no longer ruled the roost), would probably have mandated intervention. The threat of a unified and Communist Vietnam under Ho Chi Minh was quite literally waving a red flag in the face of the U.S.—though, as Howard argued, the chances for social reform and improving the lot of millions of poor Vietnamese would almost certainly be better than under Diem or Ky. But that was hardly the opinion of President Johnson: as he put it in the summer of 1965, "an Asia so threatened by Communist domination would imperil the security of the United States itself."

Howard urged that Washington discard the notion that withdrawal from Vietnam would, as a result of the often stated but never proved "domino theory," lead one Asian nation after another, with the help of China, to succumb to Communism. Attempting military solutions for the socioeconomic problems of the underdeveloped world, he argued, tended to "bring about exactly what it is supposed to prevent": the destruction wrought by war made conditions still more miserable and their amelioration more distant. Howard used the Korean War as an analogy. The U.S. had "won" that war "in the sense that we prevented the North Koreans from forcibly unifying the country. But the cost in human terms was frightful." Estimates of the number of civilians killed run into the millions, with the landscape turned into a pile of wreckage—to say nothing of the dictatorship brought into power and "the end of political democracy."

Insisting that the United States did not belong in Southeast Asia, Howard broadened his indictment to question whether our numerous bases throughout the world were, despite the official mantra, in any way necessary to our "national security." Why assume, he asked, that various upheavals in Asia resulted from the "domino effect" rather than from a home-grown attempt to topple repressive regimes and to create better living conditions? Howard made the heretical point that Marxist ideals (which he never, unlike most people, confused with Communist totalitarianism) appealed to people around the globe. "And why should they not?" he asked. "These ideals include peace, brotherhood, racial equality, the classless society, the withering away of the state." It has even been argued that some totalitarian governments do improve living conditions—perhaps Maoist China more than the preceding Chiang Kai-shek government had done, or Castro's Cuba more than Batista's.

Howard was surely on the mark when chastising the U.S. government for tending to see "every rebellion as a result of some plot concocted in Moscow or Peking." And surely, too, Howard's precocious insistence that withdrawal from Vietnam was the only sensible policy was prophetic. Withdraw we did, some five years later, though in the interim causing a vast amount of additional death and destruction. When Howard wrote *Vietnam: The Logic of Withdrawal* in late 1966 (it was published in 1967) he was far ahead of the position nearly all public intellectuals, as well as the population at large, had adopted. Whether it was Richard Goodwin or George Kennan, the emphasis among the "experts" was that full-scale withdrawal would be an abdication of responsibility. But responsibility to whom? To the Vietnamese people longing for the cessation of war? To an opinionated but badly misinformed American public for whom "victory" had become a point of national pride? To General Ky's militaristic dictatorship? To the American foreign policy establishment, who'd thus far proved immune to rational argument?

Yes, turmoil and communism would be the likely outcomes of American withdrawal. But whatever conflict ensued would be as nothing compared to the slaughter currently taking place. Apparently you can't stop killing people in the name of . . . something or other . . . until a white flag is waved—just like boys on the sporting fields.

Howard in his air force uniform, England, 1945.

The Zinn Family. Left to right: Jeff, Eddie, Jennie, Myla, Roz, Howard and his brother Shelly, early 1950s (copyright the Estate of Howard Zinn).

Howard as a young activist, aged twenty-six, addressing a "Henry Wallace for President" rally, 1948.

Howard (tallest in the crowd) marching with the American Veterans Committee, late 1940s.

Howard taught part-time at Upsala College in New Jersey while earning his BA at Washington Square College (circa 1951).

Howard with Myla and Jeff, Atlanta, 1956 (copyright the Estate of Howard Zinn).

Howard (center) teaching his course on China at Spelman College, circa 1960.

Roz and Howard at a demonstration in Boston, early 1960s.

With James Baldwin in Selma, Alabama, 1963.

Freedom Day, October 7, 1963, in Selma, Alabama.

Fannie Lou Hamer of Mississippi with Howard in Boston, 1965.

Howard and Ralph Featherstone of SNCC marching in Japan, June 1966, against the U.S. presence in Vietnam.

Howard in North Vietnam, February, 1968.

Howard with Dan Berrigan in North Vietnam in February 1968 to receive the release of three American pilots.

Howard teaching a class at Boston University, fall 1969 (photo courtesy of Elsa Voelcker).

Howard with Noam Chomsky at a meeting of the Committee to Defend the [Black] Panthers in Cambridge, Massachusetts, 1970 (photo courtesy of Michael Dobo and copyright Michael Dobo/Dobophoto.com).

Howard addressing an antiwar rally on the Boston Common, May 1971; the next day he was arrested at a sit-in (see cover of book).

5

The War in Vietnam

The slogan "Black Power" had initially become popular (among blacks) after Stokely Carmichael in a speech used the words "black power for black people"—and was greeted with tumultuous applause. The problem was that the slogan had different meanings for different people. For Carmichael, Black Power emerged out of his understandable disillusion and bitterness with how little real empowerment had resulted from the earlier biracial struggle, with its emphasis on nonviolence, the redemptive power of love, and a racially integrated democracy. But what was Carmichael calling for? Was he encouraging the expulsion of whites from the civil rights movement? A shift from nonviolence to self-defense or armed struggle? The replacement of the goal of integration with a primary emphasis on blacks safeguarding their own culture and controlling their own communities? The media, having long since discovered that melodrama pays, highlighted every racist or violent inflection and downplayed the central call for ethnic unity.[1]

Even Carmichael defined Black Power in a variety of sometimes contradictory ways. In one speech he'd highlight the call for cultural pride, in another he'd underscore the need for restructuring

capitalism, in a third he'd play up the importance of blacks consolidating their base to the point where they had enough power to
make demands rather than requests. He was far more clear and
consistent in the book (*Black Power: The Politics of Liberation in America*) he wrote with Charles V. Hamilton in 1967. The two argued
flat-out that Black Power wasn't guilty of any of the three accusations most frequently leveled at it—that it was racist, violent, and
separatist. Black nationalism, they argued, was being mistakenly
equated with racism (though admittedly the one could sometimes
spill over into the other) and refusing to turn the other cheek with
"advocating violence."

Political and cultural separatism, moreover, should be seen as
a device (much as feminist consciousness-raising groups would be
later) aimed at creating a new awareness and a new sense of community among blacks; its primary aim was the development of
psychological strength, not permanent separation. Nor did Black
Power reject coalitions per se, though it felt the most logical one for
the future was between poor blacks and poor whites. They also
looked to global coalitions in which African Americans combined
forces with African and Third World people struggling against
colonialism.

Howard was among the few whites (Staughton Lynd was another) who endorsed the Black Power movement—but with some
provisos. Howard saw its potential "as a force for beneficial change
for black Americans," a force that centered on the psychology of
self-respect. But at the same time, he was reported in the *Boston
Globe* as saying that "on the personal level" he couldn't "embrace"
Black Power. "That's too crass and too cold for me," he said. "I still
retain some of the sentimentalism that goes along with black and
white together. At my core, I'm still an integrationist . . . and I
think that at his core, Stokely Carmichael [who Howard knew well]
is still an integrationist." Yet Howard did feel a good deal of empathy for the militant turn to Black Power. After all, "the civilization
created thus far by the white Western world," he wrote, "has a long

way to go before it is truly humane, and . . . the colored people of the world—having learned from their own anguish—can be a powerful creative force pushing us all on." If nothing else, Black Power was a necessary, hopefully transient way, of "getting some dignity."

The 1964 Civil Rights Act created the appearance of making great strides forward, but since enforcement remained minimal, it was essentially toothless. Southern blacks still remained largely unprotected from physical assault and largely mired in a poverty so profound that it was marked by malnutrition. (By now, Johnson was spending fifteen times more money on the war in Vietnam as on the "war on poverty"—and the ratio would go still higher.) And in the growing black ghettos of the North, infant mortality was still rising, the maternal death rate was four times greater than for whites, and life expectancy was six years less.

Many liberal whites seethed with resentment—mostly expressed privately—at the "ingratitude" that to them Black Power represented, and they drifted away in droves from the civil rights struggle. Hadn't Martin Luther King Jr., Roy Wilkins, Bayard Rustin ("it isolates the Negro community, and it encourages the growth of anti-Negro forces"), and others told them that the younger generation of blacks had taken the wrong turn? Whites were further able to justify their disengagement by telling themselves, falsely, that when blacks said they'd no longer turn the other check if assaulted by violent whites, they were really announcing their own willingness to *initiate* violence. Few whites seemed able to recall that violence was for them a long-standing tradition, with most textbooks hailing those colonial patriots who'd taken up arms against England.

Liberal whites also claimed that the 1964 Civil Rights Act had given blacks all that they'd been asking for or needed. The rest was up to them. It was time to "pull themselves up by their own bootstraps," in accord with the good old American way. But that "good old way" was more myth than reality. A small minority of whites continued to monopolize the country's resources, to have access to the best schools, jobs, and institutions, and to harbor, in some semiconscious way, the conviction that few blacks were innately capable of measuring up to white standards. All of which meant that most blacks would continue to run up against significant stumbling blocks to advancement—no matter how many worn-out bootstraps they hoisted. A direct result of white disaffection and tokenism would be the swift spread and acceptance among the younger generation of black activists of the arguments put forth by advocates of Black Power.[2]

The Berrigan brothers, Phil and Dan, were both Catholic priests and both boldly active in the protest against the Vietnam War. In October 1967, Phil Berrigan and three companions entered the Baltimore Customs House where the draft files were kept and poured blood on them. Phil Berrigan was sentenced to six years in prison. At very nearly the same time, President Johnson began a concerted campaign to counteract the view that the war was stalemated and to convince the American people that it was being waged successfully. General Westmoreland, the overall commander of U.S. troops, gave a speech in which he announced that the enemy was "certainly losing" and the end of the war in sight. He told a *Time* reporter that he defied the Communist North to launch an attack: "I hope they try something, because we are looking for a fight."

Two months later he got his wish. Seemingly out of nowhere, the NLF struck more than a hundred control centers throughout South Vietnam—the Tet Offensive had begun, stunning the Johnson administration, the military, and the civilian population alike. On January 30, 1968, the day before the Tet Offensive, Howard was called out of class for an urgent phone call. His friend David Dellinger, a prominent activist against the war, was on the other end of the line. He'd gotten a telegram from Hanoi saying that the North Vietnamese government had decided to release three captured American pilots if the peace movement would send a "responsible representative" to collect them. Dellinger had decided to send two representatives, had already gotten a yes from Dan Berrigan, and asked Howard to be the second person.[3]

Howard wanted to know when and for how long. Dellinger's answer must have surprised him: "Tomorrow. For a week. Maybe two." Howard was sure he could get a colleague to cover his classes and that Roz would want him to say yes. He gave Dellinger the go-ahead. The very next morning Howard found himself in a Greenwich Village apartment with Dan Berrigan, Dellinger, and SDS's Tom Hayden (who'd recently escorted three NLF prisoners from Cambodia to the U.S.). Howard knew Dellinger and Hayden, both of whom had been to North Vietnam, but he was meeting Dan Berrigan for the first time. They immediately hit it off. Howard—who personified joie de vivre—felt relieved at Dan's "impish wit," not wanting to spend a lot of time with someone who "believed that fun is a bourgeois indulgence."

That same evening, Howard and Dan boarded a plane at Kennedy Airport for a difficult twenty-eight-hour trip that included some half dozen stops in Europe, the Middle East, and East Asia. At each stop, a well-dressed man from the local American embassy would board the plane and offer to stamp their passport in order to "legalize" their trip (the same thing had happened when departing Kennedy Airport). Each time, Dan and Howard politely said, "No thanks." When they at last reached Vientiane in Laos, they'd expected their timing to coincide with an International Control Commission aircraft that made six roundabout runs a month between Saigon and Hanoi. "Drunk with fatigue," they had made it on schedule to Vientiane, only to learn that the Tet Offensive had closed the Saigon airport and the ICC plane wouldn't be able to take off. A few days later, another ICC plane was canceled, and Howard and Dan were forced to spend a full week in Vientiane awaiting the next flight out.

To pass the time, they took long walks through the city, which Howard thought had the air of World War II Casablanca—spies, drugs, intrigue. They even, as Howard put it, "sampled the dark, pot-smoking cafes" of Vientiane. The long wait, Howard wrote Roz, had made him feel "gloomy," a highly unusual state for a man so free of moodiness. He actually stayed up half of one night under the mosquito netting in his shabby French hotel on the Mekong River, debating with himself about going home if the next plane was also grounded. But he then concluded that "I could not possibly go home now—to think of mundane things like my classes when this is such a unique venture, a once-in-a-lifetime thing." Having made the decision to stay, Howard felt immediately better and shifted topics when writing to Roz, telling her how much he missed her: "How I've been thinking about you. Wild dreams & fantasies & memories. What I wouldn't do to have you with me now."

He and Dan took many of their meals in the hotel's huge dining room, served by tuxedoed waiters who seemed, in their silent elegance, leftovers from an ancien régime. Dan had brought along a bottle of Cognac, and every night before going to sleep they'd have a few sips. One night, sound asleep, a knock at the door awakened them. It was a member of the hotel staff, and she quickly led them to an air-raid shelter. A former bombardier, Howard was now on the receiving end—from the same air force, he noted, "I was once so proud of."

The very next day, February 9, the ICC plane—a very old four-engine Boeing, one of only three left in the world—got special dispensation to take off from Saigon, stop in Vientiane to pick them up, and then fly on to Hanoi. They flew through the night along a narrow, prearranged corridor and on landing were warmly greeted by four members of the Peace Committee and handed bouquets of flowers. "It's hard to be unmoved," Howard later wrote, "when the people who have been bombed for three years by your countrymen extend their hands."

Three of the four members of the greeting committee spoke English, all struck Howard as "a relaxed bunch . . . great guys," and for five days the team took them all over Hanoi; Howard found it "a

fascinating, intense learning of history, politics, day-to-day living."
But he and Dan were both beginning to wonder when—or even
if—they would be meeting with the three prisoners they'd expected
to take home. One evening soon after, Oanh (one of their guides)
asked them to "please eat supper quickly. In one hour we will meet
the three prisoners."

They drove with their Peace Committee "buddies" (as Howard
referred to them) to the prison, an old French villa. Inside, there
was the expected introductory tea session, after which the prison
warden read to Dan and Howard the personal data he had on the
three Americans: Major Norris Overly, thirty-nine, Captain John
Black, thirty, and Lieutenant junior grade David Methany, twenty-
four. That done, they moved into a second room and were seated at
a table covered with cookies, cigarettes, and yet more tea. Shortly
after, the three Americans arrived through a curtained door.

Dan and Howard shook their hands and engaged them in small
talk: "You fellows are looking good," etc. Methany and Black said,
"We've been eating well—they've been treating us very well." They'd
even been given a tour around Hanoi and books on Vietnamese
history. They joked a little about how Howard and Dan, both thin,
looked worse than they did. All hands agreed that they'd been impressed with the Vietnamese, with (in Howard's words) "the calm
and confidence of the people & their efficiency." The prison warden was gracious throughout, but he did tell the three pilots that "if
Hanoi is bombed before you leave, we may reconsider our decision
to release you."

During the first five days, Hanoi wasn't bombed, but the pause
related to bad weather, not to any U.S. decision deliberately to
hold off—as became clear on the sixth day, when the sun came out
and so did the bombers. Howard and Dan went immediately into a
crowded shelter, Howard puzzling over the fact that it apparently
hadn't occurred to the U.S. government—or, if it did, had been
dismissed—that bombing Hanoi at that precise moment might
jeopardize the release of the three airmen. But Hanoi didn't, after

all, reconsider its decision, and the following day, Dan and Howard were told to prepare to leave with the pilots.

That same afternoon, they learned that five new "antisubversive" laws had been passed to block freedom of speech and the press and that several newspapers had been suspended. When they met with Pham Von Dong, the North Vietnamese premier, that day, they knew better than to refer to the repressive measures; any protest on their part might jeopardize the mission. As for the premier, they found him an impressive figure, a large man (as Howard put it) of "oceanic calm" as well as "exuberant personal warmth." His grasp of political matters seemed both firm and subtle. "It is our own efforts, our own determination," he told the Americans, that will ultimately bring victory; ". . . as war goes on . . . the social issues in the United States [will] become more difficult to solve, the war will become an intolerable burden on your society, and your people will demand the war end, for their own sake."

Shortly before they were due to board the plane out of Hanoi, William H. Sullivan, the U.S. ambassador to Laos (which the U.S. had been secretly bombing for several years, though Sullivan would deny the fact to several Senate subcommittees), crisply announced that Washington had decided they'd be transported to a base in Thailand, where they would board an air force plane for the rest of the trip home. One of their Vietnamese guides made it clear to them that Hanoi would not be pleased if the pilots returned on a military plane, though they would not make it a condition of release. Howard and Dan argued vigorously with Sullivan that using a military plane ran counter to Hanoi having initially contacted the U.S. peace mission about the release, and that the decision might prevent future releases. It was bad enough that the three airmen were likely in the future to serve on bombing missions against North Vietnam.

Ambassador Sullivan was adamant. He told them that the "people in Washington had weighed all the alternatives and come to this conclusion," feeling as well that it was desirable to avoid the press conference that would attend a commercial flight. Why? Because Howard and Dan were "tired" and the Defense Department wanted to spare them from being "harassed"—an explanation that was patently false. What the department wanted, obviously, was to avoid any positive references to Hanoi that Howard and Dan would be likely to offer the press. Major Overly added his two cents to Sullivan's: "I've been in the military seventeen years and when my government expresses its preference I know what that means. We will go back by military aircraft." The other two airmen fell into line, though Methany, for a time, argued emotionally against it.

That last day, Howard asked his guide Oanh whether there wasn't something that should be asked of the U.S. government in return for the release of the airmen. No, no, Oanh said, "You don't understand. We have released these men at the time of our lunar New Year, a very important holiday to us, very deep in our tradition. It is the time when, wherever we are, we return to our families for the New Year." So as a small gesture, in the spirit of the holiday, Oanh added, the three men were being allowed to go back to their families. The newspapers in the U.S. kept insisting that the release was mere "propaganda." Yes, Howard wrote, "but propaganda by *deed*, which, if generally adopted, would improve the world overnight." Perhaps a future generation, he thought, would better appreciate that what had happened was in "the spirit of generosity . . . that a country under daily attack delivered back to the behemoth three of its marauders."

Upon returning home, Howard's friends, even some of the radicals among them, cautioned him against sentimentality, insisting that the North Vietnamese must have had *some* political motive for the release. He reluctantly agreed that they probably did. But deep down, he wanted to argue that "all decent acts in this world are marred to some degree by selfish motivation; if we let that fact determine how we respond to such acts, the possibility of ending the cycle of reciprocal cruelty is foreclosed." Howard never found cynicism appealing. He preferred to be called a foolish utopian rather than surrender his view that *Homo sapiens* is basically benign, generous, and affiliative—which stood in opposition to the much more common view then being promulgated (by Robert Ardrey, Desmond Morris, and others) that human beings are born with the instincts of aggression and selfishness. Howard believed that "predation"—war and other aggressive manifestations—*was* deeply ingrained in our culture, but was *not* wired into our brains or our evolutionary past.

His belief in human altruism was already, in 1970, backed up with a certain amount of evidence from anthropology and primatology, though Howard seems to have been unfamiliar with it—or at least never cites any of it in support of his views. Then, in 1971, came the discovery of the Stone Age Tasaday people, who wholly lacked aggressiveness and showed no instinct for hostility and war. Today, some forty years later, the "altruism debate" has become fueled by information from a wide range of scientific sources. A number of brain researchers argue that affiliation and empathy are hardwired into the cerebral cortex. Some today even maintain that there's no such thing as "human nature" except as shaped by the social environment of a given time and place.

Dan and Howard's return was greeted with a barrage of media coverage and commentary. The dean of the College of Liberal Arts at Boston University referred disparagingly to Howard's twelve-day absence from his classes—though he'd notified his department chair in advance and had made sure that competent substitutes would take over his three lectures and two seminars. (The dean's accusation marked the beginning of what would become growing antagonism between Howard and the authorities at BU.) The government also tried to discredit the two men, deliberately lying in the effort. Dan Berrigan told the *New York Times* that the U.S. had improperly pressured the three airmen into flying home on military planes, thereby "brutally" jeopardizing the prospects of other prisoners of war being released. To which U.S. officials replied, tight-lipped, that "the men had made their own choice about their means of travel" and insisted further that Hanoi had released the men primarily for "its own political motives," in an attempt to influence world opinion in its favor.[4]

Some of the newspapers were far tougher. One suggested that "Prof. Zinn and Rev. Berrigan may want to ponder some day whether they really were negotiators—or pawns in a Red propaganda plot." That wasn't a surprise to either man. But they were taken aback when reports reached them that Major Overly was touring the country with tales of his mistreatment and torture at the hands of the North Vietnamese. He'd never said a word to Howard or Dan along those lines, though when still in Hanoi Overly may have felt it necessary to conceal the truth. Howard believed his current version; he had no doubt that brutality was endemic to prison systems everywhere.

A few months after their return from Hanoi, Dan and his brother, Phil, who'd served in combat during World War II, joined seven others in a dramatic act of civil disobedience that became a cause célèbre which became known as "the Catonsville Nine." They had entered a draft board in Catonsville, Maryland, and using homemade napalm had set fire to hundreds of draft records. In advance of that action, the group issued a statement, written by Dan: "Our apologies, good friends, for the fracture of good order, the burning of paper instead of children. . . . How many must die before our voices are heard? . . . When, at what point, will you say no to this war?"

All nine were arrested and convicted. They were given sentences of two to three years but allowed to remain free pending an appeal. When it failed, the police were sent to pick up the defendants and deliver them to jail. Three of them—Dan and Phil, plus a former nun, Mary Moylan—couldn't be found. Moylan never was, but Phil was apprehended at another priest's residence and Dan went underground. Howard and Eqbal Ahmad, a mutual friend of his and Dan's and a famous Pakistani scholar and radical, were given the address where Dan was hiding in New Jersey and, for the next four months, Howard was responsible for finding antiwar friends who were willing to take the risk of hiding Dan.

Early in 1968, Supreme Court Justice Abe Fortas, considered a liberal by many, published a widely distributed booklet, *Concerning Dissent and Civil Disobedience*, that was essentially a response to the heightening opposition to the war and the various acts—occupying campus buildings, burning draft cards, mounting protests, etc.— that expressed the shifting attitude of the American public. In his booklet, Fortas argued for a narrowing of what he believed had become a too tolerant attitude toward civil disobedience. Howard believed there were any number of inadequacies in Fortas's argument and considered his stance in general to be on the side of supporting authority, not dissent. Choosing nine of what he thought were Fortas's central fallacies, Howard wrote a booklet of his own in response: *Disobedience and Democracy*. It was a powerful little book that drew considerable attention, both positive and negative, and in its original edition sold more than seventy thousand copies.[5]

Fortas had made clear his allegiance to the "rule of law." There would be instances, he acknowledged, when a particular law—like making Jews wear armbands in Nazi Germany—should be disobeyed, but if one chose to disobey the law, one should "acquiesce in the ultimate judgment of the courts." Howard, to the contrary, felt that there could be "no moral imperative to obey an immoral law." He cogently argued that when people revere the rule of law, they're likely to minimize the injustices that exist under it, and in his view, human rights always took precedence over current laws. But wouldn't the widespread use of civil disobedience create chaos? No, Howard answered, in elevating conscience *and* remaining true to the principle of nonviolence, disobedience would make the country a better place. Or putting it another way: perpetuating the status quo should never be placed above the importance of improving human welfare.

The concept of "conscience," however, has some inherent problems. The distinguished philosopher Charles Frankel—he'd been Johnson's assistant secretary of state from 1965 to 1967 but had resigned in protest against the American role in Vietnam—challenged Howard directly on the issue. Do we grant, Frankel asked, that Governor George Wallace was acting out of his individual conscience in blocking the way to school integration? Whose conscience is to take precedence? And what do we mean by the word *conscience* anyway?

Frankel also criticized Howard for drawing "an antithesis between the individual and the government," for defining the individual (as Howard had) as seeking "health, peace, creative activity, love," and defining the state as seeking "power, influence, wealth, as ends in themselves." Was the individual all "love"? Frankel asked. "Never any fast cars that are injurious to health? No love of excitement, and even some enjoyment of violence? All creative activity and no desire just to put one's feet up?"

Frankel thought it was possible to be sentimental about the abstraction called "the individual," and that Howard was. "This sentimentality," Frankel pointed out, "has the same pragmatic consequence as cynicism: it prevents us from taking men seriously for what they are and from being attached to them for what they are." He went on to make distinctions between various kinds of civil disobedience and singled out for disapproval what he called "coercive civil disobedience"—that is, disobedience to the law that threatens other people's rights or denies them the freedom to follow their own consciences.

That last part of Frankel's argument seems the weakest. Yes, factory sit-ins in the thirties did sometimes interfere with the owner's "right" to make money or with the conscience of those workers who thought it wrong to attack property. But there was no tactic for establishing the principle of collective bargaining—essential for giving workers the chance for a better life—that all parties would sanction as "just." Howard might have further responded to Frankel that he didn't regard the principle of civil disobedience to mean that the law can be broken at all times, under all circumstances; his position, rather, was an insistence that the law should not be regarded as automatically inviolable. Should we have returned fugitive slaves to their masters because the law told us we should?

Howard defined civil disobedience as "the deliberate violation of law for a vital social purpose," and he pointed out that it was as American as baseball. At least as far back as the late eighteenth century, the colonists organized the Boston Tea Party and refused to honor the Stamp Act. The 1776 Declaration of Independence established the right of the "people" (meaning adult white men of property, of course) to alter or abolish their government if it failed to meet their needs. In the mid-nineteenth century, the Fugitive Slave Act of 1850 led antislavery sympathizers to snatch slaves away from their captors, and when put on trial for violating the law, they were usually acquitted. Howard quoted Gandhi, who believed in nonviolence but not in a doctrinaire way: "circumstances must determine tactics."

In his booklet, Fortas had argued that violence in the Korean War had been acceptable because "a vital issue" (not defined) was at stake. Yet that put him in the illogical position of denying the right of dissenters who under quite different circumstances—as in the Warsaw Ghetto uprising—were clearly justified in resorting to violence. (Fortas hadn't denied the Jews that right, but Howard felt that his arguments logically led in that direction.)

Howard used Fortas and his arguments to represent the limitations of the liberal mind in general. Segregation was a key indicator: what happens when the segregation laws are repealed and there is no specific discriminatory law left—just a widespread, bone-deep condition of racism that manifests itself in a thousand aspects of daily life? "We are reduced to the absurdity," Howard felt, "of being permitted to protest against one obvious aspect of racist society, but not against the entire body of it."

Howard was in any case departing from the orthodox pacifist position that violent tactics were always abhorrent. He was characteristically suspicious of absolutes, ideological or otherwise, and felt that "a small, focused act of violence against a monstrous evil would be justified"—and could, moreover, be effective. By way of proof, he pointed to the violent labor struggles of the 1930s, which had brought about significant gains for labor. But in regard to World War II, Howard went back and forth throughout his life on the question of whether the use of violence was justified in dealing with fascism. He did feel certain that the Allies hadn't gone to war out of compassion for fascism's victims—no more than they'd taken advantage during the war of several opportunities to rescue Jews, no more than they'd tried to intervene earlier when the Japanese were slaughtering the people of Nanking, China.

It was only "when their national power was threatened," Howard believed, that the U.S. entered World War II. As he put it years later in his autobiography, "Okay, war is bad, but what would you *do* about fascism? I could not, in honesty, pretend that I had a clear answer, but I felt sure that the answer could not be the slaughter of war." What then *was* the answer? All that Howard could do was point to instances, and there were many, when direct-action nonviolence had succeeded in toppling tyrants—such as the mass demonstrations that later led to the widespread collapse of Soviet power in Eastern Europe (or in 2011 the apparently successful "people's revolutions" in Egypt, Libya, and Tunisia). Yes, but would peaceful protests have worked against Hitler? Howard, like most of us, could never persuade himself one way or the other.

For Fortas, existing legal channels in the United States such as free speech, the right to peaceable assembly, and so forth, were sufficient to solve existing grievances. He gave as his chief example the effective way African Americans were using ordinary channels of dissent to improve their lot. Howard found that argument astonishing, coming as it did in the spring of 1968 when major violent outbreaks occurred in more than a hundred U.S. cities—thus proving, in his view, that "ordinary processes of government have *not* been sufficient to change the plight of the black person in America." He claimed that Fortas failed to distinguish between "the sufficiency of the American political system to 'trigger' a 'social revolution' and its sufficiency to fulfill that revolution."

Taking the different example of the war in Vietnam, by sending combat troops (the number by early 1968 had risen to 525,000), the U.S. had violated several international agreements—the Geneva Accords, the SEATO Treaty, and the UN Charter, to say nothing of the U.S. Constitution. Yet Justice Fortas seemed unperturbed (he'd in fact been an adviser to President Johnson), making it seem as if breaking international law was of no consequence. But he'd put himself in an inconsistent bind. Fortas was simultaneously telling blacks that "violence must not be tolerated" in protesting racism, while blandly ignoring the monstrous amount of violence we were employing in Vietnam—and *not* for some overriding moral cause (though anticommunists would claim otherwise). There were other glaring examples. The national argument over slavery had not been settled by going through traditional political channels (public debate or the electoral system) but instead by a civil war that took a deadly toll on both sides.

On the whole, Howard successfully demolished the arguments Fortas had used for adhering to "the rule of law." But when it came to presenting his own solutions for current social ills, Howard's suggestions could be vague and sometimes implausible. Because he sanctioned violence only for self-defense or in the face of terrible evil, he had to try to expand the ways in which nonviolent civil disobedience could be employed. One of his less cogent suggestions included encouraging "poor people to occupy skyscraper office buildings and live in them, in order to point up how much money is being spent on lavish" structures while far too many people "live in hot, stinking, crumbling, vermin-infested holes." Certainly true, but with the police able and willing to provide instant eviction of those "living-in," Howard's suggestion seems less than persuasive.

("Academic nit-picking," Howard might have responded, "useful primarily as a way to justify inaction.")

Some of his other tactics—like suggesting that people who couldn't pay their bills send them to the federal government, or establishing a local police force within poor neighborhoods and refusing entry to ordinary cops—were so likely to be ignored or swiftly put down that, comparably, one might as well advise releasing rats into every building on Park Avenue. Often, too, Howard would draw enticing pictures of what an ideal society might look like, though without any guidelines for how to get there. He advocated, because the other branches of government were vigorous in defending the rights of the State and of the privileged class, that the Supreme Court devote itself to defending the "natural rights" of the citizenry, "thus moving away from the deification of precedent and toward bold interpretation"—such as expanding the equal protection clause of the Fourteenth Amendment to include *economic* rights (food, shelter, education, etc.). But to rely on the Supreme Court, even during the more liberal periods in its history, to take on so radical a role was tantamount to insisting that the Mississippi River start flowing north.

Similarly, Howard urged that the Thirteenth Amendment ban on "involuntary servitude" be broadened to include military conscription and that the Eighth Amendment prohibition against "cruel and unusual punishment" be expanded to bar "*all*" imprisonment." Glorious goals, imaginative in their scope, resonant with hope for a better world—yet the question of how to achieve those goals remained unanswered. It was one thing to declare that "there is no social value in a general obedience to the law," but another to distinguish when *general* is or is not applicable. Howard advocated "a reasonable relationship between the degree of disorder and the significance of the issue at stake." But that principle would have benefited from definitions of *reasonable* and of *significance*.

Few, very few, scholars (or citizens) could match the breadth of Howard's moral concerns or the beautifully direct and passionate prose he employs in *Disobedience and Democracy*. If some of his arguments seem incomplete and some of his suggested tactics fanciful—well, those are problems inherent in being willing to take on difficult questions of large scope and investing one's own person in trying to resolve them.

At the time *Disobedience and Democracy* came out in 1968, Roz had been through two unpleasant jobs in less than three weeks. Having earlier done secretarial work to help support the family through its leanest days, she was now, approaching fifty, at the point in her life where it finally became possible to seek outlets for her own talents. The second wave of feminism was stirring and would shortly break out. Her children were no longer living at home; Jeff was enrolled in Franconia College and Myla had studied for two years at Antioch and two at Boston University. Roz confided to a close friend that she'd been feeling depressed and had to find some satisfying work to do. The friend knew what few of her other intimates ever sensed: that the warm, kind, happy face (real enough much of the time) Roz chose to present publicly was hardly the sum of her being. At middle age, some of her discontent had begun to show—that is, to those few keen enough to notice, for the facade stayed largely intact.[6]

As a younger woman, Roz had shown herself gifted in several of the arts. She now decided to volunteer for a project begun by the young Jonathan Kozol to teach reading to youngsters in Roxbury two days a week. She found it "absorbing and exciting." She also started to take a painting class; much earlier in life, she'd enjoyed working in oils but after a time had stopped. Now, along with two of her neighbors, she took it up again and found that she liked it "immensely." After class, she'd often go to the Fogg or Fine Arts museums and found the trips "mind-blowing."

In the meantime, Howard's antiwar activity began to speed up. He both wrote about Vietnam and participated in some of the major demonstrations against the war (some of the small ones, too).

Back in 1965, when he'd spoken at a rally on the Boston Common, it had drawn a very small crowd, some of whom were hecklers. In 1967, when addressing an antidraft protest, also on the Common, he drew an estimated four to five thousand. Later that same year, he took part in a massive demonstration in front of the Lincoln Memorial, which drew a hundred thousand, about half the crowd then moving to the lawn in front of the Pentagon. Later that night, the police, preceded by tear gas, roared into the demonstrators there with clubs flailing. Many protesters were badly bloodied, and many were jailed, but overall the event definitively turned the tide. The polls showed that roughly 50 percent of the country now thought that our intervention in Vietnam had been a mistake. From that point on, the continuing escalation of the war was paralleled by the continuing escalation of protest against it.[7]

Howard had left before the mayhem at the Pentagon and wasn't at the police riot in Chicago during the 1968 Democratic Party convention, which led to the 1969–70 "conspiracy" trial of the so-called Chicago Eight. But by 1968 he'd become tirelessly active in trying to stop the war. That year, to name but a few of his activities, he took part in the New England Resistance rally—again on the Common, but this time drawing ten thousand—joining Noam Chomsky (who was fast becoming a close friend and political ally) as a featured speaker. He was also one of the signers of a *New York Post* ad calling on people to refuse paying the 10 percent income tax surcharge that had been levied to help pay for the war (which as early as mid-1967 was costing the U.S. some $20 billion a year).

The more people heard Howard on a platform—deeply informed (he had a remarkably retentive memory), passionate, and trenchant—the more he was in demand to come to this campus or that rally. As invitations poured in, Howard said yes to as many as he could without jeopardizing his teaching commitments—or his family life, where some grumbling could be heard. A warm and good-hearted man in general, Howard, at times of maximum political activity, could take his family somewhat for granted, seemingly unaware that his nearly ceaseless travels and his absorption in public life might cause some resentment at home—or in Jeff's case (when younger) simply a sense of missing his father's company.

Roz, however, was much more introverted than Howard and also more thin-skinned. It took considerable effort for her to tag along to the many events that featured Howard, who could be with people hour after hour and not tire at all. Roz did her best to maintain a cheerful, contented face at the events she did attend but would sometimes complain about the stress they put on her, and the internalized strain did take its toll, tending to show up in physical ailments (and, when at home, in periodic moodiness, from which Jeff increasingly distanced himself; most of what would become a complicated family drama lay a bit further down the road).

Howard loved the platform. His immediate family all had a theatrical streak (Jeff's undergraduate absorption in folk rock gave way to a career in acting and directing), and Howard was especially adept at mixing in humor to leaven his moral intensity. Speaking to one audience, he said, "President McKinley waited for the word of God to enter the Philippines, now we are waiting for the word of God to get out. This can be very worrisome what with the present talk about God being dead." When on the BU campus meeting his classes, Howard would squeeze in as much antiwar activity as he could—even speaking at an all-night teach-in at 3:00 a.m. to a sleepy crowd in the university auditorium.

After President Johnson announced that he would not seek re-election, both Nixon and Humphrey, the 1968 presidential nominees, made noises about bringing the war to an end, Nixon claiming he had a "secret plan" to ensure success. Robert Kennedy, who'd been doing well in the presidential primaries, seems to have been a more genuine peace candidate. He called for an end to the war "as quickly as it is physically possible to reach the essential agreements," beginning with the immediate cessation of U.S. air raids on North Vietnam. He didn't want the war to drag on for another five years, he said, with the expenditure of another $100 billion "and the lives of another 25,000 of our finest sons." Robert Kennedy was shot to death in June 1968.

Howard hadn't forgotten the initial inactivity of the Kennedy brothers in regard to the beatings and killings that had characterized the early struggle for black rights, and he now fiercely attacked the outpouring of grief for Robert Kennedy as "one of the great acts of hypocrisy in world history. . . . If we were to tell the truth, we would say that murderers are wearing mourning clothes today. . . . Is murder only the killing of important men by unimportant men? Is it not also the killing of unimportant men by important men? Are not governments the greatest murderers of all?" Two months before Robert Kennedy's assassination, Martin Luther King Jr., who'd ignored many of his advisers and come out against the war in Vietnam a year earlier, had been assassinated in Memphis, his death leading to an explosion of riots across the country. In King's case, but not that of the Kennedy brothers, Howard felt deep regret and sadness.

In September, Howard was one of five American professors (the other four being Douglas Dowd, George McT. Kahin, Jonathan Mirsky, and one of Howard's good friends the historian Marilyn B. Young) who flew to Paris to meet with the North Vietnamese delegation to the peace talks. They found it in a state of distress over the lack of progress that had been made. The North Vietnamese had come to Paris with what they thought was a clear understanding that the first step in negotiations would be to determine the date on which all U.S. bombing of the North would cease.[8]

Instead, the U.S. delegation had introduced "a variety of small and large suggestions" unrelated to the bombing. Averill Harriman and Cyrus Vance, who headed the American delegation, wanted some reciprocal gesture from the North Vietnamese, and Harriman had suggested a cessation of the rocketing of Saigon. The North had at once complied, but American air raids doubled, not stopped.

Not only had President Johnson failed to ground the air strikes or to set a timetable for doing so; he openly announced that since March 31, the actual tonnage of bombs dropped on the North had "greatly increased" and had been concentrated on densely populated areas containing more than 4 million people.

Howard believed that the insurrectionary NLF in South Vietnam was "a far healthier social force than the Saigon group we have kept in power." The NLF, he felt, was much more attuned to the needs of the peasantry and "seems to be the only truly indigenous group capable of running South Vietnam today." His claim was that "those called Communists in Vietnam . . . stand best for the very principles we claim to espouse: economic welfare, political participation, self-determination." Howard urged that the U.S. reexamine the premises on which its foreign policy was based. He argued that the national interest should not be defined as the interests of General Motors, that not everything labeled "Communist" should be attacked as the equivalent of Soviet totalitarianism, and that Americans do not "save face" through butchery.

Secretary of State Henry Kissinger, whose supply of contempt was inexhaustible, told the National Security staff in August 1969, "I refuse to believe that a little fourth-rate power like North Vietnam does not have a breaking point." He had as little understanding of the antiwar movement, certain (Kissinger was always certain) that the "moral issue" in Vietnam did not warrant either civil disobedience or conscientious objection.

He was scornful—another cardinal trait—of the formation during the summer of 1969 of the committee, of which Howard was a part, to plan for a national Moratorium Day on October 15, during which everyone would stop engaging in business as usual and join protest demonstrations. Howard spoke in Boston to a crowd estimated at a hundred thousand; in New York City, Mayor John Lindsay flew the flags at half-mast; and in Washington, D.C., Coretta Scott King led some thirty thousand past the White House in a silent candlelight procession. Altogether, several million people participated in the moratorium. Nixon, having won the 1968 election, in turn stepped up the secret bombing of Cambodia and Laos. "It saved lives," Kissinger would later write in his memoir—meaning, of course, American lives, the only ones that mattered; in Kissinger's moral universe, there was no reason to mention that in the secret bombings hundreds of thousands died and half of the 7 million Cambodian people became refugees.

Vice President Spiro Agnew responded to the moratorium vituperatively. "A spirit of national masochism prevails," he said in one speech, "encouraged by an effete corps of impudent snobs." In another, he characterized the antiwar movement as "a criminal left that belongs not in a dormitory, but in a penitentiary." In 1973, during his fifth year in office as vice president, Agnew was formally charged with accepting bribes in excess of $100,000. On condition that he resign his office, he was allowed to plead no contest to a single charge of failing to list some $30,000 of income on his tax forms. Of course he never went to jail—unlike so many members of the "criminal left."

In between the rallies and speeches, Howard provided court testimony in a number of important trials—the Camden 28, the Baltimore 4, the Milwaukee 14, and so forth. He was called as an expert on social movements and civil disobedience, and once in a while a sympathetic judge would let him testify for several hours. He often spoke along these lines: "the temporary taking of the law into one's own hands, in order to declare what the law should be is a declaration that there is an incongruence between the law and humane values, and that sometimes this can only be publicized by breaking the law . . . the human value at stake must involve fundamental rights, like life, health, liberty. There is no real cause, for instance, to disobey a traffic light because it is inconveniently long."

As a witness, Howard would argue that the use of civil disobedience, which admittedly caused disruption and inconvenience, had to be weighed against the greater violations of justice that the disorder was designed to protest. At the heart of civil disobedience was the insistence that when the government itself broke the law and offended common morality—as in Vietnam, where it had ignored international treaties and killed millions—the people had no recourse but to turn to protest through acts of civil disobedience, thereby, hopefully, changing or curtailing the government's lawless behavior. Howard was a highly effective court witness. Following his testimony, prosecution lawyers often waived their right to cross-examine him, and juries often acquitted the defendants.

In the midst of his unflagging antiwar activity, or rather as a part of it, Howard somehow managed to write a fair amount, including several important essays on Vietnam. In them, he continued to stress the theme of *immediate* withdrawal and tried to respond to the most common objections to that position. To the question "Don't we have a commitment to defend Vietnam against aggression?" he pointed out that Vietnam wasn't the victim of an attack from outside: the NLF was trying to take over its own country. What we were dealing with was a popular revolution from within South Vietnam against Diem's dictatorship—80 to 90 percent of the NLF were South Vietnamese peasants. Besides, if the presence of foreign troops is by itself sufficient to demolish any claim to a legitimate homegrown uprising, then what will we do with the fact that at Yorktown George Washington's troops were outnumbered by their French allies?[9]

To the question "But isn't the NLF communist?" Howard's reply was yes as regards many of its leaders, but no when speaking of a peasantry rebelling against a regime controlled by wealthy landlords and supported by American troops. To the related objection that if all of Vietnam goes communist it would lead to a communist takeover of the rest of Southeast Asia, Howard calmly argued that such a premise was based on a misreading both of history and of communist ideology. Marxists traditionally argued that internal conditions in a given country will determine the amount of interest in communism; it cannot be exported simply by the force of arms. In fact, Howard argued, the best way to produce the spread of communism was by creating "war conditions in unstable countries." But didn't we need to contain China? In fact, Howard responded, the more we escalate the war, the more we increase the possibility of Hanoi turning to China for help.

On the matter of motives, he argued, it's always important to look to past patterns of American foreign policy. The official version has long emphasized American selflessness and altruism, our wish to help meet rising expectations throughout the world and to export our technological know-how in order to improve the material well-being of people everywhere. That, at least, has been (and continues to be) the surface rationale for our long string of interventions in the affairs of other countries.

Yet at the time of the Vietnam War, we'd recently helped prop up the dictatorship of Alfredo Stroessner in Paraguay and the Duvalier government in Haiti (after all, they were "anticommunist"). And despite the wishes of local people, we'd often been staunch defenders of corporate U.S. plunderers (Alcan, Alcoa, Kaiser) in poverty-stricken countries; we'd sent tons of military hardware to the racist regime in South Africa; and in defense of the United Fruit Company, we'd overthrown the Arbenz government in Guatemala and its promising policy of agrarian reform.[10]

The picture wasn't entirely one-sided. The Peace Corps did embody our wish to be helpful to stricken local inhabitants; the Asian Rice Institute did hold out hope for the masses; and the U.S. did support land reform in such places as Bolivia, Indonesia, and Algeria. The U.S. isn't uniquely villainous in regard to the needs of the impoverished, but it does stand out for the yawning gap between its altruistic rhetoric about spreading democracy and material well-being and its actual record of landing on the side of rapacious, brutal oligarchies.

Howard knew as well as anyone that, as he later put it, "there are things you can do in the United States that you can't do many other places without being put in jail . . . there are things that you're grateful for, that you're not in front of the death squads in El Salvador."

He felt that the U.S. did have "elements of democracy," even if it wasn't a full-bodied one—not when the brutality that goes on in police stations continues to exist, nor when the police can rough up people, especially people of color, on the streets, and certainly not when institutions like the FBI and the CIA exist, with their secret files and often murderous operations.

6

Writing History

The year 1969 had been tumultuous throughout, but its final month came close to a national brawl.

In the early morning of December 4, Chicago police quietly cordoned off a block on the city's West Side while other officers manned stations on the rooftops. Then the signal was given and the cops, armed with shotguns and one machine gun, stormed the first-floor apartment that housed the Black Panther office. Fred Hampton, age twenty-one and chair of the party in Illinois, was murdered in his bed; Mark Clark, twenty-two, another prominent Panther, was also killed. Seven Panthers survived, four were seriously wounded, one left permanently paralyzed.[1]

State Attorney Edward V. Hanrahan, at forty-eight a rising figure in the Irish police mafia that "served" the Chicago public, held a press conference later that same day. He "wholeheartedly" commended the officers involved in the action for "their bravery, their remarkable restraint and their discipline in the face of this Black Panther attack." The trouble is, there hadn't been any attack, nor any twenty-minute-long (as the police claimed) Panther gun battle.

Hanrahan's entire account was fabrication; it had been a one-sided police massacre, a deliberate, official murder.

As the facts slowly emerged over time, it became clear that the Chicago police had worked in cahoots with the FBI and the Justice Department. J. Edgar Hoover had called the Panther Party "the greatest threat to the internal security of the country," and Attorney General John Mitchell had publicly echoed that sentiment, thus opening the Panthers up to bugs and wiretaps.

The Panther party had been growing steadily nationally. Most blacks remained integrationists, despite all the deflated dreams of the past decade, but some, fed up with turning the other cheek—only to let some racist gash it—had moved over to the militantly revolutionary (and the antifeminist machismo) of the Panthers. In several cities, the Panthers had supplemented their inflammatory rhetoric with breakfast programs for schoolchildren and with small medical clinics to serve the indigent black community. The Panthers were also forming alliances (the "Rainbow Coalition") with a variety of groups, including the Young Patriots, the Young Lords, and a group of white insurrectionaries in Appalachia.

Six weeks after the Chicago raid, a special coroner's jury declared the deaths of Hampton and Clark "justifiable," a county grand jury indicted the seven survivors for "attempted murder," and a federal grand jury fully exonerated Hanrahan and the police. Thanks to the tireless work of Jeffrey Haas and several other radical young lawyers, these verdicts were reversed in 1973, though other aspects of the case dragged on until 2008.

The trouble with disproving government lies is that by the time the truth is finally known, the public's interest has waned, press coverage is slight, the survivors are deceased or despairing, and national attention has moved on to new dramas and new lies.

Meanwhile, the trial of the Chicago Seven—including the prominent radicals Abbie Hoffman, Jerry Rubin, David Dellinger, and Tom Hayden—was stumbling on. The defendants had been charged with conspiracy and rioting during the August 1968 Democratic National Convention, although the rioting had been almost entirely on the part of the police, who'd used tear gas, Mace, and beatings (frequently with batons) to disperse what had started as a peaceful protest. Originally, the Chicago Seven had been Eight—until Panther Bobby Seale, denied the right to defend himself, had called the highly prejudiced presiding judge, Julius Hoffman, various epithets, been bound and gagged in the courtroom, severed from the trial, and sentenced to four years in prison for contempt of court. The trial had begun in September 1969, heard two hundred witnesses, and dragged on till February 1970, when all seven defendants were sentenced to five years in prison.

In October 1969, Howard published, in the *Saturday Review*, an essay, "The Case for Radical Change," which unintentionally landed him in the midst of a contentious debate within the ranks of self-declared radical historians. In his professional no less than in his private life, Howard avoided heated personal clashes and controversy. Although he never hesitated in stating strong views on policy issues, he avoided tangling with individuals—maybe privately now and then of a social evening but not in terms of prolonged public argument. Unlike some leading radical historians—Eugene Genovese, say, or Christopher Lasch and Jesse Lemisch, Howard disliked and avoided personal attacks and counterattacks.[2]

Nor did he choose to participate in the necessary but time-consuming efforts that others—such as Al Young—devotedly put into establishing the Radical Historians Caucus of the American Historical Association (AHA) or the creation of the *Radical History Review*. He never once published in that journal, nor in the earlier *Studies on the Left*. The simple reasons are probably the most reliable ones: approaching fifty, he was older than most of the New Left–sponsored historians, preferred speaking and writing to proliferating meetings and interpersonal strife, and was already committed to multiple demands on his time. Besides, he wasn't much of an ideologue—which isn't to say that many of the younger radicals were.

Howard tended to like a portion of this theoretical position, the degree of attraction shifting through time. He never considered himself an ideologue in the sense that the Marxist Eugene Genovese did (before he moved to the right) or the older Communist Herbert Aptheker. Howard found the Marxian idea of redistributing society's wealth according to need a congenial one, but he also felt considerable attraction to the anarchists' antiauthoritarian stance. He was even willing to acknowledge now and then that capitalism had "developed the economy in an enormously impressive way," increasing "geometrically the number of goods available"—though failing to distribute them justly. Howard, in fact, wasn't much interested in political theory, nor did he pretend to have a creative, original contribution to make in that regard. He adapted and passionately popularized the ideas of others—a much needed role and one to which he brought modesty and humor.

But his essay "The Case for Radical Change" brought him closer to the ongoing struggle within the historical profession than he perhaps wanted. The essay began blandly enough, with Howard reiterating his long-standing view that "we [academics] are accustomed to keeping our social commitment extracurricular and our scholarly work safely neutral . . . while people suffer on earth." Knowledge, he went on, cannot itself produce revolutions, at least not directly. But in counteracting "the deception that makes the government's force legitimate" and in emphasizing the heavy weight of suffering many people endure, knowledge can feed the demand that government adjust its focus to the needs of the many.

Howard then went on to deny—and this brought him to the significant heart of the current debate among radical historians— that he was trying to "obliterate" all scholarship except for the "immediately relevant." Yet in proceeding to deplore the "endless academic discussion" of "trivial or esoteric inquiry" that goes "nowhere into the real world," Howard put himself on slippery ground.

He declared that the university "should consciously serve . . . fundamental humanistic interests," but then failed to specify what was or
wasn't "fundamental" or "humanistic." He did make a stab at it, but
not a very satisfactory one: "the university should unashamedly declare that its interest is in eliminating war, poverty, race, and national hatred [or] governmental restrictions on individual freedom."
But such a declaration—which nearly everyone could abstractly
salute—merely tagged on additional demands that were no more
precisely defined, nor were the tactics needed to achieve them specified. Who decides which topics are "trivial or esoteric"? Even if a
consensus could be reached on what is or is not "important," that
determination can, and almost certainly will, change through
time. Both women's studies and gay studies were long considered
valueless, even objectionable. Yet students of both have gone on to
produce a body of work that has importantly challenged reigning
orthodoxies.

Howard could be critical of grand generalities yet sometimes
indulge in them himself. He criticized the majority of social scientists for defaulting on the obligation to apply their specialized
knowledge to the problem of how to more equitably distribute "the
resources of the earth" and also for failing to research the central
question of which tactics were the most likely to bring about social
change. Yet Howard himself never took up his own challenge to
devote his powers of observation and his analytic skills to investigating the comparative merits of different strategies for producing
a more equitable society.

He did insist (and in this regard he has often been misinter-
preted) that objectivity—scrupulous accuracy when researching
and reporting historical data—must remain the historian's goal,
even as he warned that the Holy Grail could only be approximated, never reached: the historian's values, both buried and conscious, plus the incomplete nature of surviving historical evidence,
would always stand in the way of a fully dispassionate or fully
intact reproduction of the past. Still, there was much a historian

could accomplish by way of "exposing those facts that any society tends to hide about itself"—facts about wealth and poverty, tyranny and lies.

Howard wanted social scientists in general to apply whatever knowledge they gained to social problems in the present day: "Let the economists work out a plan for free food, instead of advising the Federal Reserve Board on interest rates. Let the political scientists work out insurgency tactics for the poor, rather than counter-insurgency tactics for the military." Howard could admonish and appeal but he couldn't force social scientists to devise programs in which they had, for better or worse, scant interest, no more than he could prevent them from identifying with the powerful rather than with the poor.

Much of this—especially arguments about objectivity and relevance—came up during the annual American Historical Association convention in December 1969. The conjunction of well-mannered historians and pandemonium isn't customary. Yet the amount of turmoil that seized the country in regard to the war in Vietnam, along with contending definitions of the historian's proper role in public life, spilled over into the annual AHA meetings, marking the convention as the most bitterly contentious one that solemn organization has ever witnessed.[3]

To be sure, the uproar was on a far smaller scale than the sweeping dramas currently convulsing the country. Still, the AHA's prolonged, agitated debate involved broad and serious issues. They ranged from questioning the very purpose of historical study to challenging the old guard's control of a profession, with important consequences for how our past was taught. As a corollary, the whole concept of objectivity came into glaring focus. Was historical writing and teaching *necessarily* skewed by the values of the historian and the limitations of evidence? And was such distortion primarily confined to the new generation of radical scholars, or were they correcting prior distortions endemic to the profession with the disfigurement of evidence as a whole?

The highly regarded historian David Donald would refer to the 1969 AHA meeting as "an attempted revolution." It was—and Howard played a role in the attempt, though not a central one. The clamor began with an unprecedented contest for the presidency of the organization. In the past, a nominating committee chose a distinguished scholar who'd run unopposed for the office. True to form, the committee chose the eminent Yale historian R.R. Palmer for the presidency, but this time the candidate did not sail to victory unopposed. The Radical Historians' Caucus presented its own nominee—Staughton Lynd.

The trajectory of Lynd's career in recent years was in many ways emblematic of the very issues that would consume the AHA meetings. Soon after Howard's dismissal from Spelman, Staughton, along with Howard's other close friends Renate Wolf and Esta Seaton, had resigned in protest against his firing. Because of Staughton's distinguished scholarship and his popularity in the classroom, he was then hired by Yale's history department. But he made no compromise with its safe centrism and to no degree trimmed his radical sails. His trip to Hanoi in 1966 was quietly deplored by his colleagues, and his substantial 1968 book, *Intellectual Origins of American Radicalism*—in which he made direct analogies between SNCC and earlier radicals as being on the same side of human rights against property rights—received substantial criticism from certain quarters.

The most influential review of Staughton's book came from Eugene Genovese, the noted historian of the antebellum South. He blasted the book in the prestigious *New York Review of Books*, calling it "a travesty of history" and Lynd an "ideologue." Staughton was up for tenure that same year, and Genovese's assault may well have influenced the Yale history department's decision against him. A letter from the history department chair explained to Staughton that "budgetary restraints" (in truth, nonexistent) accounted for the negative vote on his tenure, adding, in regard to *Intellectual Origins*, ". . . this latest scholarly evidence considerably weakened the case for your promotion and also reduced any chance we might have of securing an incremental tenure position in American history for you."

A number of history departments at other universities—some fourteen in all—offered to hire Staughton (the job market was then robust), but at the administrative level the offer was vetoed every single time. In essence, Staughton was drummed out of academia. But that didn't prevent him from continuing to write and to play an active political role at the national level. He and his wife, Alice, both subsequently went to law school and since then have devoted their talents primarily to labor law and to serving as Legal Aid attorneys for the poor.

At the 1969 AHA convention, the vote between Staughton and R.R. Palmer for the AHA presidency was a lopsided 1,040 to 396 in Palmer's favor, but that result wasn't an accurate gauge of the amount of discontent and anger at the convention. That was made clear when Jesse Lemisch delivered his rousing paper, "Present-Mindedness Revisited," and when Eugene Genovese ferociously attacked Lynd and his supporters as "totalitarians." Genovese's rage against the left in general climaxed at the organization's business meeting—which ordinarily drew only a few dozen people but this time a standing room only crowd of some 1,800—where he concluded a speech by shouting that the AHA should "put them down, put them down hard, and put them down once and for all."

Two separate motions were offered at the business meeting that would have placed the AHA on record as condemning the war in Vietnam. The radical caucus's motion was the more broad-gauged of the two. It linked the war to racism and domestic repression, with particular reference to the attacks on the Black Panthers. Those in opposition to both motions weren't necessarily hawks, though some were, like the Yale eminence Sherman Kent, who worked for seventeen years as a high-level consultant to the CIA. But the real contest within the profession was between liberals and radicals. The liberals, no less than the radicals, declared their opposition to the war in Vietnam. But they were decidedly anticommunist and against immediate withdrawal from the war.[4]

A number of them believed that scholarly objectivity wasn't chimerical and could be achieved, though endangered by transient political considerations. Genovese, for one, attacked Howard's call for "useful" history oriented toward solving present-day social problems as a form of dangerous innocence that denied the right of individual scholars to pursue what interested them; in advocating a present-ist orientation for scholarship, Genovese insisted that Howard was indulging in a form of moral absolutism. His accusation grossly distorted Howard's subtle discussion of those issues but Genovese seemed unperturbed, or unaware, of the fact.

John K. Fairbank, the well-regarded historian of Asia, took the floor that night to argue against any resolution that might "politicize" the AHA and threaten its independence as a bulwark of academic freedom (which, as Lynd could attest and Lemisch had underscored, it wasn't). The indefatigable Genovese followed Fairbank and also emphasized the danger of adopting a political resolution: it "would be an invitation to all who disagreed to resign their membership in a political purge."

It was nearly one A.M. when Howard moved to the microphone to read aloud, in condensed form, the radical resolution:

> The American Historical Association, in recognition of the atrocities committed at home and abroad, which are directly attributable to the Southeast Asian war, hereby calls for immediate withdrawal of all the United States troops and material aid.

Given the lateness of the hour, Howard and others feared that the meeting would adjourn with their resolution never considered, and he proposed postponing the vote until the next evening. What followed was the well-mannered AHA's version of gang warfare. Announcing that Howard had exceeded his allotted time, John Fairbank grabbed the mike from his hands. In a later letter to Fairbank,

Howard described (with considerable charm) what had happened: "you wandered up the aisle, came up to me at the mike, put your hand on my shoulder, fondled the mike with love, whispered a few professional nothings in my ear and then pulled the mike out of my hand with the genial ferocity of Teddy Roosevelt. . . . If I had done that to you, it would have been ascribed by some to typical radical hooliganism."

Howard then turned serious: "If you were at a meeting of historians in Germany in 1936, would you take the same position in the midst of the killing of Jews? If you were at a meeting of historians in Mississippi in the midst of the lynching of blacks, would you also insist you could not speak 'as historians' but only as individual citizens? Our silence in the face of war, racism, and other social evils is not freedom for us; it is freedom for the political leaders of the country to have their way and count on our inaction. Silence is political."

The radicals did win the vote to postpone discussion on the various resolutions until the following evening, when Howard and others spoke again. He insisted, among much else, that "being human beings is more important than being historians." Genovese again responded, vehemently, that Howard was intent on "politicizing" the AHA, but Lynd called attention to the fact that other professional associations, including the American Political Scientists and the American Sociologists, had already voted to adopt similar resolutions, not feeling, apparently, that their integrity as scholars was being compromised. Still, the motion Howard presented failed by a vote of 493 to 822. A less radical resolution that omitted all reference to the government's repression of the Panthers also went down, but by the much narrower vote of 611 to 647.

The radical caucus had failed to put the AHA on record as opposed to the war in Vietnam, but not all of its efforts had been in vain. The younger generation of historians had for several years been protesting the structural conservatism of the AHA, and in the aftermath of the 1969 convention, a number of far-reaching reforms were adopted. R.R. Palmer, president-elect, under additional pressure from the Women's Caucus, represented by Blanche Wiesen Cook and Sandi Cooper, lent his support to expanding the council by adding four new members, thereby diluting somewhat the domination of older white men.

The following year, a review board was established, and it concluded that the council needed to become more representative of the membership. In the years since then, the AHA rolls have expanded to include many more women and some minorities. And by 2007, with little fuss, a resolution against the U.S. intervention in Iraq passed on the convention floor overwhelmingly. Fear of politicizing the AHA had gone down the drain of history, defeated, perhaps, by the growing conviction in many different academic fields (including science) that what is considered truth changes through time in response to changes in the social climate.

In 1970 Howard published a collection of his essays, *The Politics of History*, that can be read as a direct extension of the struggles at the AHA convention the previous year. Nine of the twenty essays had been previously published. Of the remaining eleven, two were devoted directly to writing history and the rest partially so. In "What Is Radical History?" he began with the straight-out statement, "I am urging value-laden historiography." This focus, he argued, "does not determine answers, only questions." Yet he also believed that historical research that made no contribution to problem solving in the present day could nonetheless be justified on the grounds of aesthetics and enjoyment. Or as C. Vann Woodward, not the most radical of men, put it: "Since the historian lives in the present he has obligations to the present as well as to the past he studies."[5]

Besides, whether historians were conscious of the fact or not, Howard (and other radical historians, despite variations in their formulas) was certain that all historical writing was value-laden anyway. Until recently, the historical profession, dominated by white men, wrote and taught about the past "from the top down"; presidents, generals, and corporate heads had the profession under their spell; people of color, women, and the working poor were vaguely patronized and largely ignored—other than for those content with their lot. Because in general only the most privileged members of society leave behind substantial records, the evidence that comes down to us from the past is skewed and fragmentary even before historians select and emphasize (on the whole unconsciously) certain materials and not others from the limited stockpile, thereby inevitably distorting any reconstruction of "what actually happened."

Historians who claim that they write from a position of neutrality or who criticize their radical counterparts as ideologues don't know the history of their own profession. During World War I, a group of "objective"—so they saw themselves—historians established the National Board for Historical Service to supply the public with "trustworthy information." They churned out 33 million pamphlets stressing the righteous role the United States was playing in the war, and contrasting it to Germany's despicable aggression. During World War II, the eminent historian Samuel Eliot Morison denounced historians who had subsequently expressed disillusion with World War I for rendering the new generation "spiritually unprepared for the war they had to fight." In 1961, as president of the AHA, Samuel Flagg Bemis announced that "too much self-criticism is weakening to a people. . . . A great people's culture begins to decay when it commences to examine itself." So much for "Know Thyself." So much for speaking truth.

In the 1960s, Jesse Lemisch led the way in writing "history from the bottom up" (in his own case, colonial seamen), and the older generation labeled it "distorted," contrasting his "partisan" work with their own "dispassionate" accounts. But Lemisch already had said, "We will simply not allow you the luxury of continuing to call yourselves politically neutral. . . . You cannot lecture us on civility while you legitimize barbarity. . . . We are in the libraries, writing history, trying to cure it of your partisan and self-congratulatory fictions, trying to come a little closer to finding out how things actually were."

Howard believed that the research of Lemisch and others wasn't meant to substitute for past accounts but to augment them. He didn't want people to stop learning about George Washington but to start learning, as well, about the Ludlow Massacre of striking coal workers in 1914. Knowing about such episodes would allow for a more complete and accurate picture of the development of the American economy. As a side effect of that knowledge, new questions would be raised about the prejudicial role of government and the press, as well as about the brutal way the industrial system has sometimes treated its workers—those questions emerged from an expanded history, not from radical propaganda. "The closest we can come to that elusive 'objectivity,'" Howard wisely argued in *The Politics of History*, "is to report accurately *all* of the subjectivities in a situation." This doesn't mean, he wrote, "looking only for historical facts to reinforce the beliefs I already hold," nor "ignoring data that would change or complicate my understanding of society." He insisted on "scrupulous honesty" in reporting on the past.

Howard thought it essential to adhere to the known evidence, though it would, inevitably, be subject to variant interpretations. Accuracy remained the goal, not polemics or propaganda; subjectivity guaranteed a certain amount of bias in any historical account, but deliberate distortions of the evidence should, in his opinion, be left to the Goebbelses of the world. Howard considered a *conscious* distortion of evidence unacceptable (*un*conscious manipulations were by definition beyond control). In urging historians to focus on "relevance," Howard specified what he meant: uncover and share knowledge of how bad things have always been for the victims of poverty and oppression; compare the government's self-proclaimed benevolence and devotion to democracy to its actual policies; expose the hidden ideological pretenses that pervade our culture ("We are not like the imperialists of the nineteenth century," etc.). By calling attention to the truth of a given situation (the abolitionists were *not* destructive fanatics but idealists who wanted the public to face the horrors of slavery), historians can demystify self-serving rhetoric.

Furthermore, historians can reveal examples from the past that prove change is possible. Howard wanted to tell students about the successful anarchist communes in Catalonia, about the underground resistance to Hitler, about the New Deal's TVA project (which made life better for millions), about the nonviolent tactics of the black struggle—wanted to emphasize that part of human history, in short, that can counter widespread feelings of indifference, cynicism, or despair. Many historians would give their blessings to such goals, but far fewer to Howard's additional assertion that history should be "studied primarily for the benefit and use of men" (the second wave of feminism had barely surfaced).

His corollary that the "irrelevant" and the "trivial" were a waste of time—that present events should determine what's important to study about the past—left Howard open to some exacting criticism. What's irrelevant or trivial to one generation may not be to another. To give but one example, in the 1950s, the history of women was widely regarded as inconsequential, but by the 1970s it had become of major importance. During the Eisenhower years, the idea of gay studies would have induced mocking dismissal, though in 2012 it has significantly influenced and challenged traditional views on family, sexuality, relationships, and identity in a wide variety of disciplines.

Howard's faith that "relevant" knowledge would produce positive change led others to criticize his "naivete" about the ability of information to change values. Because Howard cared deeply about people, he wanted others to care as well, but in fact most people read history to confirm not to modify their belief system. Yet change sometimes does happen, as when Howard, as a youngster, read the muckraking books of Lincoln Steffens. The charge was also made that Howard inflated the importance of works of history to an American public that rarely read it or, if they did, converted it to their own ends, ignoring what didn't match up with their prior beliefs. Any transformation in the way history was written would, in other words, have a negligible social impact.

Most of those who reviewed *The Politics of History* were full of praise for Howard's expressive, graceful prose. But many fewer, as Howard himself probably anticipated, wrote favorably about his perspective on history. A number of critics deplored what they called his "moral absolutism." It too often led him, they charged, to either-or evaluations of events and individuals. Abraham Lincoln was a case in point. Howard did ignore Lincoln's complexity and the evolution in his view of slavery in favor of a simplistic evaluation of him as indifferent to slavery. Similarly, some historians argued, Howard too often saw liberals as *the* enemy of the good society, rather than conservatives and reactionaries. It was they, after all, who were primarily responsible for ignoring the suffering of the poor, pushing policies that favored the privileged elite, and promoting militaristic and interventionist enterprises.

Other critics took issue with Howard's proposal to single out for study certain strains in the American experience, while virtually ignoring others. This led him, they charged, to read back into the past certain descriptive categories and conflicts that didn't accurately apply to earlier periods, thereby preventing us from accurately understanding them. One critic insisted, for example, that when Howard applied the term "class struggle" to certain incidents in colonial America, he was falsely conflating colonial strife with the class conflict of a later, industrialized society, thereby preventing us from seeing either in the special context of its own times. This penchant of Howard's, his critics claimed, prevented him from understanding the evolution and mutability of such seeming constants as inequality or radicalism. The tendency, they argued, could encourage the view (which Howard did *not* hold) that historical experience in every epoch is interchangeable—a static concept that can cause even radicals to withdraw from a seemingly pointless activism. (Why struggle for change when the essentials will always remain the same?)

These critiques of *The Politics of History*, cumulative in their effect, give the overall impression that Howard's book was inconsequential.

Yet it's possible to acknowledge the cogency of some of the criticisms and at the same time to recognize the overall impact of the book. Howard had reopened questions about historical study and its potential uses that hadn't been raised since the turn of the century, when James Harvey Robinson called for a "New History," which would serve the present. Howard's insistence in *Politics* on looking to the past for inspiration in the fight against misery and alienation *did* contain a number of missteps and simplifications, but it raised the big questions regarding historical study and its potentially instrumental use in the fight against inequality and suffering. "History cannot provide confirmation," he once wrote, "that something better is inevitable; but it can uncover evidence that it is conceivable." Few historians of his generation or any other were willing to stick their necks out or risk rebuke to the same extent.

On April 30, 1970, President Nixon announced on national television that the United States had invaded Cambodia in order to attack North Vietnamese army strongholds there—a decision, he claimed, that he'd previously refrained from making "because we did not wish to violate the territory of a neutral nation." Not quite. For the previous thirteen months, the U.S. had secretly but steadily been bombing Cambodia. As documents revealed only many, many years later, Nixon had directly told Kissinger, "I want them to hit everything," which Kissinger then relayed to the Pentagon: "A massive bombing campaign in Cambodia. Anything that flies or anything that moves." In other words, Let's git us a little mass murder. General Westmoreland once openly asserted that "Orientals don't value lives." An accurate statement would have read, "The U.S. doesn't value Asian lives." The bombing raids led many Cambodians to join the anti-American Khmer Rouge, who under Pol Pot would usher in a sickening genocide of its own.

For three *years*, the Nixon administration had been bombing neighboring Laos, escalating by 1970 to the point where the Plain of Jars, previously a prosperous area, was all but obliterated. Now it was Cambodia's turn. Nixon had led the American public to believe that he was turning the war over to the Vietnamese and would be sending American troops home. But his April 30 speech, full of outright lies and overweening arrogance, declared that our "vital interests" were—again!—at stake. The speech managed all at once to stun the American public and give a shot in the arm to the antiwar movement. Nixon, predictably, denounced demonstrators against his ferocious policies as "bums."[6]

One of the hundreds of protests against the invasion of Cambodia took place at Kent State University in Ohio. None of the marchers, mostly students, carried weapons or engaged in any violent act. Yet the Ohio National Guard nonetheless fired sixty-seven rounds into the crowd in thirteen seconds, killing four and wounding nine, one of whom suffered permanent paralysis. A huge national response to the frightening event followed, some 4 million students leaving their classrooms to protest the National Guard's unwarranted attack. A Gallup poll reported that 61 percent of the country now wanted the U.S. out of Vietnam no later than the end of 1971.

One significant offshoot of the U.S. invasion was to augment the strength of Cambodia's small Communist movement, the Khmer Rouge, and in particular the faction led by Pol Pot; thousands of peasants rallied to resist the American invasion, swelling his forces. For its part, the Nixon administration no longer bothered with specific justifications for its actions, other than to reiterate pious platitudes about "defending Southeast Asia from Communism" or "spreading the blessings of Western democracy." The administration simply assumed, without inviting further discussion, that it was entitled to invade other countries, to serve as the world's arbiter and avenger—though it had proven itself incapable of arbitrating anything with an even hand, and as avenger it had developed the nasty habit of sparing the guilty and killing innocent civilians (not that combatants, fed a bunch of lies by their governments, aren't, in a somewhat different sense, also victims).

For nearly a decade, large U.S. cargo planes had been dropping more than 100 million pounds of chemical herbicides over Southeast Asia, with concentrations of deadly toxins ten times those recommended for use in the United States. Along with destroying the rural countryside, the herbicides had the secondary effect of poisoning drinking and cooking water taken from contaminated cisterns and ponds. The further result was that reports of miscarriages and birth abnormalities skyrocketed—though the evidence was largely concealed from the press and the public.

It was difficult not to become cynical or despairing about the Pax Americana. After all, the U.S. was now the leader among Western nations; every right-thinking person was expected to understand that the West was far in advance of the rest of the world and therefore knew what policies were best for everyone—never mind that those policies incidentally happened to underscore the U.S. sense of proprietorship. Howard no longer had any illusion that the U.S. government (either the president or Congress) would voluntarily do what was transparently right, that it would be guided primarily by humane concerns.

Howard's negative assessment of Nixon's foreign policy was surely on target, though he never referred to Nixon's accomplishment in opening up relations with China. He might also have mentioned that Nixon, though hardly a genuine progressive, did—under the influence of Senator Daniel Patrick Moynihan—sometimes lean toward a combination of deficit spending and wage and price controls to combat growing unemployment and inflation; he also considered (briefly) a plan for national health insurance and a guaranteed annual income to all Americans. Only recently has the country managed to cobble together a still less-than-ideal health plan, and it has yet to consider the kind of guaranteed-income idea, which might finally tame the confounding poverty—due to a lack of education, opportunities, and jobs—that for far too long has inexcusably confined many Americans to a marginal existence. Nixon—nobody's idea of Mr. Compassion—can't simply be dismissed as Attila the Hun, however tempting that may be, given his death-dealing foreign policies.

Howard continued to believe that our best hope lay in "the duty of citizens to *make* moral arguments." Before anything like a "revolution" could be achieved, it was first necessary to awaken the hearts and renovate the minds of the citizenry. Once, in a rare moment of pessimism, Howard conceded that "we don't *really* know how to affect policy," which carried the corollary that "we do not have democracy—that in a democracy there would be established ways for the desires of a large number of people to be represented." That in turn meant that Howard felt it necessary to continue to go outside standard political processes, encouraging "demonstrations, tax refusals, GI refusals, helping deserters & draft resisters," and so on. In between the large demonstrations, he also felt it was important to build grassroots constituencies for local organizing against the war in the eventual hope (Howard would never surrender hope) that opposition to it could no longer be ignored.

Howard accepted his own challenge. He spoke widely, particularly on college campuses, and to do so he often had to travel considerable distances. "If we want peace," he said in one speech, "we will have to struggle for it. If we want justice, we will have to demand it. If we want democracy, we will have to build it." He was a regular at various protests and demonstrations. One of them was out of the ordinary. Howard joined a group outside the Foreign Correspondents Club, which was in the process of giving a dinner party in honor of one of its own. The demonstrators were vociferous, but Howard outdid the others in beating wildly, incessantly, on a drum. At another protest, he was arrested and fined. Refusing to pay the fine, he was jailed overnight—which happened on eight or nine different occasions.

He was also steadfast in support of the brothers Berrigan, Dan and Phil. Back in 1968, Phil had been sentenced to six years and Dan to three for destroying Selective Service files. But when it came time for them to begin to serve their sentences at the Lewisburg

Federal Penitentiary, neither showed up. They'd decided instead to go underground, to become what Dan called "fugitives from injustice." Phil soon decided to surface at a protest rally, explaining that he wanted the FBI to arrest him on his own terms and at a place of his own choosing.[7]

Dan preferred to remain in hiding. In his support, Howard organized a demonstration of about seventy people on the Boston University campus to protest the indictments against both Berrigan brothers. For four months, Dan played a cat and mouse game with the FBI, dramatically popping up at a rally or television show, then disappearing again, as a frustrated, furious J. Edgar Hoover continued the hunt for him. Dan moved constantly, from one safe haven to another, Howard being one of the few people who usually knew where he was. He and Roz also actively helped to hide Dan several times. At one point, they drove to Dan's safe house in New Jersey, then brought him back to Boston and planned his movements for several days. They never used their home phone, assuming it was tapped (as it was). In the end, against Howard's advice, Dan decided to visit two old friends on Block Island and wrote of his plans to his jailed brother, Phil. The letter was entrusted to someone who turned out to be an FBI informant. Dan was arrested on Block Island, handcuffed, and taken by motor launch to the mainland. He was put in the same Danbury Prison that Phil was serving time in, and Howard and Roz visited them both regularly. After their release several years later, both went right back to protesting the war.

Howard's own protest activities continued unabated. Political commentators had been widely suggesting that the antiwar movement was in decline, an assessment that proved widely off the mark. Even during the winter months of 1970–71, a hastily planned demonstration in Boston brought hundreds of people out in zero-degree weather to protest in front of the Federal Building and then to march spontaneously through the streets. Only a few days later, fully five thousand turned out on the Common, though the press—

unwilling to give the lie to its own analysis of "decline"—barely covered it.

Then, when the weather began to thaw, came the "Mayday" actions in the Capitol. Thousands were arrested on the steps of Congress, Howard included. He'd made the mistake of asking a policeman why he was beating up a long-haired young man and, after being beaten himself, ended up in a one-person cell packed with half a dozen others. They stood for six hours in a pool of water several inches deep, but they were comparatively lucky: thousands of protesters were put for some thirty hours into the Coliseum stadium, so crowded and cold that there was no space on the floor to lie down at night, let alone food or blankets.

The following day, May 5, Howard was back in Boston, speaking on the Common before a crowd of some twenty-five thousand. "People who commit civil disobedience," he said, "are engaging in the most petty of disorders in order to protest against mass murder. These people are violating the most petty of laws, trespass laws and traffic laws, in order to protest against the government's violation of the most holy of laws, 'Thou shalt not kill.' "[8]

Howard had met Dan Ellsberg back in 1969 when both were speakers at an antiwar rally. The two couples—Howard and Roz, Dan and Patricia (they would marry in the summer of 1970)—gradually became friendly, now and then taking in a movie or having dinner together. Dan had graduated summa from Harvard, had joined the Marine Corps for three years, gone back to Harvard for graduate work, but then accepted an offer to become a military analyst for the RAND corporation (the Defense Department's think tank). In those pre-1969 years, he called himself "a Cold War Democrat"—meaning he believed in unions and in civil rights but in foreign policy was "realistic and tough"; his models were Hubert Humphrey and Walter Reuther. Ellsberg served under McNamara, starting in 1964, and spent two years in Vietnam, where he became convinced that the U.S. was conducting an unjust war. By the time

Howard met him in 1969, Ellsberg had moved into the antiwar ranks and had begun to think about how he might affect American policy. He was then a research fellow at MIT.[9]

Late in 1969 Ellsberg, with his top clearance and with the help of his former RAND colleague Anthony Russo, began secretly to photocopy a large number of documents. Later, in their entirety, they became known as the Pentagon Papers. In the year and a half that followed, Ellsberg treaded cautiously, knowing that when and if the papers did get released, he likely faced a lengthy jail sentence—as did anyone who helped get the material published. He showed a portion of the documents to a small number of well-connected journalists, friends, and antiwar members of Congress. After a variety of rebuffs and broken promises, the *New York Times* finally made the decision to publish excerpts from all seven thousand pages of the material.

"At last!" Howard wrote. "We have the first major rebel from those cool calculators of war," those government "whiz kids" who "unearthed the data, wrote the speeches, made the analyses, prepared the position papers, hitching their brains to the bomber planes, participating in the white-collar crimes which were the intellectual equivalent of search and destroy—searching the data to destroy a country . . . [Ellsberg] broke out of that circle which tried to hold his talent close to its murderous center . . ." Ellsberg's defection proved to Howard that "our estimate of the Establishment is too simple . . . for the gross evil of our time is not the direct product of a few bad men; it comes off a very long, very complex assembly line, in which all of us are given little jobs to do."

Ellsberg learned of the *Times's* decision to publish only the day before the first excerpts were scheduled to appear. Now that he knew publication was imminent, he put in a call to Howard and Roz, who'd been planning to join him and Patricia for a movie in Cambridge, and asked if they could come to Newton instead. Ellsberg knew the Zinns "weren't the ideal people" to avoid attracting the FBI's attention, because Howard was currently managing Dan Berrigan's journey underground. Still, he "didn't know whom else to turn to." Besides, he'd already given Howard a large chunk of the documents to read in his capacity as a historian. The Zinns immediately said yes to housing the material in their home.

The *Times* began publishing the papers on June 13, 1971. Ellsberg gave additional copies to the *Washington Post* and the *Boston Globe*, then went underground, staying with a shifting group of friends in Cambridge. After the second installment appeared in the *Times*, the Justice Department appealed for a temporary injunction in federal district court—and got it, the first time in our history that "prior restraint" of a newspaper, in violation of the First Amendment, had been sanctioned. As a result, Ellsberg scattered the Pentagon Papers to a number of other publications. With more and more papers breaking the story, muzzling the *Times* no longer made sense. The Supreme Court voted not to uphold the federal district court's injunction, and the *Times* went back to printing the papers. Ellsberg had by now been revealed as the source for the material, and he decided to turn himself in.

In his view, a sizable portion of the public—excepting, of course, those already opposed to the war—refused to believe the revelations in the Pentagon Papers that (in Ellsberg's words) "the pattern of executive deception, abuse of war powers, and the hopeless strategy of secret threats and secret and overt escalation," was continuing under Nixon, despite the administration's ongoing claim that the war was winding down and serious negotiations were under way. When Nixon revealed in July the "opening to China" and his imminent trip there, the public became even more convinced that a comprehensive deal about Indochina was all but sealed. Unfortunately, that was far from the case. Nixon was as determined as ever to force North Vietnamese troops out of the South and to ensure that the current U.S. puppet, the Thieu regime, remain the "legitimate" government there.

Ellsberg and Russo were indicted by a Los Angeles grand jury on eleven counts, including violation of the 1917 Espionage Act, which forbade disclosure of documents that might endanger national defense. If convicted, Ellsberg faced up to 130 years in prison and Russo 40 years. But conviction was far from inevitable. They were represented by an able legal team that included Leonard Boudin, the prominent civil rights attorney, and supported by a large number of distinguished official and academic witnesses. Howard was one of five designated expert witnesses (Noam Chomsky and Tom Hayden were two of the others) specifically chosen for their opposition to the war on moral grounds.

Howard was the first of the five to testify, but he flew to L.A. a week before to make sure he'd have enough time to study the documents in depth. On the stand, he spoke for several hours and was specifically asked to trace the history of U.S. involvement in Indochina from World War II to 1963. Among much else, Howard revealed that in the years immediately following the Japanese surrender, Ho Chi Minh wrote letter after letter to the White House asking that the pledges made to him for his help in the war be kept—that the Vietnamese be allowed to rule themselves. Not a single one of Ho's fourteen letters ever received a reply. Instead, during the war that followed between the French and the Viet Minh (a coalition of Vietnamese for independence, led by Ho and other communists), the U.S. was the chief supplier of guns and money to the French.

When the French were defeated in 1954 and had to sign the Geneva peace treaty promising a united Vietnam based on elections, the United States again stepped in, this time to prop up Diem as head of state in the South, to reject elections, to insist that South Vietnam had all along been an independent state and that it had called upon America to rescue it from northern "invaders." Why did we wed ourselves to such a theory? The answer, Howard testified, was right there in the Pentagon Papers, plain to see: over and over again the various memorandums refer to the basic reasons: "rubber, tin, oil, rice." And, oh yes, the little matter of the domino theory—if Indochina fell to the Communists, then the other dominoes would fall as well: Malaysia, Indonesia, the Philippines, and

Japan. Howard added that nothing in the Pentagon Papers endangered national defense—which he promptly defined as "defense of the people, not of special interests." He agreed, though, that the Papers were *embarrassing*, given the revelation that the American government had lied to its own citizens again and again. In an implicit compliment, the prosecutor waived his right to cross-examine.

Shortly after, it was revealed to the court that there had been a break-in at the office of Dr. Lewis Fielding, Ellsberg's psychiatrist, in a transparent effort to uncover material that might discredit him. Ellsberg's skillful lawyers further argued that the 1917 Espionage Act had explicitly disclaimed "any legislative intent to use it against unauthorized disclosures to the press." Additionally, it was revealed that Ellsberg was overheard on an illegal wiretap of Morton Halperin (who'd served in the Nixon administration), which had not been disclosed to the defense. At the same time, unfolding news of the Watergate scandal, involving another break-in, as well as illegal wiretaps, stunned the country. Given this fortunate conjunction of exposures and events, the judge granted the defendants' motion for dismissal and the trial was declared terminated.

Silber Versus Zinn

O il and water doesn't quite capture it. Maybe honey and battery acid comes closer. When John Silber became the new president of Boston University in 1971, leaving his post as dean and professor of philosophy at the University of Texas, he and Howard became instant antagonists. In a sense, Silber was a worthy opponent, smart, well read, articulate, and energetic—though far more wily and manipulative than the straightforward Howard, and far more conservative.

Silber could sometimes surprise. While in Texas, he'd organized a society to abolish capital punishment, energetically supported Head Start, and was also known as "good" on race, though his record in that regard is vague. And although deeply homophobic, Silber did his best to be supportive when his son David (who died of AIDS at age forty-one) came out to him. Still, in general, Silber's reputation at BU as a tyrannical reactionary seems warranted.

Even before Silber's arrival in 1971, Howard had had several run-ins with the BU administration over his antiwar activities. At one point, with Howard specifically in mind, an "investigation" was proposed to produce guidelines for faculty participation in demonstrations, but it produced such a rush of faculty support for Howard that the proposal was set aside. When Silber assumed the presidency, he made it clear that, unlike his predecessor, he wasn't one who bowed to pressure. In the spring of 1972, Silber invited the Marine Corps to recruit on the BU campus. The Marines accepted, but some of the students and faculty organized a demonstration in protest. Silber immediately called the police and, as the demonstrators were being arrested, he used a bullhorn to denounce disruption and civil disobedience.

To underscore his message, Silber wrote an article the next day for the administration's newsletter, in which he rebuked "new left intellectuals" who challenged U.S. policy in Indochina—specifically naming Howard, Noam Chomsky, and Herbert Marcuse—as threats to academic freedom and to the university as a place of free inquiry. He added that "disruptive students must be taught respect for the law." Weirdly, the three intellectuals he singled out were among the country's leading defenders of civil disobedience, free speech, and inquiry, whereas Silber would prove to be their inveterate enemy.[1]

Howard wasted no time in responding in the same determined tone Silber had used. The crucial function of the university, he wrote, was not to teach respect for the law, which usually protected the rights of the powerful and ignored the needs of the many, but rather *dis*respect for authorities or rules that served only the few. Silber seemed unable to distinguish, Howard went on, between "the right of free speech and free action." He'd muddied the distinction between the right to speak freely in defense of war with the right to recruit for an illegal war that defied the Constitution and half a dozen international treaties. Howard did mention that there were "gray areas" between speech and action, but he failed to name any or to cleanly define why we should privilege what we say over what we do—though possibly no one can. In any case, Howard's running battle with Silber would continue, with no time off for good behavior, for another seventeen years, until Howard would decide to retire.

* * *

In 1973, Howard published a short history of the twenty-five years following World War II, titled *Postwar America: 1945–1971*, as part of the History of American Society series edited by Jack P. Greene. Consisting of six essays, it was one of Howard's lesser works, covering much the same ground as his earlier, fresher, and more original *Politics of History*. His intention was to show that "greed and violence are mixed with just enough nobility and heroism to confuse any simple characterization of 'America.'" But—and this was precisely what gave the book its "tired" quality—the greed and violence were largely connected to the ruling class and the nobility to the country's dissenters.[2]

Howard's usual verve and passion appear only in diluted form in *Postwar America*. His optimism, however, remained intact—despite all the evidence he himself provided of corporate domination and endemic injustice; cumulatively, one might think, such evidence logically led to doubt, even to despair, but to Howard somehow it produced rejuvenation, and this even in the face of his own admission that "the public is not particularly well-informed about the specific issues of the day." Nor, Howard acknowledged, did the public seem ready for any dynamic, mass participation in politics.

What he did not emphasize was that most people, exhausted from the noncreative, boring, mechanical work they had to do day in and day out, had little energy left over for addressing the problems of their fellow sufferers—for delving, say, into the horrors of the prison system (like the recent September 1971 police massacre of prisoners and hostages at Attica, where 80 percent of 2,400 inmates were black or Hispanic—but not one guard); or the way in which a minimum-wage scale mired millions in poverty and hopelessness; or a racial divide that left 30 percent of the black population with incomes below the poverty line, with the deepening necessity of holding down two jobs (where jobs could be found) to feed one family, and with some African Americans seeking psychological and religious refuge in the Black Muslims or the Black Panthers.

Howard himself had understood the necessary emergence of both organizations, in that they at least emphasized dignity and independence as a counterweight to despair and fatalism. Under such nationwide conditions, "activism" held little appeal. Most people understandably preferred to expend what little leftover time they had on one form of entertainment or another—on sports, music, celebrity gossip, or TV.

Postwar America was sometimes eloquent in describing the ills that beset the country, but it had little to say about what a collective vision of the good society might look like or how to get there— except for generalized calls for "continuous organizing" and "a long revolutionary process of struggle and example." Perhaps it was too vague to declare that people had "to be drawn into active, day-to-day participation in decision-making, instead of pulling a lever once in two years." Perhaps, too, the time-worn assertion of optimism comes to sound Pollyannaish, evoking vexation, not hope. But Howard wasn't a rigid ideologue pretending to Godlike omniscience as so many others did. He preferred honest humility and flexibility.

But if the charge of vagueness can be countered, there are other omissions in *Postwar America* less readily accounted for: Howard entirely disregarded new demographic trends relating to marriage and divorce, religious affiliation, immigration, and ethnic interaction. Also, he barely mentioned the second wave of feminism that had burst on the scene a few years earlier, and he ignored the birth of the gay movement—though their combined challenge to traditional gender roles, forms of eroticism, patterns of relatedness, and family configuration held out the prospect of new ways to redistribute power and maximize human happiness.

Even as antiwar sentiment had spread to a substantial majority of the population by the early 1970s, other ongoing struggles that had engulfed the 1960s had either faded or shifted directions. The nonviolent tactics that had once overwhelmingly characterized the civil rights movement had, with a minority of African Americans turning to the Black Muslims, Malcolm X, and the Black Panther

Party, made talk of "armed struggle" far more commonplace. As the bombing of Indochina continued and expanded, the largely white New Left had increasingly broken into factions, with the Weathermen and the Progressive Labor Party holding the earlier peace movement up for ridicule as "bourgeois," lacking the needed courage to pick up arms.

As a swing to the right was already perceptible and that would culminate in the election of Ronald Reagan to the presidency, many who'd been active in the earlier struggles now backed away, discouraged and demoralized. Howard's tentative prediction of a turn to the left seems greatly mistaken. It might have seemed less so if he'd devoted any space in *Postwar America* to feminism or to a discussion of the industrial turmoil of the early 1970s, which saw the largest number of strikes and slowdowns since 1946, raising at least the possibility of a new round of class conflict.[3]

Little of that, strangely, seems to have registered enough with Howard for him to discuss labor's prospects in the book—which is especially odd since he'd previously expressed considerable concern with class oppression, and since a discussion of labor's crosscurrents in the early 1970s would have provided him with some tangible evidence that left-wing activism wasn't dead. In the 1960s, it had been precisely the left's tendency to equate the working class with conservatism, racism, and mindless patriotism that had worked against even a modest alliance among labor, left-wing, and black struggles (or the newly emergent feminist and gay ones as well).

Not that most of the working class was available for such an alliance, nor that it had achieved a unified identity or consciousness of its own—labor hadn't turned countercultural or embraced nontraditional views on gender and race. But the confusion about attitudes and alliances in the early 1970s certainly was pronounced enough to have warranted some discussion in *Postwar America*.

The 1972 presidential election somewhat settled the matter. The majority of workers voted for Nixon over McGovern (who had by far the stronger pro-labor record), with middle-class and white-collar voters siding with Nixon to a far larger degree than did union members or manual workers: 49 percent of those with little formal education preferred McGovern to only 37 percent of the college educated.

But what did those figures mean? That the majority of blue-collar workers had turned against the Indochina war that wealthier Americans still defended? That union members and manual workers had the potential to take on the corporations? Or was the opposite closer to the truth—that labor held blacks, women, gay people, welfare "cheats," communes, and the counterculture in heightened contempt? Neither? Both? The ambiguities of the early 1970s clarified somewhat when the economic boom ended in the mid-'70s. Whereas unemployment had been at a historic low and strikes and organizing drives at a historic high, the figures had swiftly reversed by mid-decade. Wages fell, inflation rose, plant closings increased, the outsourcing of production accelerated, and the general climate shifted to a sense of disarray, even to fear of the disaster of nuclear war. Economic and cultural conservatism strode back to center stage.

Shortly before Nixon's reelection, Howard joined four other anti-war activists (including Tom Hayden) on a return trip to Hanoi in early November 1972. Their mission had originally revolved around the prospect of an additional release of American prisoners of war, but Hanoi had linked that to the successful conclusion of cease-fire negotiations, which had been secretly under way since May. The U.S. agreed to terms three times, and three times backed away, Kissinger vaguely explaining to the press that "ambiguities of language" had unexpectedly surfaced—though peace, he assured them, was still at hand. What had in fact surfaced was doubt in the administration that peace would be good for Nixon's reelection bid. The consensus that seemed to emerge was that it would not. Nixon resumed saturation bombing of Hanoi and Haiphong.

By then, Howard and the rest of the peace delegation had returned to the States, empty-handed. But while still in Hanoi, the

Americans had been taken to the remote village of Thuan Thanh, twenty-seven miles north of Hanoi, and shown the horrifying results of an American bombing raid a few weeks before. It had left behind little more than rubble, along with the bodies of twenty-two people, twelve of them children. The villagers had never seen Americans before, and they took them through the rice paddies and a field of vegetables to the grave sites of the victims, the mounds of earth still fresh.

From that scene, Howard returned to the U.S., where he listened with a different ear to Silber defending the right to offer an ROTC program on the BU campus. The stale academic discussions about military recruitment "suddenly seemed absurd"; thinking about the graves of the dead children in Vietnam, Howard found the cool, detached debates "grotesque." It all reminded him of what his father had told him as a boy: "Go to school—but don't become an educated dummy."

Congress finally threatened to cut off further funding for the war unless negotiations were again picked up with Hanoi. Military victory having eluded the U.S., and with more than 58,000 Americans and well over 3 million Vietnamese dead, the U.S. signed a peace treaty with North Vietnam in Paris in January 1973, agreeing to withdraw its forces. A mere month after the agreement, Nixon rerouted the B-52s to Cambodia and in the following six months dropped a quarter of a million bombs on military sites and civilians alike. In addition, war continued between Hanoi and the Saigon government, with the U.S. still providing South Vietnam with military and economic aid. Real peace did not come until the fall of Saigon two years later.[4]

A different kind of crisis—a domestic kind—took place around this same time. Roz had been somewhat unhappy and discontented of late. She'd initially been excited about her teaching job, but by 1973 she'd come to feel that "too much stress" was attached to it, and she quit; she told one friend that she was "depressed," and also socialized a good bit less than earlier; due to go to dinner somewhere or to attend a party, she increasingly stayed only briefly or canceled plans at the last minute, pleading a sudden headache or stomach upset.

Most people who met Roz casually saw her as a radiantly happy, kind, and generous-hearted woman, one deeply contented with her life. Her close friends knew that her many virtues were real. But they also knew that, at certain times, she could be dispirited and moody. Roz wasn't nearly as gregarious as Howard, who "always seemed the same" and was almost never low in spirits or ill at ease. Roz also enjoyed getting together with friends, but it took increasing effort for her to participate in large, hectic social events. She did her best to present herself as outgoing—which allowed many people to misread her. It was mostly at home that she'd allow her distress to show. Her son, Jeff, a lively young man, reached the point where he grew tired of his mother's "negativity," and for a time he kept her at a distance.

What undoubtedly contributed to Roz's darker moods was her discovery in the early 1970s that Howard had been having an affair with another woman that had become serious. The few details we know come not from the vacuumed Zinn Archives but from material in the archives of others and from a few close friends who've spoken frankly (and anonymously)—though without, understandably, providing many details. Howard initially chose to confide in Myla, when she was in her midtwenties, telling her that he'd fallen in love with another woman—though he still loved Roz as well. If he expected understanding, he was quickly undeceived. Myla (in her own words) "was shocked and upset not only because I had had no idea that anything like this had ever happened, but also because he hadn't told my mother. His seeking my support and approval showed me how little he knew me and how little he understood what a huge betrayal this was of my mother."

She told her father that he simply *had* to tell Roz, which he did soon after—that is, told her about the several affairs he'd had but not (he wasn't remotely a cruel man) that he'd recently found "true love," in the words of an anonymous friend. Indeed for a time he considered divorcing Roz. Possibly, both women gave Howard an ultimatum; in any case, he did finally choose to stay with Roz, but did continue to have "flings," making sure that Roz didn't find out about them. They were both "deeply sensuous" people, and when Roz took some courses at Goddard College, she herself had a little flirtation—but quickly drew back from it.[5]

All of which poses some profound and long-debated issues regarding relationships that can only be discussed, not settled, because different cultures and value systems produce quite different codes for moral behavior and the codes change through time. That alone should give pause to any assured labels or quick judgments. The dynamics of long-standing relationships vary considerably among couples. Some people think that promising lifelong commitment to one's partner ideally should entail making a clearly understood distinction between an emotional commitment and a sexual one. Nor, in the United States at least, does it usually include the knowledge that relationships change over time. The needs of the other person, along with one's own, continue to evolve and cannot, without resentment, always be contained within the boundaries originally set.

With Roz and Howard, we simply don't know if they initially and explicitly committed to sexual monogamy. A good guess—given the traditional "till death do us part" families they both grew up in—is that the assumption of sexual exclusivity was there from the beginning (even if never articulated or explored). Currently, many studies of sexuality conclude that monogamy is neither natural nor easy—but that people who opt instead for an "open" marriage are no happier. There are those who choose to ignore their partner's infidelities even if they're hurt by them and prefer to remain monogamous themselves. There are as well some partners who feel that emotional monogamy plus short-term sexual relationships can be a highly successful formula for maintaining a good lifelong relationship. Of course, these days women are no longer assumed to be indifferent to sex or innately committed to monogamy, but if many more women are today having affairs outside of their marriages, it seems safe to say (for now) that the wish for sexual variety still derives primarily from a gendered (male) script.

Certainly that was true of Howard and Roz. The fact that Howard, and not Roz, periodically had affairs, calls for some explanation, however speculative. Yet none of the theories about extramarital sex currently prominent in our culture seems applicable to Howard, the individual. He obviously wasn't the kind of macho man who needs to boast about his frequent conquests.

Then there's also the common view that erotic excitement and domesticity can never coexist for very long, but we know literally nothing about the actual pattern of Howard and Roz's sexual relationship (or Howard's inner life). Some prominent psychologists—preeminently Stephen A. Mitchell, one of the founders of relational psychoanalysis—believe that in our culture many men cannot risk monogamy. They prefer to separate sex and love because to combine the two puts them in danger of heightened vulnerability, of being (as Mitchell puts it) "easily destabilized by dependency longings," by the threat of deep intimacy. While it's true that Howard mostly kept his inner feelings to himself, that isn't the equivalent of being afraid of closeness. His, it seems, was a generational male style of avoiding *talk* about intimate matters, not of avoiding *feelings* of intimacy.

But the bottom line is that we lack the kind and amount of evidence that might allow further speculation about what led to Howard's affairs and the way he and Roz understood them, separately or together. It does seem necessary to add that Howard's decision not to remain faithful wasn't an indicator of the failure of his relationship with Roz. There is, after all, the little matter of loving each other—of real companionship and shared values, of understanding and caring—and the fact that they decided to stay together for the rest of their lives.

Which isn't to say that Howard's philandering had no negative impact on their relationship, at least in the short run. Roz had been deeply, deeply hurt, and that known fact is of bottom-line importance. Myla was upset by her mother's pain and her father's "duplicity" (as she called it) and for a time felt alienated from her father. We cannot measure, even broadly, the extent to which time healed all wounds. Deception and secrecy do produce distrust, and it seems unlikely that such scars would ever entirely fade. What we do know is that Howard and Roz successfully reconstituted their marriage; several of their close friends have used nearly the same language in describing their later closely interwoven bond as among the strongest they'd ever seen.

In 1973, the University of Paris at Vincennes invited Howard to teach for one semester—two courses of three hours each on Marxist and anarchist theory, carrying a salary of $9,000 (about average in Europe at that time). Howard immediately accepted and assumed that a three-month leave of absence without pay would pass through the assorted faculty and administrative procedures automatically. He arranged for Herbert Marcuse, one of the world's most distinguished political philosophers, to take over his classes. Howard thought BU would jump at the chance to get Marcuse on campus—especially because he himself would pay Marcuse's salary and his leave wouldn't cost the university a cent.[7]

But Howard hadn't counted on the depth of Silber's antagonism. To almost everyone's surprise, the dean of liberal arts turned down Howard's request for leave; the reason given was that his absence would burden the university with incidental expenses totaling $2,000—a sum that the dean himself had earlier called "modest." What followed the announcement was a week and a half of special faculty meetings, during which there was a shouting match between Howard and the dean. A subsequent deal, which would have apparently led to official approval of Howard's absence, required him to submit a memo "requesting permission to leave." He point-blank refused. "See how starved we are," Howard wrote his close friend and colleague Frances Fox Piven (*Poor People's Movements*), "when crap like this becomes important!" The administration, for once, made no further objections, and when the time came, Howard and Roz simply left for their three-month stay in France.

Silber had his own ways of getting even. Though he was an excellent fund-raiser and increased BU's endowment considerably, Silber was simultaneously given to large hikes in tuition and small raises in faculty salaries. And toward his "enemies," he could be downright harsh. BU's faculty wages compared badly with average salaries nationally and were still further behind when compared with other Massachusetts colleges. The average BU full professor in the early 1970s earned $21,200 compared to the state's $24,800; the junior ranks were even harder hit. From 1970–1974, faculty compensation remained a small percentage (17 percent) of the BU budget, "while tuition and income skyrocketed." For the same years, there'd been "a dramatic increase" in administrative expenses—and also in the nation's inflation, with prices going up 8 percent in 1973 alone and with the Boston area having one of the nation's highest costs of living.[8]

Howard's case was special. His department recommended him for a $1,000 raise in 1974, but Silber overrode the recommendation and reduced the figure to zero. There was a larger issue, besides personal enmity, at stake. In most universities, salaries were determined by the executive committee of each department; it was one's immediate colleagues, after all, who were the most familiar with the merits of a given faculty member. But at BU, the president played the key role in allocating funds to a department and in deciding salaries. In a formal complaint to Silber, Howard charged him "with flagrant disregard . . . for democratic process," and further accused him of being "unable to deal with men and women who voice opinions that differ from yours or who object to your own policies." All of which had led, in Howard's well-documented opinion, to an administration staffed with "sycophants, panderers, and incompetents." Many on the faculty agreed with Howard's analysis, but only a few dared to adopt such boldly accusatory language. Howard would pay for it—literally.

As Silber's dictatorial style became increasingly apparent, the faculty did manage occasionally to find its voice. When he rejected the idea of a faculty union, it passed the faculty Senate by the substantial vote of 395–260—about 60 percent of those voting. "Not overwhelming," Howard wrote Frances Fox Piven, "but decisive, clearcut . . . Silber had obviously lost & the next step will be negotiations. He will undoubtedly be a *tough* negotiator, knowing how the word *strike* scares faculty people." Along with Piven, Howard's closest ally on the faculty was Murray Levin, a colleague in political science. Individually and collectively, they were quite as formidable as Silber.

The three put together an alternate manifesto detailing what their kind of university might look like. They renounced those standards "of excellence shoved down on us from above," elite standards that adhered to nonpolitical goals. The "in" group employed "the haughty academic style, the esoteric language systems, the ritualization of argument," that help to perpetuate class divisions. The three also indicted BU's dominant "cults of success and hierarchy," offering in their place the encouraging of "scholarship not only more penetrating in its criticism of existing ideas and institutions, but also more ready to explore visions and projections of a new society," one that would explore the "potentialities of the human race, so far imprisoned and distorted inside corrupt systems."[9]

They denounced the kind of university—BU for one—that encouraged the centralization of power as a training ground for students modeling deference to authority and traditional values. They wanted the classroom, now dominated by a single "expert" handing down purported "truths," to evolve into an informal, democratic setting, in which a single authority, ruling without challenge, would be displaced by an exchange of differing views, the collective questioning of authority, and the dawning realization that truth is elusive and unstable.

Silber responded with a lengthy essay in which he reiterated his traditional views on education and the purpose and structure of the university. In the piece, he specifically named Howard for "poisoning the well and cheapening the standards of discourse," even as he, Silber, presented himself as a champion of free speech. Further, he deplored the "increasing difficulty in maintaining even the most footloose standards of academic duty, as obligations increasingly fail to be correlative to rights." The two men would never remotely see eye-to-eye on such issues. Nor would the antagonism between them ever diminish—and a long road of mutual recrimination lay ahead.

Howard agreed to become an occasional columnist for the *Boston Globe*. He enjoyed having a platform and using it to comment on a wide range of issues. His political values had long since been set, and his columns contain few surprises, though they were often expressive and eloquent. When Nelson Rockefeller headed a commission to investigate the CIA and issued a report that read in part: "There are things that have been done which are in contradiction to the statutes, but in comparison to the total effort they are not major," Howard, in his column, acidly named among the CIA's "little faults," keeping secret files on ten thousand American citizens, running Operation Phoenix (a program of assassination, torture, and imprisonment in Vietnam, 1967–1971), and plotting to overthrow left-wing governments, including those in Guatemala, Iran, and Cuba. Yet despite this record of murder and deceit, nothing had been done to dissolve the CIA or even curtail its power. Why? Because the organization was essential to our fight against "Communism," which Howard sardonically remarked "roams the earth, conspiring to overthrow other governments. . . . Once, there was the Stone Age. Now, the Age of Irony."[10]

Similarly, as economic conditions in the country continued to worsen and Congress failed to find enough votes to override President Ford's veto of a $3 billion jobs creation bill—while overwhelm-ingly passing legislation to give the Pentagon an additional $25 billion—Howard, reflecting the view among the ever diminishing group of radical critics of national priorities, bitterly asked whether the federal government could any longer be trusted to serve the needs of the people rather than those of the plutocracy. He re-minded his readers that the government had spent $150 billion and 58,000 American lives on the war in Indochina, all in the name of "national security." But had it succeeded in ensuring our security? Hardly. The war had weakened us, made us hated all over the world.

What Howard's columns did not reflect was the growing dismay by the mid-1970s among radical dissenters over the lack of signifi-cant social change that two decades of protest had produced, plus the loss of confidence that any shift in tactics held out any greater hope of producing better results. But anguish wasn't intrinsic to Howard's personality. Confidence and good spirits were. As more and more social critics retreated toward the center—or to their studies—Howard remained positive about future prospects.

One day he jotted down this note to himself: "there is only one theory of man which explains his behavior on earth thus far, and which is a useful guide for social action: he is incredibly open to every possibility." No, alas not every person remains "incredibly open"—far from it, and few people over thirty, given the multiple problems that consume their own lives, ever have much energy left over for dealing with political issues. The irony is that if they *could* deal with them, their lives would stand some chance of getting easier. In the mid-1970s, more than usual, there were too many dark clouds on the horizon, too much despondency in the heart-land. By mid-1975 the unemployment rate had shot up to 9.2 per-cent—13 percent among blue-collar workers—and because inflation had outstripped wages, real earnings had dropped by 4.1 percent in a single year.

Instead of organized labor upping its demands, the earlier rash of strikes fell off dramatically, and the AFL/CIO leadership—and in particular its president (from 1955–1979), George Meany—stood as if paralyzed, imprisoned by its own ideological centrism. Union members were to some degree protected by previous collective-bargaining agreements with management that provided for some unemployment benefits and for "early retirement" plans, but non-union workers—a growing percentage of labor—had little to fall back on other than, when they could find them, menial or part-time jobs. Public employee unions were more militant in making demands, but they lacked the numbers (and enough popular support) to push for any federal legislation that smacked of "socialist" solutions like nationalization and planning.

But why didn't the labor movement move further to the left, as it had during the depression of the 1930s? The answer is contested and complex, but two explanations stand out. Foremost is American mythology—the insistence that if one "failed" in life, the responsibility was primarily due to the individual; as every indoctrinated American knew, if you worked hard enough, you could achieve whatever you wanted to. Sure—go tell it to blacks, single mothers, or gay people (who back in those prehistoric years seldom dared even to come out publicly). Or try telling it to Howard's own father, denied education, hardworking but forced to become a window washer or waiter, dying at the comparatively young age of sixty-seven, having gotten nowhere (at least as society believes is somewhere).

The second explanation for organized labor failing to move to the left involved the new cultural formations and issues that had emerged in the early 1970s, in particular the women's and gay movements, as well as the rise of ethnicity as a political force. The second wave of feminism found some allies among workers—job opportunities for women actually rose in the 1970s, in contrast to the general downturn—but the gay movement found none. Also, certain specific solutions for deep-seated social problems—such as the use of busing to solve ongoing school segregation, or gun control to contain violence, or a woman's right to choose abortion as a necessary adjunct to her freedom—infuriated many working-class whites and helped to drive them into the arms of a rising conservative tide. Thus oppressions based on race and class (to say nothing of gender and sexuality) were unable or (for whites) unwilling to combine forces in the name of combating their common enemy: the solidified alliance between the federal government and the corporate world. The "freaks," not the CEOs, became labor's enemy.

In his *Boston Globe* columns for 1975–76, Howard had little to say about the current recession or the changing culture. The issues of primary interest to him remained what they had long been: race and class. Though sympathetic to the New Left (unlike most radicals over fifty), Howard was late in acknowledging feminism or ethnicity as primary aspects of identity, and even later in regard to sexual orientation. He never wrote negatively about any of these newer developments, but neither did he ever devote even part of a column or essay to any of them. In his heart of hearts, he couldn't imagine comparing the deprivation of African Americans and the poor to that of essentially white middle-class women and gay people. But oppression and suffering take their toll wherever found, though when viewed from the outside it may be difficult to recognize, especially when disposable income and a high level of education are present. In fact, many women and LGBT people were working-class poor, and many in the middle class had been psychologically socialized to feel second-rate and marginal in the "real" world. Besides, feminism and homosexuality, along with abortion, constituted the triumvirate of evil at the heart of the Culture War, turning the country in an ever-deepening conservative direction—a development that Howard, after all, cared about a great deal.

But Howard's house was already built and fully furnished; the idea of adding new rooms seemed unnecessary. An old engine isn't in charge of pulling spanking new Acela passenger cars. Howard's dream of ending injustice was based on solidarity, not on finding, Oprah-like, one's "real" self in the therapeutic looking glass. He ascribed the suffering of his own parents to restricted education and poverty, not to their being Jewish ethnics. He saw his mission as helping to eradicate discriminations based on race and class. Though he was never contemptuous of other sources of injury, he could never wrap his mind around the importance of an individual's search for his or her "specialness."

For Howard, whether the focus was on gay rights or Polish rights, such emphasis was mostly diversionary. He couldn't get himself to care much about whether a man should be punished for having sex with another man, or whether a transgendered woman was psychologically better off with or without surgery. He felt that the enormity of oppression based on race or class transcended the "search for self." It doesn't necessarily take Howard off the hook to point out that the concerns of each generation (or rather, a small portion of each) often center on issues distinctive to that generation. More obvious, perhaps, is that no one can be simultaneously active in all possible causes. At different times, to different people, certain matters seem more immediately pertinent than others. Where Howard can be considered unusual is in his declared sympathy—sometimes, to be sure, limited—for the newer concerns of the most recent generation. Unlike most of his contemporaries, he never described women as "intrinsically less analytic" than men, or gay people as "contrary to nature."

His sense that issues relating to race and class remained the essential ones can't be contradicted as somehow wrong, but his unchanging focus did mean that Howard had, by the mid-1970s, little left to add by way of commentary that was fresh. Yet he did continue to write, even if his columns and articles of the mid-'70s were too often stale and repetitive—in no sense a match for the passionate clarity of his earlier work, possibly the plight of anyone who writes continuously on public affairs.

In his seventies articles, Howard continued to defend "socialism" but defined it without reference to nationalizing the means of production and distribution or to championing federal economic planning—Marxism's classic precursors to a classless society. He *was* careful to distinguish what he meant by "socialism" from the totalitarian usurpation of Marx that characterized the Soviet Union. An interviewer once asked Howard directly if he considered himself a Marxist. Howard's response was, "Yes, I'm something of a Marxist," the "something" deriving from the fact that "people have so many different notions about what a Marxist is."[11]

True enough, but what was Howard's "notion"? He gave various answers to the question throughout his political life, many of them distinguishing between the young Marx and the older Marx. He thought Marx had been needlessly "dogmatic" in regard to the necessity of progressing through various stages in dislodging capitalism. Further, Howard thought Marx's economic analyses "unnecessarily dense," in contrast to the lucidity and eloquence of his critique of capitalism—which Howard felt was equally true of the works of the young and older Marx. (The great economist John Kenneth Galbraith also felt that Marx's economics was doctrinaire.) Yet despite all of Howard's criticism, he believed that the liberating powers of Marxism, "especially in its motivating quest to escape from alienation," were its overriding value.

Yet at certain periods in his life, especially during his later years, Howard thought philosophical anarchism still more potent, especially in its dismissal of nation-states as a barrier to the development of humane values—though he certainly didn't mistakenly equate the capitalist notion of globalization with bringing people together internationally. Howard dismissed the popular (and false) association of anarchism with violence and chaos. He'd been drawn to anarchism because it rejected authoritarianism, especially that of church and state, and because of its notion that localized collectives of various sizes, without national borders, passports, or boundaries, best served the widest possible dispersal of power and entitlements.

In this regard, Howard looked back for inspiration to Thoreau and Emerson, with their skepticism toward authority and government. And he looked back to SNCC as having had an essentially anarchist spirit, in utilizing direct action against segregation instead of waiting for the government or the courts to take up the cause, and in insisting that if your end is an egalitarian society then so must your means be. Howard had retreated from his earlier calls for federal intervention and turned instead to championing "a democratically-organized economy in which work cooperatives and consumer cooperatives control things at the local level, yet coordinate what they do nationally." He now called *that* "socialism." His newfound utopia of decentralized economic planning and decision making at the local level, however, had one—hardly minor—drawback. The very problems of national scope that Howard cared most about—racism and poverty—seemed to require considerable federal intervention. As the black struggle had demonstrated, discriminatory practices couldn't always be left for solution to local initiative, resources—and prejudice.

Which brought everything back full circle: how do we get the federal government to focus on the needs of the least fortunate of its citizens? Through armed struggle? Of course not, Howard would have replied—there was no constituency for it, and even if there was, it was immoral. Reinvigorating the nonviolent tactics of the black struggle—the "long march through the institutions"? But the country was sick of marches and protests, and how would we decide on which were the most salient structures to march against—Goldman Sachs? Congress? The International Monetary Fund? And where were the troops for doing battle against whatever target was chosen? Was it any wonder that Howard—in order to remain hopeful—sometimes retreated to tired rhetoric?

Howard was well aware of the cynicism spreading throughout the country and of the nation's marked turn to the right. But the best he could come up with were rather limp, rhetorical counterarguments for why we should nonetheless retain our optimism. Yes, 1 percent of the population in 1974–75 owned 33 percent of the wealth, and those below the poverty line had *no* representatives in Congress. And yes, the tax system supported the growing gap between rich and poor. *But*, Howard pointed out, the polls showed a mounting distrust of the federal government, too. Ergo, the people would soon turn against it, and possibly against corporate aggrandizement (capitalism), too. If so, there were few signs of it on the horizon.

Americans have generally been a good deal less class-conscious than Europeans. A number of surveys have shown that Americans are twice as likely to blame themselves if their income remains low than they are to cite the structural obstacles kept in place by the wealthy that for most people block the path to greater success. Throughout U.S. history, there have been outbreaks of class-based rebellion, but both white and black workers have more consistently identified with issues relating to race. In the 1970s, unfortunately, class and race were moving further away than ever from any alliance against corporate capitalism. The labor historian Jefferson Cowie has put it well: "In the 1970s, race and class were often at odds, trumping any possibility of drawing together the class-based politics of the thirties with the racial freedom of the sixties into that most elusive of things in American history—an interracial class identity."

Union busting, not building, was becoming the mantra of the day. Labor's "excessive" wages, according to the Nobel Prize–winning economist Milton Friedman and his conservative buddies, were chiefly responsible for the rise of inflation. Union demands could be best curtailed by convincing workers that unions were not in their best interest; the leadership was purportedly corrupt and predatory (unlike corporate leadership?) and worked *against* the interests of its own members. Corporate propaganda, in combination with the anger of the white working class over newfangled notions like busing and new cultural formations like feminism and gay rights, made arguments from the right seem increasingly attractive, and mounting numbers of white workers shifted their political allegiance. The country was heading into twenty-five years of conservative domination that in regard to domestic policy would make Richard Nixon look like a flaming liberal.

Howard wasn't about to give up, but he did turn some of his energy to issues that hadn't previously engaged him much. Foremost among them was the horror of the prison system. As early as 1974, he'd put together an anthology of writings by others (and a few short ones by himself), *Justice in Everyday Life*, that featured articles on the courts, the police, and the prisons but also included pieces that examined justice (or the lack of it) in housing, the workplace, health care, and schools. The book represents Howard taking his own new advice: go local.

The institutions he examined were in Boston, and he enlisted students from his BU course Law and Justice in America in the research. Still creative and enthusiastic as a teacher, he felt his class would better understand case histories and constitutional law if they recognized how those formal texts got translated into everyday life. Most of the students were deeply shocked when they tried to match the stated law with the way it was put into practice. It was the power of the policeman on the beat, not the Supreme Court, that determined how everyday justice was meted out. It was a jolt for the students to read the essays in the anthology and to see with their own eyes that although we had constitutional guarantees and a Bill of Rights, elections, and representative government, in reality they had little impact on how our democracy worked on a daily basis. The match-up between statute law and how it was defined on the street by the police was slight. Regimentation, wealth and status, hierarchical authoritarianism—plus downright whim—turned out to be significant arbiters of how justice was executed.

In reality, the formal guarantee of a trial by jury meant that many defendants were badly represented by incompetent or overworked legal counsel and that some 90 percent of arrestees never got tried by a jury but were persuaded to enter guilty pleas after being falsely informed that the judge would thereby hand down a lighter sentence. Then they ended up in a brutal prison system, in which they lost all control over their lives, the arbitrary power of the guards determining whether they would undergo physical or mental abuse.

Many of the same indignities and deceptions were an intrinsic part of other social institutions. Residential segregation remained a fact of life, and housing stock for the poor was characteristically awful—firetraps with little heat in winter, little air in summer, little privacy anytime, with vermin as co-habitants, and danger omnipresent. For the poor, housing wasn't necessarily the equivalent of having a home: it had less in common with a comfortable private retreat than with a reproduction of the dismal working conditions many had to face during the day. The nonunionized worker was often under the constant surveillance of a boss and his assistants, which for many could mean grueling rules, low pay, few time-outs, barked orders—and the steady fear of unemployment.

Nor was first-rate health care available for many of those who were poor. Hospital wards were sometimes left unattended; medical records scattered and unavailable; unnecessary surgical procedures performed or, when actually needed, not performed; infant death rates high; the brusque nursing staff more prone to rebuke than ministration; the doctors more sniffily cautious about handling the unwashed than doing sterilizations. As for the public school system, the occasional creative teacher wasn't enough to make a dent in a bureaucracy dominated by rote, discipline, rules, and racism. In the 1970s, few public schools prepared poor children for college and good jobs, tracking them instead for trade school, blue-collar jobs, or the armed forces—thereby perpetuating the inequalities already current.

Unlike the 1960s, there wasn't much optimism that the chasm between the lives of the well-off and the poor could be lessened. Although Howard's 1974 book *Justice in Everyday Life* was a grim compilation of the serious and mounting injustices in the country, he closed it in typical fashion: with examples of people fighting back and accomplishing change. That section of the book was comparatively small, since Howard wasn't given to outright invention, but he managed to point to a community organization that had driven a corrupt, authoritarian judge from the bench, a successful tenant organizing effort, and an aggressive student-faculty coalition that had saved the jobs of several radical professors. Slim pickings, perhaps, in a national scene dominated by right-wing confidence and left-wing gloom, but enough to give some cheer to those already inclined toward optimism.

As for the future, Howard advised that we shed some traditional mythology: namely, that those in power deserve to be there, that failure is due to an individual's lack of effort; that antagonisms between ethnic and racial groups would always prevent the discontented from unifying and achieving power; and that changes on the local level can't possibly make a significant dent in problems of national scope. Essentially Howard was issuing a call for continuous organizing. But in the wake of disappointment over how little apparent change the sixties had produced (though the shifts in values went deeper), lethargy and indifference had largely taken over, blocking movement to the left.

Characteristically, Howard acted on his beliefs. It wasn't enough to deplore the prison system; one had to help individual prisoners suffering under it. He visited them, sent books, looked over their writing, exchanged letters, and recommended them for parole. With a few prisoners, Howard remained in touch for long periods. A case in point is Jimmy Barrett. Howard wasn't always allowed into "murderers' row" in the Charles Street jail, but when barred he'd stand outside the gray stone fortress and wave up to Jimmy. Howard couldn't make him out but knew that Jimmy could see him.[12]

Jimmy had grown up in the South End of Boston, a poor kid in a large Irish family. When he was twenty-two, a man had lunged at him from a doorway at night, beaten him, and threatened to shoot him on sight the next time. Terrified, and believing that he was acting in self-defense, Jimmy had killed the man, having bought a gun just three days before to protect himself on the South End's rough streets. The prosecution had offered him a deal whereby he'd serve "only" seven years, but Jimmy, convinced of his innocence, had turned it down. His court-appointed defense lawyer never answered

Jimmy's letters, and a jury, acting on confusing instructions from the presiding judge, found him guilty and sentenced him to life in prison. His lawyer never appealed the case.

In prison, Jimmy became a reader (in solitary, the only book available was the Bible, so Jimmy read it five times) and also an organizer for prisoners' rights—double grounds for getting close to Howard's heart. He was thrown into "the hole," Ten Block, a hellish place where the guards beat Jimmy repeatedly. It isn't clear when and how Howard first met him, but Jimmy had started to keep a diary and, after reading and admiring something of Howard's that he'd read, sent him a few pages. Howard thought they were "remarkable," and it may well have been at that point that he sought Jimmy out in prison (by then, Jimmy was in his midthirties). Howard found him a decent attorney, worked hard for his release (writing to the governor and encouraging others to do so), and worked equally hard at trying to get Jimmy's diary published as a book. Jimmy's appeal went through, he was retried, and set free in January 1975. He'd had almost no formal education but, in Howard's opinion, had "great intellectual curiosity and a powerful desire to learn." Howard set up a study plan for him, and within a short time Jimmy was admitted to Goddard College.

Still acting locally, Howard continued to follow his own new prescription for social change: put down your bucket where you are. And where Howard was much of the time was Boston University. Throughout the early seventies, he and Silber had continued to lock horns, though some periods were more fraught than others. Back in 1972, antiwar students had demonstrated in front of the building where Marine Corps recruiters were holding court, and Silber had called the police on the demonstrators and shouted at them through a bullhorn—forever the symbol of the Laurie Pritchetts and Bull Connors of the world.[13]

Howard was in bed at the time, ill with a viral infection, and hadn't been part of the demonstration. But the next day, when

the administration's in-house paper came out with the headline
DISRUPTIVE STUDENTS MUST BE TAUGHT RESPECT FOR LAW, SAYS DR.
SILBER, Howard got himself to the typewriter and wrote a widely
reprinted article about civil disobedience and the need for an
"open university" that challenged "the rule of obedience to legal
authority."

The next major confrontation with Silber came over the Health
Service workers' battle, beginning in spring 1975, for better wages.
Within six months, Silber had fired twelve of the sixteen workers.
An appeal was made to the National Labor Relations Board (NLRB),
which held hearings on campus that fall. In Howard's opinion, the
administration "put on a very weak case." Then a student referen-
dum voted to appropriate $1,000 to help the health care workers
with their legal fees, which the administration vetoed. But the NLRB
ordered the workers reinstated, ruling that the university had "co-
erced employees in the exercise of rights" guaranteed by law. Soon
after, the secretaries on campus organized through District 65 and
threatened a legal battle of their own.

Silber was a wily opponent, loved a fight, and was resourceful
in outwitting opponents. He advised all departments to plan for a
budget cut of 25 percent over the next two years, the equivalent of
wiping out all nontenured positions. The departments of psychology, political science, and sociology promptly called emergency
meetings, and all three unanimously passed resolutions declaring
their refusal to comply with the edict from on high, insisting it had
been arbitrarily declared without any consultation with a faculty
body. Silber held to his views that "there is a natural hierarchy
among men," that egalitarianism is "destructive," and that "no university can be run except on an elitist basis."

Howard was hardly alone in his opposition to Silber's philosophy and policies. When his five-year contact as BU's president ran
out in 1976, there was an outpouring of opposition to his reap-
pointment. The students demonstrated against it, the faculty voted
overwhelmingly against it, and most of the deans also expressed

their opposition. In the end, none of this registered. The university, as Silber had said, is not a democracy. All final decisions rested with the Board of Trustees. In 1976 there were still some members who disliked Silber, but he rallied his forces, appeared before the board to argue his case, and sealed the deal behind the scenes by arranging the appointment of a new chair, Arthur Metcalf, a right-winger and a close friend. Silber's contract was renewed. Henceforth he had nearly absolute power, the Board of Trustees serving as a mere rubber stamp.

Howard backed down not an inch, even as faculty opposition to Silber eroded out of fear of reprisal. Howard was especially unyielding in defense of BU's students. He protested when they were denied the right to leaflet, and he went to the American Civil Liberties Union when a student involved in trying to get the university to divest its stocks in South Africa as a protest against apartheid was told to remove the DIVEST sign from his window or face eviction from his room. The ACLU took that case—and won it, on the grounds of free speech. In a more personal incident, when an honors student being interviewed for a university brochure was asked to name her two most inspiring professors and picked Howard as one of the two, she was told to either remove his name or her interview wouldn't be published. She refused, and the penalty was exacted. And so it went over the next few years. In the late 1970s the Zinn-Silber battle would again boil over.

Howard had always had the capacity to enjoy life. Now he had more leisure time to do so, especially during summers, when he was free from classes. He'd always liked going to the theater and the movies and, in warm weather, biking to class and regularly playing tennis. But in 1975 came a whole new order of pleasure. He and Roz made a down payment on a house in Wellfleet, on Cape Cod. They'd already spent some time on the Cape and had loved it. The house was about fifty years old, an "old-fashioned" two-story shingled place, very plain, surrounded by other houses, with a porch and fireplace and situated right on Wellfleet Bay. To complete the purchase, they had to borrow money and take out a mortgage, but "Roz has never been so happy," Howard wrote to Frances Piven. She adored swimming—Howard came to adore floating—and went into the Bay several times a day. Having tried social work and been only briefly engaged by it, Roz quit her current job and decided to complete her teaching practicum at Goddard; her aim was to get certification to do a combination of counseling and teaching children on a one-to-one basis.

On top of their happiness with the Cape house, Roz and Howard were thrilled to become grandparents for the first time. Both of their grown children had married, and in 1975 Myla gave birth to a son, Will, the first of her three children. Howard thought him "a terrific little boy," and he and Roz both delighted in the fact that the family had re-knit. Myla and her husband, Jon Kabat-Zinn (a molecular biologist whose work led to the field of mindfulness-based health interventions), lived near Boston. Jeff and his wife (they would later divorce, and Jeff would remarry, becoming a father for the first time at age forty-four) lived in New York, where Jeff frequently acted Off-Off-Broadway in the Theater for the New City (TNC), one of a handful of places devoted to new work by a new generation.

Beginning in 1975, Jeff came to the Boston area more often in order to have production conferences with Howard on a political play he'd written about the radical anarchist Emma Goldman, which Jeff was going to direct at TNC. Howard was the only one in his immediate family who hadn't already exhibited some talent for the theater. During the years at Spelman, Roz had acted several times with Theater Atlanta, and Myla had appeared in the lead role in *The Diary of Anne Frank*—winning Best Actress of the Year. Her first two years of college had been at Antioch, but she'd then transferred to study drama at BU, though neither she nor her mother pursued acting careers.

Jeff, on the other hand, did. He worked initially as both an actor and director in New York City, and thereafter became the artistic director of the now well-known Wellfleet Harbor Actors Theater. Jeff and his father would periodically have friendly arguments about the value of "political" or "message" theater, Howard championing it, of course. He'd later trace his interest back to 1938, when he saw a Federal Theater production of *One Third of a Nation* and claimed he'd ever after longed to become attached to the theater in some way. In fact he had—though not in the sense he meant. When speaking on a platform to audiences, Howard was a consummate performer—speaking without notes (the script), his presence warm and informal yet charismatic, his rich and resonant voice carrying to the balcony.

Howard had long been attracted to Emma Goldman as a person and to anarchism as a theory—not to the bomb-throwing, nihilistic caricature of the textbooks, but to the philosophy (as exemplified in the writings of Pierre-Joseph Proudhon and Prince Peter Kropotkin) of opposition to traditional authority and distrust of the State. The federal government's initial failure to protect civil rights workers in the South and its ugly war of terror against Vietnam, Laos, and Cambodia had further weakened Howard's trust of centralized authority. He knew that the New Deal had accomplished considerable good, but he also knew that by the 1950s the regulatory agencies set up to supervise corporate malfeasance had been taken over by representatives of the corporations themselves, that farm-subsidy programs had benefited the largest operators while giving minimal or no support to sharecroppers and tenant farmers, and that urban renewal and poverty programs had produced more corruption than relief. Big business and big government had joined forces, becoming allies more concerned with their own prestige and power than with the multiple needs of the people.

Howard's recent emphasis on decentralized organizing, building collective action on the local level, was a mark of his own migration away from reliance on state-sponsored socialism and toward the principles of anarchism. (Starting in the late 1960s, he began using anarchist writings in his course on political theory.) As he later told a newspaper reporter, he was drawn to Emma Goldman because of "the combination of sex and politics, love and anarchy." Howard didn't think that his work on the play about her life was "an entirely different activity from his usual historical work." Its focus on radical activism remained, and on seeking the truth about Emma Goldman's life by relying on traditional forms of evidence.

Yet playwriting in fact freed him to commit all sorts of cardinal sins, as the historical profession would define them: a bit of invented dialogue, the injection of humor, and an emphasis on telling an absorbing story rather than on relentless analytic detail. He enjoyed, too, the fact that putting on a play was a collective enterprise. He found an excitement in "working with all these other people, intensely, in close quarters, with a warmth and affection foreign to academe. People arrived for rehearsal and hugged one another. It was not a scene one encountered in the university."[14]

How good was Howard's first play? It depends on who you ask, which performance and version (there were many) you saw, and what you yourself brought to it in terms of political conviction and personal experience. The reactions to *Emma* range from "tedious speechifying" to "deeply engaging," and both contain a measure of truth. In the final version of the play, performed in London in 1987, Howard introduced for the first time the character of Ben Reitman. The love letters between him and Emma had only recently been discovered and published, and somehow Howard found the irresponsible, philandering, grandstanding Reitman fascinating and wrote him into the final version as a major character.

To make room for Reitman, Howard diminished the role of Emma's early love and comrade Alexander Berkman, so markedly that, for a long stretch of the play, he virtually disappears. Yet Berkman's real-life story is far more dramatic than Reitman's. As a young man, Berkman believed in the symbolic importance of "propaganda of the deed" (the assassination of a leading "enemy of the people"), and he attempted, but failed, to kill Henry Clay Frick, head of U.S. Steel. Tried and convicted, he had a number of extraordinary prison experiences and wrote a brilliant book about them. After his release, Berkman again became Emma's trusted companion (but not lover).

In terms of both historical importance and intrinsic personal interest, Berkman far outshines Reitman, yet in the final (and printed) version of the play, Howard chose to let the less impressive and electrifying man dominate much of the second half of the play. The first act's central focus on the Goldman-Berkman relationship dissipates in the second into a string of events that lack an energizing center and become discursive and talky. Even in the earlier version, the play—unlike the real-life events it describes—doesn't build sufficiently. Howard ignored the theater's most venerable and valid injunction: "Show, don't tell." Far too much of the central action in *Emma* takes place offstage, with the audience subsequently *told* about it instead of seeing it. And some of the scenes, moreover, simply don't work: Berkman's attempt on Frick's life is so brief that it's over before any dramatic impact has been realized.

Yet Howard did succeed in keeping polemics to a reasonable minimum—not easy for a committed political person—though in a few spots they could have been reduced still further. The character of Emma herself is well drawn; her many dimensions—except her orneriness—all come through, and the varied colors mix coherently. Howard's first attempt to write a play wasn't a triumph, but it wasn't an embarrassment either. It reads like the effort of a seasoned writer for the theater, and the best proof is that it found a considerable audience. After the initial run of three weeks at the Theater for the New City, under Jeff's direction, Howard spent many months doing rewrites. The new version was then produced in Boston's the Next Move theater, where it was directed by Maxine Klein (who taught drama at BU) and ran for an impressive eight months— the longest run of any play in the city for 1977. In the early 1980s, Howard would write a second play and, in the mid-1990s, a third.

In the summer of 1977, after their rent had abruptly doubled, Howard and Roz moved to a two-family house in Auburndale, at the edge of Newton. Initially they shared it with the likable young couple who owned it. But within a few years, the Zinns bought it from them, sharing the purchase price with an old friend, Hilde Hein, who taught at Brandeis and Holy Cross. Hilde had grown children but was currently living by herself. She and the Zinns shared left-wing views, and the three frequently went to political events together. Howard and Roz took the smaller, first-floor apartment, Hilde the second, and the third floor served multiple functions—storage, guest room, and later a studio for Roz. When Howard called the bank to arrange for a mortgage, the person who answered the phone said, "*The* Howard Zinn, the one who believes property is theft?"[15]

At about the same time, Roz and Howard took on their old friends from Spelman Pat and Henry West (then teaching at Macalester College in St. Paul, Minnesota) as equal owners of the house on the Cape. The Zinns had originally paid $55,000 for the house, but then, due to repairs and storm damage, had to put in an additional $10,000; the two couples split all costs equally. Over the years, the Wests' relationship with Howard and Roz would at times become a bit bumpy—mostly because there were occasional disagreements about who had the Cape house during which months—yet the two couples would remain good friends. Sharing property with other people, of course, invariably produces *some* conflict and irritation. Hilde got along very well with the Zinns, but even she complained that they didn't like her—or any—dog, and regretted that she couldn't ask them to take care of him when she was away. She also felt that Howard and Roz took "the high moral ground" too often when discussing politics and weren't willing to compromise. It would also get Hilde's back up a bit over Roz and Howard never speaking well of *any* politician (and particularly not Barney Frank or, later, Hillary Clinton).

Howard enjoyed biking and playing tennis, and he sometimes joined Roz tending her tomato and basil plants (she was a fantastic, self-taught cook). As Howard wrote to a friend, "I'm enjoying more freedom than I've had in a long time, to relax with no real commitments." He did do a bit of shingling on the Cape house roof and other repairs—and even enjoyed that: "I love doing all sorts of things connected with using hammers and pliers and screwdrivers." Most important, as he wrote Frances Piven, "Roz seems not as troubled by the 'what will I do with my life' problem." She loved the Cape house and was "so happy" when they were out there that she "never wants to return to Boston." From time to time, when she felt like it, Roz would pick up secretarial work from a temp agency but would otherwise enjoy her freedom instead of fretting about not having a career. Later Roz's discontent would resurface, and when it did, she would at last find a creative solution for it.

Neither Howard nor Roz was much interested in "things." They dressed simply, disdained gadgetry, and tended to patch up worn linoleum or a rickety old chair rather than make new purchases. The interior of their homes could be characterized as somewhere between modest and cozily informal. That was due in part to the fact that professors back then didn't make much money, but probably due even more to having grown up in poverty, with every nickel pinched. They'd early on learned to make do with only absolute necessities, not mere adornments. In any case, they cared little about material possessions, feeling it important to keep *down* with the Joneses. Yet Roz had a great sense of color and which pieces of furniture best fit together, which made the interiors of their homes welcoming and attractive. Devoted to her friends, Roz put up a wall of photos of them and their children in the kitchen of the Newton apartment.

When at the Cape, they loved having breakfast on the porch, picnic lunches on the sand, and quiet evenings reading. Friends and family would drop by for a few days, but it was the peace and quiet of being alone together that they relished. Carol and Noam Chomsky had a place nearby on Gull Pond and would occasionally sail into their beach on the bay just to say hello or to share in the oysters Roz and Howard had harvested from the water that morning.

Howard liked teasing Noam about the mounting number of boats in his "oceanic fleet," and "the gross inequity between their armada and our inflatable raft in the closet." But the day came when Carol Chomsky called to say that she'd seen an ad in the *Cape Codder* for a $495 Sunfish. The two couples went to have a look and found that it was ten years old but nonetheless in "remarkable condition." They bought it on the spot, and Howard in particular immediately loved it; Roz, too, but she preferred her minimum of two swims a day in the bay.

Idyllic as these summers were, Howard—who was still, after all, in his "prime," his midfifties—was always mulling over in the back of his mind a possible large-scale new writing project. For a time he thought he might embark on a book tentatively titled "The Case of the Pentagon Papers," and went so far as to draw up a proposal. But he couldn't drum up much excitement for it in the publishing world.

And then it came to him: what he really wanted to do was an "alternate" history of the United States—alternate in the sense that, unlike the traditional textbook, which had a patriotic, not to say jingoistic, gloss and dwelt primarily on the experiences of presidents, generals, and the privileged class, his book would feature precisely those ordinarily ignored by historians—the people themselves. It would take him nearly three years of hard work, but when *A People's History of the United States* was finally published in 1980, it would become by far his most successful book: a dozen translations, sales in the millions, and—for a professional historian, anyway—genuine renown.

Howard giving an antiwar speech, Boston Common, May 1971.

Howard (middle, with left hand on leg) with antiwar group in Washington, D.C., in the spring of 1971. Marilyn B. Young is on the far left, Noam Chomsky is second from the right, and Daniel Ellsberg is behind Chomsky.

Howard around age fifty, circa 1972.

Roz and Howard at their summer home in Wellfleet, on Cape Cod, early 1970s (copyright the Estate of Howard Zinn).

At a clerical workers strike at Boston University for a union around 1974; Murray Levin is in the middle; Frances Fox Piven is on the right.

Left to right: Jeff, Howard, Roz, and Myla in the early 1980s (copyright the Estate of Howard Zinn).

Jennie with her four sons in the early 1980s. Left to right: Bernie, Shelly, Jerry, Howard (copyright the Estate of Howard Zinn).

On the back of the photo: "writing on my old typewriter on which I wrote A People's History of the United States," late 1970s (copyright the Estate of Howard Zinn).

With Alice Walker, late 1980s

Self portrait painted by Roz in the 1990s, when she was in her seventies (photo courtesy of Keitaro Yoshioka).

Howard in the fall of 2000, at age 78 (photo courtesy of Robert Birnbaum).

Howard with the cast of *Voices* at the Japan America Theatre, in Los Angeles, California, October 2005. Left to right: Viggo Mortensen, Marisa Tomei, Sandra Oh, Christina Kirk, Josh Brolin, Howard, Leslie Silva, Floyd Red Crow Wester-man, Kerry Washington, Danny Glover, and Anthony Arnove (photo by Frazer Harrison, courtesy of Getty Images).

Front of the Wellfleet house (photo courtesy of Paul Allen Smith).

Howard, Marisa Tomei, and Anthony Arnove at a performance of *Voices of a People's History* on April 26, 2006, at the Lannan Foundation (photo courtesy of Don Usner).

Howard on the telephone in Wellfleet, October 2009, the year before his death (photo courtesy of Paul Allen Smith).

A People's History

During the three-year period that Howard was at work on *A People's History of the United States*, he often broke away to give a lecture, join a political protest, or take part in a panel. And twice, accompanied by Roz, he went abroad—to teach for a term at the University of Paris in 1978 and to spend a week in Cuba in 1979. In Paris, his teaching load was light (two classes on consecutive days), with virtually no preparation needed. He taught his course on "American Imperialism" "off the top of my head," for his students (thirty-five of the fifty were Africans) knew little American history, though they "love to argue" about it.[1]

Howard was alone in Paris for the first month, until Roz joined him, and he loved walking the streets, having coffee or lunch with a friend, and getting some work done on the new book. He felt "happy Roz is coming," he wrote a close friend, though "it's been very good being alone—a rare experience, including both the luxury of freedom and single-ness and the loneliness from time to time which makes you appreciate having someone." Through a mutual friend, he met a true counterpart: Harvey Goldberg, well known as an extraordinary teacher at the University of Wisconsin (where he spent most of his academic career) and as the author of a highly regarded biography, *The Life of Jean Jaures.*

Like Howard, Goldberg was far more interested in the radical movement than in the profession of history and believed his teaching was a *political* activity. Howard described him as having "a classical Jewish-comedian's face, a kind of male Molly Picon . . . a really nice person." Goldberg had been coming to France for half or more of each year for twenty years, and he invited Howard to his apartment for dinner. Another guest was a young, "good-looking, clean-cut" American philosophy student. It slowly dawned on Howard that the student and Goldberg were "a homosexual pair"—though in writing that to a friend, Howard humorously added that he wasn't mentioning it "to prove how enlightened I am." But to a limited degree, he was. Howard wasn't judgmental about someone being gay, but it didn't interest him one way or another, and the original version of *A People's History* didn't mention gay people as a repressed minority or gay rights as part of a general struggle for liberation. By the second revised edition, in 1995, he did devote three short paragraphs to the gay movement, admitting in an afterword that he'd "neglected groups in American society that had always been missing from orthodox histories"—including Latinos and LGBT people.

The weeklong holiday in Cuba proved just as enjoyable. He and Roz bypassed any official tour that would march them around from factory to hospital to farm, all the while subjecting them to polemical lectures about the glorious revolution. Instead they spent mornings on the beach and afternoons and evenings wandering around Havana, taking city buses and getting into conversations with people. (They'd learned a little Spanish before taking the trip, and as Howard put it, "17 words of Spanish can get you a long way.") He and Roz found the Cubans "incredibly friendly, warm, helpful and, when asked directions would insist" on *taking* them to where they were going.

They thought Cuba was "a very equalitarian society," with "no conspicuously wealthy people . . . or beggars or prostitutes . . . everybody decently dressed, everyone employed." They realized, not being ideologues, that the island was "technically backward—most people don't have phones or TV, certainly not cars or washing machines." But what they did have, in contrast to the U.S., were totally free education, medical and dental care, rents that never exceeded 10 percent of their income, and basic food items available at low cost. Howard and Roz didn't romanticize the Castro regime; they were well aware that there were political prisoners in Cuba, that only a few newspapers were allowed, and that in general a party line prevailed—no criticism could be heard of the Soviet Union (which was helping economically to counteract the effects of the American embargo). "If you look on these socialist revolutions as steps in the right direction," Howard wrote a friend, "Cuba is one of the most attractive examples."

The solitary scholar working alone year after year in manuscript archives was far from Howard's idea of the good life. He was much too gregarious and political, too open to new experiences, too fond of people to adopt the kind of monastic life that sustained archival research requires. Out of necessity—to get his doctorate—he'd done it for his first book, *LaGuardia in Congress*, but thereafter he primarily relied in his writing on a combination of secondary sources and personal experience. He worked hard on *A People's History* in the late 1970s, but was temperamentally unable to let the book become his sole preoccupation. Besides, he would have thought himself derelict in his political obligations.

Above all, he continued to play a leading role in the ongoing tensions at Boston University. The late 1970s saw another crescendo of charges and countercharges in the battle against Silber's authoritarian policies. It was a battle that for a time consumed a good deal of Howard's energy. Back in 1975, the BU faculty had voted to unionize because of their fear of Silber's arbitrary power. The administration fought unionization relentlessly for more than three years—until the U.S. Court of Appeals in April 1978 finally denied its claims.[2]

Silber refused to modify his style, and for years kept battling with his critics, the focus of disagreement periodically shifting. At one point it would center on his attempts, despite the vote of a department, to deny promotion, leaves, salary raises, or even tenure to a faculty member who'd spoken out in opposition to him. Then the central conflict might change to Silber's censorship of the university radio station and student newspapers, or to the administration's assorted mistreatments of groundskeepers, secretaries, and librarians, leading to the contested formation of unions. When Silber refused to sign union contracts, four separate strikes were needed to force his hand. Even the Massachusetts Civil Liberties Union got involved, issuing a report criticizing the administration for its various violations.

But Silber, like the Energizer Bunny, kept popping back up after each defeat or reprimand. What enabled him to stay in power was his ability, whenever a dissident member of the Board of Trustees—the final authority on all matters—resigned, to replace him with a fellow conservative. That Silber's control of the board was complete was demonstrated in late 1978, after two thirds of the faculty voted in favor of removing him as president. The board responded, with only one dissenting vote, by passing a vote of confidence that renewed his contract. At that point, BU became Silber's personal fiefdom.

At every turn, Howard continued to lead the opposition, pouring just as much energy into incidents where he himself wasn't Silber's principal target as when he was. Howard had a stubborn streak that refused to yield to an act of injustice, but he wasn't nearly Silber's match in resourceful manipulation. Each confrontation over the years had its special texture or configuration, and a mere listing of the number and variety of clashes would be tediously long. But several of them represent matters of larger scope, illuminating issues or values that provide insight into both men.

In 1977, for example, a strike broke out and picket lines were set up to protest Silber's refusal to sign union contracts. Howard was insistent, in the face of opposition, that the faculty union had to establish from the start that any individual member could file a grievance, but only the union could take it to arbitration, and that the union had to make it clear it would fight the grievances of *all* its members. That was typical Howard: he was a leveler at heart, despising the prerogatives of any privileged group.

In that same year, Silber withdrew all advertising from the nationally known campus newspaper, the *BU News* (which under the writer Ray Mungo's editorship had pioneered criticism of the Vietnam War), causing it to close down. A new student paper, *Exposure*, took its place and from the start was anti-Silber. Howard became the official faculty adviser to the *Exposure* staff. He saw his job as reading every issue of the paper carefully to ensure a high level of journalistic integrity and "the exemplary responsibility of a free press—to be critics of officialdom and guardians of the public interest."

Silber saw Howard's role differently. After *Exposure* published an article critical of the administration, he withheld the funds that the Student Allocations Board had already voted for the paper. The dean of student life, Johan A. Madson, informed Howard that the administration was not engaging in censorship but was simply protecting the university from prospective libel suits. He pointedly reminded Howard that his primary job as the paper's faculty adviser was to stop in advance of publication any potentially libelous material. The suggestion infuriated Howard. He informed Madson first of all that "the present definition of libel by the courts is such as to make the commission of libel difficult to prove in the case of public figures"—for example, John Silber.

As for the insistence that Howard exercise "prior restraint" in regard to articles in *Exposure*, he flatly refused to do so as a violation of the First Amendment. Ordinarily tolerant and relaxed, Howard proved immovable on the issue. *Exposure* brought a lawsuit to get the release of its allocated funds, but instead of getting its money *Exposure* was banned—which had a chilling effect on *all* exercise of free speech and free press on campus. While he was at it, Silber took over control of the BU radio station, WBUR. An attorney friend of Howard's at the Civil Liberties Union told him they got so many complaints about Silber that they'd opened a special Silber File.

The next important round came in 1979 and focused on the administration's habit of overriding departmental decisions on salaries, hiring, firing, and granting promotion or tenure. Silber, in justifying the attempt to clasp all control over these matters to his own bosom—an all but unheard-of prerogative for a university president—likened himself to a surgeon, "superior to his patients" in making decisions about their welfare. Even as Silber engaged in inflammatory language and behavior, he refused salary raises to his antagonists while investing large sums of (presumably nonexistent) funds in buying up additional land and constructing a huge (and ugly) new building—even though enrollment in BU was shrinking. The university's salaries in 1979 were in the bottom 10 percent nationally for comparable universities. Yet Silber managed to find $250,000 to hire Modern Management Methods, a union-busting consulting firm.

In Howard's case, his department had recommended a $2,400 raise. The provost cut it in half, giving as his reason that Howard's favorable student evaluations couldn't be trusted because he gave high grades to almost everyone. Before Howard could answer the provost's argument, Silber cut Howard's raise down to zero. He treated Murray Levin, Howard's close friend and fellow radical, exactly the same way. Cleverly, Silber gave Frances Fox Piven and others not friendly to the administration merit raises—a neat tactic for forestalling any charge of political discrimination.

When the clerical workers went out on strike late in 1979, several faculty members, to show support for the workers, met their classes on the lawn outside the building they ordinarily taught in—a time-honored practice in the academic world, though usually to enjoy good weather, not as a gesture to workers. In November 1979, Silber initiated proceedings against the four professors (Howard, journalist Caryl Rivers, historian Fritz Ringer, and psychologist Andrew Dibner), all of whom had or believed they had tenure, for failing to meet their classes at assigned times and places during the weeklong clerical strike. He construed meeting classes off campus or on the lawn as interference with university operations and brought the four professors up for disciplinary charges that could lead to their dismissal.[3]

But teaching classes out of doors to avoid crossing picket lines hardly constituted either a "sympathy strike" or "gross neglect of duties." Besides, Silber made no charges against the estimated ten to fifty other professors who'd also taught outside. Obviously Silber was singling out for punishment those on his long-established enemies list. Silber claimed, preposterously, that it wasn't that "Mr. Zinn's views are particularly antagonistic to me" but rather "his methodology: his apparent belief that it is proper to distort the truth for political purposes." He added that he didn't think Zinn's "standards of scholarship were very high." Silber gave no examples, though he did claim that Howard had, back in 1970, joined some students in trying to set fire to the administration building. With the charge of arson, Silber had overreached and he was forced to make a public apology, which Howard calmly accepted.

Being an equal opportunity oppressor, Silber also had a history of belittling women faculty members. Few ever got tenure positions at BU—especially if their politics were left-wing. But Silber met his match in Julia Brown, who'd written an admired book on Jane Austen. Her department voted her tenure but Silber vetoed it; in the process, he dismissed Jane Austen as a "lightweight" among novelists. Brown, unlike most of those denied tenure, refused to go quietly. She sued Silber and, after six persistent years, won her case: she was awarded $200,000 and tenure.

Silber's abrasive, petty retaliations produced widespread protest. Within days of his action, three hundred students staged a protest rally, and offers of support from fellow professors from Oregon to Paris poured in. And the protest continued to spread. Nobel laureate Salvador Luria of MIT circulated an anti-Silber petition, and five hundred faculty members in the Boston area signed it. Then three others—Noam Chomsky, historian John Womack of Harvard, and historian of science Everett Mendelsohn of Harvard—started circulating a second petition nationwide. The national press—including the *New York Times*—also began publishing articles that further spread word of Silber's various malfeasances. Only a slick pro-Silber profile on *60 Minutes*, which referred to him admiringly as "the General Patton of academe," helped to counter all the negative publicity—but hardly stopped it.

Both the Boston University chapter and the statewide branch of the AAUP issued statements reminding everyone that until just a few years ago there had been exactly *one* union on campus. In 1979 there were five, four of them forced to strike in order to win "legitimate demands." This ran counter to a degree to the national current. Strikes and unions were definitely on the decline across the country. Even at the federal level, Jimmy Carter, who'd barely squeaked into the presidency in 1976, had little enthusiasm—or sympathy?—for improving labor's standing. Those who saw him as more liberal than not were bitterly disappointed when he failed to advance labor's claims.[4]

The anti-Silber movement came to a climax when the BU faculty in mid-December 1979 voted 457–215 to ask the trustees to fire him. Silber dismissed the vote by pointing out that some nine hundred part-time faculty (mostly doctors at the medical school, who weren't involved enough in campus affairs to vote) hadn't attended the meeting. Enter the Board of Trustees. In an attempt to argue their case before the scheduled board meeting of February 7, 1980, the protesters wrote to Arthur Metcalf, chair of the board, requesting an opportunity to meet with the trustees. "The tone of the reply," according to Frances Piven, was "extremely insulting"; the delegation was limited to six (one of whom was Howard), and their combined time for addressing the board was set at forty minutes. They were then cross-examined—but denied the right to enter into dialogue or to reply to anything the trustees said.

The following day, the board—led by Metcalf, an ardent militarist (he wrote for *Strategic Review*) and a leader in the right-wing Valley Forge Freedom Foundation—unanimously passed a vote of confidence in John Silber, issuing a statement that declared its full support for his administration. For as long as the board continued to function as Silber's lapdog, which it did for a very long time, no amount of protest would lead to his replacement. And there it stood. Howard turned his focus back again to *A People's History*.

In 1979, just as Howard was completing *A People's History*, Jean Anyon of Rutgers published a long essay reporting on her examination of seventeen widely used textbooks on U.S. history. Her analysis revealed that the books were grossly subjective, clearly serving the interests of those already in dominant positions in society. (Earlier, Émile Durkheim had drawn similar conclusions for France, and Raymond Williams for England.) The textbooks examined by all three made it obvious that approved knowledge provided a primary foundation stone for maintaining the position of those in power.[5]

Anyon concluded that with rare exceptions the U.S. textbooks ignored evidence that didn't support the authors' preexisting assumptions, thereby producing many badly distorted, ideologically driven conclusions (precisely the charges that would be leveled against *A People's History*). It was true, as the textbooks claimed, that the Progressive Era produced legislation aimed at reforming the concentration of economic power, but they failed to mention that the actual results from the legislation were meager. Twelve of the seventeen texts failed to include anything about the Socialist Party; of the five that did, four made derogatory remarks.

It was the opposite story when dealing with industrialists; fourteen of the seventeen books depicted them as admirable. In one, Andrew Carnegie—his exploitation of labor never mentioned—is described as spending all of his time after selling his company "helping other people with his money and writing. He helped build libraries, improve schools and keep peace between the countries of the world." Apparently the more Andrew Carnegies we have, the more the country benefits.

Similarly, when discussing the period of rapid industrialization between the Civil War and World War I, the textbooks minimized the success of workers' efforts to combat low wages and wretched working conditions through strikes and unionization. Of the thirty thousand strikes during the period, the texts mentioned a grand total of three, all of which failed, thus giving the impression that strikes are not only an ineffective tool but often lead to deplorable violence, hurting labor's cause. All of the books, moreover, made unsympathetic remarks about the more radical unionizers, like the Knights of Labor or the Industrial Workers of the World (IWW).

Taken together, such textbooks acted as a deterrent to social action, preaching the gospel that disputes between management and labor are best resolved through negotiations—as if the two groups have equal power. The books also inculcate the message that workers have mostly themselves to blame for their poverty, for failing to—here comes the quintessential American myth—"pull themselves up by their own bootstraps." To people indoctrinated to blame themselves rather than the "system" for their failure to prosper, collective action has been made to seem a problematic, even misguided tactic—thus helping to account for the fact that among industrialized nations the U.S. has uniquely failed to produce a militant, sustained labor movement.

The biased indoctrination of most textbooks was one of the goads that led Howard to write *A People's History*. He wanted to fill in what the standard texts left out, skimmed over, or demeaned—the stories and perspectives of Native Americans, immigrants, slaves, and factory workers and the many protests and struggles that had aimed at improving their lot. His intention was to include major events—the great railroad strike of 1877, say, or the savage suppression of the Philippine independence movement—usually ignored or distorted as incidental to the Great Advance of the United States as Leader of the Free World. As Howard once put it, "It became clear to me that the really critical way in which people are deceived by history is not that lies are told, but that things are omitted. If a lie is told, you can check up on it. If something is omitted, you have no way of knowing it has been omitted."

Howard also made clear at the beginning of his book what almost all historians know but choose to conceal: that an *individual* is deciding which part of the available evidence to emphasize, downplay, or omit, and that the historian's own experiences and values will have much to do (sometimes unconsciously) with the decision about what is important or unimportant material. In addition, only a limited amount of evidence for what actually happened in the past ever exists, and it usually reflects the experience of the literate class much more than others.

Howard openly acknowledged at the beginning of *A People's History* that he made no claim to neutrality, to an impersonal account; he focused on what interested him. He did believe that remaining true to the known evidence was the true goal of writing about the past, but also felt that no matter how scrupulous the effort, that goal could only be approximated, not achieved. He wasn't alone in writing "advocacy" history—that's what all historians have always done, though back in 1980 almost all of them kept it a kind of semiconscious secret. The open acknowledgment of built-in distortion in the historical profession was about as rare as an alligator off the coast of Maine.

Howard's primary goal in writing *A People's History* was to include those portions of U.S. history ordinarily passed over as irrelevant to the "grand picture." It was precisely the stories of those "irrelevant" people that Howard wanted to reclaim and emphasize—not always as noble but as real. What further distinguishes Howard's book from most attempts to present on overview of U.S. history is its readability: in clean, concise prose, he creates a dramatic narrative totally accessible to the average reader. He felt it urgent to reach the general public, not merely other academicians.

When Howard first thought about doing the book, he intended to organize it by topics: race, class, war, etc. Then he realized he should write it chronologically, the way other textbooks did, so that teachers could use it alongside a traditional text for comparison purposes. He knew from the start that he'd be relying on secondary sources, as well as on his own files of assorted clippings and articles; along with his temperamental distaste for archival work, it would have been overkill, and likely impossible, to dig his way through primary sources for an entire history of the United States. Howard also relied on his trusty old Royal manual typewriter—and he wrote the first draft rapidly, completing the six hundred pages in six months. When he got to the end of the first draft, he went back and, with pen and ink, revised it. He then typed it up a second time—and that was that.

It was easier for him to write the history of the era he'd lived through simply because he could draw on personal experience, and more than half of the book covers the 1930s to the present day. He was aware that during the socially conscious '30s there had been a few popular, progressive histories—preeminently the work of Charles and Mary Beard and James Harvey Robinson—that actually explored issues relating to race and class. But Howard also knew that once that activist decade had passed, so had the committed scholarship he admired, and with a very few exceptions—Ray Ginger's books or H. Larry Ingle and James Arthur Ward's *American History*—the historical profession had once again settled for bland, congratulatory overviews with scant attention paid to the nation's blunders and shortcomings.

Then in the 1960s a new generation of historians, many of whom had been movement activists, once again took up the cudgels and turned its focus to history "from the bottom up," challenging official justifications for some of the country's most grievous acts of destruction. Most of their elders, predictably, denounced the "revisionists" as lacking in balance and objectivity. The implicit (and wrongheaded) assumption behind the charge was that their own scholarship was free of such blemishes. Obviously Howard preferred the work of the younger group, of left-wing historians, and his aim was to synthesize it and to present it in the "easy-going conversational style" that was accessible to more than fellow scholars.

Given his sympathy for contemporary movements of liberation, Howard wanted to highlight the ways that the ruling class had masterfully alternated between outright repression and seeming concessions to maintain its structural control. Among the major achievements of *A People's History* was Howard's unusual ability to analyze the past in such a way that its patterns illuminated present-day concerns. He also succeeded in his objective of "disclosing those hidden episodes of the past when, even if in brief flashes, people showed their ability to resist, to join together, occasionally to win." And in the process he revealed a great deal about those ordinarily passed over in the standard textbooks of the day—the Cherokees, black soldiers in the nation's wars, sharecroppers, Chinese laborers, landless farmers, and the radical Wobblies (IWW organizers). Two difficult feats, successfully executed.

And Howard did still more: through his eloquent descriptions of the wretchedness of slavery and the immiseration of the working class, he made the reader *feel* their suffering—and empathy encourages action. Yet as in any synthetic historical work—or indeed as in *any* work of history—there are some peculiar emphases, simplistic generalizations, and questionable judgments. There are even some surprising omissions—like the struggle of Latinos or Howard's failure to discuss the role of religion in American life, despite its foundational importance. The Salem witch trials and the Great Awakening of the midnineteenth century provide important insights into the American character and all but demand *some* commentary, yet they got none. Nor do many of the major religious figures in our past, whether Jonathan Edwards, Charles G. Finney, Reinhold Niebuhr, or Henry Ward Beecher, get any mention at all. Similarly, if more surprising, the long history of communal experiments, ranging from the eighteenth-century Moravians to Brook Farm and Oneida, is entirely omitted, though it is evidence of idealism and experimentation vital to our history.

Initially, *A People's History* dealt substantially with nineteenth-century feminism, but the second wave of feminism was given but a few pages (expanded in the 2003 edition). Those few pages were a surface recounting, even in later editions, of several key events or personalities, without any substantive discussion of whether gender itself is a social construction or a biological given. And the gay movement, ignored in the earlier versions, at least by the 2003 edition gets three short paragraphs.

It needs to be said in Howard's behalf that few straight men of his generation, including those on the left, ever treated the feminist and gay movements as holding potentially transformative social information or were nearly as worthy of attention as problems based on race or class. Howard at least stood among the small minority—especially in 1980—who treated the plight of women and gay people as real and the movements to change attitudes about them with respect. Nor did he, like most of his compatriots, belittle their plight or treat them with condescension.

Sometimes *A People's History* lacks nuance, with the world divided into oppressors and oppressed, villains or heroes; the history of the U.S. is treated as mainly the story of relentless exploitation and deceit. Demonic elites are often presented as repressing the helpless masses, even robbing them of cultural vitality. Yet just as often the masses are portrayed as fully aware of their plight and determined to combat it; they persistently rise up to struggle against their oppressors. The middle ground disappears in *A People's History*. In truth, the workers in this country *haven't* been in a state of constant agitation. Howard needed to have distinguished more between issues relating to the local workplace, which often did arouse worker discontent, and overall anger at the country's class divisions, at "the system"—which, in the abstract, American workers have greeted more with indifference than anger.

The question that needed raising is why the working class hasn't been more class-conscious. A short answer might be that it's been too internally divided, capable of periodic localized unity (as in the Colorado coal strike of 1913–14) but in between such dramatic episodes, ideologically, racially, and ethnically riven. Workers, like most good Americans, in the past have often conflated the unemployed with the unworthy; unions harshly discriminated against blacks, Asians, and others, and were no less indoctrinated and deluded than the rest of the citizenry into believing that in our "free" country anyone could rise from poverty to riches (and once in a great while some few did, thereby substantiating the myth of upward mobility).

Howard's overriding theme in *A People's History* is that the American experience from start to finish has essentially been the story of how the powerful few have deceived and dominated the many. From the Founding Fathers on, the elites have hoodwinked the ordinary citizen into believing that they act for the common good, shrouding their self-interested activities in patriotic rhetoric—sometimes true, but considerable qualification is needed. Freedom of the press and of speech, for example, are genuine virtues of the "system" and not commonly found elsewhere, even if periodically curtailed and often controlled and distorted by the interests of the ownership class.

A People's History deserves praise for including a great deal of material ordinarily left out of standard texts, especially in 1980. Still, Howard's version of our past has been justly criticized as leaving out too much, of presenting a partial and thereby distorted account—just like other historians. It's as if a photo of the Empire State Building showed the first thirty floors but nothing of the structure's soaring height—though Howard had been clear that his intent was to write an alternate not a comprehensive history.

It isn't possible to list every example of this throughout his book, so two prominent ones—the Constitution and Abraham Lincoln—will have to suffice. Howard's description of the motives of the Founders at the Constitutional Convention go back to Charles Beard's 1913 historic debunking, *An Economic Interpretation of the Constitution*, a work that still has admirers for its key assertion that political decisions are to varying degrees linked to economic interest, but overall the book no longer has many defenders. Howard, in large measure, was one of them. He puts his Beard-like view of the Founders succinctly: "The Constitution was a compromise between slaveholding interests of the South and moneyed interests of the North." As much scholarship since Howard's day (and especially George William Van Cleve's *A Slaveholders' Union*) has shown, this basic statement isn't wrong but it does stand in need of considerable modification.[6]

In a limited way, Howard partly anticipates the scholarship that postdates him. The Constitution, he writes in *A People's History*, "serves the interests of a wealthy elite, but also does enough for small property owners, for middle-income mechanics and farmers, to build a broad base of support." Yet he then modifies that statement to say, "the prosperous people who make up this base of support are buffers against the blacks, the Indians, the very poor whites." Does he mean that this was self-consciously and successfully done or rather that the "buffers" were an unconscious offshoot, not a primary intention? Or something in between? Howard doesn't say—and possibly no one can.

Most current scholarship agrees that the Founders' primary purpose *was* as Howard had more or less stated it: to curtail direct democracy in favor of indirect republicanism (the Electoral College, the Supreme Court, and senatorial elections by state) and to encourage investment (as Woody Holton's recent book on the origins of the Constitution has put it). But due to the state ratifying conventions' insistent demand for the addition of a Bill of Rights, the people managed to modify in their favor the original draft of the Constitution, and most students of the Constitution do credit the Founders (as Howard did not) with "an ardent desire to serve the common good" (which certainly did *not* include that of slaves or Native Americans). Among other staunch Federalists at the Constitutional Convention, James Madison expressed considerable concern over the plight of those without money or property. That can, of course, be argued away as simple hypocrisy, but then so can any expression of common feeling with the less fortunate anywhere at any time; cynicism can always find supportive evidence and frame its argument with cogency.

It might be added that some debtors, along with creditors, avidly favored the Constitution; the battle over ratification wasn't a simplistic struggle between those who had property and those who didn't, nor was it the creation of a cabal of creditors determined to collect monies owed them—which is pretty much Howard's position. Yet the Constitution *was* designed to set up a much stronger government than had previously existed, and a major reason for that was to protect property rights, including in slaves. But it wasn't the sole reason. Many patriots, well aware that the weakness of the preceding Articles of Confederation was likely to lead to a partition of the states into a number of separate confederacies, and believing that the Revolution had been fought for the rights of man as well as property, felt it imperative to maintain the union intact as a standing example for people everywhere. The protection of property rights, in short, wasn't the sum and substance of the Constitution's design. Its adoption may have profited bondholders, but a description that reduces it to the wealthy consolidating their power leaves out a good deal.

Turning to Abraham Lincoln, Howard scoffs in *A People's History* at the traditional notion of the Great Emancipator; he credits Lincoln with employing moral rhetoric against slavery but not with any real concern for its abolition. It's of course true that Lincoln wasn't an abolitionist in the strict sense meant by William Lloyd Garrison ("Free all the slaves *now*") but his repugnance for the institution can be traced far back in his political career. Eric Foner, in his balanced account, *A Fiery Trial*, properly places Lincoln in the context of his times and carefully traces the transformation of his views on slavery and blacks. He had always condemned the physical brutality of the institution, and for half a dozen years prior to the outbreak of the Civil War he had always opposed measures that threatened to expand slavery's current borders. Believing that white Americans would never accept blacks as their social or political equals, he thought that freed slaves, for their good, ought to emigrate out of the country.[7]

Howard will have none of it. He insists in *A People's History* that when the "American government . . . set out to fight the slave states" it wasn't "to end slavery, but to retain the enormous national territory and market and resources." Although the Civil War did end up freeing the slaves, Lincoln (according to Howard) deserves no credit for the result. It was only when his hand was forced, when the war was going badly and casualties were mounting, and when "the criticism of the abolitionists threatened to unravel the tattered coalition behind Lincoln that he began to act against slavery." In other words, politics not morality forced his hand. And when he finally issued the Emancipation Proclamation, "it was a military move."

But this is a one-dimensional view of a complex, cautious man. Howard ignores the fact that unlike most people, Lincoln's capacity for growth was impressive. He stood at a substantial distance from the outright racism that dominated Northern opinion (during the 1863 draft riots in New York City, blacks were literally hunted down and killed). Lincoln, on the other hand, was in a decided minority in believing that natural rights belonged to all human beings. Howard also accepts what was a common view at the time he was writing: the Emancipation Proclamation applied only to areas under Confederate control—meaning it freed no one. But that was a limited view of the proclamation, which did free slaves in some areas under Union control. Moreover (a sign of Lincoln's growth), it made emancipation immediate, not gradual, and made no mention of any compensation (which had been much bandied about earlier) to slaveholders. Earlier, too, Lincoln had rejected the idea of blacks serving in the Union army, but he then changed his mind, and shortly after the proclamation black troops were enlisted.

Howard's disparagement of Lincoln is part of a general problem with the way he assigns motivation to individuals. With few exceptions, only members of the working class or minorities (or their champions) are allowed to represent human nobility and selflessness. In his earlier book *New Deal Thought*, Howard had described the New Dealers as "articulate, humane and on occasion profound." But in *A People's History*, Roosevelt and his advisers aren't allowed to rise above any concern other than the determination to save capitalism by instituting a certain number of reforms—most of which were soon corrupted: the National Recovery Act "from the first . . . was dominated by big business," with corporations and trade associations overriding the needs of the public. Concessions made to working people, like the minimum wage act of 1938, "helped enough people to create an atmosphere of progress and . . . to restore some faith in the 'system,'" but "didn't solve basic problems."

Howard's repeated tales of high hopes dashed, labor unions crushed, reform movements thwarted, and industrial strikes defeated can for some readers have unintended consequences. Though he conceived his book to inspire activists—and that *has* been its dominant impact—all the past failures to produce significant change lead some readers to throw up their hands and exclaim, "It's all been tried before and failed to work, so why bother? Miserable as this system is, it looks like we're stuck with it." *A People's History* does sometimes read like a pageant of triumphant cupidity. Too often individuals, rather than the economic system that spawned them, are held responsible for the wrongdoing committed. Henry Clay Frick is flayed alive, but U.S. Steel, which he ran, was embedded in a capitalistic structure (which isn't given a single listing in the index) that controls production and distribution and makes working-class resistance an unequal struggle.

Still, it's important to remember that most previous historians had treated the many oppressions Howard describes in passing or not at all. And if *A People's History* does sometimes read like a polemical text, Howard—unlike the vast majority of historians—acknowledges his bias up front, tipping off readers to proceed with caution, alerting them to remain aware that his own focus will be on the suffering and courage of the powerless and on keeping alive the memory of their resistance, even if it's spasmodic and often unsuccessful. The whole point of *A People's History*, after all, is to include the very stories historians have often omitted or minimized—the struggle of the oppressed to resist their onerous circumstances and the substantial evidence of governmental and capitalistic malfeasance and deceit.

Howard aimed to deflate the usual exaggerated claims that equate the United States with a mythical land of opportunity, democracy, and justice. That said, the fact remains that the American Dream isn't entirely fiction. There *has* been social mobility, though not nearly as much as the average high school text claims. Not all of the immigrant poor remained forever stuck in poverty; for some there was genuine advancement—better wages and a higher standard of living.

A People's History may omit or distort some of the record, but it does rest on the faith that ordinary people are of great worth and on the hope—perhaps utopian—that the day may yet come when they will permanently triumph over the system that oppresses them. Though Howard is careful not to overplay the extent of the oppositional spirit or to sugarcoat its many failures to secure change, he somehow maintains faith in "a powerful human impulse to assert one's humanity." And his hope for *A People's History* was that it would act as a guide to radical action in the present and encourage the growth of the idealistic spirit he himself deeply valued. The many testimonies we have from high school history teachers and their students make clear that Howard's hopes have been fulfilled.

As one teacher has written from Oregon, "this history changed my students' lives in profound ways." Another thanked Howard and *A People's History* "for lighting a fire in my students and giving us all a critical eye for the past."

Despite its mix of strengths and shortcomings, overall *A People's History* has marked and encouraged a profound shift away from the tone of triumphalism that before 1980 was the defining feature of most full-scale works on U.S. history. By gathering up much of the inaccessible scholarship produced by the new generation of radical historians in the 1960s and 1970s, Howard produced an alternative version of our past that proved an impressive counterweight to the downpour of patriotic misinformation that had dominated people's understanding—and still afflicts it through the media.

The initial press run of *A People's History* was a modest five thousand copies. As Howard's editor Cynthia Merman remembers it, Howard's original proposal for the book (which she thought "brilliant") hadn't garnered "a whole lot of enthusiasm from the powers-that-be at Harper and Row," but she and Hugh Van Dusen (another Harper editor) went to bat for it. Rick Balkin, Howard's affable and skillful agent, had originally asked for a $20,000 advance, but Harper honchos had held the line at $10,000—not at all bad back then, especially because Howard's previous books were out of print and the Harper brass didn't have very high expectations for his new one. The two sides seemed stalemated until Cynthia came up with the idea of "front-loading" the advance, giving Howard $7,500 on signing. That had sealed the deal.

When *A People's History* was published, early in 1980, the reception was mixed. Some well-known historians gave the book a drubbing in various journals, though the majority of fellow scholars, critical to varying degrees, admired the undertaking and recognized it as a game changer. For a while, the book chugged along at a modest clip. There was something of a spike in sales when it was nominated for an American Book Award (though it didn't win). Then came two lucky breaks. A decade after publication, in the film *Good Will Hunting*, Matt Damon (who grew up as a neighbor of Howard and Roz) gave it a considerable plug. Then, some two decades after publication, an episode of *The Sopranos* made more than a passing reference to the book.[8]

Those two mentions turned the trick. Sales soared, and from then on, more copies of *A People's History* were sold each year than in the preceding one—all but unheard of in publishing. As of 2012, the book has passed through several revisions, sold more than 2 million copies, and shows no sign of slowing down. Rick Balkin took advantage of the multiple opportunities that poured in, and a whole cottage industry of translations (at least twenty), audio and visual materials, and spin-offs were developed, along with many requests for high-fee lectures, book signings, and appearances. Though his own disposition was friendly and warm, Rick sometimes had to play "bad cop" to offset Howard's generous tendencies to settle for less.

Whenever a potential deal appeared, Howard learned to defer to Rick ("whatever you think is right"). Except he sometimes—out of sympathy, say, for a small, left-wing publisher—made deals of his own, without letting Rick know, and often got the worst of it. Later, when he let one of those poverty-stricken houses publish *The Zinn Reader* and *Voices of a People's History of the United States*, he failed to include the clause that Rick always did: if royalties weren't paid in a timely manner, the license would be terminated. Sure enough, the point arrived when the publisher owed Howard $75,000—but claimed he had no money. Instead, he offered Howard 4 percent ownership in the company—the hitch being that the house habitually claimed it made no profit.

For "at least ten years" Rick sent Howard about $200,000 a year in royalties, though the money did little to change the way he and Roz lived. Howard's "letterhead" stationery continued to be ruled yellow paper, and only rarely would they buy clothing or a new piece of furniture. Their downstairs quarters in the Auburndale house remained, as it had been for years, unpainted, and when their Honda passed its tenth birthday, they didn't replace it with a fancy new model. Howard and Roz put money aside to help pay for their grandchildren's education and contributed to their son Jeff's annual fund-raising drive for his theater, the Wellfleet Harbor Actors Theater.

But that was about it. Roz and Howard had both grown up making do with little, settling for cast-offs. Some people who grow up in poverty and then become prosperous quickly buy two of everything. Howard and Roz were of a different breed. Totally unassuming, they'd never learned the habit of building their identities on conspicuous consumption, the acquisition of "things." Howard's sole concession to newfound riches, as he grew older and continued to give lectures widely, was occasionally to fly other than economy class and to stay in a good hotel.

9

The Eighties

H oward was, lucky man, all but devoid of a dark side. Oh, he had the necessary drops of anger and disappointment to qualify as human—but not enough to congeal into something resembling a "bad patch" or a depression. On the personal side, but not the political, he disliked conflict and "unpleasantness," and in distancing himself from them, he could disconnect from someone else's unhappiness. He and Roz both presented themselves to the world as happy, contented people. Howard actually was, but Roz concealed beneath her smile a considerable amount of emotional distress. Howard had the sunnier, but also the more remote, disposition. No one was more present and vitally engaged during political argument than he, but like many men of his generation (and still too many in the present one) he was often uncurious about someone's private turmoil and unresponsive to it. As he once wrote Frances Fox Piven, "Myla & Jonny are of the generation that believes in talking out strong feelings, and Roz *has* the strong feelings, [but] my tendency is to want everybody to forget unpleasant things."[1]

With *A People's History* completed and successful, Howard even withdrew somewhat (certainly in comparison with his earlier output) from sustained writing and, to some degree, from direct participation in politics. Though still only fifty-eight, and with nearly thirty more years of life ahead of him, Howard never again undertook a major writing project (the one exception, it might be argued, was his 1990 *Declarations of Independence*). Yet there was an inverse relationship in the latter part of Howard's life between his output and his influence. After *A People's History*, his renown and impact grew exponentially. Besides, he did continue to turn out a number of short pieces on issues of the day as they arose—the movement against nuclear weapons, Israeli nationalism, the U.S. invasion of Panama, etc.—but nothing that approached his solid earlier work (*SNCC*, say, or *Vietnam: The Logic of Withdrawal*).

This was due in part to the shift in the country's attention away from black and working-class struggles to more recent and hotly debated cultural issues—preeminently the feminist and gay movements. Howard's deep concern for the plight of the poor always remained intact, and unlike so many whites once active in the movement, the turn to black nationalism (Malcolm X and the Muslims), with its overtones of separatism and violence, didn't lead him to turn his back. He was no fan of Elijah Muhammad but did greatly admire Malcolm's courageous, ardent journey. He didn't believe that separatism was the solution but did feel that "it has to be listened to because if you don't listen to it you cannot understand the depths of anger behind it." He even went so far as to say, "I am very suspicious of violence . . . as a means of achieving social change," but "if you want to say to people, 'You mustn't do anything that will provoke violence,' there's no way you can avoid that unless you want things to remain as they are."

The continuing loss of job growth, outsourcing, a heightening of corporate antiunion sentiment, the growing conservatism in the Republican Party, and the growing indifference of the new generation of Democrats to pro-labor policies all added up to a significant decline in union strength. This troubled Howard far more than did the rights of women or of gay people (or Asian Americans or Hispanics, for that matter). These newer struggles *did* relate profoundly to Howard's long-standing concern with race and class, but that only became apparent when one dug beneath the surface unity of the gay and women's liberation movements. (Why, for example, weren't more black women, especially those from the working class, involved in NOW or reading *Ms.*?) Howard wasn't interested enough in either issue to do more than turn over the topsoil. He did pay dutiful, though constrained and belated, attention to second-wave feminism and gay rights, but he couldn't seem to locate any connections—or therefore any sustained interest—between the older movements and the newer ones. His passion was reserved for the working class and black people.[2]

The downturn in the fortunes of those overlapping groups did put a dent in Howard's previously steadfast optimism, though he admitted as much only to a few close friends. "We persuade people," he wrote Frances Piven, ". . . that struggles are worthwhile, but their achievements, though valuable, still leave us in a terrible state. People need to be able to imagine that the same energy that brought small reforms can, if multiplied, bring big changes . . . the history of other countries is better than our own in showing that mass movements can overturn systems of control—but this also is not easy, because this hasn't happened in sophisticated liberal countries, and where it's happened in developing countries the revolutions have been perverted." This was Howard's version of pessimism.[3]

But a bit later in the same letter, he quickly backtracked when recounting to Frances what he'd attempted to accomplish in *A People's History*. "What I tried to do was more emotional than analytical, to throw at people enough instances of people continuing to fight, despite repression, despite containment of reform, to suggest that the energy is there for even more." His critics would accuse him of "manipulating" the past in order to polemicize about the future. The accusation, if meant to characterize Howard's conscious purpose, was unjust. He tried his best "to be honest about history," to show "how these victories don't last, how they are controlled, how people have to go at it again and again . . . what I wanted to do was have a mix of history and hope (that is, of control-history and revolt-history in which the latter dominates, if not by hard count, by emotional effect)." He acknowledged that his weakness was for "soft inspirational stories," but insisted he wasn't "bold enough to go *beyond* an 'accurate' recounting of the past."

Absorbed as he had been in the late 1970s in writing *A People's History*, Howard rarely commented, at least publicly, on developments during Jimmy Carter's administration (1977–1980). In retrospect, he made it clear that he didn't admire Carter, but at the time, his public criticisms were few—perhaps he didn't think it worth the effort. He did fault Carter for increasing defense spending and for allowing the Gulf Oil Corporation in 1978 to avoid going to court by paying $42 million of the $79 million it had falsely claimed to have paid for crude oil—and then passing the costs on to consumers. Howard's dry comment: "One wonders if a bank robber would be let off if he were to return half his loot." The following year he also excoriated Carter for reinstating the draft of young men for military service, and further for applying pressure on the *Washington Post* not to print a story about CIA payments to King Hussein of Jordan.[4]

But Howard put next to nothing on the record about Carter's still more egregious abandonment of Hubert Humphrey's earlier efforts to achieve full employment, or for failing to come up with an effective anti-inflation strategy (in one year, 1979, inflation had spiraled to 13.5 percent, the price of food going up faster than wages). Nor, with unemployment at a new postwar high, did Carter expend much energy on beating back the business lobbyists who successfully defeated labor law reform, thereby contributing to a tidal wave of plant closings and consequent loss of union power in the 1980s. Essentially, Carter left intact the power of the corporations and *increased* the already huge military budget.

Carter's pious hectoring about the country's "spiritual crisis" took up much more of his time than labor's sinking fortunes. He talked a great deal about "human rights" but rarely about equality, though he did send UN ambassador Andrew Young on a goodwill trip to Africa. His human rights mantra was rarely invoked in regard to such brutal regimes as Somoza's in Nicaragua or Pinochet's in Chile. Nor was self-determination cited as a critical part of human rights—Carter essentially ignored the near-annihilation in Indonesia of the citizens of East Timor.

His resounding loss to Ronald Reagan in the 1980 presidential election ushered in a frightening rise in economic inequality. Reagan's brand of conservatism accepted major lineaments of the welfare state like Social Security and Medicare but despite the abiding twinkle in his eye, he proved less than kindly about a host of mounting ills for the working class—corporations moving overseas, technology increasingly replacing employees, unionization falling to a new low. When the air controllers union, PATCO, went out on strike in 1981, the twinkle disappeared and Reagan peremptorily dismissed all eleven thousand union members—and for toppers banned them from future federal employment. That fierce edict did its work: henceforth the strike rate plummeted, further weakening labor's bargaining power. Likewise, Reagan worked congenially with the CIA in trying to destroy, especially in Latin America, popular insurrections against tyrannical regimes.

One such instance—the U.S. reaction to the left-wing uprising in El Salvador in 1979—particularly roused Howard's anger. The Reagan administration backed and helped to train (under the guise of "promoting democracy") a counterinsurgency movement, notorious for their brutality and death squads (in Guatemala and Honduras too). Howard joined a Boston rally in April 1980 and the large protest in Washington, D.C., in July against these policies, though not relishing the prospect of another arrest and jailing—which indeed did happen. Howard and others were locked up in cells wretchedly hot and crowded; they had to take turns sitting. The first food was provided only after nine hours—two baloney sandwiches, two stale doughnuts, and a plastic cup of very sweet, lukewarm tea. The "bed" was a perforated steel plate with no mattress, blanket, or pillow;

there were roaches everywhere and the noise so loud that sleep proved impossible. The statute they'd broken called for a sentence of six months, but the lenient judge let them go—*if* they didn't get arrested again for a year.

Both parties in Congress, continuing to equate "left-wing" with "Communist," backed up the president. Even the mainstream human rights organizations Amnesty International and Americas Watch (not to be confused with the peace movement) essentially gave Reagan a free hand by announcing that they took no position on U.S. actions in Central America—which was akin to declaring impartiality about whether to call an ambulance for a child lying in the street after being hit by a car.[5]

Howard, now free of *A People's History*, decided to link up with the Committee in Solidarity with the People of El Salvador (CISPES). Heir to 1960s organizations like SDS in its tactics of direct-action nonviolence and in its sharp critique of U.S. interventionism, CISPES issued a pamphlet denouncing U.S. imperialism in El Salvador. Howard joined CISPES when it mounted the first large demonstration in protest against the Reagan administration's policies, some five thousand people on the Boston Common—the largest turnout since the protests against the Vietnam War. The following week in Boston there was a citywide march to the statehouse; Howard felt Reagan "is both scaring people and bringing them out angry."

In the March 1982 election in El Salvador, the U.S. intervened to ensure that its ally José Napoleon Duarte won the presidency over the "Marxist-Leninists." In an editorial, the *New York Times* applauded the intervention: "If there is a center in El Salvador, Mr. Duarte alone seems able still to define it. . . . he will need the energetic encouragement of Americans and democrats everywhere." Beyond military help, Reagan's economic aid to Duarte would eventually come to an additional $350 million.

Secretary of State George Shultz claimed that the additional aid was warranted because the Duarte government "had made progress in curbing human rights abuses." Reagan, for his part, also spoke of the "progress" in El Salvador. Since there was much evidence to the contrary, these statements outraged Howard. He cited, in rebuttal, testimony from former soldiers in the El Salvador army that U.S. advisers were present at torture sessions conducted by the "Treasury Police," a group notorious for its involvement with the death squads. The 1980 U.S. Arms Export Control Act had forbidden U.S. advisers from engaging in a combat role, yet Americans were flying reconnaissance flights from Honduras over El Salvador.

The use of Honduras as an American staging area, with some five thousand U.S. troops in continuing maneuvers, made a mockery of the U.S. claim that it was deeply concerned about self-determination. Moreover, the "Kissinger Commission on Central America" (on which John Silber sat), formed to look into current developments in that region, reported its fear that there was a general "proliferation of Marxist-Leninist states" in the area—which meant, of course, that self-determination couldn't be allowed to serve as a top priority. As Howard shrewdly commented, "given the record of intra-Communist rivalry in the world—Sino-Soviet, Yugoslav-Soviet, Sino-Vietnamese, Vietnamese-Cambodian—how can such proliferation suggest a fearsome monolith?"

John Silber joined the fray with an article in the conservative *Boston Herald* applauding the Reagan administration for not abandoning El Salvador to "a communist takeover." As usual, Silber and Howard were on opposite sides of the fence. And as usual, Silber dealt with opponents ruthlessly; as the *Boston Globe* put it, "Silber is . . . still a faithful practitioner of that old maxim of political hardball: Reward your friends and punish your enemies." In the early 1980s, Howard described the scene at BU as "a kind of stabilization of low morale among tenured faculty, while non-tenured faculty live in fear they will be denied tenure for no good reason." Howard's own morale remained high, though his salary stayed low. In the academic year 1982–83, Silber once again turned down an increase in pay for him recommended by the various committees that passed on such matters. Howard asked the AAUP to investigate, and it concluded that "the administration improperly deprived Professor Zinn of an earned and deserved merit increase of $750." This wasn't exactly extravagance, given Silber's rent-free mansion and an annual salary that approached half a million dollars (it would go still higher).[6]

Howard didn't believe in "merit" raises anyway. He thought the cases rare when you could distinguish between a faculty member who produced a large amount of scholarly writing versus one who produced very little. Even in those disparate cases, it didn't follow, in his opinion, that output ought to determine salaries. It would do little to stimulate better teaching and better research. Bad teachers didn't become good ones if raises were dangled in front of them. Nor did good teachers cease to be good if denied raises. Howard also felt it untrue that scholars produced in order to get higher salaries: "People who are impelled to write do so; people who can't produce good work still can't even when merit raises are made available." Howard was in all areas an egalitarian: though he knew he was a good writer and a far more productive one than most faculty at BU, he rejected the notion that salary raises should be based on such standards. Besides, he believed that teaching "is what we are in the university for; otherwise we could be in a think tank somewhere. Research and publication are admirable and desirable, but have always been over-emphasized."

Additional bad news came when an administrative law judge of the National Labor Relations Board (NLRB) ruled that the BU faculty union did not come under its protection because the union had "managerial" power—that is, it played a "predominant role in faculty hiring, tenure, termination and promotion." That was a grotesque conclusion for anyone who knew the actual situation at BU, where faculty were regularly terminated and tenure denied solely by administrative fiat even when every faculty committee member opposed the decision. Yet the NLRB ruling wasn't a major surprise. Reagan had been packing it with appointees who reversed or recast decisions made since the mid-1970s, surrendering its prior role as a neutral defender of the law to become a weapon wielded by employers against unions.

A few years later, still more trouble arrived in the form of a watchdog lobby called Accuracy in Academia (AIA), an offshoot of Accuracy in Media. AIA was a sort of counterpart to the publication *Red Channels*, which in the 1950s had hounded various left-wing Hollywood actors and writers for their purportedly Communist activities. The founder of AIA, Reed Irvine, was on the masthead of the *Conservative Digest*, recently purchased by a group of John Birch supporters, and was close spiritual kin to John Silber. (In an op-ed piece in the *New York Times*, Irvine wrote that he "strongly agreed" with Silber's declared view that "professors' errors" required "public exposure.") Silber, in turn, defended AIA on television—the only college president to do so. Irvine was additionally convinced that alleged liberal bias in the press had its origins in the universities. He announced that "there are 10,000 Marxist professors on U.S. college campuses," but he singled out a small group—including Howard, Salvador Luria of MIT, and Nobel laureate George Wald of Harvard—for particularly venomous attack (all of whom would have been astonished to learn that the media favored liberals).[7]

Howard had made clear in *A People's History* his belief that "information" is processed through an individual's prior experience in the world and that no "social scientist" was without bias. AIA, on the contrary, was based on the assumption that "facts" were freestanding, independent of any individual's values. The group directly attacked Howard as "anti-American" and *A People's History* as portraying "American heroes as villains, if it mentions them at all . . . Gen. Douglas MacArthur is not mentioned . . . as the revered architect of the remarkable transformation of Japan under American occupation." AIA also attacked the historian Linda Arnold of Virginia Polytechnic for using one of Howard's books in her introductory course. Irvine told her that she "should be teaching about the entrepreneurial spirit, for instance the people who created McDonald's."

Howard fought back directly. He denounced AIA as the sort of group one associates with "a police state," and pointed out that the organization was redundant: "There is a permanent political bias in the university against teachers who go against the ongoing shibboleths and slogans of the culture." In his opinion, AIA had emerged at this point in time because its members were "worried about the New Generation . . . it might not be accepting everything that is being said by the establishment . . . by 1975 all of the surveys showed that Americans had lost their great respect for authority." The current polls showed, for example, that the citizenry was against American military intervention in Central America and believed in general "that we are spending too much money on the arms race."

There were protests against AIA on campuses throughout the country, and the *New York Times* ran a strong editorial denouncing AIA's "political intimidation," saying the project carried "echoes of the 1950s, when professors were hauled before state and Federal investigators seeking Communists and other subversives . . . campuses should be protected from external political hurricanes." The *New Republic* joined the *Times*: there "is no excuse for an offensive enterprise in policing thoughts."

Just in time for Howard's sixtieth birthday, he received an invitation from the South African Department of Interior inviting him to deliver the T.B. Davie Memorial Lecture at the University of Cape Town, an antiapartheid stronghold, on July 23, 1982. He accepted with pleasure. He had never before been to South Africa, where there had been a series of bombings in the earlier part of the year, designed to discourage the mounting movement against apartheid. After a twenty-one-hour flight, Howard was taken to a "Graham Greeneish" small hotel and was left to rest till the following morning. He used the time to write Roz; the first line, underlined, was "*I miss you*," and the last, again underlined, "*I do love you.*" In another letter, he wrote, "It's crazy that I should miss you so much after being away 5 days, but I do." They'd weathered well the worst period in their marriage, even though now and then a residual undercurrent would surface.

The next morning, he was picked up at ten A.M. and given a walking tour around the campus. He learned that in the last ten years, the percentage of students of color (which included African and Asian) had gone up from 5 percent to 12 percent, and he had lunch with three or four young faculty members. Then it was on to a series of informal meetings and a seminar with a group of students. The following day, he delivered his formal lecture. In the opening section, he told his audience how much he'd looked forward to coming to South Africa as "an occasion for protest against a government . . . in such a violation of democracy, such an infringement of liberty, that men and women of good will everywhere must condemn it." Then he brought up the name of the black activist Steve Biko, who'd been tortured and beaten to death five years earlier while in police custody, linking the horror of Biko's story with what takes place in police stations everywhere, including socialist ones. The lecture was well received, and his South African hosts were enormously kind throughout the weeklong visit.

On returning home, Howard went straight to the Cape Cod house, in need of some respite from the scenes he'd witnessed and the grim stories he'd heard. Ever since they'd purchased it, the Cape house had served them well as a place of recuperation and solitude. Howard would wade out into the bay with what he called his "awesome equipment"—sneakers, a rake, a pail—to gather oysters for dinner, and Roz would cultivate "with Japanese-like care any ten square feet of land" she could find on their tiny property. Howard described himself as her "Caucasian assistant," applying tape measures and diagrams with "such application . . . as to impress any neighbor who did not know I am just contemplating a small deck on the back side of the house." After a period of quiet and peace, they'd invite some selected close friends—like Marilyn Young, Frances Fox Piven and her husband (and co-author), Richard Cloward, and Myla, Jon, and their children and Jeff and his wife.[8]

Wellfleet was the favored watering hole of a veritable troupe of artists and intellectuals, and Roz and Howard got to know a fair number of them—though Howard continued to be much more social than Roz. Once he went off for a full three days to the home of the writer Betty Lifton and her husband, the psychiatrist Robert Jay Lifton, for a conference on the rising threat of nuclear war and what could be done about it. Dick Falk (the radical professor of international law at Princeton), and his wife, the writer Florence Falk, were there, along with the eminent theologian Harvey Cox and chemist George Kistiakowsky (eighty-two and dying of liver cancer but determined to devote his remaining time to warning against the nuclear arms race). Erik Erikson, a major psychoanalytic theorist, was also in attendance but talked mainly about a book on Jesus he was working on, leaving it to the rest of them, as Howard put it, "to figure out its connection with the nuclear arms race."

Given the nationalistic nature of the arms race, Howard thought it was up to ordinary people, not governments, to meet the threat. In the early 1980s, he found signs of growing popular resistance to the irrational, not to say demented, behavior of warlike governments. The most encouraging signal was the turnout of some three quarters of a million people for a march for world peace in New York City in June 1982. A broad-based coalition—the Nuclear Weapons Freeze Campaign—called for the United States and the Soviet Union to halt the testing and production on all nuclear weapons. The freeze advertised itself as an orderly middle-class movement that avoided the "excesses"—i.e., the militancy—of the 1960s, and it did successfully enlist in its ranks citizens who spanned the spectrum of American life. Plus, the movement had significant counterparts throughout Europe.[9]

That hopeful beginning, however, ran smack into Reagan and the national security establishment's Cold War rhetoric. Conservatives both here and abroad rallied support for the view that a true system of verification was impossible and that a freeze on nuclear weapons would in essence give the Soviets an advantage, because the

U.S. would be unable to upgrade its weaponry. Further, the administration encouraged the public to believe the mad message that the U.S. could survive and win a nuclear war. To underline his point, Reagan announced his plans for the Strategic Defense Initiative to intercept ballistic missiles before they could reach American shores, in essence proclaiming the equally mad message that the threat to the U.S. of nuclear weapons would thus be ended. Reagan's policies sent a chill through the nuclear freeze movement, and its momentum faltered, especially after he was reelected in 1984, yet the movement did continue to be a force throughout the 1980s.

Because the freeze movement was silent on the issues central to Howard's concerns—an end to militarism and to U.S. interventionism—he never became involved to the degree he had in regard to the black struggle and the war in Vietnam. He saw nuclear weapons as a threat *from* governments and the destructive nationalism they generated, and he didn't believe they could be counted on to tell the truth about their stockpiles and nuclear sites. Later events would prove him right—the building of the Trident multiple-warhead missile, allowing one submarine to carry hundreds of nuclear weapons (at a cost of billions), and the revelation in 1988 that the U.S. had concealed from the public the explosion of 177 nuclear devices in the Nevada desert.

Early in 1984, Howard received news that he was the recipient of the Eugene V. Debs Award given annually since 1965 "in recognition of an individual's efforts in the cause of labor, social justice, and peace." Previous recipients had included Norman Thomas, Dorothy Day, Coretta Scott King, and Pete Seeger. Though pleased with the honor, Howard didn't dwell on it; instead he focused on yet another indefatigable round of courtroom testimonies and political rallies. He'd long corresponded with and visited prisoners and had testified at any number of trials involving Movement people. Back in 1980, Dan and Phil Berrigan, among others, had started the Plowshares Movement (still beating swords into plowshares today), beginning by damaging nuclear warhead nose cones and pouring blood on draft board files.[10]

In 1984, a Plowshares group hammered an estimated $114,000 worth of damage into air force equipment; arrested, they were charged with conspiracy and the destruction of national defense material. Testifying (over the objections of the prosecuting attorney) at their trial in Syracuse, New York, Howard declared that the Plowshares action was an example of the many civil disobedience acts that "historically have been proven necessary"—he highlighted the abolitionists' aid to fugitive slaves and the protests against the Vietnam War—"and today are absolutely vital."

A few months later, Howard was in Burlington, Vermont, testifying in a similar vein on behalf of a group (the "Winooski 24") from Peacework Network, who were charged with criminal trespass in the office of Republican senator Robert Stafford (he'd rebuffed all their requests to discuss Central American policy). Fortunately, the group drew a rare judicial liberal, Judge Frank Mahady, for their trial; he allowed them to use the so-called necessity defense— namely, that they'd had to do what they did in order to avert a larger catastrophe. That ruling enabled them to put a variety of witnesses (including Dick Falk and Ramsay Clark) on the stand, as well as, on the trial's final day, Howard. As usual, he testified on the history of civil disobedience and was able to cite the many times in the past that juries had acquitted people (as in fugitive slave cases) who'd broken the law. One of those on trial later told Howard that he'd had such a "great impact" on the jury that it stayed in deliberations for only an hour—and decided to free the Winooski 24.

Though Howard testified with some frequency (in 1987 he spoke on behalf of Abbie Hoffman and Amy Carter after they'd been arrested during an anti-CIA demonstration at the University of Massachusetts at Amherst), he was under no illusion that the courtroom was a neutral field or that all persons were equal before the law. He co-authored a paper arguing that the concept of "due process" concealed the fact that the legal system had a distinct class bias. It wasn't that the courts always decided in favor of the rich or powerful but that they did so much more often than they decided for the poor or marginalized. When the National Labor Relations Act (the Wagner Act) had been passed in 1935, its intent was pro-labor, but subsequently the courts had made a number of key decisions that soon weakened the rights of workers and left-wingers under it. Nor had the Smith Act trials in 1949 been models of neutrality. Nor were the lenient sentences or outright acquittals frequently given to corporate defendants. As Howard wrote, "in eight years of violations of the Sherman Antitrust Act, executives received prison sentences in only three cases . . . typically, we find fines for corporate offenders, prison for lower-class offenders." Yet where, other than the courts, is one to go for justice? Presidential pardons are reserved for the likes of Richard Nixon and his vice president Spiro Agnew.

In the mid-1980s, as if getting his second wind, Howard started to write again with something of his old appetite. He finished his second play, *Daughter of Venus*, about a generational conflict between a daughter and her physicist father over his temptation to go to work again for the federal government on a new weapons system. Howard's son, Jeff, directed an early version in 1984 at the Theater for the New City and the following year at Connecticut's White Barn Theater. The revised script had two more productions in 2008, but unlike his previous play, *Emma* (and his later one, *Marx in Soho*), it did not find much of an audience. However, Jeff's later production in Wellfleet at WHAT in 2010, which restored the original script, received strong reviews and was also a popular success.

The play reflects Howard's deep concern over the nuclear arms race (then at its height) and has its share of astute insights and emotional impact. Too often, though, the polemics are flat-out—the audience told, lecture style, rather than shown through character interaction, the political and generational conflicts at work. Nevertheless, in Myla's view, *Daughter of Venus* is her father's "most emotionally intelligent play," one that "brought to life very real family dynamics and conflicts." Howard wrote that the physicist's wife, Lucy, was "modeled after my wife, Roslyn" (Paolo: "She was disappointed in the world." Aramintha, the daughter: "She was disappointed in you"). During the summers of 1957 and 1958, the Zinns spent time at the University of Colorado in Denver where Howard had a Ford Foundation Fellowship and Myla remembers her mother jumping into a very cold lake in the Rocky Mountains; "she loved to do that," according to Myla. In the play, Paolo, the father, says: "The summer we drove to California—there was a pearl of a lake, eight thousand feet up into the Sierras. Your mother didn't hesitate. She took off her clothes, dove into that ice-cold water. But every time we came back, her wonderful laughter disappeared. She would read the newspapers and every horror in the world became a part of her own life."

This was a time when Roz was in a far better place in her life than had been true for some time. Her previous stints at social work and teaching hadn't given her much satisfaction. But in 1987, having dabbled a bit earlier, she decided to formally enroll in painting and watercolor classes at the Museum of Fine Arts in Boston. Her gift was considerable, and over the final twenty years of her life she had half a dozen exhibitions. She also donated paintings to the Art Connection of Boston, which gave work out on loan to public and nonprofit agencies, including shelters for the homeless, elder services, and group homes for battered women. "What I see in the world," Roz once wrote, "so burdened and troubled, and yet beautiful in nature and in the human form, impels me to seek to create images that give the possibility of hope."[11]

In the second half of the 1980s, Howard wrote more opinion pieces and essays than he had in some time. They were usually on the same issues that had long absorbed his attention, as if he wanted to restate the major themes that had ruled his political life, and even, here and there, to reexamine some of those positions.

Probably the top issue among Howard's political priorities was U.S. interventionism in the sovereign affairs of other countries. It was apparent by mid-1985 that the U.S., in supporting the Contras in Nicaragua, had chosen to side with corruption and brutality. No one was more committed to the Contra cause against the left-wing Sandinista government than Reagan himself, and the following year a supine Congress voted to provide the Contras with an additional $100 million. In a reversal of the truth, the administration insisted that the Nicaraguan government had rejected all attempts to negotiate. The U.S. didn't want to negotiate; it wanted to "disappear" the Sandinista government. Reagan was quick to demand that all Soviet and Cuban military personnel be expelled from Nicaragua, but he rejected any proposal that the U.S. withdraw its own forces or close its bases in Honduras.[12]

Yet war followed on war, while at home only the most miserly sums were set aside for the needs of the poor. Howard held firmly to his ingrained optimism, but he now based it on an argument he hadn't previously stressed: the utter unpredictability of past events (previously it had been the inherent compassion of people and their rejection of injustice). It was true enough that time and again in the twentieth century, events hadn't turned out the way they were "supposed" to. Few had predicted the Russian revolution, fewer still that Stalin would pervert it, that Khrushchev would expose Stalin's crimes, that China would break with the Soviet Union, or that Gorbachev's reforms would bring the whole system down around his ears.

Given all the evidence of the unexpected in human history— how he would have rejoiced in the unpredictable rise in 2011 of the Arab Spring and Occupy Wall Street—Howard concluded that "the struggle for justice should never be abandoned on the ground that it is hopeless . . . no cold calculation of the balance of power need deter people who are persuaded that their cause is just." He would have been delighted that the demonstrations in 2011–12 seemingly sprang up from nowhere. Evidence from the past was robust with similar examples of spontaneous uprisings, and they "give hope, because for hope we don't need certainty, only possibility."

Just a few years earlier, a number of anthropologists and theorists of altruism began to construct a radical and persuasive model of human nature as innately affiliative, egalitarian, sharing, and trusting. It was Howard's old claim, now bolstered by new data. At the University of Zurich, to give but one example, various studies found that by age six or seven, "children are zealously devoted to the equitable partitioning of goods," and they'll punish those who attempt to grab more than their proper share. Curiously, Howard, as earlier, seemed unaware of this latest body of evidence, though it provided strong support for his belief in people's innate goodness.[13]

In the years of Ronald Reagan's guileful administration, many people gave up their earlier activism and glibly dismissed the current generation of college students as preoccupied with a combination of materialism, celebrity, sports, and the self. Not Howard. In 1986 he'd seen and sometimes participated in demonstrations on campuses across the country calling for divestment from South Africa. At Wellesley half the campus boycotted classes, and at Harvard a black-tie dinner for alumni had to be called off because of a large protest against the university's holdings. He didn't feel that his students in the eighties were "different human beings than those I knew 20 years ago."[14]

Howard despised Reagan's policies yet wrote comparatively little about them. He did single out the administration's lowering of standards for cotton fiber inhalation, which causes brown lung, and its having pamphlets describing the disease withdrawn from circulation—Reagan cited the pamphlet's cover, showing a sick textile worker, as "biased against business." There was much else to fuel indignation about the Reagan presidency, and if Howard didn't write extensive, detailed critiques of Reagan's policies (except for the administration's support for the Contras), he did make some scathing, if brief, comments on many of them. Howard called Reagan's support of Guatemalan strongman General Rios Montt genocide, for example, because the general directed the murder of some two hundred thousand people, most of them Mayan Indians. (In 2012 Montt has finally been brought to trial.)

Reagan's supporters then and now often credit him—not Mikhail Gorbachev, the man actually responsible—with dismantling the Soviet Union, just as they often assign him the major role in toppling the Berlin Wall. Reagan himself spoke of having liberated certain concentration camps (he didn't mean Hollywood, where he spent all of World War II), and of the pope approving his policies in Central America (he hadn't). Weirdest of all was his insistence that the apartheid regime of P.W. Botha had eliminated segregation in South Africa—as if Reagan wasn't responsible for even *approximating* the truth. Nor did he ever mention AIDS until five years into the epidemic, then coldly refused to provide federal assistance for the afflicted—the degenerates had brought the scourge on themselves. It needs to be added that Howard himself rarely mentioned the topic of AIDS.

Howard was among the few American historians ever to have had much interest in theories of knowledge or the philosophy of history, and in his case it was mostly the result of defending himself against charges of being a "mere propagandist." He'd already written a considerable amount on objectivity in historical writing, but in the late 1980s he returned to the topic as the result of reading Peter Novick's remarkable book *That Noble Dream*. He reiterated his view that any claim by the *New York Times* or, for that matter, by a historian, to be printing "all the news that's fit to print" was an absurdity; the *Times* was publishing "all the news that its *editors*" thought fit to print. He also repeated his frequently stated view that any historian worthy of the name had the obligation to try to remain as honest as possible about interpreting the known evidence. This meant, for instance, forewarning the reader (as he had done in *A People's History*) about how the historian's experiences or values might well be contaminating to some degree the evidence presented.[15]

Howard thought journalism and historical writing were somewhat similar. The reporter might be writing about the present and the historian the past, but both were *selecting* which part of the evidence to introduce and with what degree of emphasis. No such thing as entirely objective history or reporting exists, though some writers scrupulously try to minimize their own subjectivity and straightforwardly call the issue to the reader's attention. In illuminating the point, Howard returned to his treatment of the Constitution in *A People's History.* He now rephrased his earlier question about how "good" the document was to "What effect does it have on the quality of our lives?" His own answer was: "Very little." The Constitution "made promises it cannot keep, and therefore deludes us into complacency about the rights we have." Plus, the document was wholly silent "on certain other rights that all human beings deserve."

Howard gave several examples of what he meant: the Constitution's silence on any rights relating to economic entitlements (a sustainable income, decent housing, medical care); or its rejection of any effort to put slavery on its way toward extinction, however gradual; or its failure to establish standard procedures, including one for the often ignored requirement that Congress be consulted before we go to war. True, someone might pipe up and say, "no single document can deal with all imaginable circumstances, especially those that haven't yet arisen"—but that someone wouldn't have been a black slave.

Howard had always been a greatly admired teacher. A colleague who sat in on several of his classes in the 1980s found no trace of the boredom that often emanates from those who've been teaching for a long time—and from their catatonic students. In his notes, the colleague emphasized Howard's "outgoing, tolerant and relaxed" style—"he has a way of teaching that is disarmingly open," welcoming interruption, disagreement, and controversy. Nor did Howard believe in grades, though because of administrative pressure he gave them—nearly always high ones. He knew that made him a "soft touch" but didn't care: "there are people who don't deserve the grades they get [but] they are not cheating him, they are cheating themselves." Many students, Howard felt, "must be helped to find their own ways and standards at their own pace . . . if you put them in your own pace . . . they are not their own people."

Howard cared deeply about his students and never grew tired of teaching. But he had grown tired of John Silber and Boston University. Howard was elsewhere an active citizen, but at BU he'd come to respond not on a daily basis but mostly during a crisis. He'd never been an organizational type, not at least since the days of SNCC. At BU he never served on committees and wasn't active in the faculty union. Some called that irresponsible, but both Howard's temperament and his experience at BU had taught him to keep his distance. His anarchist side kept him away from any sort of commitment to the nitpicking of committee work, and his extended mistreatment at BU had finally taught him, for self-protection, to stay apart, conscientiously doing his teaching but not putting himself in Silber's gun sights. (In the 1980s, Howard noted, "the controls at B.U. have become much, much tighter.")

None of which kept him entirely free from Silber's ongoing attempts to dishonor and damage him. Indeed, a kind of peripheral skirmishing between the two men went on right through the decade. When in 1986 Howard requested a grader for one of his courses—350 students had enrolled, making it the largest class in the university— he was advised to limit the number of students allowed in. That same year, antiapartheid demonstrations had spread to include more than one hundred universities and, unlike the earlier civil rights and anti–Vietnam War protests, these were aimed directly at the power of college trustees and administrations. Howard, of course, applauded the demonstrations (the students have "the courage to do what they feel they need to do. They haven't been silent"). And Silber, of course, called in the police—to "restore free speech," no less.

While in the early 1980s Howard remained the lowest-paid full professor in his department, Silber cashed in $2 million in stocks he owned in a corporation headed by Arthur Metcalf, chair of the

Board of Trustees. In the 1980s, the board also authorized the expenditure of $2.5 million to pay a lobbyist in Washington to get grants for BU—and to push for Silber to become Reagan's Secretary of Education (it didn't happen). Next up on Silber's agenda was the award of a BU honorary degree to Mangosuthu Buthelezi, chief minister of KwaZulu land and at the time a leading opponent of Nelson Mandela and the African National Congress. At the ceremony, five hundred students turned out to protest against the award, the largest rally BU had seen in years.

Howard began to feel, as he wrote Frances Piven, "a small urge, starting with wanting a semester off, and in a matter of weeks developing into an overwhelming desire to be free." He was still "having a lot of fun teaching"—he now had four hundred students in his day course—but was also feeling "a great fatigue." He wanted more time to write, without having to squeeze it in between courses, and after twenty-four years at BU (and thirty-four years in all as a teacher), he no longer felt willing to be hemmed in by an academic calendar—or to keep dodging John Silber's bullets. Having been among the 15 percent lowest-paid full professors on campus in 1982, Howard, through the AAUP, finally got merit and equity back pay in that year. He had also accumulated enough money from his pension and Social Security, to say nothing of the large sums that *A People's History* would later bring in, to afford to live comfortably without worry. When, almost twenty years later, Silber himself finally retired (having long been among the highest-paid university presidents), his loyal Board of Trustees put together—to considerable outrage among academicians—a $6.1 million package to ease his later years.

Colleagues who'd taken early retirement told Howard that they'd usually gotten a full year's salary. Howard coolly decided that Silber would be so delighted to get rid of him that he should ask for *two* years' salary. It was, according to Howard, "the fastest negotiation anyone had seen." He got a settlement of $90,000, spread over a three-year period. Two weeks later, in the middle of April 1988, Howard gave his final lecture to his Introduction to Political Theory

class, telling them that he was retiring "from your [the students']
university, not theirs [the administration's]. Act as if it was yours. . . .
I'll be around." He then led the class to a picket line in front of the
School of Nursing in support of the eight tenured faculty who'd
been fired when Silber closed the school down.[16]

Howard wondered in advance whether he'd have any regrets, but
instead he felt "just great," buoyed by the flood of letters he received expressing sadness *and* congratulations for having gotten
out from under. One of them was from his old friend Staughton
Lynd, who wanted to tell him "how much influence you have had
on [my] life. . . . And as they say in Nicaragua, 'va bien' ['go well']
in this new beginning." Roz was as pleased with Howard's resignation as he was. She, too, was having a much better time of it, taking
two art classes and playing with a recorder ensemble once a week.
Late in 1987, she'd had trouble with the vision in her right eye, but
successful cataract surgery restored it to 20-25.

Howard wasn't retiring in any ordinary sense. At age sixty-six,
he remained healthy and vigorous and maintained a full schedule of
lectures around the county. He and Roz did a fair amount of
traveling—first to a SNCC reunion conference at Trinity College:
"A wonderful meeting with old friends. Great stories were told,
songs were sung," making him feel "energized, even inspired." Then
it was trips to London, Budapest, Tuscany, and Paris (several times)—
sometimes tied to a lecture or a brief course. When in the States,
they continued to love their summer weeks at the Cape Cod house,
and Howard continued to speak throughout the country on various
subjects—the First Amendment, the interventions in Vietnam and
Central America, a comparison between the 1960s and 1980s, "the
political uses of history," and civil disobedience and democracy.

He began to think about a new writing project more substantial
than the occasional pieces he'd been turning out of late, and he
came up with a proposal for something called "Taking Off from
La Guardia." But Hugh Van Dusen, his editor at Harper, turned it
down: he thought it read like "a scissors and paste book, culled from

your past writings, and of varying interest." The Guggenheim Foundation also turned him down for the fellowship he'd applied for, though it's unlikely, since Howard was financially secure, that that alone would have caused him to abandon the project. Maybe, he wrote Frances Piven, he'd continue to "enjoy the luxury of pretending to be planning some profound, important work without facing the threat that it is available to be read and criticized."

Instead, Howard bought a computer and what he called "the arrogantly-titled" WordPerfect program. His son, Jeff, skilled in such matters, taught him proficiency, and before long he was writing to Frances, "No more of these curt though affectionate notes from me . . . set some solid time aside for reading my letters."

Unfortunately, Howard's resignation coincided with the death of his mother, Jennie. She'd grown lonely in her apartment in the Bronx (Howard had helped to support her financially since the death of her husband, Eddie) and, always insistent on her independence, she decided to move to a trailer park in Florida, where she became the warmhearted, much beloved center of community life. When Howard visited her there, he discovered "there were always people from the neighboring trailers in hers, having coffee and cake, people of all ages and backgrounds." But she then decided that she missed New York and moved back to a small apartment in Co-op City in the Bronx. Though Jennie was inescapably Jewish, "she was always totally open to all sorts of people, and she seemed oblivious as to whether they were black, white, Christian, Jewish, young, old." It was an attitude toward people and life that she'd passed on to Howard, who'd mirrored it exactly.

Jennie's final years (she died at ninety) were contented ones, though there'd been too many operations, too many hospitals, too much pain. Howard delivered the eulogy at his mother's funeral. He said that all of her sons had seen her as "an extraordinary person . . . she had such charisma that people were attracted to her in whatever situation she was."

10

The Nineties

Though he'd retired from BU, Howard hadn't quite put himself beyond the reach of John Silber's tentacles. A militarist, a defender of American interventionism, and a strong supporter of Ronald Reagan, Silber was in the process of seeking the Democratic nomination to run for Governor of Massachusetts. Because his politics coincided with the conservative climate in general, he actually won the nomination (though he lost the 1990 election). In recognition of Silber's breakthrough into politics, the *New York Times* ran a puff piece ("Crusader on the Charles"!) on him. In it Silber took square aim at Howard, describing him as "not worth a damn . . . an incompetent teacher . . . the enemy of truth, of scholarship, of civility and decency in a university."[1]

Silber's words were defamatory, to say nothing of being brazenly wrongheaded. Howard had been an inspiring teacher, insistent on accuracy in his historical scholarship (even as he rightly stressed that every historian inescapably contaminates the evidence), and had always tried—except with Silber—to argue without attacking opponents personally. Howard was the embodiment of "civility and decency"; it was Silber who embodied pugnacity, manipulation, and scurrility.

Though Howard didn't have the stomach for a drawn-out libel suit, he hardly took the attack lying down. To the *Times* he sent a letter to the editor calmly pointing out that, among much else, Silber had a long history of censoring student newspapers, that the Massachusetts Civil Liberties Union had stated publicly that it "had never received such a volume of complaints about deprivation of free speech as it had about Boston University," and that Silber had further interfered with its expression by having the security police regularly take photos of both faculty members and students who peacefully protested against his policies, most recently about BU's investment in apartheid South Africa. When it became known that Silber was writing a book, the joke around Boston was that he'd call it *Mein Kampus*.

Howard also wrote a strong response to Silber in *Newsday*. He pointed out that Silber had supported the war in Vietnam, had urged aid to the death-squad government of El Salvador (and awarded an honorary degree to Duarte), and had opposed the "Marxism-Leninism" of the African National Congress. When students, following a national trend, put up a few shanties on campus to symbolize apartheid, Silber had the police tear them down and arrest the students. He was, Howard wrote, "the J. Edgar Hoover of higher education."

The *New York Times* credited Silber with elevating BU above its prior reputation as "a streetcar college," but Howard felt the *Times* failed to understand that "the most important thing about a university is not the size of its endowment but the feeling of faculty and students that they teach and study in an environment that respects their freedom, that treats them as human beings." Howard did credit Silber with enormously increasing BU's endowment but pointed out that he'd also raised the university's debt over the past twenty years from $8 million to $240 million. Further, Howard underscored the fact that Silber had held "the salaries of secretaries and staff to subsistence levels," had tried to destroy employee unions, and had held down the average faculty member's salary to $40,000—but made sure that he himself got a hefty raise every year.

Silber had also persuaded his friendly Board of Trustees to lend him, by 1990, $638,000 at low or no interest and allowed him to buy real estate below market value from the university. Then there was his 40 percent bonus called "deferred compensation," which had already accumulated $2 million, plus a year's salary for every five years he worked without taking a leave. By 1990 his salary had shot up to $441,000, more than the presidents of Harvard, Yale—and the United States. "To his credit," Howard wrote, Silber did "beautify his plantation." He'd also gotten a special deal from Arthur Metcalf, the right-wing chair of the board, to purchase stock in his company, Electronics Corporation of America, which would have made Silber wealthy all by itself.[2]

Soon after Silber began his 1990 losing campaign for governor, he made the inflammatory remark at a news conference that Massachusetts had become "a welfare magnet" that has "suddenly become popular for people who are accustomed to living in the tropical climate." Called out by a reporter for his words, Silber angrily replied, "It is scurrilous to use my remarks to accuse me of racism." Soon after, when addressing a group of the state's mayors, he asked, "Why should Lowell [Massachusetts] be the Cambodian capital of America? It is extraordinary. Why should they all be concentrated in one place? This needs to be examined."

As if he hadn't done enough damage, Silber next took a potshot at Jews. He told a reporter from the *Jewish Advocate* that as a young man he'd "thought about it and then found out that the racism of Jews is quite phenomenal." (Silber's father was Jewish, and an aunt and uncle had been killed during the Holocaust.) Besides, he went on, "I also thought Judaism made a great mistake in not recognizing Jesus as one in the line of the great Hebrew prophets." The series of racist, bigoted remarks made Silber seem out of control, but he made no public apologies and sailed blithely on, as autocratic despots do. The man was certainly charismatic, his presence magnetic—but so was Darth Vader. Howard summed it all up succinctly: "What Silber lacks is a kind of common sense intelligence, a sense of proportion, an understanding that human beings have to be treated with decency."

In retiring from teaching, Howard wasn't retiring from writing or activism. In 1990 he published *Declarations of Independence*, a collection of his essays, primarily on war and justice—his first book in a decade. Most of the ideas and some of the actual articles were retreads from an earlier period. Yet for a "midlist" book, *Declarations* sold reasonably well (some fifteen thousand copies) and was reissued in 2003 under the title *Passionate Declarations*. But Howard himself wasn't particularly enthusiastic about the book, and a number of reviewers agreed with him, though almost all continued to admire his clean, simple, direct prose.

The *New York Times* critic Herbert Mitgang, himself on the left, found the entire book "remote" and felt that Howard, in place of analysis, too often settled for "simply moral and personal outrage." Even H. Bruce Franklin, though a political radical, accused Howard of proposing "merely a reform of capitalism . . . while studiously avoiding any fundamental challenge to the nation-state." But Franklin was mistaken. While it's true that Howard rarely attacked nationalism at length, he makes it clear throughout his work that his preference is for "a world order." Besides, he was hardly a proponent of reformed capitalism. Variations on "our economic system has failed" pepper Howard's work, and his preference for some form of socialism is repeated so often in his writings as to be emblematic. The critical reception of *Declarations* came down to, as is often the case, a series of other people's projections.[3]

In 1990, Reagan was succeeded in office by his vice president, George H.W. Bush, guaranteeing considerable continuity in policy. Bush approved new weapons systems for nuclear warheads (of which we had a mere thirty thousand) and refused to accept the Soviet Union's suggestion that all nuclear testing be abolished. The critical year in Bush's presidency was 1990: U.S. troops invaded Panama and jailed its leader, Manuel Noriega, on drug charges; Mikhail Gorbachev won the Nobel Peace Prize for his role in dismantling the Soviet Union and ending the Cold War; Nelson Mandela was released from prison in South Africa; and Iraq invaded Kuwait. The Reagan and Bush administrations had facilitated Iraq's military buildup, but the UN now gave Saddam Hussein an ultimatum for withdrawing his troops.

Hussein ignored it, and the UN sanctioned a "coalition" to force the Iraqis to leave. Bush claimed that Saddam had left no choice but war—a lie, since he'd made a number of overtures for negotiation. The U.S. led the invasion and contributed by far the largest number of troops; second was its oil-rich ally Saudi Arabia, the feudal monarchy where women weren't (and in 2012 still aren't) even allowed to drive cars. The coalition that set about "liberating" Kuwait—or, to be more precise, its monarchy, not its people—then launched Operation Desert Storm, which began with an aerial bombardment of Iraqi troops in January 1991.

Peace activists managed to organize some of the largest demonstrations since the war in Vietnam. But most Americans cheered the war on, apparently unaware or not caring that only 8 percent of the men and no women were allowed to vote in Kuwait. Nor was the information widely disseminated that Kuwait's royal family owned the world's tenth-largest oil company and were invested in no fewer than seventy of the largest corporations in the world. But no, officially we were protecting a tiny, defenseless country from being swallowed up by the tyrant Saddam Hussein's aggressive invasion.

When Secretary of State James Baker was asked by a reporter why we were in Kuwait, he answered, because it was "important to the average, everyday American—in terms of what will happen to his pocketbook, to his standard of living . . . if a dictator succeeds in putting himself astride the economic lifeline of the industrial world." Yet in 1991 Bush decided *not* to help the Kurds in their uprising against Iraq's tyranny on the grounds that the U.S. did not interfere in the internal affairs of another country. To get away with so grotesque a lie, he could count on the American public not knowing its own history. Bush also decided to sell ballistic missiles to Iran, Syria, and Egypt—those bastions of democracy.

Howard, to no one's surprise, wasn't among those cheering on the invasion. He thought it was right for Iraq to get out of Kuwait— just as "it is *right* for Israel to get out of the occupied territories" (though a deracinated Jew, Howard felt far more sympathy for the Palestinians than for Israel). He had no doubt that Saddam was "a tyrant and an aggressor," but the world was full of them and "if we must engage in the mass slaughter of war" to get rid of them all, "we will be in perpetual war." He felt there were alternatives, other means: "boycotts, embargoes . . . , diplomacy, negotiations." The rejection of military solutions would "make available a trillion dollars a year to eliminate hunger, homelessness, disease—a far more worthy project of long-term value than the toppling of this or that tyrant of the year."

Desert Storm was quickly over and Iraq successfully pushed out of Kuwait. Many hailed the result as a smashing victory and a "just" war. Among them was John Silber: he applauded Bush for having drawn the line "right here and now and put an end to the kind of tyranny and terrorism that Saddam Hussein would impose on the world." For Howard, there was no such thing as a just war—as opposed to a just *cause*. World War II was often held up as "the good war," and Howard had eagerly participated in it, but the toll of 40 million dead had soon afterward raised his doubts, and they never receded. The question, Howard asked, is, How do you combat injustice, how do you defend against attack, without going to war, which involves massive and indiscriminate violence?

Howard battled the question throughout his life. He believed in a nonviolent approach to conflict but wasn't an out-and-out pacifist; he'd never joined the War Resisters League, SANE, or other comparable groups (of course, he wasn't much of a "joiner" in any case). In *Declarations of Independence*, Howard devoted two of eleven essays to the troubling question of "just and unjust war." As a young man, he'd had no doubt that fascism had to be resisted and defeated through force of arms.

Yet Howard now asked that if the U.S. had truly been concerned with fascism why, after Italy invaded Ethiopia, did Washington continue to send Italy oil to facilitate the war? Why during the Spanish Civil War, when Franco was receiving aid from Hitler and Mussolini, did Roosevelt sponsor a Neutrality Act that effectively blocked supplies to the antifascists? And between 1938 and 1940, when Hitler seemed focused not on extermination but on forcing all Jews to leave Germany, why was no country in the West willing to take them? The "good" war, it seems, was initially committed neither to saving Jews nor to destroying fascism. And one can hardly claim that World War II had the moral purpose of defeating the Nazi notion of "superior" and "inferior" races, not when the U.S. Navy continued to allow blacks to serve only as mess men, the Red Cross refused to accept blood from blacks, the craft unions were for whites only, lynching continued in the South, and segregation reigned in the North and South.

Besides, how just was a war in which the Allies employed saturation bombing of German cities at night, with no attempt to avoid civilian targets? And what about the atrocity of dropping atomic bombs on Hiroshima and Nagasaki, killing hundreds of thousands of civilians and maiming just as many? As Howard put it, "we were victorious over fascism, but this left two superpowers . . . armed with frightening nuclear arsenals . . . dominating the world, vying for control . . . Hitler's aggression was over but wars continued," and millions continued to die in them.

Perhaps Howard's strongest point in championing nonviolence over combat was his reminder that the results of war were unpredictable, its original goals (usually muddy) mostly unachieved. A million died in the Spanish Civil War, but Franco's fascism continued for another forty years. "Millions," Howard wrote, "were killed in the Soviet Union [and China] to 'build socialism'" but the result was totalitarian state control—not exactly what Marx had in mind. Plus, the cost and waste of military weaponry were phenomenal—$28 billion spent on building a hundred largely ineffective B-1 bombers, $12 million for every nuclear weapons test, and that's but two of the many projects of the arms race. The money spent on nuclear testing alone, as Howard put it, "would train 40,000 community health workers." After the disintegration of the Soviet Union, Americans were promised a "peace dividend." Somehow it never arrived, perhaps because not enough Americans ever demanded it.

The nonviolent approach to conflict did not, in Howard's view, "mean acceptance, but resistance—not waiting, but acting. It is not at all passive. It involves strikes, boycotts, non-cooperation, mass demonstrations, and sabotage [to property] . . . the means for achieving social change must match, morally, the ends." Besides, he emphasized, advanced military hardware was not necessarily protection against an aroused populace determined on toppling a tyrannical regime—recent examples being the ousting of Somoza in Nicaragua, of Marcos in the Philippines, and the shah of Iran (in 2012 we can add Tunisia, Egypt, and Libya). Howard remained convinced that ordinary people can nonviolently achieve remarkable results in situations that seem immovable—though the many examples are usually absent from history books, especially in a society devoted to the notion that military might is the most reliable means for achieving its goals. "Those of us," Howard wrote, "who call for the repudiation of massive violence to solve human problems must sound utopian, romantic" to those who believe violence is not only innate to human nature but optimally effective.

Though nearing seventy, Howard continued to crisscross the country giving lectures, serving on panels, doing book signings. No matter where he went, he drew packed houses, with hundreds sometimes being turned away. On one trip to Santa Cruz (a benefit for the Resource Center for Nonviolence), six hundred people crowded into a church, and the mayor (a Socialist!) gave Howard the key to the city and issued a proclamation announcing Howard Zinn Day. "How," Howard wrote his agent Rick Balkin, "can one maintain modesty in the face of that?!" Somehow he managed it.

In the 1990s, Howard still hadn't tired of travel, but Roz certainly had. She would sometimes accompany him—on a visit to Spain in 1990, for example, to attend a Basque conference and to vacation in Barcelona—but usually Roz preferred to work in the garden, paint, or join her recorder group to make music. These days she felt (in her own words) "pretty well," sometimes even "great," but a new condition—"this fibrillation mishegas"—continued to bother and worry her.[3]

Currently absorbed in issues relating to violence and war, Howard never lost his profound concern for the ongoing plight of black Americans. He was well aware that the civil rights struggle had produced heightened opportunities for maybe 10 to 20 percent of the African American population only. Yes, more blacks were attending college and entering the professions, but many more were in prison, and still more remained mired in poverty and marginalized in ghettoes. It had become fashionable to ignore the extent of institutionalized racism that continued to block their paths and blame blacks themselves. The mantra went something like this: "We're tired of hearing about black grievances. We've done all we can for 'you people' . . . You have to stop being lazy and start behaving like the rest of the country—work hard and pull yourself up by your bootstraps."[4]

Such a mind-set refused to absorb a slew of studies that challenged the current indifference. As far back as 1986, a *New York Times* investigation concluded that "young black men from the inner city are as willing to work . . . as are white youth . . . at jobs and with wages that are comparable." In the late 1960s, three fourths of all black men had been employed; by the end of the 1980s only 57 percent were. Yet many works of (purported) scholarship appeared in the 1990s that underscored and tried to justify mounting white disengagement: Alan Wolfe's *One Nation, After All*, Jim Sleeper's *Liberal Racism*, Shelby Steele's *A Dream Deferred*, and a book that quickly became the bible for whites suffering from "race fatigue," Stephan and Abigail Thernstrom's *America in Black and White*. Fortunately a number of other books—by Andrew Hacker, William Julius Wilson, Derek Bok and William G. Bowen, Patricia Williams, Derrick Bell, and David Shipler—also appeared and trenchantly countered the dominant white attitude of patronization.

During the Reagan and Bush administrations, issues relating to race were simply swept under the carpet, along with any number of other social issues like education, housing, medical care. From 1980 to 1995 the Dow Jones average went up 400 percent, but the real wages of most working people went down 15 percent. Yet it was widely proclaimed in the media that the economy was "in a thriving state." If so, Howard asked, "Are not our urban centers really two cities, one of comfort, one of desperation? Since too many of our countrymen are not at all 'in a thriving state,' can we leave it to the wonders of the 'free market,' which historically has created wealth at the top, poverty at the bottom, and insecurity in the middle, to fulfill the American Dream?" The U.S. government was unresponsive; its preoccupation was on enhancing the killing machine known as the military and using its shiny new weapons to topple left-wing regimes in other countries.

The Physicians Task Force on Hunger had reported in 1985 that at a conservative estimate some 15 million American families earned less than $10,000 a year, were unable to get food stamps, and were chronically hungry—a large percentage of whom were black. The Reagan administration's response had been to cut back on welfare. When Bush became president, he declared a war on drugs but made no mention of tobacco or the corporations that produced it, even though deaths from tobacco outnumbered those from cocaine roughly seventy to one. In his 1990 book *Declarations of Indepen-*

dence, Howard passionately called for a turnabout in national priorities, with a new emphasis on meeting social needs, not maximizing corporate profits.

By that year, particularly in the Northeast, racial segregation in the schools was *greater* than at the time of the Supreme Court's *Brown v. Board* decision in 1954. As for the segregation of housing, the only places that showed a decline were in metropolitan areas with small black populations, places like Albuquerque and Phoenix; three quarters of all African Americans in the 1990s were still living under highly segregated conditions. Throughout the decade, moreover, more than 25 percent of all blacks continued to lack even a high school diploma, and there was a decline in the number of blacks entering college. One third of black men in their twenties were in jail, on probation, or on parole. The number of poor whites declined by 4 million, but the number of poor blacks rose by 700,000 from 1970 to 2000.

Only a scant amount of white sympathy remained to be drawn upon. In its place was a deepening amount of white smugness about the "pathology of the ghetto." Instead of offering sustained help, many whites preferred to stigmatize blacks and the poor in general for failing to mimic middle-class values and behavior. Very little was any longer said about the entrenched psychological heritage of slavery and second-class citizenship, and even less about opening up more job opportunities for blacks. Instead of tackling the durable patterns of poverty and segregation, most whites chose to ignore them and to point the finger at blacks themselves for their ongoing problems. As Howard put it, "it will take a massive redistribution of resources to do away with this situation"—as true as it was unlikely.

But if Howard believed that the goal was transparently clear, what tactics held out the most hope for reaching it? *Not* the ballot box, *not* initiatives from the president, the Congress, or the Supreme Court—not if the hope was for "truly important change." Howard believed that the country's history suggested instead that crucial social change "depended on the concerted action of citizens, on social movements acting outside the framework of governments, sometimes even outside the law." He took as his examples the anti-slavery movement and the bitter, prolonged labor strikes against corporate power in the late nineteenth and early twentieth centuries. Howard argued that a few presidents (Lincoln, FDR), a few acts of Congress (the laws and constitutional amendments passed by the post–Civil War Radical Republicans), and even a few Supreme Court decisions (*Brown v. Board*) had to some degree advanced the cause of social justice, but he would have assigned credit for those accomplishments not to the standard "great man" but to pressure from below, to social struggle.

How to make additional progress? Howard's answer was that those who remained concerned about persistent injustice should "build a new national citizens movement dedicated to political and economic democracy—a force so widespread, so powerful, that whoever is in office, attention will have to be paid." He pointed to the "important victories" currently being won "by movements for gender equality, for disabled people, for the rights of gays and lesbians, for protection of the environment."

What Howard failed to question was how stable and extensive such advances had been. The Equal Rights Amendment had failed to pass, the gay rights movement had shifted from a radical early agenda to one that primarily served the needs of the white middle class, and environmental issues like global warming had largely been ignored or disputed. The 1990s were not the 1960s, as Howard well knew. Where would the troops come from to form a substantial new "national citizens union"? The working class had turned away from unions, the feminist movement had weakened, and racial progress—with a third of young black men in prison and a third of blacks still living below the poverty line—had been limited. True, some Americans remained angry, yet immobilized politically, about the huge sums of money still being committed to wars, but most were seemingly indifferent to the ways in which the concentration of wealth had destroyed the American Dream. If, somehow (through a major depression?), a powerful new protest movement does arise, à la Occupy Wall Street, Howard may still be proven right in the long run.

When Bill Clinton was elected president in 1992, there was some giddy hope for a while that this young and purportedly liberal leader would produce a shift in direction for the country. To his credit, he did defend Medicare and Medicaid, education, and environmental programs from the Republican Congress's demands for deep cuts. But Clinton's "progressivism" soon turned out to be paper thin. He maintained the same swollen military budget that had characterized Republican administrations, escalated the racist dope war, and made no significant effort to address the growing gap between rich and poor.

In terms of foreign policy, when some sixty generals and admirals from around the world called for the total elimination of nuclear weapons, the White House coldly dismissed their call, stating that the nation's current policy, holding on to tens of thousands of nuclear weapons, would remain unchanged. Clinton also held firmly to the aggressive unilateralism that had become a hallmark of U.S. international policy. After American embassies in Kenya and Tanzania were attacked, the administration promptly bombed what it called a nerve gas plant in Sudan—which turned out to be a pharmaceutical factory.[5]

Howard did credit Clinton with at least one positive foreign policy decision. To get rid of a brutal military regime in Haiti, Clinton in 1994 sent in a limited number of troops to restore the duly elected but deposed Jean-Bertrand Aristide to power. "I think that was justified," Howard said. "I'm not an absolute pacifist." Yet in sanctioning that invasion, Howard was contradicting his usual stand against intervention in the internal affairs of other countries.

Clinton had earlier supported the Gulf War, so it should have come as no surprise that his foreign policy mirrored the preceding Republican administrations. He kept the military budget at the same level, and though he came into office soon after the end of the

Soviet Union and the Cold War, his foreign policy closely resembled interventionism. Besides Haiti, he sent troops to Somalia and Bosnia and rained down cruise missiles on much of Iraq, killing many civilians, which he justified as necessary to discourage Iraq from rebuilding its arsenal of weapons and to punish it for its purported refusal to allow UN inspectors to monitor its missile test sites. Yet the U.S. stood aside during the horrendous tribal warfare in Rwanda and opposed international action.

Like Bush and Reagan, Clinton retained close ties with governments already in power, ignoring their record on human rights. Indonesia is a case in point. U.S. aid continued despite that country invading East Timor and killing nearly a fourth of its population. By the end of Clinton's presidency, the United States was, as Howard accurately put it, "selling more arms abroad than all other nations combined." In regard to Israel, Clinton continued Bush's policy of turning a blind eye to its nuclear weapons arsenal while reiterating his predecessor's promise to maintain a "partnership" with Israel in developing and producing "high technology goods." Clinton even stated that the U.S. had the right to use military force "to ensure uninhibited access to key markets, energy supplies, and strategic resources." The liberal Democrat sounded no less the bully than Reagan or Bush.

At home, Clinton endorsed and signed the cruel congressional "welfare reform" bill, declaring that its determination was to "break the cycle of dependency." What it broke was the more than sixty-year-old Aid to Families with Dependent Children program designed to assist families living in poverty. In its place, he substituted a program that gave block sums to the states without detailed instructions on how the money should be spent. In addition, the new program established a five-year lifetime limit for assistance and allowed food stamps for adults without children for only three out of every thirty-six months—despite polls that showed that 65 percent of the public felt it was the responsibility of the federal government "to take care of people who can't take care of themselves."

On the floor of Congress, Representative John Lewis denounced the new program, which would take a heavy toll on single-parent and African American households, as "mean, base . . . lowdown." Of all the senators up for reelection, only Minnesota's Paul Wellstone voted against the enabling bill. As usual, the move toward a balanced budget came on the backs of the poor, not the military or the for-profit prison system, which got $8 billion of taxpayer money to build new units, giving the United States the highest rate of incarceration in the world. On the positive side, it should be noted that Clinton did sign the Family and Medical Leave Act, cut taxes on 15 million low-income families, and claimed credit for creating 6 million new jobs.

The beginning of Clinton's presidency coincided with the fervent, though contested, celebration of the five hundredth anniversary of Columbus's arrival in the already inhabited New World. Howard's *People's History* had continued to sell remarkably well (by 1994 it was in its twenty-fourth printing). Its opening chapter had carefully detailed the way Columbus had returned the kindness and hospitality of the Arawaks (Tainos) with genocidal cruelty. But in Howard's opinion, the truth about Columbus hadn't sufficiently sunk in. There *were* a number of anti-Columbus protests, and Howard delighted in them. Yet a significant number of parades and celebrations still sounded the theme (but not by Native Americans) that Columbus's voyage marked the transition in the New World from savagery to civilization, dismissing the importance of the Indian civilizations built up over thousands of years.

Though most historians have adopted Howard's critical view, some scholarly publications persisted in proclaiming Columbus an untarnished hero. The 1986 edition of the widely used *Columbia Encyclopedia* typified the country's entrenched attitude: its lengthy entry on Columbus makes no mention at all of the gruesome atrocities he committed against the Arawaks. Then there's Ronald Reagan's response when he was president to an audience question about the wretched conditions on the reservations: "Let me tell you just a little something about the American Indian in our land. We have provided [them with] millions of acres of land. . . . We have done everything we can to meet their demands as to how they want to live. Maybe we should not have humored them in that . . . some of them became very wealthy because some of those reservations were overlaying great pools of oil . . . I don't know what their complaint might be."

Howard did his best to counteract such ignorance by giving a batch of speeches during the Columbus celebration. Whether they did much to dispel the country's ahistorical mind-set is open to question. Yet there *is* a significant amount of evidence that both teachers and students are far more critical these days of standard accounts than previously, and for that Howard could take a sizable share of the credit. A considerable number of textbooks do now mention Columbus's cruelties, even if they still don't say enough about the subsequent mistreatment of Native Americans—the many wars of annihilation or the tragic removal via the the Trail of Tears of the Cherokees and the Choctaws from their homes in the Southeast to Indian Territory in Oklahoma, thousands dying during the journey.

Howard was ready for a new writing project. At first he thought it was the right time to update *A People's History*, including a new final chapter, to take advantage of all the hoopla surrounding the Columbus quinquecentennial. But he was willing to undertake the task only if his publisher HarperCollins would guarantee "a substantial advertising campaign." They wouldn't, telling Howard that "ads don't work"—a bit of standard publishing dogma Howard disagreed with. Given the large, ongoing sales figures for *A People's History*, HarperCollins did change its mind, and revised editions appeared in 1995, 1998, and 1999. Howard's agent, Rick Balkin, suggested he might want to try his hand on a book about historians, but Howard didn't take to the idea.[6]

Just as it seemed a new project was unlikely, Howard got the idea of doing a memoir. At this point in his life, he'd become accustomed to success and acclaim, with many a publisher suggesting this or that idea, none of which he liked. But when he did finally come up with a possibility that excited him—he managed to complete the memoir rapidly—the widespread lack of interest in it came as a considerable surprise to him. When Rick Balkin began to send the manuscript out, he got back one rejection after another, a few rather curt and dismissive. Peter Davison of Houghton Mifflin struck a theme common to several of the turndowns: Howard "transforms his human concerns into a reductive political screed, without managing to describe his personal reactions to those around him . . . indeed, to Roz Zinn! . . . people are treated like puppets in a morality play."

Little, Brown, Simon and Schuster, and Viking Penguin rapidly followed suit. One editor, echoing Peter Davison, wrote that "there's a lot of good stuff in here, but there is also a good deal that's missing. First, the personal stuff . . . we hardly hear anything about his wife, except in passing . . . he doesn't tell us much about his children . . . everyone in the Movement was a nice guy . . . they all seem to be without a flaw, but this couldn't be . . . he seems to be holding back. . . . I can't help thinking that if Zinn weren't such a nice person he could have written a much better memoir." Rick and Howard decided to go with Beacon Press, the only publisher to express interest.

The memoir appeared in 1994. Beacon had wanted to call it *Original Zinn*, but Howard thought that title "terrible." He came up with *A Life Out of Order*, which Beacon disliked. Finally entitled *You Can't Be Neutral on a Moving Train: A Personal History of Our Times*, the book can be characterized pretty much the way Peter Davison and others did—not nearly enough of Zinn the person and already familiar political events too repetitively told. The structure of the book is also peculiar. The first two thirds proceed chronologically, but after his discussion of the Vietnam War Howard shifts to thematic chapters ("the court system," etc.), which contain some material from after 1975 but not much. The emphasis on the pre-1975 period does reflect the arc of Howard's political life, since he was most active politically during the black struggle and the protest against the war in Vietnam. After 1975 he'd remained somewhat active but not nearly to the same degree that had characterized the earlier years. The two decades that followed the end of the Vietnam War presented Howard with an ideal opportunity to tell us more about his relationships and inner feelings. But it was an opportunity he clearly did not want.

All that said, *You Can't Be Neutral* is a good read—Howard was incapable of writing an awkward sentence—and several of the book's chapters are particularly moving. Perhaps the standout is the one on Mississippi in 1963–64; the prose is lucid, lean, and emotionally eloquent: "not to believe in the possibility of dramatic change is to forget that things *have* changed, not enough, of course, but enough to show what is possible. We have been surprised before in history. We can be surprised again. Indeed, we can *do* the surprising." As one reviewer of the book remarked, Howard's "real métier [is] the popular narrative . . . novelistic . . . [and with] a burning sincerity."

At the beginning of March 1995, Howard and Roz headed off for Italy. He'd applied for a Fulbright scholarship and gotten it—at the University of Bologna. Before leaving, both studied Italian (Howard could already speak French and Spanish reasonably well). They spent three months in Bologna, with grandson Will joining them for a week. He'd already been visiting them regularly at Wellfleet, and "they always had a great time" together. As far back as when Will was still a preteen, he and Howard had formed an especially close, even unique, bond. Though Howard typically distanced himself from "messy feelings," he let Will (who later became a therapist) ask him all sorts of intimate questions about his life. Will adored and admired his grandfather and describes him as "an incredible being, an electric, unruffled presence, full of humor and 'spaciousness,'" who "knew how to have a good time." Will was also very fond of Roz, though he recognized that she was more "introverted," less gregarious, than her husband, and as she grew older she disliked much socializing and became better at saying no to it.[7]

In Bologna, all three had a "simply wonderful" vacation, though for the first two weeks Howard was quite ill with some flulike bug. They'd rented a "very nice," quiet apartment in the center of the city, the living room window looking out on "a garden with trees and old statues." Howard could walk from the apartment to work in ten minutes, and since he was required to teach for only two hours on one day a week, they had plenty of free time to wander the city and to make a number of side trips—to Venice, Florence, Siena, Turin (where Howard gave a speech), the Tuscan hills, and the Adriatic and Ligurian coasts.

Roz quickly took to Bologna, enrolled in art classes, and turned out a fair number of oils and watercolors (which Howard thought "really good"). They both found the Italians "wonderful, gracious, good-humored"—and they ate "luxuriously." Howard would often make them breakfast, and Roz, an excellent cook, made dinner for them on most nights. They took long walks through the city (the Piazza Maggiore was only ten minutes from their apartment), soaking up its sights and smells. Two outdoor markets were also nearby, and the produce led Howard to wax eloquent about the availability of "the freshest, mouthwatering fruits, vegetables, cheeses, breads, meats [and] fish." But about a month into their stay, Roz developed "sharp, piercing pains in the right ear and temple, especially during the night," and that cramped their style for a while. Then, as suddenly as it had arrived, the pain "miraculously and inexplicably disappeared," and to celebrate they hopped over to Paris for a few days.

They returned home in late May and, soon after, Howard attended a dreary-sounding conference in Boston sponsored by the National Coalition of Education Activists—dreary, that is, after the wonders of Italy. They went to Europe again in 1998, though Howard worried "about whether Roz would be up to it—she hates air travel, and foreign beds, and usually on the first day abroad she says, in the middle of the night: 'I want to go home.' But she loved this trip." Howard gave a talk on the sixties at a huge book fair in Göteborg, Sweden, where they were put up in a posh hotel and given lots of free time to wander the city. Then they spent four days in Spain, hosted by a tiny publishing house that had translated one of Howard's books. Again registered in a luxury hotel, they went to see the magnificent collections in Madrid's Prado Museum and the National Museum of Fine Arts (where they saw Picasso's *Guernica*). From there they spent a few days in Paris, visiting their old haunts, including the street market at the corner of rue de Seine and rue de Buci, from which they gathered up fruits, cheeses, and breads and had a picnic in the Luxembourg Gardens. For Roz, the nontraveler, the trip "was all rather magical."

Back home, Howard was soon absorbed in writing a new play, *Marx in Soho*. He'd had the idea for it as far back as 1991; his original draft had included Marx, his wife, Jenny, their daughter Eleanor, Friedrich Engels, and the anarchist Mikhail Bakunin. That version had a reading in Boston that Howard himself decided didn't work. Roz, always his most astute critic, urged him "to make the play more directly relevant to our time and to turn it into a one-person show." He felt she was right and came up with the idea that Marx, "in a kind of fantasy," would show up in New York City in the present day. He also rewrote the script as a one-man show, confining it to Marx himself. His intentions were multiple: to portray Marx "as a passionate, engaged revolutionary," to subject his ideas "to an anarchist critique," to show that Marx's analysis of capitalism still remains largely valid (though many have distorted and tried to discredit it by equating Marxism with Stalin's crimes), and on top of all that to show Marx "as a family man"—a very tall order.[8]

In his revision, Howard decided to put the other four characters offstage. Marx reminisces *about* them instead of letting the audience directly see and hear their interactions—the essence, most feel, of drama. Still, Howard carried off the tough assignment he'd given himself exceedingly well in the first half of *Marx in Soho*, which is full of wit and political insight. Perhaps the theme that comes across strongest is his criticism of dogma, including certain aspects of Marxism. But Howard's sympathies overall come across as more with Marx than with the anarchist Bakunin, the cogency of whose ideas is compromised by buffoonery.[9]

Unfortunately, the second half of the play is more talky, sinking too often into polemics, turning in spots into a political screed. ("The workers of all countries must unite against foreign policies which are criminal.") Howard's rich sense of humor sometimes flattens, degenerating into mere foolery. Yet many consider *Marx in Soho* the best of Howard's three plays (though Myla and Jeff prefer *Daughter of Venus*). Certainly *Marx in Soho* has been the most successful, having had several hundred staged readings and productions and having been translated into half a dozen languages. When it was done in Greek in 2009, Howard—aged eighty-seven—flew to Athens to see it.

11

Final Years

In the late 1990s, the United States was hardly the sole perpetrator of atrocities. In October 1998, the Turkish army launched another of its murderous efforts to drive the Kurds from eastern Turkey. For years the Serbs had been attempting to suppress, at the cost of many lives, ethnic Albanian rebels in Kosovo. Israel repeatedly bombed and invaded Lebanon, killing a large number of civilians. The Suharto regime in Indonesia committed a genocidal war in East Timor. And the royally despotic ruling family of Saudi Arabia routinely tortured and killed dissenters. All this went on without a peep of protest, and sometimes with enablement, from the U.S.—the aggressors, after all, were U.S. allies.[1]

What made the targets of American bombing and the invasion of selective targets reprehensible to a humanist like Howard was that they ran counter to the country's pretense that it, above all others, stood for democracy and human rights. When the United States and Great Britain launched a four-day bombing and cruise missile attack on Iraq in 1998—ostensibly for its lack of cooperation with UN inspectors and to "degrade" its alleged stockpiles of weapons of mass destruction (WMD)—Howard wasn't alone in protesting the action. Representative Cynthia McKinney may have been the lone voice in Congress to speak out against it, but France, Russia, and China—three of the five permanent members of the UN Security Council—called for lifting the eight-year-old oil embargo on Iraq, accurately denying the U.S. claim that Saddam Hussein had forced out the last of the UN inspectors. Henry Kissinger's objection to the bombings was on different grounds: they hadn't gone far enough to make "a decisive difference."

Howard presciently wrote that "there is not even certainty about the existence of such weapons in Iraq, or, if they do exist, about their location." He also pointed out that Turkey, Saudi Arabia, Indonesia, Pakistan, and China possessed weapons of mass destruction, "but we do not speak of that because they are 'friends'—either military allies or profitable markets." Howard and Roz personally knew Representative Barney Frank, and Howard wrote to him asking why he hadn't joined Cynthia McKinney in protesting the bombing of Iraq. Howard pointed out that "there is general agreement, although the Administration has ignored it, that Iraq simply does not have the delivery system to do anything with whatever it has in the way of chemical or biological weapons. It can hide those weapons, but it cannot hide delivery systems."

Barney Frank quickly responded, but not in a way that pleased Howard. Frank stated flat-out that it seemed to him "very important for the U.S. and other governments to do everything possible to force Iraq to continue to comply with the inspection," adding that the loss of civilian lives in the bombings was "inevitable." "Sorry," Howard candidly responded to Frank, but that explanation "is not satisfying." He still wanted to know why Frank believed that bombing was an appropriate solution: "Any reasonable doctrine of 'just war' requires a condition of 'proportionality' between the human cost of war and the likely result. . . . The spirit and letter of [the UN] Charter is that no one country will take it upon itself to make war on any other country, unless it is directly attacked. To legitimize the idea of preventive war is a very dangerous thing for world peace." He plaintively added, "Barney, you know better! What is going on?" Barney rather weakly replied that Saddam's case was unique because his "appetite was insatiable . . . I believe he would have invaded Saudi Arabia." Frank seems to have meant that as a conclusively decisive point, which of course it wasn't, especially when coupled with his final insistence that "the policy of threatening force worked very well here"—though the policy had been *actual* force, and it would be continued in the future without ever working "very well."

Roz and Howard went off for a month of rest—with no lecture gigs—on Long Boat Key in Florida. But when they returned, Howard found himself in more demand than ever. Matt Damon had grown up next door to the Zinns in Newton, and as both co-writer and title character of the 1998 film *Good Will Hunting* he praised *A People's History* to his therapist in the film as a book "that will knock you on your ass." Thanks to that reference, book sales "increased considerably," according to HarperCollins, and at Howard's lecture bureau, Speak Out, the phone started "ringing off the hook." Howard said that Matt was "paying me back for all the cookies we gave him when he was a kid."[2]

Among the new perks that came Howard's way was writing a regular column ("It Seems to Me") for the *Progressive*, with the perhaps secondary benefit of allowing him to justify not starting a substantial new book. In December 1998, Howard learned the additional good news that he'd been chosen to receive the 1998 Lannan Nonfiction Literary Award (Howard's friend Noam Chomsky had won the award six years earlier, along with Chet Raymo and Lawrence Weschler). It came with $75,000 and the offer of a residency at the foundation's house in the well-known arts center in Marfa, western Texas, to allow him "a period of time wholly dedicated to writing"—precisely what Howard didn't want. He accepted the award gratefully and turned down the opportunity to write in isolation in a hot small town.

Even if unsure whether or not he again wanted to devote himself to a lengthy writing project, the events of the day did continue to capture Howard's attention, and he did want to stay politically engaged. He attended a demonstration against capital punishment in Philadelphia, was part of a conference on economic justice on Cape Cod, and participated in a "labor assembly" in Lawrence, Massachusetts. He continued, as well, to cite events from the past in ways that would be "a part of social struggle" and would inspire optimism for the future. In one of the many interviews he gave, he said that his goal had always been to look at history from "the point of view of people who have not had a voice, people who have been oppressed, and people whose struggles have not been noticed."

In one of his short pieces, he wrote: "People in power seem invulnerable, but they are in fact quite vulnerable. Their power depends on the obedience of others. . . . Don't look for a moment of total triumph. See it as an ongoing struggle, with victories and defeats." For such exhortations, of course, some historians would, in a conservative era, continue to dismiss him for writing "shoddy, ideologically distorted history." The well-known historian Eugene Genovese, for one, told a reporter that "Zinn's ideology slants the facts . . . it basically transforms history into a good guys–bad guys view of the world." To which Howard indirectly responded in one of his first columns for the *Progressive*, "I would not have become a historian if I thought that it would become my professional duty to never emerge from the past, to study long-gone events and remember them only for their uniqueness, not connecting them to events going on in my time."[3]

Much of Howard's—and the world's—attention in 1998–1999 was focused on the Serbia-Kosovo conflict in the Balkans. Yugoslavia, a federation of six republics and two autonomous provinces (one of which was Kosovo), had collapsed along ethnic lines in 1992. Almost immediately, the Serbs launched what became a nearly four-year seige of the predominantly Bosnian city of Sarajevo, finally broken early in 1996 by NATO air strikes. The complex events that followed are much contested, but most agree that hostility between Serbia and the dominant population of ethnic Albanians in Kosovo was at the core of the next stage of the conflict. Howard, often more critical of his own country than others—and often rightly so—blamed the Clinton administration for the many lives subsequently lost. And, again with reason, though the United States probably bears no more of the responsibility than do the Serbs and the Kosovo Liberation Army.

What happened, in brief, was that the dominant ethnic Albanians in Kosovo declared their independence from Serbia. When the Serbs rejected the notion of an independent Kosovo, the Kosovo Liberation Army (KLA) in 1998 turned to armed struggle and began to wage guerrilla attacks on Serbian targets. The Serbs responded brutally, and a spiral of violence followed. The United States blamed the Serbs alone and declared its opposition to Serbia's attempt to put down what it called the "insurgency"—but confusedly, the U.S. also announced that it opposed Albanian demands for independence, thus thoroughly muddying the waters. An attempt at a cease-fire was rejected by the KLA, and it was back to the pattern of KLA attacks and, under Slobodan Milošević, Serbian reprisals.

The U.S. simultaneously established diplomatic channels to the KLA and led a successful campaign for NATO intervention—thus again opening itself to charges of inconsistency. With scant attempt at diplomacy NATO, in March 1999, began a series of air strikes—ultimately thirty-one thousand over seventy-eight days, killing four times as many civilians (both Serbian and Albanian) as soldiers. Fear of the increasing casualties led to the Rambouillet negotiations. The United States and its allies in the West pushed through an agreement, but both the Serbs and the KLA refused to sign it. The *New York Times* reported that the Clinton team, led by Secretary of State Madeleine Albright, was "flabbergasted" at the rejection. But it should not have been, given its mixed signals to the warring parties. The U.S. finally got the KLA to accept the Rambouillet pact by declaring that NATO would otherwise be unable to justify the bombing of Serbia—hardly an impartial stance, for the administration made no comparable approach to Serbia, merely giving it an ultimatum. When Belgrade continued to reject Rambouillet, the air war against Serbia began. As it had throughout, the United States and its creature NATO seriously miscalculated.

At this point, in a column for the *Progressive*, Howard—acknowledging that the Serbs had committed atrocities—wrote that the KLA was "ruthlessly putting its countrymen at risk," even though "a protracted nonviolent campaign of resistance" existed in both Serbia and Kosovo. He reminded his readers that back in 1995, the West had stood apart when the Serbs massacred seven thousand Bosnian men in areas that the UN had declared "safe zones." Why was it not standing apart now? He argued that instead of siding with the KLA and bombing Serbia, NATO should have sided with the groups favoring nonviolent resistance.

All that the bombings accomplished was to goad Serbia to apply to Kosovo the ethnic cleansing tactics it had earlier used in Bosnia, and the Serbs forcibly expelled ethnic Albanians from Kosovo. President Clinton insisted that the NATO bombings had prevented genocide, and then turned around and accused the Serbs of exactly that. The NATO bombings had killed fifteen hundred civilians. "There is no way you can avoid killing non-military people," Howard wrote, "when you drop bombs." As he'd often argued, a cause may be good (like toppling Hitler), but there's no such thing as a good war: "The strike is a much more powerful weapon than the guerrilla attack." He acknowledged that "it's hard to argue against those who take up arms against a brutal terrorist regime, but they have to be very careful to avoid indiscriminate violence and thereby lose the people they are trying to help." Yes, but that old chestnut had never been resolved: could "discriminate" violence have brought down a Hitler?

Alternating his attention to the Balkans with the situation in Iraq, Howard, along with Noam Chomsky and the cultural critic and author of *Orientalism* Edward Said, in April 1999 issued a declaration on the Internet calling for the end of the U.S. economic sanctions against Iraq, which were killing more than four thousand children under the age of five each month. "This is not foreign policy," the statement read, "it is sanctioned mass-murder that is nearing holocaust proportions. If we remain silent, we are condoning a genocide that is being perpetrated in the name of peace in the Middle East, a mass slaughter that is being perpetrated in our name." The declaration in part blamed the media—which as usual had run the stars and stripes up the flagpole—for creating a virtual embargo on news of the tragic number of deaths that were resulting from American policy.[4]

CNN finally did air a prime-time special about the situation in Iraq, but the largest portion was devoted to promoting a one-sided case for bombing the country. When President Clinton justified the escalating air war against Iraq, he acknowledged that other countries had stockpiles of weapons of mass destruction but insisted that Iraq alone had used them. To Howard, that was an outrageous distortion. Had Clinton forgotten about Hiroshima and Nagasaki? Did he, like most Americans, obliterate the past so fully that the fact that the United States had killed millions of people in Korea and Vietnam no longer registered? Howard didn't doubt that Saddam Hussein was evil, but he insisted that he did not represent a "clear and present danger" to world peace.

Diane Wachtell of The New Press came up with the idea for a series of short books, to be written by various hands, to carry forward the idea behind *A People's History* of giving voice to "common people and to economic struggles usually left out of standard history texts." The series would cover various time periods in American history— *A People's History of the Civil War* and so forth. Howard agreed to serve as the series' "adviser," but he was very clear about the limited extent of his commitment: he would be happy to advise and consult on topics and writers but would not read or edit manuscripts, though he'd consider—not promise—writing brief introductions. Within the year, the first book in the series appeared: Ray Raphael's *A People's History of the American Revolution*. Howard thought Raphael had "done a superb job. . . . I believe it is the best single-volume history of the Revolution I have read."[5]

The floodgates were open. Throughout the decade that followed, several other small, left-wing publishing houses—Seven Stories, Charta, Paradigm, Common Courage, South End, and City Lights—issued short books that excerpted material from Howard's writings—articles, pamphlets, lectures, reviews—of the past thirty-five years. Sleek and brief, they attracted fans from various phases of Howard's now well-known career, even if their titles were usually more consequential than their contents—*Just War*, *The Bomb*, *Uncommon Sense*, *A Power Governments Cannot Suppress*, and *Artists in Times of War*. To a significant degree, the downpour had been prefigured by the success in 1997 of Seven Stories' *The Zinn Reader*, a much larger collection of reprints that by selling well had spawned this proliferating breed of reproductions. Howard took some pleasure, of course, in seeing his out-of-the-way, out-of-print work again made available.

The Zinn Reader was an ambitious (746 pages) compilation of short essays Howard had written over the years. He himself put in considerable work on the book. Dan Simon, the Seven Stories publisher, remembers his shock when, after many editorial conversations (with all final decisions left to Howard), "several hundred little bundles," each with a paper clip and a neatly typed one-paragraph introduction attached, came in the mail one day. The shock resulted from Dan's expectation that at this stage in his life Howard would supply "something sloppily presented," which many other, younger hands would convert into a finished product.

After the happy experience with the *Reader*, Dan suggested that Howard start work on "A People's Economics," but Howard didn't feel he was the right person for that topic and turned it down. He suggested instead that they take primary sources—speeches, letters, newspapers, debates, and the like, such as those previously mentioned in *A People's History*—and make a separate book of them (which would appear in 2004 under the title *Voices of a People's History*). But this time around, Howard made it clear that he wasn't prepared to take on the role as sole editor or to do the bulk of the work.

Initially, Dan hit on the idea of sending one of his editors off to the library several days a week to locate possible sources, with Howard then making final choices as to what to include. But the editor produced so much material that Howard balked at reviewing it all, and the entire project ground to a halt. For several years it remained dormant. But then Dan came up with the idea of hiring Anthony Arnove, a young writer, editor, and activist who'd been a member of the Boston-based publishing collective South End, as a possible co-editor. Howard and Anthony had met back in 1998 and worked well together on the publication of *Marx in Soho*.

Arnove accepted the offer, and the two began to talk on the phone about the project nearly every day, eventually becoming good friends. Anthony and Dan agree that Howard shared fully in the collaboration. "It was Howard himself," according to Dan, who "led the charge, championing certain texts, telling us to discard others, effortlessly agreeing with or overriding" suggestions made by the others. As Anthony has put it, Howard "worked like a dog on this for the next year." By February 2003, enough material had been agreed upon to hold a reading at the 92nd Street Y, with Patti Smith, Kurt Vonnegut, Danny Glover, and Marisa Tomei, among others, contributing their talents. By the following year, not only was the *Voices* project completed but Anthony did a series of interviews with Howard following the 9/11 attacks on the World Trade Center that were separately published—two years before *Voices* came out—as *Terrorism and War*.

The only glitch came over money. Some of the small publishers who turned out these assorted collections of Howard's work were reluctant to pay him his earned royalties, causing him and his agent, Rick Balkin, some grief. But Howard wasn't one to brood about such matters, especially as he was sensitive to the difficulties any left-wing press faced in trying to survive. Besides, Howard's main attention was focused, as always, on current political events.

The presidential election in the year 2000 particularly exercised him. "There came a rare amusing moment in this Presidential race," he wrote in the *Progressive*, "when George W. Bush (who has raised $177 million) accused Al Gore (who has raised only $126 million)" of appealing to "class warfare." Neither our leaders nor our textbooks are allowed to talk about class; when, like Bush, they slip, they invariably misapply the term. They *are* allowed to speak of our "national" interests, as if matters like war were in *all* our interests.

At election time, Gore received hundreds of thousands more votes than Bush, yet the electoral count was close, with Florida the pivotal state. The voting there had seemed tainted; in many districts where blacks were in a majority and had for many decades voted Democratic, their ballots had been mostly disqualified. Katherine Harris, a Republican and Florida's secretary of state, rushed through an incomplete recount that made Bush the winner by 537 votes. With Gore ready to challenge the results, the Republicans took their case to the Supreme Court, where a 5–4 decision—the five had all been Republican appointees—forbade the recounting to continue, thereby handing George W. Bush victory. To many, the result seemed a calculated fraud.

Once installed as president, Bush immediately put his conservative, probusiness agenda into play. He increased the military budget and decreased spending on social services and environmental issues (giving in to the fossil fuel lobby, he refused to support any cut in power plant emissions).

Nine months into Bush's presidency, two hijacked jets slammed into the World Trade Center towers, killing some three thousand people. Another hit the Pentagon and a fourth crashed near Shanksville, Pennsylvania, killing all on board, after the passengers had succeeded in foiling the hijackers. Bush immediately declared a "war on terror," and Congress all but unanimously (Barbara Lee in the House was the sole vote against) gave Bush the power to proceed with any military action he thought appropriate. Assuming (wrongly) that Saddam Hussein and al-Qaeda had been in cahoots in the attacks, Bush promptly ordered the bombing of Afghanistan, where bin Laden was thought to be hiding. Five months later, with the bombing still in progress, Bush announced that "we are winning the war on terror." He and his advisers were apparently oblivious to the considerable historical evidence that terror produces terror.[6]

Howard was appalled that Bush, having lost the popular vote in 2000, could proceed with such a deadly combination of arrogance and ignorance. "My feeling," he wrote, "is that we're living in an occupied country . . . that a junta has taken power and now the problem for the American people is to do what people do in an occupied country." He wasn't suggesting that everybody should buy a gun, though he did maintain his faith that "the public is ahead of both major parties"—a dubious assumption at the time. Whenever the United States goes to war, the country responds, at least initially, with a knee-jerk burst of patriotism. The dominant public view is that the United States always takes the high moral ground and that since our leaders have greater access to information than the average person does and therefore must have made sound judgments, the duty of the citizenry is to support them.

Perhaps a few trembled in their allegiance when Bush announced that he planned both to build a massive missile defense system and to develop a new generation of nuclear weapons. During the presidential campaign, he'd suggested that the nation's current arsenal of 7,500 strategic warheads was overkill, that they needed to be taken off of high-alert status and reduced to 2,500. But the campaign was over, and Bush's natural belligerence once again surfaced.

In thus backtracking, Bush was no different from his predecessor Bill Clinton. Once *his* campaign was over, Clinton had resisted all efforts to reduce carbon dioxide in the air and arsenic in the water; further, he made no effort to encourage the auto industry to produce cars with better fuel-efficiency standards. Clinton had strategically waited until the very last days of his presidency to sign various resolutions to improve the environment and provide safer working conditions. Bush, predictably, overturned every single one of the last-minute regulations. But Clinton and his administration were on record as having made the attempt to liberalize policy, his "legacy" enhanced.

Bush's attack on Afghanistan had done nothing to weaken terrorism; if anything, the anger it sowed throughout the Middle East increased the number of jihadists. Undaunted, Bush and his close advisers Dick Cheney, Donald Rumsfeld, and Condoleezza Rice began to spread the word that Iraq was a growing menace to the United States, accusing Saddam of hiding weapons of mass destruction and secretly planning to build nuclear arms. The following year Bush upped the ante. He claimed that the International Atomic Energy Agency had issued a report showing that Saddam was only months away from having nuclear weapons. "I don't know what more evidence we need," Bush said. The answer was "a lot more"—the Atomic Energy Agency had said no such thing.[7]

Saddam had undoubtedly committed many atrocities, including the use of chemical weapons to kill some five thousand Kurds. But given the fact that Iraq had been devastated by wars against Kuwait and Iran (the United States had *supported* Saddam in the Iran war), as well as by U.S. economic sanctions, Howard believed that the real animus against Iraq grew from the fear that its oil reserves (second only to Saudi Arabia's) might not be available to the U.S. in the future. Oil had dominated U.S. policy in the Middle East for fifty years, and even during the "liberal" Carter administration, the president had bluntly declared that the United States would continue to defend its interest in Middle Eastern oil "by any means necessary, including military force."

But the UN Security Council refused to support the U.S. war against Iraq—even after Colin Powell gave a notorious speech at the UN that claimed, falsely, that Iraq was already in possession of "weapons of mass destruction." Despite worldwide protests, the immovable Bushites, having been brought up always to expect "yes," stomped their feet and early in 2003 launched a massive attack on Iraq, daring to call it Operation Iraqi Freedom. Within a few years, hundreds of thousands of Iraqis would die, along with forty-five hundred American soldiers, yet Congress continued to pass military budgets that soon topped half a trillion dollars—the largest in history. Military contracts brought huge profits for U.S. corporations and their executives, while cuts were made in many social justice programs, including health care and education.

CBS news anchor Dan Rather echoed on TV the sentiments of many: "Bush is my president. When he says get into line, I get into line." Yet the country was beginning to awaken to the needless horror of the war. The veteran journalist Helen Thomas asked a critical question: "Where is the opposition in the opposition party?" Well she might ask; in 2002 a number of prominent people on the left (including Richard Falk and Christopher Hitchens) supported Bush's war, and although many pockets of resistance were beginning to form, Howard expressed disappointment initially at the limited opposition, even as he remained confident that protest would grow.

"I do believe," he eloquently wrote early in 2002, "that if people could see the consequences of the bombing campaign as vividly as we were all confronted with the horrifying photos in the wake of September 11, if they saw on television night after night the blinded and maimed children, the weeping parents . . . they might ask: Is this the way to combat terrorism? Surely it is time, half a century after Hiroshima, to embrace a universal morality, to think of all children, everywhere, as our own."

Howard was tireless in his opposition, traveling the country to give speeches denouncing the war and writing a number of columns in sickened protest against the ongoing killing and destruction. "We need new ways of thinking," he wrote in one. "We need to stop sending weapons to countries that oppress other people or their own people. We need to decide that we will not go to war, whatever reason is conjured up by the politicians, because war in our time is always indiscriminate, a war against innocents, a war against children. . . . Our first thoughts should be not of vengeance, but of compassion, not of violence, but of healing." In another piece Howard put it even more bluntly: "war is itself the most extreme form of terrorism." He added a quote from a CIA senior analyst of terrorism that "U.S. policies are completing the radicalization of the Islamic world."

The Bush administration would have none of it. To counteract such sentiments, the president, acting on "intelligence" that was flawed or outright wrong, issued a number of false statements in defense of U.S. policy in Iraq. He claimed that Saddam "has a growing fleet of manned or unmanned aerial vehicles [UAVs] that could be used to disperse chemical or biological weapons" and was working on unmanned UAVs "for missions targeting the United States," failing to mention that no drone can fly the six thousand miles to the U.S. coast. Similarly, Colin Powell told the UN Security Council that by conservative estimates Iraq had a stockpile "of between 100 and 500 tons of chemical weapons. That is, enough to fill 16,000 battlefield rockets." A frightening estimate when presented as fact, but in truth not a single shred of such a stockpile was ever found. Nothing daunted, Bush in 2003 made the flat-out assertion that "a biological laboratory has been found in Iraq." It turned out to be two trailer trucks used to fill weather balloons.[8]

Bush had used September 11 to justify his belligerent foreign policies of bombing Afghanistan and declaring a "war on terrorism." Were there no alternatives? Howard thought so. He deplored, of course, the 2001 attack and the "enormous grief and suffering" it had caused, but he also thought that Bush had chosen exactly the wrong set of responses. He believed that "terrorism does not stem from any one country that you can then make war on. Terrorism comes from many, many different sources. . . . There are tens of thousands of trained terrorists around the world and terrorists in at least a dozen countries . . . in bombing Afghanistan . . . we picked out this ravaged land . . . a spot on earth which we could bomb with impunity."

As far back as 1997, the Defense Science Board had issued a report that showed "a strong correlation between U.S. involvement in international situations and an increase in terrorist attacks against the United States." But Bush preferred his own experts, who assured him that tearing apart people's bodies was the sure way to defeat our enemies. If Bush wanted to do something effective about terrorism, Howard suggested that he deal with the roots of it—namely, "the grievances that huge numbers of people in various parts of the world . . . feel against the foreign policy of the United States."

Howard felt that the media, by parroting the administration's line and minimizing coverage of the horrors that bombing had caused, were complicit in keeping the public uninformed. Eight countries in the world had nuclear weapons (as Iraq did not), but there was no talk of waging war against any of them—perhaps, Howard suggested, because they lacked huge oil reserves essential to the American economy. To make sure that the oil kept flowing, the U.S. government was spending a billion dollars a day—which would go higher, making companies like Boeing and General Dynamics huge profits, while the needs of the poor went unattended and the moral corruption of our own soldiers, forced to kill and maim, continued unchecked. In 2002 Bush's approval rating stood at 75 percent, though by 2005 it was 50 percent.

In the fall of 2002, an episode on the hugely successful TV series *The Sopranos* depicted Tony Soprano's son reading a copy of *A People's History* and telling his father that Columbus murdered and tortured Indians. Tony—Italian, of course—is outraged, and a family conflict ensues, ending with Tony yelling that he doesn't care what his son's teacher or his book says, "To me, Columbus will always be a hero." The episode led to a large surge in book sales (it passed the million mark in 2002). Rupert Murdoch's Fox network had optioned *A People's History* for a miniseries on TV three or four years earlier, but before long Fox dropped the project—Murdoch must have realized what the book actually said.

The bolder HBO (owned by AOL–Time Warner) was quick to pick up the option. Yet after commissioning three scripts (from Howard Fast, John Sayles, and the Scottish writer Paul Laverty), HBO soon backed out too. A lull followed. To celebrate having passed the million-copies mark, Howard and Anthony Arnove put on an evening of readings early in 2003 at the 92nd Street Y in Manhattan and subsequently other performances around the country. The gilded cast included several who would ultimately be in the final production: Danny Glover, Marisa Tomei, etc. But it would take five more years to successfully execute the project.[9]

The previous year, 2001, had seen the publication of *Three Strikes*, with Howard, Dana Frank, and Robin D.G. Kelley each contributing one of the short book's three essays. The collection was designed to pay tribute to labor's combative spirit in the past, to inspire its revival, and to fill in the shameful absence from most history textbooks of instances of the working class fighting back against the combined power of industry and government. Howard chose to write about the Colorado Coal Strike of 1913–14, which ended in the Ludlow Massacre, the subject of his 1952 MA thesis and one of the most dramatic instances of class conflict in labor's history. He retooled his treatment of it for *Three Strikes*.[10]

The late nineteenth and early twentieth centuries were a time when the working class was more militant and large-scale strikes far more frequent than in 2002. Howard's essay wasn't particularly analytic, but it was dramatic and moving—probably just as he intended, knowing as he did that the public memory needed to be viscerally reawakened if the current plight of unskilled workers and the union movement itself were once more to become the focus of concern. Howard did vividly evoke the squalid conditions of the Colorado mining camps and the pitiless hazards of working in the mines (owned by John D. Rockefeller Sr.'s Colorado Fuel and Iron Corporation) that led to the walkout of eleven thousand miners, about 90 percent of the total. They gathered into the Ludlow colony, where they threw up makeshift tents that provided scant protection from the deep mud and the snow that began to fall.

The violence between miners and representatives of the corporation began almost immediately—a matter of rifles against machine guns. The governor of Colorado soon began to arrest strikers and also sent in the Colorado National Guard, which quickly laid siege to Ludlow. Government and business leaders joined hands, as they typically did, and a reign of terror followed. Over the course of the strike, hundreds were killed by machine-gun fire into the tents. Then, on April 20, 1914, the soldiers drove the strikers from the encampment in a daylong battle and set fire to the tents, under one of which two women and eleven children were burned alive.

The miners sent out a call to arms to other nearby mining camps, and throughout the country hundreds of mass meetings were held to protest the slaughter. The Colorado governor asked President Wilson to send in federal troops, a request he quickly heeded. With that, the fighting ended. Predictably, a Colorado investigating committee exonerated the National Guardsmen. The strikers weren't so fortunate: several were tried for murder and convicted. As for the lesson learned, Howard as usual chose to emphasize the positive: "We are inspired by those ordinary men and women who persist, with extraordinary courage, in their resistance to overwhelming power."

Another of his short books, *Artists in Times of War*, came out in 2003, and then in 2004, Howard and Anthony Arnove edited the anthology *Voices of a People's History of the United States*. Howard had sounded most of the themes in *Artists* a number of times before. After all, he was now eighty-one years of age, and it's the rare octogenarian who can find new ways to say new things. He focused on activists and writers who'd challenged authority—Dalton Trumbo, Langston Hughes, Joseph Heller, Kurt Vonnegut (who was a friend), though he'd periodically slide off into a familiar minilecture on, say, Emma Goldman and the Haymarket affair, Kosovo, or the immorality of bombing Afghanistan and Iraq. Nowhere in the hundred-page booklet did Howard offer his definition of *artist*— possibly because too many of his long asides would fail to qualify. He was at that stage of life when he'd many times over earned the right to dwell on some of his favorite topics, even if the reader might puzzle over their relationship to the subject at hand.

As for *Voices*, it was the opposite of slim, running as it did to 650 pages. The emphasis, once again, was on those voices from the past that had been largely shut out from standard histories—which is to say, public memory. During his own education, Howard had never heard the name Emma Goldman until after he completed his doctorate in history. Nor had he heard about the 1637 massacre of six hundred men, women and children of the Pequot tribe in New England, nor the slaughter of black people in St. Louis in 1917 during the so-called Progressive Era. *Voices* is a rich, varied selection of materials documenting the stories and struggles of American outsiders. Both comprehensive (it runs from Columbus to George W. Bush) and moving, it got an excellent critical reception and sold well.

Through all these years, Howard had remained committed to prison reform and had continued to correspond and occasionally visit (Roz sometimes accompanying him) several individual prisoners. In contrast to most of western Europe, which had eased the length of sentences and ended execution, in the United States building prisons had become a growth industry, the number of people incarcerated (especially among juveniles and blacks) had skyrocketed, and executions—briefly banned by the Supreme Court in 1972—had also soared. Back in 1996, Howard had participated in the meeting that had launched the Campaign to End the Death Penalty, and in December 2009, when he was eighty-six, he keynoted in Chicago the campaign's annual convention.[11]

He began, "I don't trust the government. I don't trust the judicial system. I don't trust district attorneys. I don't trust judges. And so, why should I accept any judgment they make against a human being?" And that was just for starters. Howard went on to underscore the fact that people put in prisons were "mostly poor; they're people of color; they're troublemakers politically." He then talked about the prisoners he'd corresponded with for years, "magnificent people" all. "Somewhere back there maybe they did something, maybe they didn't . . . when they were 18 years old." Howard was particularly close to Kevin Hicks, an African American man who'd been involved in a shoot-out when he was a teenager. In prison he taught himself to read and had written novels, plays, and an autobiography, all of which he'd sent to Howard. "My God," Howard thought, "they're keeping this guy in prison, and there are all these idiots up there in high office.'"

Howard wrote to and visited another of his prison friends, Tiyo Attallah Salah-El, for twenty-five years. Tiyo had organized a campaign within his own prison against incarceration and had also written an autobiography. An impressed Howard took the manuscript to his brother Jerry, who was a typographer, and Jerry—free of charge—converted it into a disc, formatted it, and sent it off to iUniverse for publication. Howard paid for the incidental expenses, like binding the finished books. Tiyo was thrilled, but he was incarcerated, alas, in a Dallas maximum security prison, which didn't allow prisoners to receive books, let alone write them.

When still a mere eighty-one, Howard continued to speak widely against the Iraq War; in the single month of November 2003, he conducted no fewer than seven teach-ins—traveling as far as Miami and California. Everywhere he spoke, Howard reiterated his core theme: war is terrorism. Negotiations, not war, had "solved the problem of the hostages in Iran" back in 1979. "We've drawn a line around this little country [Iraq] in the Middle East and said, 'This is where all evil reposes.'" He reminded people that "the history of military occupations of Third World countries is that they bring neither democracy nor security."

Howard also went (with Anthony Arnove and grandson Will) to Cuba and then later, with Roz, to Paris in order to collect the Les Amis du Monde Diplomatique prize he'd been awarded. The trip to Cuba in 2004 was for the book launch during the Havana book fair of the Cuban edition of *A People's History*, and to attend the opening of his play *Marx in Soho*. It was Howard's second trip to Cuba, and it proved tumultuous. At the book launch, people fought so loudly over the chance to buy the book that Howard's brief speech (in which he lauded the revolution's achievements in literacy, education, and health) was partly drowned out. To top off the visit, Havana University surprised him with an honorary degree for "Historical Sciences."[12]

During the presidential campaign of 2004, John Kerry, the Democratic candidate (Howard had preferred John Edwards), failed to oppose the war in Iraq. He spoke instead of doing a better job than Bush had done in waging it—more U.S. troops and bigger contributions from the other nations in the so-called coalition. Howard decided to write an open letter and send it directly to Kerry, who he'd met years earlier. If Kerry really wanted to defeat Bush, Howard suggested, he had to use his "trump card" and come out against the war (as he previously had in regard to Vietnam).

In response to Kerry's statement that "we can't leave a vacuum" in Iraq, Howard forcefully reminded him that the Iraqi people would still be there "and will have to work things out themselves, but without an American army bombing and shooting and imprisoning them by the thousands." Let our military presence "be replaced by an international group, including people from the Arab countries, of peacekeepers and negotiators." He acknowledged that such a group wouldn't easily be formed and that the bottom line was that we couldn't be certain what would happen if the U.S. left. "What is certain," he added, was that "our presence is a disaster, for the Iraqis, for us."[13]

Kerry ignored Howard's letter, but in a series of hard-hitting columns for the *Progressive* Howard continued to argue against the war. "Those who died in this war," Howard wrote, "did not die for their country. They died for their government. . . . They died to cover up the theft of the nation's wealth to pay for the machines of death." The common argument that we had to "stay the course" was the same one used to prolong the war in Vietnam—and by the time we were finally defeated there 58,000 Americans and 3 million Vietnamese had lost their lives.

Going back still further in history, Howard tried to remind people that the U.S. occupations of the Philippines, Haiti, and the Dominican Republic (to name but three) had led not to democracy but to military dictatorships. It saddened him that in 2004 the American public still supported Bush and his policies. He blamed the media for not making clear the "human consequences of the war" and the Democrats and their candidate John Kerry for failing to provide counterarguments for withdrawal. Howard, as well as Noam Chomsky, decided to vote for Ralph Nader. Bush slid in with 51 percent of the votes cast.

In another of his columns for the *Progressive*, Howard wrote that "the definition of fanaticism is that when you discover you are going in the wrong direction, you redouble your speed." He called for the United States to leave Iraq and for an international team of negotiators, largely Arab, to "work out a federalist compromise to give some autonomy to each group" (Sunnis, Shiites, and Kurds). But before that could begin, the U.S. had to withdraw. Howard and Noam Chomsky tended to agree politically about everything—but withdrawal proved the exception. When they spent an evening together in June 2005, Noam said that he never told "my audiences that we should leave." To which Howard replied, "I always tell my audiences we should leave Iraq."

What followed, in Howard's words, was "probably the only time Noam and I have ever disagreed so strongly." Noam kept repeating that we couldn't "leave the Iraqis to the mercy of these gangs," and Howard would go only as far as agreeing that "we must leave a force there, and U.S. troops must be the main part of that, but under UN command." He also agreed that the United States must help Iraq after the war—but not with military aid. Noam then argued that it wasn't "clear that Iraqis don't want us there," though a recent poll had shown that 82 percent of Iraqis wanted us gone. Noam challenged the poll's "reliability." Howard, who rarely criticized anyone, described Noam as being "on Mt. Olympus"; when thus ensconced, as Howard put it, he could be "ferocious and intimidating."[14]

Howard and Roz decided to return to Spelman College, where Howard had been invited to deliver the commencement address. It had been more than fifty years since he'd been fired, and very few of the people they'd known were still there (Dr. Beverly Tatum was the current president). Still, they greatly enjoyed the visit, and Howard gave the graduates an inspirational speech. He told them not to be discouraged at the way the world looked at the moment, recalling for them the 1950s and 1960s, when the consensus was that the white South would never tolerate changing its position on segregation. But it had, even if incompletely, and Howard predictably gave the credit to "ordinary people [who] organized and took risks and challenged the system and would not give up." He added, "those years at Spelman were the most exciting of my life, the most educational certainly." The current generation, he emphasized, had to "demand an end to war . . . [and] wipe out the national boundaries that separate us from other human beings on this earth."[15]

He also devoted one of his *Progressive* columns to nationalism, calling it "one of the great evils of our time." He felt there hadn't been any significant protests around the issue because "our citizenry has been brought up to see our nation as different from others, an exception in the world, uniquely moral, expanding into other lands in order to bring civilization, liberty, democracy." An explanation that was on the mark, but perhaps Howard was being too confident in predicting that a "citizens protest movement" would arise bearing the antinationalism banner. The belief in the moral uniqueness of the United States was so profoundly ingrained in its citizens that it helped to sustain our belligerent foreign policies on the grounds that the wickedness of other countries was the root cause. The country could be massively aroused against government policies only when enough body bags had arrived home and when the lies of the administration had reached a deafening crescendo.

Gino Strada, the Italian doctor who'd spent the last fifteen years operating on war victims around the world, wrote a book about his experiences, *Green Parrots* (the reference is to a certain kind of land mine with little wings designed to entice children to pick them up, thinking them toys). Strada's book had become a best seller in Europe and, for the English edition, he asked Howard (who he already knew) to write the introduction. Howard did, and when the English-language version came out Strada invited Howard and Roz to spend a week in Italy at his expense.

They accepted and had a wonderful time. He and Strada spoke to some twelve hundred people in Rome's new municipal auditorium, but that was the sole public engagement. Most of the time, Roz and Howard were free to roam a city they loved, to visit art museums and stumble into a series of wonderful trattorias. When the week was over, they flew home and almost immediately went to the Cape Cod house they co-owned with Pat and Henry West but occupied at different time periods. The Zinns had the place to themselves for July and part of September. "Life is too full (but wonderful)," Roz wrote Frances Piven. She was now deeply into painting, and the results pleased her more and more. In September 2006, she had a showing at the Wellfleet Public Library, and it was well received. As for Howard, at age eighty-three, he still played tennis and rode his bike, wrote his monthly *Progressive* column and gracious introductions to the books his friends and political allies produced—and in his spare time set about organizing a worldwide petition denouncing war.[16]

On August 3, Human Rights Watch announced that the Bush administration "appears poised to resume the production of anti-personnel mines," for the first time since 1997. Howard was appalled. The U.S. already had a stockpile of some 10 million mines yet had refused to sign an international treaty banning them, the administration explaining that "the terms would have required us to give up a needed military capability." Since the early 1990s, forty mine-producing countries had stopped making them, reducing annual casualty rates (especially among children) from 26,000 to somewhere around 17,500—still quite enough to leave a legion of people without arms, legs, or eyes. The cynical military phrase "inevitable collateral damage" reduced such people to the category of garbage disposal.

In mid-2006, neither Roz nor Howard felt particularly well. They were both eighty-three, and some aches and pains were to be expected—though Howard had been remarkably healthy throughout his life. He now got "miserably sick" for a few days with stomach problems and also developed a hematoma on his leg, which took the doctors somewhat longer to get under control. Roz had a worse time of it. She and Howard were three fourths of the way up the escalator at a railroad station when they heard screams from below. "Some old guy (probably younger than us!)," as Howard later described it to Pat and Henry West, had fallen on the escalator. Roz instinctively turned to help—and she also fell. Howard managed to pull her up and off the escalator as it reached the top, but "she had cuts, bruises and bleeding all over her legs, arm, hip." An ambulance was called, and they spent three hours in the emergency room at the Newton-Wellesley hospital, with Howard reading to her the entire time.[17]

They went out to the Cape Cod house to recuperate but after a few days had to return home because Roz felt unwell (though they did make it to Dan Berrigan's eighty-fifth birthday celebration). But home didn't help. Roz couldn't sleep and had severe back and upper chest pain. Her doctor ordered X-rays and found "muscle-nerve problems" centered in her spine. He gave her a painkiller and scheduled a CAT scan for the following week. She felt considerably better by August 2006 and thought she'd accompany Howard to Vienna—though in the upshot she didn't feel up to it—where he and David Barsamian (the founder and director of Alternative Radio) were to do two performances with the celebrated Kronos string quartet. (Howard and David talked together, unscripted, about war and related topics for four minutes on one side of the stage, and then the quartet played for four minutes on the other, the pattern repeated a number of times.) Returning home, Howard found Roz still in considerable pain. But it would be another six months before a firm diagnosis would finally be made.

A long-dormant idea of a TV series based on *A People's History* and including material from *Voices of a People's History* awoke from its slumber in mid-2006. Back in 2003, Chris Moore (producer of *Good Will Hunting*) had seen one of the readings from *A People's History* that Howard and Anthony Arnove had put on and told Howard that they should do the project independently as a feature-length documentary. He agreed, and they then brought Arnove on board. Later, Josh Brolin and Matt Damon joined up as co–executive producers. A number of stars including Danny Glover, Viggo Mortensen, Matt Damon, David Strathairn, and Marisa Tomei also made firm commitments to participate once the production finally got rolling in 2007. Called *The People Speak*, the documentary was taped live in January 2008 at the Cutler Majestic Theatre in Boston (Morgan Freeman, Don Cheadle, Bruce Springsteen, and Bob Dylan later joined the cast). Additional shoots, in which Howard participated, were done in California, Toronto, and at Springsteen's home recording studio in New Jersey.

Howard thoroughly enjoyed the process; he loved "the affection, the teamwork and the camaraderie—it becomes less a cast than a social movement, like people on a picket line together. That's the spirit we felt backstage." Indeed, at one of the 2003 performances,

Arnove had had to tell the sound technicians to turn off Howard's microphone during the rehearsals and readings because his "grunts of pleasure" were being picked up on the tapes. *The People Speak* ultimately premiered on November 19, 2009, at Jazz at Lincoln Center, and then on the History Channel, with 9 million people watching, on December 13, 2009.[18]

Roz was in the audience throughout the taping, but it couldn't have been easy for her. She'd by now gotten her diagnosis, and it was terrible—ovarian cancer, for which the survival rate was notoriously low. Her doctors were divided about treatment: drastic surgery followed by months of recuperation, followed by five months of chemotherapy, or chemotherapy without the surgery. Roz rejected both options. She wanted to live her last days—and no doctor would venture a guess as to how long she had—"normally" and in peace. Howard reported to Noam and Carol Chomsky that "she is in good spirits, has no pain, some discomfort, gets tired easily." Roz was open to reevaluating her decision about treatment, though in the upshot she didn't.

Once *The People Speak* was behind him (it was released in 2010 as a DVD), Howard canceled all appointments to lecture, attend meetings, give interviews—or even to go out at night. He and Roz were able to spend seven weeks on the Cape in the summer of 2007 ("the best summer of my life," Roz declared). Howard did all the shopping, and Jeff's wife, Crystal, would bring additional food down from time to time. Roz went swimming every day, and when the tide was right she and Howard would go digging for oysters. They hoped to do the same during the following summer, but by the end of the year Roz had taken a turn for the worse.

By January 2008, never a whiner, she understatedly wrote Pat West that she was "not at my best." She'd developed "an itch which is malignancy-connected, in the torso section of my body, which drives me up the wall. Who knows," she spiritedly added, "miracles can happen, and we may have a lovely visit together at the Cape and swim together and laugh together." It was not to be. From that point on, Roz failed rapidly. Myla, Jeff, and their families were called to her bedside (Howard described Myla as "a nurse and angel throughout"). Roz seemed at peace at the end, and gradually she slipped into unconsciousness. She died two days later. Her ashes were buried in Newton Cemetery, under a tree near a small pond. Only the immediate family was present, and Roz's eldest brother, Ben, recited Kaddish, a Jewish prayer for the dead. Howard thought it "was just right, added just the right amount of Jewishness to the day." Then everyone came back to the house, where Myla had prepared food; Howard thought "it was a sweet gathering." When Howard's old Spelman student Alice Walker heard the news, she wrote him to say "Roz's smile made the plants grow."[19]

A memorial confined to family and friends was held at the Parish Church in Harvard Square. Howard spoke to the gathering, describing Roz as "luminous, smiling, joyful, and a more rounded person than I was . . . for the past six months we enjoyed a wonderful tranquility together. . . . At the very end, lying in bed, she was concerned about me: would I have enough to eat? Would I be able to take care of myself?" Anyone who wished to was welcome to speak at the memorial, and a number of friends did. The *Boston Globe* printed an extensive obituary, and Roz's friend Elly Rubin later wrote a brief remembrance and asked a few others, including Roz's three brothers, to contribute a few more.

In the months following Roz's death, Howard—unaccustomed to grief, except when his mother died—felt desolate and dull, unable to do much of anything. Family and friends provided what comfort they could, but no one could substitute for the intimacy he and Roz had shared. During the final period of her illness, Howard had taken charge of many household chores, though until the very end of her life Roz had still managed to do some of them, especially cooking. Howard slowly began forcing himself to learn some of the basic tasks Roz had always done, like taking care of the house and putting together a decent meal. Gradually, he began to revive, but as he wrote Pat West at the close of 2008, "I never remember my dreams so I don't know if I've dreamt of Roz. But I have mystical experiences when I'm awake, or half-awake. I'll get up in the morning, and look over to see if Roz is next to me. At odd times I'll hear her voice calling to me from the next room. I'll come home from something and expect her to be sitting in the living room. . . . I'm cool most of the time, but then something happens to trigger off my emotion . . . this friend we knew many years ago came up to me and said, 'How is Roz?' That broke me up."

Determined to push through the pain, Howard began to go out a little, but he'd find himself calling Roz at home to report how things had gone—only to hear the phone ring on and on. Yet his resilient temperament and strong ego stood him in good stead and led him to heed the advice of those close to him to start getting busy again. "I have to decide not to think about Roz's death," he told his grandson Will. And he did slowly begin to pick up his ordinary routines, though not with the same enthusiasm or energy. Years before, he'd had a pacemaker installed (twice, in fact) and had successful hip replacement. But he now developed back pain that was sometimes severe enough to interfere with his walking, and not even surgery provided much relief. In addition, the macular degeneration he'd had for some time worsened. Yet even in the eye that was most compromised, he retained some sight, and against the advice of friends he insisted on still driving his car. He also turned to putting his own affairs in order and spent a great deal of time removing from his archives nearly all personal material. "He just seems obsessed with getting everything settled," one close friend wrote to another.

As Howard gradually began to revive, he managed to write a few articles, mostly short ones. A number of them focused on Barack Obama's 2008 candidacy; early on, Howard characterized him as a centrist. The realization came to him when Obama went to Connecticut to support Joe Lieberman, the war hawk, in the primary instead of his opponent, Ned Lamont, a progressive who was against the U.S. presence in Iraq. Howard also distrusted Obama's record as a senator: he'd voted in favor of resuming construction on additional nuclear power plants and continuing to fund the war, and had opposed John Murtha's call for immediate withdrawal. Obama had also favored reauthorizing the Patriot Act (a decided threat to civil liberties), had voted against a bankruptcy bill that would have capped credit card interest rates at 30 percent, had supported the death penalty, and had worked tirelessly to pass a bill that would effectively shut down state courts as a venue to hear most class-action suits—a cherished goal of the Bush administration and large corporations.[20]

On all these matters, Howard's views were opposite to Obama's. But the differences between Obama and John McCain seemed more important still—"not a significant enough difference for me to have confidence in Obama as president, but just enough for me to vote for Obama." This time around, Howard didn't consider Ralph Nader a viable alternative, so he did give his vote to Obama—anything to get rid of the Republicans. Once in office, Obama proceeded to raise the military budget and send even more troops to Afghanistan than Bush had. Yet Howard felt that Obama "has a certain instinct for people in trouble," and could only hope that it would influence his future policies. It continued to puzzle him why, with the successful precedent of the New Deal to point to, Obama had failed to respond to the economic crisis by putting millions to work rebuilding the nation's infrastructure.

When, after the election, Obama was awarded the Nobel Peace Prize in 2008, Howard was "dismayed" that a president carrying on two wars would be considered worthy of such a prize. Even during his short amount of time in office, Obama had increased rather than reduced the already huge military budget. When campaigning, he'd said that "it's not enough to get out of Iraq; we have to get out of the mindset that led us into Iraq." Yet once in office, he seemed bent on maintaining a militaristic mind-set, including the unreported "secret war" begun after 9/11 and a drone campaign that the CIA claimed hadn't killed a single noncombatant—though other studies drew quite different conclusions. "Have we destroyed terrorism?" Howard asked. "No, but we've killed a lot of people."

A political animal to the core, Howard soon began writing somewhat longer pieces, and to give interviews and public lectures again. As he wrote to one friend: "I'm keeping busy, traveling, speaking, having lunches and dinners with friends—all that helps, though in-between the busy times, yes, I have to struggle against the profound sadness, and try all sorts of psychological tricks, like thinking of all the things that made Roz happy . . ." In June (approaching his eighty-seventh birthday) he went all the way to Athens, Greece, to see the production of a shortened version of his play *Emma*. He found, too, that he was able to enjoy the Cape Cod house again. In September, he reported to a friend that he was "having glorious days in Wellfleet . . . enjoying solitude, eating my meals on the porch looking out at the sea," even oystering—with the help of a cane chair, the gift of a friend, that he could drag out into the water.[21]

Yet Howard was physically wearing down, hobbled by back pain and the deterioration of his eyesight—particularly awful for someone whose primary activities were reading and writing—and his naps grew longer. As was typical with Howard, he enveloped his various symptoms in humor: "I am declining in many ways that are invisible over e-mail!" Howard wasn't a complainer, but Noam Chomsky gave a starker version of his condition: "In Howard's last year he was suffering from severe infirmity and personal loss, though one would hardly know it when meeting him." Howard did his best to soldier on, delivering a lecture as late as November 2009 to the newly formed Coalition for Social Justice. He reserved what turned out to be his last article in the *Nation* for expressing disappointment in Obama: his foreign policy was "no different from a Republican," in that he was "nationalist, expansionist, imperial and warlike," and his proposed domestic policies were "limited" and "cautious."

In January 2010, Howard decided to spend a few weeks in Santa Monica to give some lectures, avoid the worst of a Boston winter, and visit with two grandchildren (Will and Naushon), who lived in the East Bay. Though his memory was still keen, he somehow forgot his wallet and checkbook and had to call Hilde Hein from the airport to say that he needed her to FedEx the items to him. Fortunately he did have his plane ticket, along with some identification, and was met by a friend at the airport in California. Howard's intention was to stay at his Santa Monica hotel for several weeks and then go to the San Francisco Bay Area to visit his grandchildren.

But it was not to be. The day after he arrived, on January 29, 2010, Howard moved from his second-floor apartment to one on the first floor, shopped for some groceries, and decided to put on his swimsuit and sit by the hotel's small pool. He'd long ago taught himself how to do a slow sidestroke, but soon after getting in the water he had a heart attack. A young Hispanic workman saw him go under and—though he couldn't swim himself—jumped into the pool and somehow managed to pull Howard out and put him in a lounge chair. Still conscious, Howard reassured everyone: "I'll be OK, I just need to rest a bit." A woman who worked at the front desk held Howard's hand, and an ambulance was called, but before it could arrive Howard died. Myla and Jeff flew out to the West Coast to handle all arrangements. Howard was cremated and his ashes brought back to Massachusetts to be buried next to Roz.[22]

Coda

Howard had been a person of considerable modesty, neither devious nor manipulative, an "innocent" in the sense of always thinking the best of people. He had scant drive for personal power and few if any self-serving motives behind the political stances he took. Never self-centered, he could be, which is quite different, self-absorbed—so involved, say, in a given public issue or event that he tuned out those around him, especially their needs. But he was

basically kind and generous, in person deeply engaging, more interested in persuasion than in confrontation—though with the Sil-
bers of the world quite capable of determined resistance. When
an interviewer asked Daniel Ellsberg who his own heroes were, he
had no hesitation in answering, "First, Howard Zinn." Noam
Chomsky sounded a similar note: "He was devoted, selflessly, to
the empowerment" of those who had little. As a teacher, Howard
was all but unanimously beloved and revered by his students—
even, as a person, by some of the conservative detractors who would
unexpectedly appear in his classes. He cared about them, and they
knew it.

His legacy as a historian has been more contested, and his radical
activism deplored. With *A People's History*, Howard became a public
figure, greatly admired among leftists, greatly denounced by those
on the right and even, to a lesser degree, among those who considered themselves liberals or centrists. Nor can those who were
critical of his work be simplistically labeled "a bunch of conservatives." The majority of them—Oscar Handlin, for one—spoke from
the right. But even among the many liberals who now inhabit history departments—far more than, say, fifty years ago, though
radicals remain somewhat scarce—there are pronounced divisions
over Howard's work. Outside the historical profession, his ador-
ing fans rank in the millions—and even in his eighties Howard
was able to connect with young people. His impact was, and is,
multigenerational (in Boston, the Occupy Wall Street camps named
their libraries after him). But within the historical profession, Howard has nearly as many detractors as admirers.[23]

One historian has said that Howard had "a very simplified view
that everyone who was president was always a stinker and every
left-winger was always great. That can't be true." No it isn't—and
Howard never made such a flat-out claim, though his books, taken
together, do lean strongly in that direction, and younger historians
generally agree with his evaluations. Another historian has argued
that, contra Howard, we have many instances of people at the bot-

tom or in the middle directly challenging the powers that be and also have multiple examples of "the masses of people going along with those in power or even leading the charge in the wrong direction. History is full of people rooting against their own class."

Again, true enough. But it also needs to be said that Howard's work has played a crucial role in providing a corrective to the traditional accounts that omit discussion of the lives of ordinary people or of those who protest against the status quo. Too many high school textbooks continue to emphasize and glorify government, military, and business elites, tout the United States as God's gift to the planet, and ignore or dismiss the suffering of the underclasses as "their own fault." Most college-level books about American history have today shifted to a more balanced account, and many historians give Howard (though not Howard alone; he did have a few predecessors, as well as a number of contemporary co-conspirators) the lion's share of credit for the shift.

Focusing on the book he is best remembered for, *A People's History*, a number of historians have faulted it as being insufficiently nuanced and complex, and simply wrong in some of its particulars. That assessment has some truth to it, though it needs to be added that by the 2003 edition of the book Howard had softened some of his indictments and corrected all factual errors that he'd been made aware of. Still, as late as 2010 several critiques appeared insisting that *A People's History* failed to offer "a compelling explanation of past events or present conditions," nor could it have, given the author's commitment "to insisting on the nobility of the exploited many at the hands of a nefarious few . . . [a point of view] that doesn't come near to being the whole story about the United States."

Yet that same critic added that although he regarded Zinn as essentially "a popularizer and agitator," he had helped many historians to see that they had a responsibility to act as citizens, not simply as specialists who "research, write, think and teach." His writings and public appearances—emotionally powerful, sensitive to suffering—"have helped people to wake up to the fallacies and brutalities of U.S. military and economic power," to bring the struggles of previously unheard voices into the history books, and to challenge the triumphalist version of American history.

Those accomplishments alone should be enough to secure Howard's reputation. And although *A People's History* brought fame and fortune, several of his other books—in particular *SNNC*, *Vietnam: The Logic of Withdrawal*, and *The Politics of History*—were way ahead of their times and may well retain their historical importance. What will most certainly come down to future generations is Howard's humanity, his exemplary concern for the plight of others, a concern free of condescension or self-importance. Howard always stayed in character—and that character remained centered on a capacious solidarity with the least fortunate.[24]

Note on Sources/Acknowledgments

The central source for this biography has been the Howard Zinn Archives (abbreviated throughout as HZA). They were unprocessed when I read through them but are now fully processed and available for use at the Tamiment Library, New York University. As I've said in the preface, Howard himself thoroughly screened his archives, removing virtually all references to his personal life.

Fortunately, I've been partly able to reconstruct it—though not in the detail I'd like—through three other sources: interviews; the papers of several of the Zinns' friends and colleagues on deposit in various manuscript libraries; and the willingness of a number of the Zinns' close friends to share with me—usually asking for anonymity—their own recollections and correspondence.

The secondary sources I consulted are cited in the endnotes. Of the several dozen people I interviewed, I want to single out a few as having been of special importance: Howard's brothers Bernie Zinn and Jerry Zinn; Howard and Roz's daughter, Myla Kabat-Zinn, and their grandson Will Kabat-Zinn; Robert Cohn; Henry and Pat West; Anthony Arnove; Hilde Hein; and Marilyn B. Young. I also want to thank several people at The New Press who went out of their way to help get the manuscript in final shape: Maury Botton, Tara Grove, Jason Farbman, Ben Woodward, and Julie McCarroll. I'm also grateful to Gary Stimsling for an unusually thoughtful copyedit.

In regard to primary sources held in various manuscript libraries, the most significant, aside from the Howard Zinn Archives and collections that are privately held, have been the Staughton Lynd Papers at the Historical Society of Wisconsin (SHSW), the Frances Fox Piven collection at Smith College (FFPS), and the Archives of the Association of University Professors, George Washington University (AAUPGW); my thanks to Ellen Schrecker for leading me to the latter. The staffs at all the manuscript libraries have been uniformly helpful, but I want to single out Jan Hilley at Tamiment, who processed the Zinn Archives, for alerting me to certain material I might otherwise have overlooked. I also want to give special thanks to Cassandra ("Ryan") Coletti for her reliable research assistance with several collections.

As to the privately held material, several collections of letters and other items were very large, and in that regard I want to give special thanks to Anthony Arnove, Dan Simon, and Henry and Pat West. Of the other Zinn friends who shared material with me, I'm grateful to Rick Balkin, Noam Chomsky, Hilde Hein, Myla Kabat-Zinn, Nancy Carlsson-Paige, and Marilyn B. Young. I'm grateful to Myla Kabat-Zinn for giving me permission to include several personal photographs from the Zinn family photo albums.

A number of people—my partner, Eli Zal; Ellen Adler and Marc Favreau of The New Press; Anthony Arnove; Myla Kabat-Zinn; Leon Friedman; and Marilyn B. Young—have read the manuscript in its entirety, and I'm grateful for their astute comments and corrections. Staughton and Alice Lynd read the two chapters on Spelman, and Jesse Lemisch read the chapter "Writing History," and their thoughtful critiques have made a significant difference. Howard and Roz's son Jeff also read the manuscript, offered comments, and shared some of his memories.

Notes

Each note gives the citations for the material between that note and the one following.

Chapter 1: The Early Years

1. For the description of early family life in the pages that follow, the major sources have been Jennie Zinn's 1973 tape (courtesy of Howard's daughter, Myla Kabat-Zinn), her e-mail to me, Jan. 4, 2012, and my Sept. 21, 2010, interviews with Howard's two brothers Bernie Zinn and Jerry Zinn. For Eddie and blacks: HZ, *Boston Globe*, Sept. 19, 1975.

2. For a rich history of Yiddishkeit, see Irving Howe, *World of Our Fathers*, 2d ed., Schocken, 1989. On being a waiter, etc., David Barsamian's interviews with HZ, Nov. 11, 1992, Feb. 7, 2005, Howard Zinn Archives (henceforth HZA).

3. Oct. 15, 2011, interview with Howard and Roz's grandson Will Kabat-Zinn; Sept. 21, 2010, interviews with Bernie Zinn and with Jerry Zinn; interview with Myla Kabat-Zinn, Mar. 23, 2011; interview tape with HZ, Dec. 2008 about Brooklyn Navy Yard (courtesy Myla Kabat-Zinn); HZ to Nancy Carlsson-Paige, June 29, 2004, courtesy Carlsson-Paige; HZ, *You Can't Be Neutral on a Moving Train* (henceforth *Neutral*), 2d ed., Beacon, 2002; Julian Schlossberg's interviews with HZ, July 13, 2006, Dec. 2007, DVD; scattered, undated notes in HZ's hand, HZA; Roz to Pat West, Aug. 29, 2007, courtesy West; HZ to Rick Balkin, June 4, 1997, courtesy Balkin.

4. As later recounted by Zinn in his book *The Southern Mystique* [henceforth *Mystique*], Knopf, 1964, 24; HZ, *Neutral*, ch. 7; HZ, *Just War*, Charta, 2005, 30–42; Eleanor Rubin, "Sanctuary" (about Roslyn), n.d., HZA; HZ to Edward W. Wood Jr., n.d., HZ to Pat West, n.d., courtesy West.

5. Col. H.A. Schmidt to HZ, Nov. 9, 1967, HZA; *New York Times*, May 3, 1996, Dec. 12, 2010; HZ, "A Mess of Death and Documents," *Columbia University Forum*, Winter: 1962; HZ, *Vietnam: The Logic of Withdrawal* (henceforth *Vietnam*), Beacon, 1967, 4; HZ, *The Politics of History*, 2d ed., Univ. of Illinois, 1990, 258–74; HZ, *The Bomb*, City Lights, 2010, especially 42–44; HZ, *Just War*, 14–15, 42; HZ, *Neutral*, 11; HZ, "Private Ryan Saves War," *Progressive*, Oct. 1998; HZ, "The Bombs of August," *Progressive*, Aug. 2000. The literature on the atomic bomb is vast. David McCullough's much-admired biography of Truman skirts the issue of the atom bomb. I myself am much more in agreement with the revisionist histories of Gar Alperovitz, *The Decision to Use the Atomic Bomb*, Knopf, 1995; Gabriel Kolko, *The Roots of American Foreign Policy*, Beacon Press, 1969; Walter LaFeber, Richard Polenberg, and Nancy Woloch, *The American Century*, 6th ed., M.E. Sharpe, 2008; and Lloyd C. Gardner, *Three Kings: The Rise of an American Empire*, The New Press, 2009. For the counterargument that dropping the atomic bombs was necessary, see Max Hastings, *Retribution*, Knopf, 2008.

6. HZ to Muirhead, Sept. 16, 1952, HZA; HZ, *Neutral*, 15–17; HZ, *Failure to Quit: Reflections of an Optimistic Historian* (henceforth *Failure*), Common Courage Press, 1993, 30–31. For the definitive study of how academia gave in to McCarthyism and dismissed faculty members even suspected of being "red," see Ellen W. Schrecker, Oxford, *No Ivory Tower*, 1986. For a scholarly justification of U.S. policies during the Cold War, see John Lewis Gaddis, *We Now Know: Rethinking Cold War History*, Oxford, 1997.

7. HZ, *Postwar America: 1945–1971*, Bobbs-Merrill, 1973; Wilkes & Adler to HZ, Jan. 4, 1950, Howard Horton to Michael Straight, chairman of AVC, Mar. 6, 1950, plus one letter n.d., HZA. In 1952, Howard attempted to write a novel set during the 1913–1914 Ludlow coal strike (his description of it is in HZA).

Howard's voluminous FBI file was released in 2010. Since the file is now readily available, there seems no point in providing full citations for every reference in the reports. One exception does seem necessary: the encounters with the FBI agents are in two reports, dated Nov. 25, 1953, and Feb. 24, 1954.

8. The most important reviews were in the *Nation* and the *Mississippi Valley Historical Review*, both June 1960; the *American Historical Review*, July 1960; *Phylon*, 2d qtr., 1960; and the *American Political Science Review*, June 1960. When yet a third book, Charles Garrett, *The LaGuardia Years*, Rutgers, 1961, on LaGuardia came out, Howard reviewed it in the *American Historical Review* and made an arresting comment about the motivation of reformers that would prove emblematic of the "revisionism" about to sweep the historical profession: "Garrett's . . . professional delight in accounting

for the reformist drive by such psychological factors as egotism and a hunger for power based on 'a deep inferiority complex'—may help explain the volume of energy expended, but hardly explains its direction."

Chapter 2: Spelman

1. HZ, ms., "Alice at Spelman," HZA; Myla Kabat-Zinn e-mail to me, July 4, 2011. As an example of white Northern opinion, Adlai Stevenson, the liberal Democratic candidate for president, told a *black* audience early in 1956 that "as President he would not cut off Federal funds from segregated schools nor use Federal troops to enforce integration. . . . We must proceed gradually," he went on, "not upsetting habits or traditions that are older than the Republic." How desegregation and "traditions" were both to be served, Stevenson failed to say (*New York Times*, Feb. 8, 1956).

At the beginning of 1963, the gallery of the Georgia legislature was finally desegregated. In celebration, Howard, Roz, and three Spelman students attended the opening session. Seeing them, the Southern liberal Pat Watters looked up and chuckled. Howard thought the atmosphere was "resigned, resentful acceptance," a far cry from the "hate bordering on violence" that had greeted them earlier (HZ, occasional diary notes, Jan. 14, 1963, courtesy Myla Kabat-Zinn).

The books and articles central to the background discussion that follows have been: Marybeth Gasman, "Perceptions of Black College Presidents . . ." *American Educational Research Journal* 20, no. 10, 2011; HZ, "A New Direction for Negro Colleges," *Harper's*, May 1966; Clayborne Carson, *In Struggle: SNCC and the Black Awakening of the 1960s*, Cambridge, 1981; Albert Manley, *A Legacy Continues*, Univ. Press of America, 1995; HZ, *Mystique*; HZ, *SNCC: The New Abolitionists* (henceforth *SNCC*), Beacon, 1964; David J. Garrow, ed., *Atlanta Georgia, 1960–1961*, (henceforth Garrow, *Atlanta*) Carlson, 1989; HZ, *Neutral*; Marian Wright Edelman, *Lanterns: A Memoir of Mentors*, Beacon, 1999 (henceforth Edelman, *Lanterns*); Barbara Ransby, *Ella Baker and the Black Freedom Movement* (henceforth Ransby, *Baker*) Univ. of North Carolina Press, 2003; Harry G. Lefever, *Undaunted by the Fight* (henceforth Lefever, *Undaunted*), Mercer University Press, 2005; Tomiko Brown-Nagin, *Courage to Dissent: Atlanta and the Long History of the Civil Rights Movement* (henceforth Brown-Nagin, *Courage*), Oxford, 2011. In the section discussing the response of intellectuals to the Supreme Court decision, I've relied heavily on Carol Polsgrove's splendid *Divided Minds: Intellectuals and the Civil Rights Movement* (henceforth Polsgrove, *Minds*), Norton, 2001.

2. HZ journal notes, May 19–20, HZA; Watts to Zinn, May 26, 1959, Staughton Lynd Papers, State Historical Society of Wisconsin (henceforth SHSW); *Atlanta Journal*, May 25, 1959; HZ, "A Case of Quiet Social Change," *Crisis*, Oct. 1959; HZ, *Neutral*, 22–23; HZ, *Mystique*, 4–5; Garrow,

Atlanta, 129. For Ella Baker, I'm deeply indebted to Ransby's brilliant and subtle *Baker*, especially chapter 6.

3. HZ, "Finishing School for Pickets," *Nation*, Aug. 6, 1960; Lefever, *Undaunted*, 26–27; "Chronology (Southern Regional Council—SRC)," SHSW.

4. "Appeal for Human Rights," *Atlanta Journal-Constitution*, Mar. 9, 1960; also in Lefever, *Undaunted*, pp. 268ff; Edelman, *Lanterns*, 59–62—the photo of Marian Wright in jail follows p. 102.

5. HZ, "Pickets," *Nation*, Aug. 6, 1960; *Richmond News Leader*, Feb. 22, 1960; Garrow, *Atlanta*, 67–70, 129–34; "Chronology—1961," Lynd Papers, SHSW; Myla Kabat-Zinn e-mail to me, July 19, 2011. After attending a performance of *Aida* by the Metropolitan Opera touring company, Howard wrote to an official of the Atlanta Music Festival to say that the one thing that marred his enjoyment was the inability of black music lovers to attend because they "cannot reconcile themselves to the humiliation of segregation." He reminded the official that at Atlanta University and several other places, blacks and whites had been attending plays and concerts on a nonsegregated basis for a number of years. He suggested the Music Festival adopt the same policy (HZ to Draper, May 4, 1958, Lynd Papers, SHSW).

6. Myla Kabat-Zinn e-mail to me, July 19, 2011; HZ, *Neutral*, 30–31; Wesley C. Hogan, *Many Minds, One Heart: SNCC's Dream for a New America* (henceforth Hogan, *Minds*), Univ. of North Carolina Press, 2007.

7. HZ introduction to Carl Mirra, *The Admirable Radical*, Kent State Univ. Press, 2010; Alice Lynd and Staughton Lynd, *Stepping Stones*, Lexington, 2009; Andrej Grubacic, *From Here to There: The Staughton Lynd Reader*, PM Press, 2010; HZ to Alfred Hero, n.d. [1962], Lynd, SHSW; Henry West to me, Sept. 14, 2010, in my possession. This seems the appropriate place to express my gratitude to Alice and Staughton Lynd for reading the manuscript versions of chapters 2 and 3 and giving me the benefit of their wise counsel.

8. Ransby, *Baker*, especially 256–59; Hogan, *Minds*, ch. 2.

9. Hogan, *Minds*, 67–72; HZ, "Albany," HZA; HZ, *Mystique*, part 3 (which reprints his Southern Regional Council report "Albany"); David Barsamian interview with HZ, Sept. 18, 2002, HZA; HZ's FBI file, 1962–64, especially Rosen to Belmont, Dec. 3, 1962; HZ, "The FBI and American Democracy," speech, Community Church of Boston, Feb. 26, 1987; HZ, "Changing People: Negro Civil Rights and the Colleges," *Massachusetts Review*, Summer, 1964; HZ, "The Southern Mobsters and Their Federal Friends," *Worker*, Dec. 2, 1962; HZ, *Neutral*, 46–55; *Student Voice* (SNCC), Oct. 1962; Tom Hayden to HZ, Aug. 14, 1962, HZ to Hayden, "Aug–Sept.," 1962, Lynd Papers, SHSW.

10. HZ, "Kennedy: The Reluctant Emancipator," *Nation*, Dec. 1, 1962; HZ, "A Question of Action," *Correspondent*, Nov.–Dec. 1963; HZ, "The Limits of Nonviolence," *Freedomways*, Winter, 1964; Ransby, *Baker*, 300–301; HZ, *SNCC*, 96–101. Robert Kennedy did wage a consistent fight from the

early 1960s on for a meaningful antipoverty program (see Edward R. Schmitt, *President of the Other America*, U. of Mass Press, 2010).

11. *Atlanta Journal-Constitution*, Mar. 3, 1961; notes dated March 1963, Lynd Papers, SHSW; *Student Voice* (SNCC bulletin), Apr., 1963; HZ, *Mystique*, 188–91; Brown-Negin, *Courage*, ch. 8.

12. HZ, diary entries, Jan. 13, Apr. 12–14, 1963 (courtesy Myla Kabat-Zinn); 1963 was the only year during which Howard kept a relatively full diary. HZ "Nov. 1963" notes during a "Mississippi Staff Meeting," SLSW; David Barsamian interview with HZ, part 2, Sept. 18, 2002, in HZ, *Original Zinn*, HarperCollins, 2006 (henceforth Barsamian, *Zinn*); *Atlanta Journal-Constitution*, May 20, 1963; set of undated notes in Howard's handwriting in HZA, likely a partial record of the April 1963 SNCC conference but can't be assigned with certainty. Robert F. Williams, a somewhat earlier figure, analogous to Malcolm X, pointed out that armed self-defense was a fact of life in rural areas of the Deep South. Williams founded the Deacons for Defense and Justice but was forced to flee to Cuba in the early 1960s (for more details, see Timothy B. Tyson, "Robert F. Williams, 'Black Power,' and the Roots of the African American Freedom Struggle," *Journal of American History*, Sept. 1998).

13. For sample reviews of *SNCC*, see *America*, Oct. 24, 1964, and *Phylon* 27, no. 2 [1966].

14. HZ diary, Jan. 2, 3, 5, 16, Feb. 4, 5, 14, 22, Mar. 3, 7, 11, 14, 16, 17, 18, 24, Apr. 14, 15, 1963, courtesy Myla Kabat-Zinn (now in HZA).

15. HZ diary, Jan. 18, 20, 1963, HZA. A sympathetic faculty member reported to Howard that several black professors also "believed dissidence comes from a white group" whose goal was "to replace Manley with me as president! And that communism in the backgrounds of one or more of these conspirators is a factor." (HZ diary, Apr. 30, 1963.)

16. Angus Cameron (Knopf) to HZ, July 25, 1963, HZ to Cameron, Oct. 21, 1963, HZ to Llewellyn Howland (Sterling Lord Agency), Sept. 17, Nov. 8, 16, Dec. 4, 1963; HZ, *Mystique*, 5, 7–8, 11, 34, 35, 38, 53, 64, 83–86, 92–99; HZ had prefigured many of the arguments he used in *Mystique* as far back as his article "A Fate Worse Than Integration," *Harper's*, Aug. 1959; Martin Duberman, "The 'New' (1997) Scholarship on Racism," in Duberman, *Left Out*, South End Press, 2002; Eric Foner, "Today's Color Line," *Nation*, Jan. 24, 2011. For a recent study that shows school and residential segregation weakening in some areas but unchanged in others, see the *New York Times* summary, Jan. 31, 2012.

17. See, for example, any of Frans de Waal's books, as well as Matt Ridley, *The Origins of Virtue*, Penguin, 1997; Eliot Sober and David Sloan Wilson, *Unto Others*, Harvard, 1997; Randall Kennedy, *The Persistence of the Color Line*, Pantheon, 2012.

18. Lillian Smith, *Chicago Tribune*, Oct. 18, 1964; C. Vann Woodward, "Southern Mythology," *Commentary*, May 1965; Ralph Ellison, "If the Twain

Shall Meet," *New York Herald Tribune*, Nov. 8, 1964. I myself favorably reviewed both of Howard's books in *Partisan Review*, Winter, 1965.

Chapter 3: The Black Struggle I

1. Myla Kabat-Zinn e-mail to me, July 22, 2011. Even before 1963, Howard had written at least one short play that we know about, based on the Abraham-Isaac sacrifice (HZ diary, Jan. 24, 1963, HZA). Lebs, etc.: HZ diary, April 12–13, May 1–2, 17, 18, 1963, HZA.

2. HZ diary, May 17–20, 22–23, 24, 31, HZA.

3. Alice Lynd and Staughton Lynd, *Stepping Stones*, Lexington, 2009, 4, 174–75; HZ diary, April 9, 10, 24, 26, May 16, June 4, 1963, HZA. Alice and Staughton have "no memory of Howard and Roz coming to Grady Hospital" on the day of Lee's accident (Lynds' e-mail to me, June 2, 2011).

4. HZ, *Neutral*, 42–45; Hogan, *Minds*, 146; Lefever, *Undaunted*, 161–64; HZ diary, June 20, 1963, HZA; Alice Walker to HZ, June 20–21, 1963, HZA.

5. Manley to HZ, June 1, 1963, HZA; HZ to Spelman Board of Trustees et al., July 1963, Zinn file, archives of Association of University Professors (AAUP), George Washington Univ., Washington, DC (henceforth AAUPGW); SNCC news release, June 7, 1963, Staughton to HZ, "June 1963," HZA; *Atlanta Inquirer* (an African American newspaper), June 8, 1963; *Atlanta Journal-Constitution*, July 18, 1963; HZ, *Neutral*, ch. 6; Renate Wolf to Zinns, June 9, Sam DuBois Cook (black political philosopher at Atlanta Univ.) to HZ, June 10, Staughton to HZ, June 12, 19, 23, July 1, 2, 23, Aug. 3, 5, Sept. 20, Oct. 18, 23, Jim Laue to the Zinns, June 16, Betty Stevens to HZ, June 19, July 12, 24, Oct. 21, Vincent Harding to HZ, June 19, HZ to Betty Stevens, July 21, Esta Seaton to "Howie and Roz," n.d.—all 1963, all HZA.

6. HZ to Spelman Board of Trustees et al., July 1963, AAUPGW; Esta Seaton to Judge Tuttle, June 30, Aug. 11, Manley to HZ, June 15, 26, 1963, Tuttle to Seaton, July 2, HZ diary notes, July 10, 13, 14, Carl and Anne Braden (prominent white activists for racial justice), July 15, 25, Anne Braden, "How the South Is Knocking Its Brains Out," *Gazette and Daily*, Sept. 11, HZ, "To Whom It May Concern," Aug. 31, Alice Walker to Zinns, July 8, Sept. 19, 20, [plus 4 to Howard, n.d.]—all 1963, all HZA; *Jet*, June 27, 1963.

In a 1987 interview, Manley claimed that he "never tried to stop" students from civil rights activism (Marybeth Gasman, "Perceptions of Black College Presidents," *American Education Research Journal*, 2011), but as Lefever makes clear in *Spelman*, Manley was usually conflicted and vacillating on the issue. In his own autobiography, *A Legacy Continues*, Univ. Press of America, 1995, Manley makes no mention of his contentious relationship with Howard or of his dismissal.

7. HZ diary notes, July 10, 1963; Sinclair [?] to ?, June 21, 1963, HZA; Staughton to me, Aug. 23, 2010, in my possession. HZ to Hollowell, June 21, Lynd to Manley, July 8, HZ to Manley, July 2, 29, Aug. 25, HZ to Betty Stevens, July 21, HZA; Robert Van Waes to Lionel Newson, June 24, Van Waes to Manley, July 23, Manley to Van Waes, Sept. 26—all 1963, all HZA; Van Waes to Howard, July 23, Aug. 1, Nov. 14, Van Waes to Manley, July 23, Manley to Van Waes, July 26, Nov. 20, HZ to Van Waes, July 31, Aug. 2—all 1963, all AAUPGW.

8. Manley to Van Waes, Sept. 26, Nov. 20, 1963, Jan. 25, 1964, Van Waes to Manley, Jan. 3, Van Waes to HZ, Jan. 23, Manley to HZ, Jan. 25, HZ to Van Waes, Jan. 30, Van Waes' 3-page "CONFIDENTIAL MEMORANDUM, Interview with Professor Zinn," Feb. 12, Maurice Maloof to Van Waes, Feb. 18, HZ to Manley, Mar. 5, Manley to Van Waes, Mar. 19, Manley to Ehrmann, May 8—all 1964, all AAUPGW.

9. Polsgrove, *Minds*, 225. The post-May exchange of letters was considerable but mostly repetitive of what had preceded. (HZ to Ehrmann, May 17, 1964, Ehrmann to HZ, June 1, 1964, AAUPGW.) Manley initially agreed to the settlement, but he'd assumed that the AAUP meant the check for 1963–64 already given Howard. When it became clear that a second check was required, Manley balked. (Manley to Ehrmann, May 8, June 5, July 7, Ehrmann to Manley, June 12, July 19.) For the highlights of the last six months of the dispute, see Ehrmann to HZ, July 10, 1964, Zinn to Ehrmann, July 13, 1964, HZ to *Book Week*, Nov. 9, 1964, HZ to Louis Joughin, Nov. 13, 1964, Van Waes to Groton, Feb. 24, 1965, Van Waes to HZ, n.d. [1965]—all in AAUPGW.

Chapter 4: The Black Struggle II

1. HZ, *Neutral*, ch. 5.

2. Ransby, *Baker* 314–17; *Hattiesburg American*, Jan. 21, 1964; HZ to John O'Neal, Jan. 30, 1964, HZA; *Atlanta Journal-Constitution*, Feb. 2, 1964; Marian Wright to HZ, Mar. 12, 1964, HZ, "Proposed Educational Program," 2 pp., HZ, 11 pp. ms. "A 'Hot Line' from Mississippi" [on the bloody beating in the Hattiesburg jail of Oscar Chase, a Yale law school graduate working with SNCC], Mar. 11, 1964, HZA; Waskow to HZ, Feb. 13, 1963, HZ to Harold Taylor, Mar. 2, 1964, Taylor to HZ, Mar. 5, 1964, HZA.

3. Lynd to Waskow, Mar. 29, 1964, Waskow to Lynd, Apr. 13, 22, 1964, typed notes of Feb. 9–10 meeting, Charlie Cobb's ms. "Prospectus for a Summer Freedom School Program," Lynd to Waskow, Mar. 29, 1964, Lynd to HZ, June 12, 1964, Lynd Papers, SHSW; Mirra, *Radical*, ch. 3; HZ, handwritten notes on meeting, HZA.

4. SNCC executive committee minutes for the April 18–19, 1964, meeting in Atlanta, HZA; HZ to Julian Bond Apr., 26 1964; Noel Day to Clifford

Alexander, June 9, 1964, signatories of petition to President Johnson, June 9, 1964, HZA; HZ to Clyde Ferguson, May 4, 1964, Lynd Papers, SHSW.

5. Thelman to Robert Harris, May 19, 1964, Charles Black to HZ, May 25, 1964, Harris to Thelwell, May 25, 1964, Thelwell to HZ, [1964], HZA; HZ, 19 pp. ms. article, Lynd Papers, SHSW; HZ, ms. "Lyndon Johnson and the Mississippi Summer," HZA.

6. HZ, "What Tactics for Civil Rights?" *Current*, June–July, 1964; Mendy Samstein to "Dear Friend" (summer 1964), "Some proposals for a Mississippi Summer Project," Lynd Papers, SHSW. Howard wrote a letter to the editor of the *New York Times* protesting the failure of the Justice Department to investigate the disappearance of the three civil rights workers on the grounds that they lacked the constitutional power to intervene. In his letter, Howard reiterated, as he had several times before, the sections of the Constitution and statute law that made such intervention legal and mandatory (HZ to *Times*, June 27, 1964, HZA).

7. HZ, 26 pp. ms. notes, n.d., HZA; Ransby, *Baker* 309–29.

8. Harold Taylor to HZ, June 20, Lynd to HZ, June 12, July 10, Adlai Stevenson to HZ, July 22, HZ to Stevenson, July 24, "Confidential Freedom School Report," July 10, "Jackson Freedom School Teachers," Aug., "Freedom School Data," 4 pp. typed ms.—all 1964, all in Lynd Papers, SHSW; *New York Times*, July 23, 1964; Mirra, *Lynd*, 51–64. Sponsors of the Free Southern Theatre included James Baldwin, Langston Hughes, and Lincoln Kirstein.

9. Lynd, "Mississippi Freedom Schools: Retrospect and Prospect," July 26, Lynd, "Freedom Schools—Final Report, 1964," Lynd, *From Here to There: The Staughton Lynd Reader*, Andrej Grubacic, ed., PM Press, 2010, 74–84; *Atlanta Inquirer*, Aug. 8, Grenville Clark letter to *New York Times*, Aug. 16, Bob Zangrando to HZ, Aug. 20—all 1964, all Lynd Papers, SHSW; Christopher Jencks, "Mississippi: From Conversion to Coercion," *New Republic*, Aug. 22, 1964; HZ to Dorothy Height (president, National Council of Negro Women), Sept. 28, 1964, HZA; HZ, "The Mississippi Idea," *Nation*, Nov. 23, 1964; HZ, "Notes On 'Action-Research' Project Meeting," Oct. 10, 1964, HZA; Irving Howe to HZ, Oct. 15, 1964, HZA; Hogan, *Minds*, ch. 8–9; Ransby, *Baker*, ch. 11; Brown-Nagin, *Courage*, 340–43; *Boston Traveler*, June 24, 1964; HZ, "Don't Call Students Communists," *Boston Globe*, Nov. 19, 1965.

10. HZ, "The South Revisited," *Nation*, Mar. 20, 1965; HZ, untitled 9 pp. ms. [1965], Lynd Papers, SHSW; Andrew Kopkind, "New Radicals in Dixie," *New Republic*, Apr. 1, 1965; Staughton Lynd, "Coalition Politics or Nonviolent Revolution?" June–July 1965, *Liberation*; Peter Osnos, "Getting Negroes to Register in the South More Than a Legal Problem," *I.F. Stone's Weekly*, 13, 1965; HZ to Lynn Nesbit, Mar. 1, 1965, HZA.

11. I take this argument from my essay "Black Power and the American Radical Tradition" (henceforth Duberman, "Radical") in *Dissent: Explora-*

tions in the History of American Radicalism, Alfred F. Young, ed., Northern Illinois Univ. Press, 1968.

12. HZ, "Negroes and Vietnam," *Commonweal*, Feb. 18, 1966; HZ, *Neutral*, ch. 8; Mark Philip Bradley and Marilyn B. Young, *Making Sense of the Vietnam Wars*, Oxford, 2008, and especially the Fredrik Logevall article, "There Ain't No Daylight: Lyndon Johnson and the Politics of Escalation"; David Elliott, *The Vietnamese War*, Sharpe, 2003; Christian G. Appy, *Working-Class War* (henceforth Appy, *War*), Univ. of North Carolina Press, 1993; Murray Polner and Jim O'Grady, *Disarmed and Dangerous* (henceforth Polner/O'Grady, *Disarmed*); Basic Books, 1997; Michael S. Foley, *Confronting the War Machine* (henceforth Foley, *Confronting*), Univ. of North Carolina Press, 2003; Charles DeBenedetti, *An American Ordeal: The Antiwar Movement of the Vietnam Era*; HZ, "Negroes and Vietnam," *Commonweal*, Feb. 18, 1966.

13. HZ, "Don't Call Students Communists When They Protest Against the Vietnam War," *Boston Globe*, Oct. 24, 1965; Foley, *Confronting*, 30–31; Appy, *War*, ch. 1; Polner/O'Grady, *Disarmed*, chs. 6, 8–9; Hogan, *Minds*, appendix H; Chris Myers Ash, *The Senator and the Sharecropper* (henceforth Asch, *Senator*), The New Press, 2008.

14. Martin Duberman, *A Saving Remnant: The Radical Lives of Barbara Deming and David McReynolds* (henceforth Duberman, *Saving*), The New Press, 2011, 90–91; HZ, "Should Civil Rights Workers Take a Stand on Vietnam?" *Village Voice*, Aug. 30, 1965; Young, *Vietnam*, 62–63; Leslie Dunbar, 4 pp. ms., Sept. 14, 1965, Lynd Papers, SHSW; Hogan, *Minds*, 291–92, n. 31, 391–92; Asch, *Senator*, 231–33, fn. 21, 341; John Lewis to HZ, n.d. (1965), HZA; HZ to Muriel Tillinghast, Sept. 30, 1965, HZ to *New York Times* articles editor, [July?] 1965, in which he flatly states that "the overwhelming sentiment in SNCC [is] against American policy," Lynd Papers, SHSW.

15. HZ to Norman Cousins, July 10, 1965, Skillin to HZ, Dec. 10, 1965, Lynd Papers, SHSW; *New York Times*, May 24, 1966; "What's Happening in SNCC?" June 3, 1966, HZA; Stokely Carmichael, "What We Want," *New York Review of Books*, Sept. 22, 1966; C.E. Wilson, "Black Power and the Myth of Black Racism," *Liberation*, Sept. 1966; editorial, *Nation*, June 6, 1966; Lewi Tonks to Ruby Doris Robinson, June 12, 1966, HZA; "Black Power," *New Republic*, June 18, 1966; Lynd to HZ, July 8, 1966, HZA; memo from Elizabeth Sutherland of SNCC's New York office, "Press Survey, May 17–August 17, 1966," HZA; Carmichael speech at Howard University, *Barrister*, Oct. 14, 1966.

16. Douglas Dowd to HZ, Feb. 21, 1966, Yoshiyuki Tsurumi to HZ, Apr. 30, 1966, HZ to Roz and Jeff, 5 letters, some undated, [June–July, 1966], HZA; HZ, "Setting the Moral Equation," *Nation*, Jan. 17, 1966; Arthur Schlesinger Jr., "A Middle Way Out of Vietnam," *New York Times Magazine*, Sept. 18, 1966; interviews with Anthony Arnove and Will Kabat-Zinn, 2011.

17. HZ, *Vietnam: The Logic of Withdrawal*, passim, Beacon Press, 1967; Marilyn B. Young, *The Vietnam Wars: 1945–1990*, passim, HarperCollins,

1991; HZ, "The Healthful Use of Power," *Fellowship*, Mar. 1967; HZ, ms. speech, "The Case for Unilateral Withdrawal," HZA; HZ, "Violence and Social Change in American History," *Boston University Graduate Journal*, fall 1968. Unlike Howard's earlier books, *Vietnam* was a commercial success. It quickly went through eight printings (HZ, *Neutral*, 110–13).

Almost simultaneously with the publication of *Vietnam*, Howard edited an anthology of writings of the 1930s under the title *New Deal Thought* (Bobbs-Merrill, 1966). In his twenty-page introduction, he made his own position on the New Deal clear. It was both appreciative and critical. He acknowledged that much was accomplished under FDR (Social Security, the TVA, minimum wage laws, farm subsidies, the National Labor Relations Board, etc.). He nonetheless regretted that FDR never aimed for a more thorough reconstruction of the social order that would have included national economic planning and redistributing the wealth (HZ, "Beyond the New Deal," *Nation*, Apr. 7, 2008). Howard lamented, too, that the middle class had been given far more help than the poor—blacks, tenant farmers, slum dwellers, and sharecroppers. The New Deal went no further than it did because FDR had no interest in or mandate to repudiate capitalism. Still, Howard's essay preceded the work of other New Left scholars who challenged the extent of FDR's reforms, and it became something of an ur-text for them. A revised excerpt from Howard's introduction appeared as "The Grateful Society," *Columbia University Forum*, spring 1967.

Chapter 5: The War in Vietnam

1. Brown-Nagin, *Courage*, 274–75; Duberman, "Radical," 234–41; Andrew Kopkind, "The Lair of the Black Panther," *New Republic*, Aug. 13, 1966; Stokely Carmichael and Charles V. Hamilton, *Black Power: The Politics of Liberation in America*, Vintage, 1967; Robert Levey interview with HZ, *Boston Sunday Globe*, Aug. 4, 1968; HZ, *Book Week*, Mar. 27, 1966; HZ, "Black Power & American Liberalism" (excerpts from texts of his lectures), *Pratt Alumnus*, fall 1968. As evidence that black power was affirmed by only a segment of the younger generation, when Carmichael spoke at Spelman late in 1968, his reception was raucous and hundreds of students walked out during his talk (Mel [?] to HZ, Dec. 13, 1969, HZA).

2. Jeffrey A. Turner, *Sitting In and Speaking Out: Student Movements in the American South 1960–1970*, Univ. of Georgia Press, 2010, ch. 6; William L. Van Deburg, *New Day in Babylon: The Black Power Movement and American Culture, 1965–1975*, Univ. of Chicago Press, 1992; Bayard Rustin, "Black Power and Coalition Politics," *Commentary*, Sept. 1966; Howard's lengthy taped interview with Carmichael is in HZA; that liberals were not all soulless compromisers, see David Farber, "The Radical Sixties," *Reviews in American History* 39 (2011).

3. HZ, *Neutral*, ch. 10; Murray Polner and Jim O'Grady, *Disarmed and Dangerous*, Basic Books, 1997; HZ, "The Petty Route Home," *Nation*, Apr. 1, 1968; HZ to Roz, Feb. 3, 8, 1968, HZ ms. notes about trip, Ray Mungo telegram to Roz, Feb. 13, 1968, HZA; Berrigan to "Dear Friends," Mar. 3, 1968, Berrigan to Dave [Ronk] and Howard, Aug. 6, 1968, Berrigan Papers, Cornell (henceforth BPC); HZ to Frances Fox Piven, Papers at Smith (FFPS).

4. HZ, ms. "An open letter to the B. U. Community," HZA; *Morning Union Leader*, Feb. 23, 1968; *New York Times*, Feb. 25, 1968; *Hartford Times*, Feb. 19, 1968; HZ, "A Holy Outlaw," *Progressive*, Feb. 2003.

5. HZ, *Disobedience and Democracy*, Vintage, 1968; Charles Frankel, "Some Civil Thoughts About Civil Disobedience," HZ, "More on Civil Disobedience," *Dissent*, Mar.–Apr., 1970, in response to Michael Walzer's "Corporate Authority and Civil Disobedience," *Dissent*, Sept.–Oct., 1969. Among the many reviews and comments Howard got, Jessica Mitford [Treuhaft's] must have been particularly satisfying: "I've just read your book . . . and I think it is splendid. . . . Many, many congratulations . . . I hope it will be read by a million people." For Howard's position on nonviolence, see HZ, *Neutral*, 98–102, and HZ, *Terrorism and War*, Anthony Arnove, ed., Seven Stories, 2002.

6. The "close friend" has requested anonymity; Roz to Pat and Henry West (twice), n.d. [mid-1960s], Howard to the Wests, Nov. 30, 1965, courtesy Wests; interview with Jeffrey Zinn, Jan. 14, 2011.

7. HZ's FBI files, HZA; interview with Jeffrey Zinn, Jan. 14, 2011; HZ, *Neutral*, ch. 9; Duberman, *Saving Remnant*, ch. 6–7; Marilyn B. Young, *The Vietnam Wars: 1945–1990* (henceforth Young, *Vietnam*), HarperCollins, 1991, ch. 11, 12; an undated 3 pp. speech on Robert Kennedy's death, HZA. Myla Kabat-Zinn e-mail to me, Aug. 27, 2011; Howard was himself arrested, along with approximately one hundred other people, for sitting down and blocking buses carrying inductees to the Boston Army Base.

8. HZ, 3 pp. ms. dated Sept. 9, 1968, HZA, describing the Sept. meeting in Paris with the North Vietnamese. When he got home, Howard wrote to Senator Ted Kennedy, n.d. [Sept. 1968], detailing his thirteen hours of talk with the North Vietnam delegation. He offered to make his extensive notes on the conversations available to Kennedy; there's no record of any response.

9. HZ, "Vacating the Premises in Vietnam," *Asian Survey*, Nov. 1969; HZ, "Napalm, the University, and Civil Liberty," 10 pp. ms., HZA; HZ, "Vietnam: The Moral Equation," and HZ, "The Prisoners: A Bit of Contemporary History," originally published in the *Nation*, were reprinted in HZ, *The Politics of History* (henceforth HZ, *Politics*), Univ. of Illinois Press, 1970; 7 pp. ms. of HZ speech on Moratorium Day, Oct. 15, 1969, HZA.

10. This and the following paragraph are partly taken from my essay "Vietnam and American Foreign Policy," *Village Voice*, May 11, 1967, reprinted in Duberman, *Left Out*, South End, 2002; Young, *Vietnam*, 239–41; HZ, "Federal Bureau of Intimidation," *Covert Action*, winter 1993–94.

Chapter 6: Writing History

1. Christopher Chandler, "Black Panther Killings in Chicago," *New Republic*, Jan. 10, 1970; John Kifner, *The Story of the Murder of Fred Hampton*, *Scanlan's* [1970].

2. Some of the critical documents that inform the following discussion of the 1969 AHA meeting are: "Minutes of the Annual Business Meeting, December 28–29," *AHA Newsletter*, Feb. 1970; Lynd to "Friends," Feb. 26, 1970, Rumbarger to HZ, Feb. 2, 1970, HZ to Fairbanks, draft, n.d., HZA; "Toward History: A Reply to Jesse Lemisch," and Lemisch, "New Left Elitism: A Rejoinder," *Radical America*, Sept.–Oct. 1967; Eugene D. Genovese, "Abolitionist," *New York Review of Books*, Sept. 1968; HZ, "The Case for Radical Change," *Saturday Review*, Oct. 18, 1969; Lynd to HZ, et al., Apr. 19, 1970, Lynd Papers, SHSW; Newsletter of the Radical Historians' Caucus, Spring 1970; David Donald, "Radical Historians on the Move," *New York Times*, July 19, 1970; Lynd, "Intellectuals, the University, and the Movement"; Lynd, "The Responsibility of Radical Intellectuals," *NUC Newsletter*, May 24, 1968, with Lemisch's response, "Who Will Write a Left History of Art While We Are All Putting Our Balls on the Line?"; Lemisch, "2.5 Cheers for Bridging the Gap Between Activism and the Academy," in Downs and Manion, *Taking Back the Academy* (2004), and Lemisch paper, "History at Yale in the Dark Ages, 1953–76," AHA, 2007; Lemisch, *On Active Service in War and Peace*, New Hogtown Press, 1975; Jonathan M. Weiner, "Radical Historians and the Crisis of American History, 1959–80," *Journal of American History*, Sept. 1989; Lemisch to me, July 3, 4, 20, 2010, May 10, Sept. 20, 2011, in my possession, Al Young to me, Aug. 17, 20, 2010, in my possession, Lynd to me, Aug. 21, 23, 25, 2010, in my possession.

3. Lynd to me, Aug. 21, 23, 25, 2010, in my possession; Mirra, *Lynd*, 129; Eugene D. Genovese, "Abolitionist," *New York Review of Books*, Sept. 26, 1968; Jim O'Brien, "'Be Realistic, Demand the Impossible . . .'," *Radical History Review*, winter 2002; Jesse Lemisch to me, July 20, 21, 2010, Sept. 20, 2011; me to Lemisch, July 20, 2010, in my possession. Earlier, in 1961–62, Staughton had been brought to the Yale campus for a job interview. The professor who showed him around advised him not to leave his briefcase in the car because they were in "darktown," and not to consider buying a home in a certain suburb because "the sons of Abraham are numerous there" (Lynd to me, Aug. 23, 2010).

4. "Minutes of the Annual Business Meeting," *AHA Newsletter*, Feb. 1970; Mirra, *Lynd*, 150–65; Peter Novick's splendid *That Noble Dream*, Cambridge Univ. Press, 1988, 435–38; draft letter HZ to Fairbanks, n.d., HZA; *Newsletter of the Radical Historians' Caucus*, Spring 1970; David Donald, "Radical Historians on the Move," *New York Times*, July 19, 1970; Fairbank to HZ, n.d. [1970], Lynd to HZ, et al., Apr. 19, 1970, Palmer to Lynd, Jan. 23, 1970, Lynd to Palmer, Feb. 5, 24, 1970, Lynd to "Friends," Feb. 26, 1970—all

in HZA; Jim O'Brien, "'Be Realistic, Demand the Impossible': Staughton Lynd, Jesse Lemisch, and a Committed History," *Radical History Review*, winter 2002; Carl Mirra, "Forty Years On: Looking Back at the 1969 Annual Meeting," *Perspectives on History*, Feb. 2010.

5. HZ, "Objections to Objectivity," *Z Magazine*, Oct. 1989; Ronald Radosh, "Historian [Arthur Schlesinger Jr.] in the Service of Power," *Nation*, Aug. 6, 1977, "Boorstin," *Nation*, Sept. 26, 1987; HZ, "Born Yesterday," *Tikkun*, May 2002; HZ, *The Politics of History*, Univ. of Ill. Press, 1970. Some of the more significant reviews: David Leonard, *Harvard Educational Review*, May 1971; Herbert Aptheker, *Political Affairs*, Oct. 1970; Gerald W. McFarland, "Notes on the New Left Historians," *Soundings*; Robert Allen Skotheim, "Two Challenges to Historians," *Historian*, May 1971; David Osher, *Win*, Oct. 15, 1970; George M. Dennison, *Rocky Mountain Social Science Journal*, Apr. 1971.

6. Young, *Vietnam*, 235, 245–48; Orville Schell, "Cambodian Civil War," *New Republic*, June 6, 1970; Henry Kamm, *Cambodia*, Arcade, 1998; Rick Perlstein, *Nixonland*, 2008; Cook, Haseltine, and Galston, "What Have We Done to Vietnam?" *New Republic*, Jan. 10, 1970; *Boston Globe*, Dec. 5, 1970; HZ, speech excerpt? n.d. [1970?], HZA; HZ, handwritten notes, n.d. [1970?], HZA; HZ, "The Art of Revolution," Oct. 1970, HZA; Zinn FBI files.

7. *Newsweek*, May 4, 1970; *Boston Herald Traveler*, Jan. 23, 1971; *New York Times*, May 9, 1971; Polner and O'Grady, *Disarmed*, ch. 11; Zinn FBI files; Dan Berrigan, "From the Underground #1," HZA; HZ to Dan, Aug. 15, 1970, a second one n.d., Roz to Dan, Mar. 6, 1972, Dan to HZ, Nov. 22, 1970, Feb. 19, 1971, Berrigan Papers, Cornell.

8. *Boston Globe*, May 9, 10, 1971;*Washington Post*, May 5, 1971; transcript of HZ's May 1971 speech, HZA.

9. Daniel Ellsberg, *Secrets*, Penguin, 2002, 24–25; HZ, *Neutral*, ch. 12; Young, *Vietnam*, ch. 12–13; Sophie Quinn-Judge, "Through a Glass Darkly," 111–34, Lien-Hang T. Nguyen, "Cold War Contradictions," 219–49, Mark Philip Bradley and Marilyn B. Young, *Making Sense of the Vietnam Wars*, Oxford, 2008; HZ, "The First Major Rebel," *American Report*, July 2, 1971; HZ, "Pentagon Papers: Break the Circle," *Phoenix*, June 29, 1971; HZ, "Testifying at the Ellsberg Trial," *Real Paper*, Apr. 11, 1973. Howard and Chomsky together edited *The Pentagon Papers* in the Senator Mike Gravel edition, along with a fifth volume of essays analyzing their meaning (courtesy Arnove), Beacon, 1971. I'm grateful to Leon Friedman for the information about the Halperin wiretap (Friedman was his lawyer).

Chapter 7: Silber Versus Zinn

1. Lynd to "Friends," Feb. 26, 1970, HZA; interview with Bob Cohen, Aug. 31, 2010; *Daily Free Press* (BU student newspaper), Mar. 16, 1972; HZ,

"Silber, BU and the Marines," *Boston Phoenix*, Apr. 12, 1972, reprinted in the *BU News*, Apr. 20, 1972; Silber to "Colleagues," May 23, 1973; HZ, "Freedom Where It Counts," *Civil Liberties Review*, fall 1973.

2. *Postwar America* (Bobbs-Merrill, 1973) wasn't widely reviewed, and the few reviews that did appear were largely negative; see, as an example, William L. O'Neill, *Progressive*, June 1973.

3. Silber to "Dear Colleague," May 9, 1975, HZA. My discussion of labor relies heavily on Jefferson Cowie's fine study *Stayin' Alive: The 1970s and the Last Days of the Working Class*, The New Press, 2010.

4. *Evening Star* (Washington, D.C.), Nov. 2, 1972; HZ, draft of a 1972 speech, HZA; Young, *Vietnam*, ch. 13; Lien-Hang T. Nguyen, "Cold War Contradictions," in Bradley and Young, *Vietnam Wars*; Myla Kabat-Zinn e-mails to me, Aug. 27, Sept. 12, 2011; interview with Jeff Zinn, Jan. 14, 2011.

5. My interview sources on this subject were all close friends of Howard and Roz's and have requested anonymity; their accounts do agree in broad outline. My single most important source believes that the crisis took place in "the early '70s," and in the absence of evidence to the contrary that's where I've placed it. Besides the interviews, there are a few important references to Roz's state of mind in two letters (dated Nov. 10, 1973, Mar. 31, 1974) from HZ to his good friend Frances Fox Piven in her (closed) papers at Smith College (FFPS); I'm grateful to her for giving me access to them.

6. David P. Barash and Judith Eve Lipton, *The Myth of Monogamy*, Macmillan, 2002; Ulrich H. Reichard, Ulrich Reichard, and Christophe Boesche, *Monogamy*, Cambridge Univ. Press, 2003; Stephen A. Mitchell, *Can Love Last? The Fate of Romance over Time*, W.W. Norton, 2002; Michael Kimmel, *The Sexual Self*, Vanderbilt Univ. Press, 2007; Robert M. Sapolsky, *The Trouble with Testosterone*, Scribner, 1997. The discussion of Mitchell's work largely comes from my essay "Jewish Radicals, Effeminacy, and the Rise of Gay Chauvinism," *Nation*, May 20, 2002, as reprinted, with slight changes, in Duberman, *Left Out*, South End, 2002.

7. HZ to Dan Berrigan, Mar. 10, 1974, Berrigan Papers, Cornell; Pierre Dommergues to HZ, Nov. 16, 1973, HZ to Dean Trachtenberg, Nov. 21, 1973, Jeffrey Kaplow to HZ, Jan. 18, 1974, HZA; *Daily Free Press*, Nov. 27, 1973; HZ to Piven, Nov. 10, 1973, Mar. 31, 1974, Piven Papers, Smith.

8. "Statement on Economic Situation of Faculty," Mar. 17, 1975, BU chapter, AAUP; HZ to Dean Trachtenberg, July 28, 1974, HZA; HZ, "Remembering Murray Levin," 2000, HZA; HZ to Piven, June 9, [1974?/5?], Piven Papers, Smith.

9. Piven, Levin, Zinn, "Pursuing Excellence at Boston University," Jan. 23, 1975, *BU News*; John R. Silber, "Poisoning the Wells of Academe," *American Chronicle* [1975]. I'm sure most readers realize that I'm on Howard's side in these debates over education, but just to be sure, see Duberman, "On Misunderstanding Student Rebellion" and "An Experiment in Education," in Duberman, *Left Out*, 197–228.

10. HZ *Globe* columns of Jan. 3, Feb. 7, 20, 28, June 7, 20, Sept. 15, Dec. 2—all 1975, plus Mar. 5, Apr. 16, 1976; Arnold R. Weber, "Labor: Hard Times, Little Radicalism," *New York Times*, June 12, 1975; HZ review of Herbert Gans, "More Equality," *Political Science Quarterly*, winter 1974–75, 854–55; David Brody, *Labor Embattled*, Univ. of Illinois Press, 2005; and especially, Jefferson Cowie, *Stayin' Alive*, ch. 5, The New Press, 2010 (henceforth Cowie, *Stayin'*).

11. HZ, ed., *Justice in Everyday Life*, Morrow, 1974; HZ to Piven, Feb. 8, 1988, Piven Papers, Smith; HZ, "Letters to Zeta," *Z Magazine*, Oct. 1988.

12. HZ, "To Whom in May Concern," Dec. 1, 1974, HZ, "Study Plan for Jimmy Barrett," ms., HZ, diary entry, Jan. 23, 1975, HZ, 2 pp. ms.—all in HZA.

13. Interview with Robert Cohen (who co-taught a course with HZ at BU on Marxism and the New Left), Aug. 31, 2010; HZ, "Repression Goes Back to College," *Real Paper*, May 9, 1973; HZ, *Neutral*, ch. 14; HZ to Piven, Aug. 3, 1974, Nov. 14, 1975, Mar. 28, June 9, 14, 1976, Oct. 24, 1987, #1 Memo from the Chair of the Political Science Department, Mar. 25, 1976—all in Piven Papers, Smith.

14. HZ, *Three Plays*, Beacon Press, 2010; Eric Leif Davin, "Howard Zinn's Anarchist Theater," *New Sun* (Pittsburgh), Oct. 18–30, 1979; Bob Emmett to HZ, Mar. 6, 1978, HZA; HZ to Piven, June 26, Nov. 14, 1975, May 7, 1977, Piven Papers, Smith.

15. Interview with Hilde Hein, Sept. 16, 2010; HZ to Piven, May 7, 1977, June 14, Aug. 24, 1977, June 16, Aug. 16, 1979, Piven Papers, Smith; lengthy correspondence between Pat West and the Zinns, courtesy Pat and Henry West; interviews with Marilyn Young.

Chapter 8: A People's History

1. HZ to Frances Piven, Mar. 20, 1978, FFPS; HZ to Pat and Henry West, Dec. 1, 1978, Jan. 2, 1979, courtesy Pat West.

2. HZ to Piven, Apr. 6, 1976, Feb. 19, Nov. 12, 1978, Jan. 7, 1980, FFPS; Dean Madson to HZ, Dec. 21, 1977, HZ to Madson, Dec. 7, 1977, HZ to Reinstein, Nov. 12, 1978, HZA; booklet [1977] "Who Rules BU?" drawn up by the Ad Hoc Committee for a True University, consisting of some dozen names, mostly of students but also Howard's, HZA; HZ to Wests, Nov. 12, 1978, courtesy Wests; *New York Review of Books*, June 20, Oct. 23, Nov. 6, 1980.

3. HZ to Piven, Nov. 23, 1979, June 27, 1980, Piven to Einstein and Roberts, Apr. 26, 1980, FFPS; HZ to Dean Bannister, May 31, 1979, Silber to Hazel Hopkins, Nov. 28, 1978, BU-AAUP to Dear Colleague, Dec. 1979, HZA; editorial "How to Re-Heat BU," *Boston Globe*, Apr. 6, Nov. 9, 16, Dec. 9, 18, 1979; Laura Barrett transcript of interview with Silber, Dec. 3, 1979

(LBS); O'Brien and Ajemian, "The Strike at BU," *Boston Phoenix*, Apr. 17, 1979; *New York Times*, Dec. 19, 1979; *Saturday Review*, Mar. 15, 1980; Janny Scott, "It's the BU Faculty vs. Silber, and Silber vs. the World," *Real Paper*, Dec. 1, 1979; *Daily Free Press*, Feb. 6, 15, Dec. 4, 1979. An arbitration committee finally gave Howard his raise in the early 1980s (HZ, *Neutral*, 192, 195–96).

4. Cowie, *Stayin'*, ch. 6; W. Carl Biven, *Jimmy Carter's Economy*, University of North Carolina Press, 2002; *Boston Globe*, Dec. 1979; William Worthy to HZ, Jan. 8, 1981, HZA; Silber, "1948–1984: Visions of the Apocalypse in the Post-War Era" (part of a Tufts Univ. symposium, Nov. 18–19, 1981), HZA. I'm indebted to Anthony Arnove for certain critical correctives in this section.

5. Jean Anjon, "Ideology and U.S. History Textbooks," *Harvard Educational Review* 49, no. 3, 1979; Nat Segaloff interview with HZ, July 26, 2003, Audiobooks Today; James Nuechterlein, "Radical Historians," *Commentary*, Oct. 1980.

6. For high school history teachers' experience with *People's*, see "Teachers' Stories," http://zinnedproject.org/why/teachers-stories; HZ, *People's*, 98ff; Woody Holton, *Unruly Americans and the Origins of the Constitution*, Farrar, Straus, 2007; Joseph J. Ellis, *American Creation*, Random House, 2007; George William Van Cleve, *A Slaveholders' Union*, Univ. of Chicago Press, 2010; Jack Rakove, *Revolutionaries*, Houghton Mifflin Harcourt, 2010; Richard Beeman, *Plain, Honest Men*, Random House, 2009; David Walstreicher, *Slavery's Constitution*, Hill and Wang, 2009. Curiously, Howard doesn't cite his close friend Staughton Lynd's early critique of Beard: *Anti-Federalism in Dutchess County, New York: A Study of Democracy and Class Conflict in the Revolutionary Era*, Loyola Univ. Press, 1962.

7. *People's*, 187–92, 198; Eric Foner, *The Fiery Trial: Abraham Lincoln and American Slavery*, Norton, 2010; Interview with Rick Balkin, Oct. 2, 2010; Cynthia Merman to me, Aug. 12, 2010, in my possession.

8. HZ to Piven, Mar. 23 [1981], FFPS; Cynthia Merman to HZ, Mar. 18, 1981, HZA; HZ to Dan Simon, Oct. 12, 1979, Berrigan Papers, Cornell; HZ to Simon, June 16, July 1, 2008, Balkin to Simon, June 23, 26, 2008, Simon to Balkin, June 24, 2008—all courtesy Dan Simon. *A People's History* was widely reviewed. Among the most astute reviews, in my opinion, are: Mike Wallace, "A History of Class, Race, and Sex Struggles," *Monthly Review*, Dec. 1980; Michael Kammen, "How the Other Half Lived," *Book Week*, Mar. 23, 1980; and Bruce Kuklick, "The People? Yes," *Nation*, May 24, 1980. For sheer (conservative) savagery, see Oscar Handlin, "Arawaks," *American Scholar*, 2001, and as a close second: Joseph R. Conlin, *Wisconsin Magazine of History*, winter 1980–81; Michael Kazin's patronizing *American Dreamers* (Knopf, 2011) is also an overstated indictment though its tone is more temperate.

Chapter 9: The Eighties

1. HZ to Piven, Aug. 6 [1980], Piven Papers, Smith. On black nationalism: HZ's lecture notes [early 1980s], HZA. He excoriated Israel's invasion of Lebanon in 1982 as "a particularly horrifying episode," HZ ms on "Israel for *Tikkun*"; HZ lecture notes, "Nationalism and Terrorism," 1983, HZA. In October 1983, the U.S. invaded the island of Grenada, off the coast of Venezuela, charging that it was constructing an airport to assist Soviet-Cuban forces in transporting weapons to insurgents in Central America; Howard spoke at rallies and meetings nearly every day for several weeks protesting the action (HZ to Pat and Henry West, Nov. 7, 1983, courtesy Pat West).

2. HZ to Piven, Aug. 25 [1981], Piven Papers, Smith.

3. HZ to Piven, Aug. 25 [1981], FPPS; HZ, *Declarations of Independence* (later reissued as *Passionate Declarations*; henceforth *Declarations*), Harper-Collins, 1990, 114, 157, 216; the *New York Times*, Oct. 15, 1984.

4. In regard to the discussion of the Carter and Reagan administrations that follows, a large number of secondary sources exist. For me, four works have stood out and in the discussion that follows have deeply informed my perspective: Jefferson Cowie's already cited *Stayin' Alive*, James Peck *Ideal Illusions: How the U.S. Government Co-opted Human Rights*, Henry Holt, 2010, Bradford Martin, *The Other Eighties*, Hill & Wang, 2011, and David T. Courtwright, *No Right Turn: Conservative Politics in a Liberal America*, Harvard, 2010 (Courtwright's full endnotes contain many additional source citations for the various presidential administrations). HZ discusses the Carter and Reagan administrations at some length in later editions of *A People's History*, where he credits Carter with making some effort to hold on to social programs, though the effort was "undermined by his large military budgets" (2003 edition, 571–73). In regard to the feminist and gay movements, the Zinns' close friend Hilde Hein has told me (Sept. 16, 2010), "Howie wasn't interested in the gay movement—never talked about it"; and as for feminism, she commented, "Roz wasn't a feminist either, though more sensitive than Howie to 'equal rights.'"

5. Cheryl Hudson and Gareth Davies, *Ronald Reagan and the 1980s*, Palgrave, 2008. Doug Matthews to HZ, Apr. 3, 1984, Ngo Vinh Long to HZ, May 8, 1984, HZ, ms. "Morality and National Interest: Vietnam and Central America," HZA; HZ, ms. "Conversations (mostly with yourself) While in Jail . . ." HZA; John Silber, "The 'Right' Lesson of Vietnam Applies to El Salvador," *Boston Herald*, Apr. 8, 1983; *New York Times*, May 5, 8, 1984; *Capital Times*, Apr. 12, 1985; HZ to Piven, Mar. 23, Apr. 1, 1980, Piven Papers, Smith.

6. *Boston Globe*, May 9, July 4, 1982; Zinn 1982–83 Merit Grievance, BUC-AAUP; BU Trustees to Faculty, July 11, 1984, BUC-AAUP, vol. 6, no. 1, July 17, 1984, HZ to Chris, Oct. 27, 1984, HZA.

7. Ms. of the Cape Town lecture, HZA; HZ to Roz, July 18, 20, 1982, HZA; Mark Reader to HZ, Nov. 17, 1985, transcript of HZ's appearance on the *CBS Evening News* with Dan Rather, Nov. 6, 1985, HZA; *New York Times*,

Oct. 21, 27, 1985; *Daily Free Press*, Dec. 2, 1985, Mar. 14, 1986; *New Republic*, Nov. 18, 1985; *Campus Report* (AIA), Mar. 1986; HZ, "War in the Classroom," printed in bulletin of the Community Church of Boston, Apr. 1986; Jon Weiner, "Reed Irvine Rides the Paper Tiger," *Nation*, Apr. 5, 1986. It should be noted that AIA is still in existence in 2012, despite Reed Irvine's death in 2004.

8. HZ to Piven, Aug. 25, 1981, June 4 [n.y.], Piven Papers, Smith; HZ to Pat and Henry West, Aug. 24 [n.y.], courtesy Pat West; Balkin to me, March 15, 2012, in my possession.

9. Martin, *Other Eighties*, ch. l; HZ, *Passionate*, 282–288; HZ, ms. "Does Civil Disobedience Work?" [1983], HZ, ms. "What Will it Take to Prevent Nuclear War?" HZA.

10. T.J. Kelley to HZ, Jan. 25, 1984, HZA; HZ to Pat and Henry West, May 1, Nov. 17, 1984, June 22, Oct. 3, 1986, Roz to Pat West, Aug. 28, 1984, courtesy Pat West; *Post-Standard* (Syracuse), June 7, 1984; one of HZ's trial affidavits (Oct. 25, 1987) is in HZA; Ellen Dorsch to HZ, Dec. 12, 1984, Eqbal Ahmad to HZ, Sept. 24, 1985, HZA; HZ and Laura Stewart, "Ideology in the Courtroom," *New England Law Review*, 1985–86; *Daily Free Press*, Apr. 12, 1988; *Boston Network*, Apr. 28, 1988. To give just a few more examples of Howard's many courtroom appearances: in 1986 he flew to Minneapolis to testify for people who'd gone into Sen. Durenberger's office to protest his support for Contra aid (Howard was amazed at the size and spirit of the antiwar movement there), then went on to Kansas City, Missouri, to support a group who'd gone into a missile silo and were facing a heavy sentence. He also gave vital help to the international effort to gain the release of the Pakistani attorney Raza Kazim, who'd been arraigned, along with some 155 others, before a secret military court for "treason" and had collapsed several times during the proceedings. Although some of those charged ended up with life sentences, Kazim was acquitted and released.

11. Roz to Frances Piven, Jan. 27, 1988, HZA; "Roslyn Zinn's Artist's Statement: Introduction to 'Painting Life' (2007)," Jewish Women's Archive.

12. Peter Kornbluh, "What North Might Have Wrought," *Nation*, June 27, 1987; *Daily Free Press*, Apr. 15, 1987; HZ, "Learning by Doing," *Boston Globe*, May 1988.

13. HZ, "Optimistic Uncertainty," *History Handbook* [1988]; HZ, "Failure to Quit," "Nothing Human Is Alien to Me," "Objections to Objectivity," *Z Magazine* [1988], the latter two subsequently reprinted (along with other HZ reprints) in HZ, *Failure to Quit*, Common Courage Press, 1993. In 1986 scholars from around the world (not including HZ) gathered in Seville, Spain, to discuss the so-called propensity of human beings for violence. They subsequently issued a statement—the well-known Seville Statement on Violence—that concluded with "biology does not condemn humanity to war." For a recent summary (including the Univ. of Zurich findings) of some of this anthropological evidence, see Natalie Angier, "Thirst for Fairness

May Have Helped Us Survive," *New York Times*, July 5, 2011. For the greatly expanded literature on altruism, see especially any of the works of Frans de Waal and Matt Ridley. In 2011, Steven Pinker's book *Better Angels of Our Nature* expanded the argument further.

14. Eric Alterman, "Ronald Reagan Superstar," *Nation*, Mar. 7–14, 2011; Kevin Drum, "Ronald Reagan's Real Legacy," *Mother Jones*, Oct. 14, 2011; HZ's teaching notes (Reagan), Mar. 31, [1982?]; Peter Novick, *That Noble Dream: The 'Objectivity Question' and the American Historical Profession*, Cambridge Univ. Press, 1988; HZ, "Objective History a Myth," *Michigan Daily*, Dec. 13, 1988; HZ, "Some Truths Are Not Self-evident," *Nation*, Aug. 1–8, 1987.

15. "Robert Cohen Interview," Aug. 31, 2010; Eilts to HZ, Apr. 25, 1986, HZA; *Christian Science Monitor*, Mar. 20, 1986; *Daily Free Press*, Apr. 17, 1986; HZ to Frances and Richard [Piven and Cloward], Dec. 5, 1986, Piven Papers, Smith.

16. *Daily Free* Press, Dec. 7, 1979; HZ to Piven, June 27, 1980, Fran and Richard [Piven and Cloward], Apr. 16, 1988, Piven Papers, Smith; Mayfield to HZ, Dec. 19, 1980; Mittenthal (AAUP) to HZ, Mar. 15, 1985, HZA; *New York Times*, May 10, 2006; HZ to Eilts, May 16, 1985, HZA; HZ to "the Internal Arbitration Committee," Mar. 18, 1981, HZA; Lynd to HZ, May 17, 1988, HZA; HZ to Pat and Henry West, Nov. 17, 1984, Oct. 3, 1986, Sept. 14, 1988, courtesy Pat West. The letters to HZ on his retirement (in HZA) are too numerous to cite individually.

Chapter 10: The Nineties

1. *New York Times*, Apr. 23, 1989, Feb. 9, 1993; HZ, "Will Mass. Dems Pick an Anti-Democrat?" *Newsday*, July 27, 1990; HZ, "Not Exactly Mr. Civil Liberties," *Lies of Our Times*, May 1993; HZ to Lydon, Dec. 13, 1989, HZA; *Boston Globe*, Jan. 27, 1990; *Jewish Advocate*, Feb. 13, 1990. Silber also published a book, *Straight Shooting*, which Jacob Weisberg characterized (in "Troubling Questions," *New Republic*, Dec. 11, 1989) as "a tired screed against homosexuals, the media, and BU historian Howard Zinn."

2. *New York Times*, Jan. 5, 1991; *Bulletin of Atomic Scientists*, Sept. 1991; *Los Angeles Times*, Oct. 17, 1990; Osha Gray Davidson, *In These Times*, Dec. 12–18, 1990; HZ, *Newsday*, Feb. 12, 1991; *Daily Free Press*, Feb. 6, 1991; HZ speech at Univ. of Wisconsin, Mar. 21, 1991, reprinted as Pamphlet #8 in *Open Magazine*'s pamphlet series; HZ to Henry Klein, Nov. 8, 1991, HZA. For a sample of one of the more positive reviews, see Erwin Kroll, editor of the *Progressive*, in the *Progressive*, Feb. 1991, who thought Howard at his "exemplary best" in sections of *Declarations*. The historian Edward Countryman wrote Howard a disquieting if even-tempered letter pointing out that his discussion of northern land rioters in the eighteenth century had used the ideas

and sometimes even the wording of one of Countryman's articles—without citing it. He added that he had "no intention of going public on this. It would be petty and uncomradely." Howard immediately responded with an apologetic letter and blamed his appropriation on "inefficiency, negligence, oversight." This kind of "borrowing," conscious or not, is fairly common, though Howard's inattention to primary sources may have been partly responsible (Countryman to HZ, Feb. 24, 1989, HZ to Countryman, Feb. 28, 1989, HZA).

3. Roz to Frances Piven, Jan. 20, 1991, Piven Papers, Smith; HZ to Carol and Noam Chomsky, Mar. 22, 1990, Chomsky to HZ, Apr. 16, 1990, courtesy Chomsky; HZ, *Declarations*, 174; Randall Kennedy, "*Brown* Plus 35," *Nation*, May 29, 1989; Adolph Reed Jr., "The Liberal Technocrat," *Nation*, Feb. 6, 1988; Wajahat Ali interview with HZ, Apr. 19–20, 2008; HZ, "A Tale of Two Cities," ms., HZA; HZ to Balkin, Nov. 2, 1996, courtesy Balkin; HZ to Parole Commission, Aug. 13, HZ to Assoc. Warden Gallegos, Sept. 13, 1996, HZA. Howard also spoke out at several public meetings on behalf of the imprisoned Mumia Abu-Jamal.

4. Richard B. Freeman, *New York Times*, July 20, 1986. For a similar conclusion, see a later work: Katherine Newman, *No Shame in My Game: The Working Poor in the Inner City*, Knopf, 1999; Martin Duberman, "The New (1997) Scholarship on Race," in Duberman, *Left Out*, South End, 2002; HZ, ms. "Beyond Voting," courtesy Balkin.

5. Taylor Branch, *The Clinton Tapes*, Simon & Schuster, 2009; HZ, *A People's History*, 2–21; edited transcript of HZ speech, Apr. 12, 1991, Univ. of Minnesota, HZA. Howard refers repeatedly to Columbus's "journal," but as David Henige (*In Search of Columbus: The Sources for the First Voyage*, Univ. of Arizona Press, 1991) makes clear, no such item exists. It was the compassionate Franciscan priest Bartolomé de Las Casas, a firsthand witness to many of the atrocities, who transcribed and added to Columbus's log, so that the extant "journal" is essentially the work of Las Casas, not Columbus. Garry Wills, "Man of the Year," *New York Review of Books*, Nov. 21, 1991; HZ, *Open Magazine* pamphlet, *Columbus, the Indians, & Human Progress*, 1992; HZ to Van Dusen, Feb. 3, 1992, courtesy Rick Balkin. For someone in his early seventies, Howard did a remarkable number of speeches, signings, and interviews for *Neutral*. In October 1994 alone, he had nineteen engagements. One of them, in San Francisco, was at the request of Ron Kovic, the wheelchair-bound veteran of Vietnam who wrote the remarkable *Born on the Fourth of July* (Kovic to HZ, Oct. 28, 1994, HZA); he told Howard "how important and inspirational you have been to me."

6. HZ to Van Dusen, May 16, 1992, HZ to Rick Balkin, May 16, Oct. 25, 1992, Dec. 21, 1993, Aug. 31, 1994, May 2, 1995, May 28, Dec. [n.d.], 1996, HZ to Van Dusen, June 6, 1994, Mar. 15, 1995, HZ to Pfund, June 10, 1965—all courtesy of Balkin; HZ to Hrycyma, Apr. 21, Davison to Balkin, Apr. 28, May 6, Josephy to Balkin, May 7, Bender to Balkin, May 10, Dorman to

Balkin, May 28, Bakalar to Balkin, May 31—all 1993, all HZA; Paul Buhle, "He Shall Not Be Moved," *Nation*, Nov. 21, 1994.

7. Interview with Will Kabat-Zinn, Oct. 15, 2011; HZ to Piven, Feb. 9, 1994, FFPS; HZ to Balkin, Mar. 15, 1995, courtesy Balkin; some fifteen e-mails from Roz to Elly and David Rubin, dated Mar. 7–May 9, 1995, some dozen e-mails between Howard and his son, Jeff, mostly Apr. 1995, HZA; and a few to Henry and Pat West, especially Nov. 4, 1998, courtesy West.

8. Shawn Setaro, "A People's View of Howard Zinn," *Political Entanglements* [1994]; HZ, ms. "The Diverted Left," [n.d., 1994?]; HZ, ms. "Ten Real Reasons to Impeach Clinton," fall 1998, HZA; HZ, *A People's History*, ch. 24; Neil deMause, "Mean, Base, Downright Lowdown," *Z Magazine*, Oct. 1996; Joseph Gerson, "Desert Storms, Deadly Connections," *Peace Review* [1994]; Martha Honey, "Guns 'R' Us," *In These Times*, Aug. 11, 1997; HZ, "A View from the Bridge," *Peacework*, Jan. 1997; Piven to Howard and Roz, May 1, 1995, FFPS.

9. HZ's plays are published in *Three Plays: The Political Theater of Howard Zinn*, Beacon, 2010; his preface to *Marx in Soho* is particularly rich.

Chapter 11: Final Years

1. Edward S. Herman, "Bombing à la Mode," *Z Magazine*, Dec. 1998; Deborah Isser and Suzanne Nossel, "Terror Can't Defeat Terror," *New York Times*, Nov. 5, 1998; Danny Schechter, "War . . . and Peace," *Nation*, Mar. 16, 1998; HZ ms., "On the Iraq Crisis" [Feb. 1998]; HZ to Barney Frank, Feb. 11, Frank to Howard and Roz, Mar. 9, HZ to Frank, Mar. 21, Frank to HZ, Mar. 27—all 1998, all HZA; Frank to Howard and Roz, Nov. 2, 2001, HZA.

2. HZ e-mail to Balkin, Dec. 7, 1997, courtesy Balkin; Saskia Hamilton to HZ, Dec. 18, 1998, May 13, 1999, HZA.

3. *Los Angeles Times*, Dec. 14, 1998; HZ, ms. "On Getting Along," HZA; Raymond Lotta interview with HZ, *Revolutionary Worker Online*, Dec. 20, 1998; Christopher Layne and Benjamin Schwarz, "For the Record," *National Interest*, fall 1999; Ed Herman and David Peterson, "The NATO-Media Lie Machine," *Z Magazine*, May 2000; HZ, "A Diplomatic Solution," *Progressive*, May 1999, HZ, "Words of Encouragement," *Progressive*, Sept. 16, 1999; Wien to HZ, Nov. 1, 1999; Anthony Lewis's column "Proof of the Pudding," *New York Times*, June 5, 1999; Mark Danner, "Kosovo: The Meaning of Victory," *New York Review of Books*, June 15, 1999; Joel Bleifuss, "Truth, the First Casualty," *In These Times*, June 27, 1999.

4. Internet statement from EBSCOhost, Mar./Apr., 1999; Mohammed Al-Obaidi to HZ, Dec. 20, 1998, Feb. 26, 1999, HZA; Danny Schechter, "War . . . and Peace," *Nation*, Mar. 16, 1998; Charles M. Young, "Howard Zinn's Rage Against the Machine," *Rolling Stone*, Oct. 17, 1996.

5. Dan Simon to me, Dec. 27, 2010, in my possession; interview (plus e-mail correspondence) with Anthony Arnove, Oct. 24, 2011; HZ to Diane Wachtell, Sept. 10, 2000, Marc Favreau to HZ, Sept. 29, 2000, HZA; HZ, "A Campaign Without Class," *Progressive*, Nov. 18, 2000; HZ interview with Robert Birnbaum, identitytheory.com, 2001; HZ, *The Unraveling of the Bush Presidency*, Seven Stories Press, 2007; HZ, *A People's History*, 2003 ed., ch. 25.

6. Michael Moore, "Give the Devil a Bone" *In These Times*, June 11, 2001; HZ, *The Unraveling of the Bush Presidency* (44 pages), EBSCOhost.com, June 15, 2010; HZ speech, "Artists in a Time of War," to Mass. College of Art, Oct. 10, 2001, Jeff Zinn e-mail to HZ, Oct. 1, 2001, Marilyn B. Young to HZ, Oct. 5, 2001, Chomsky to HZ, Oct. 29, 2001, HZA; HZ, "Opinion," *Prince George's Post*, n.d., HZA; HZ, "The Old Way of Thinking," *Progressive*, Nov. 8, 2001, HZ, "Changing Minds, One at a Time," *Progressive*, Mar. 24, 2005; *Cape Codder*, Oct. 19, 2001; Anthony Arnove e-mail to HZ, Sept. 28, 2001, courtesy Arnove.

7. Paul Krugman, "Matters of Emphasis," *New York Times*, Apr. 29, 2003; HZ, "A Kinder, Gentler Patriotism," commondreams.org, Aug. 17, 2010; Nicholas D. Kristof, *New York Times*, May 7, 2003; David Wise, "If Bush Is Lying, He's Not the First," *Washington Post Outlook*, June 15, 2003; HZ, "The Others," *Nation*, Feb. 11, 2002; Sharon Basco interview with HZ, TomPaine.com; Theodore Hamm interview with HZ, brooklynrail.org, Sept. 2002; HZ, "A Chorus Against War," *Progressive*, Dec. 16, 2002; HZ, "The Poisons of Nationalism," EBSCOhost.com, May/June 2008.

8. Craig O'Hara e-mail to various people, "The Truth Does Matter . . . Doesn't It?" June 30, 2003 HZA; David Barsamian interviews with HZ, Sept. 18, 2002 Mar. 25, 2003 (all of Barsamian's interviews with HZ [2002–5] are reprinted in *Original Zinn*, Harper, 2006); HZ article in *Peacework*, Sept. 2002; HZ, *Terrorism and War* (edited interviews with Anthony Arnove), Seven Stories, 2002.

9. Program at 92nd Street Y for Feb. 23, 2003, HZA.

10. Zinn, Frank, and Kelley, *Three Strikes*, Beacon, 2001; HZ, *Artists in Times of War*, Seven Stories, 2003; HZ and Anthony Arnove, *Voices of a People's History*, Seven Stories, 2004. Back in 1999, Howard's series of six interviews with David Barsamian was also reprinted by Common Courage Press.

11. Carol S. Steiker, "Why We're So Tough on Crime," *Boston Review*, Oct–Nov 2003; James Q. Whitman, *Harsh Justice*, Oxford, 2003; *New Abolitionist*, Jan. 25, 2010; New Lab 50: Layout 1, which includes a conversation with Dave Zirin; HZ contribution to the symposium, "How to Get Out of Iraq," *Nation*, May 24, 2004; HZ to Tiyo, Apr. 22, 2005, Apr. 6, 2007, Tiyo to HZ and Roz, Sept. 20, 2005, Apr. 25, 2006, Tiyo to Howard, Sept. 29, 2005, HZA; HZ to Balkin, Mar. 4, 2005, courtesy Balkin.

12. Michael Laine to HZ, Nov. 4, 2003, HZA; HZ ms. speech in Paris, Dec. 1, 2003, HZA; Common Ground Travel to HZ, June 28, 2004, Jorge Luna, "Howard Zinn," June 29, 2004, HZA. Howard also appeared on the

Bill Moyers show in 2003—the transcript of the conversation, plus Moyers to HZ, May 15, 2003, in HZA; HZ to Nancy Carlsson-Paige, Feb. 20, 2004, courtesy Carlsson-Paige.

13. HZ to Kerry, n.d. [2004], HZA; HZ, "Dying for the Government," *Progressive*, June 2003, HZ, "What Do We Do Now?," *Progressive*, June 14, 2004, HZ, "Our War on Terrorism," *Progressive*, Nov. 2004, HZ, "Harness That Anger," *Progressive*, Jan. 2005; HZ, "Kerry Needs the Courage to Walk Away from Iraq," commondreams.org, Aug. 17, 2010.

14. HZ, "Bring U.S. Troops Home from Iraq," *Progressive*, Jan. 20, 2005; Marilyn Young to HZ, June 7, HZ to Young, May 4, June 7—all 2005, all in HZA.

15. Transcript of HZ's Spelman speech, HZA; HZ, "The Scourge of Nationalism," *Progressive*, June 2005; HZ to Vonnegut, July 31, 2005, Arundati Roy to HZ, Nov. 3, 2005, HZ to Eduardo Galeano, Nov. 20, 2005, HZ to Alice Walker, Nov. 19, 2005, HZ to Thich Nhat Hanh, June 3, 2006—all in HZA; Roz to Piven, n.d., FFPS. Howard's account of how he, Roz, and Vonnegut became friends is in his *Progressive* column for June 2007.

16. HZ, "A Surgeon's Touch," *Progressive*, Sept. 2005; Lorne Lieb to HZ, May 23, 2006, Chris Moore to HZ, Aug. 24, 2006, HZ to "Al & Lorne," Aug. 24, 2006, HZA; *Daily Variety*, Dec. 11, 2007; *Boston Globe*, Jan. 4, 10, 2008; *Boston Phoenix*, Jan. 18–24, 2008; AlterNet.org, Jan. 26, 2008.

17. HZ to Pat and Henry West, May 30, June 5, 8, 9, Nov. 13, Dec. 3, 4, 2006, courtesy Wests.

18. Interview with Arnove, Oct. 24, 2011; HZ to Pat and Henry West, Jan. 30, 2008, Pat to HZ, Jan. 31, 2008, courtesy Pat West; HZ to Alex MacDonald, e-mail Oct. 1, 2007, HZA; HZ e-mail to Chomsky, Aug. 7, 2007, Chomsky e-mail to HZ, Aug. 8, 2007, Roz e-mail to Chomsky, Aug, 8, 2007—all courtesy Chomsky. I'm extremely grateful to Anthony Arnove for alerting me to a number of errors in my manuscript account of *The People Speak*.

19. Interview with Will Kabat-Zinn, Oct. 15, 2011; HZ to Noam and Carol Chomsky, May 15, 2008, Noam to HZ, May 15, 2008, courtesy Chomsky; *Boston Globe*, May 21, 2008; Pat West to me, Oct. 26, 2010, Pat to HZ, July 30, 2007, HZ to Pat and Henry, July 23, Aug. 29, 2007, Mar. 3, 2011, Hilde Hein to Pat, Aug. 6, 15, 2007, HZ to Pat, Jan. 19, Sept. 9, 17, 19, 2007, Dec. 11, 2008, Roz to Pat, Jan. 25, 2008—all courtesy Pat and Henry West; Rubin's eight pages of tribute by various people, courtesy Jeff Zinn.

20. HZ, "Obama & McCain," *Progressive*, Aug. 2008; HZ, "The Poisons of Nationalism," *Tikkun*, May–June 2008; HZ, "The Obama Difference" and "Changing Obama's Mindset," *Progressive*, Oct. 2008, May 22, 2009; HZ ms., "Obama's Peace Prize," meant for the *Guardian* (UK), Sept. 2008, HZA; HZ, "What Next for Struggle in the Obama Era?" and "Standing Up for Justice in the Age of Obama," socialistworker.org, Nov. 5, 2008, Mar. 13, 2009; Amy Goodman interviews with HZ, Jan. 2, May 13, July 7, 2009, democracynow.org.

21. Interview with Anthony Arnove, Oct. 24, 2011; HZ e-mail to Aris [?], June 8, 2009, Aris e-mail to HZ, June 11, 2009, HZA; Hilde Hein to Pat West, Jan. 25, 27, 29, 2010, Hilde to Pat, Jan. 27, 2010, courtesy Pat West; interview with Henry and Pat West, Sept. 26, 2010; HZ to Nancy Carlsson-Paige, Sept. 22, 2009, courtesy Carlsson-Paige; HZ to Candace Falk, n.d., courtesy Myla Kabat-Zinn.

22. HZ to Pat and Henry West, Nov. 28, 2009; Hilda Hein to Pat West, Jan. 29, Feb. 9, Pat West to Alexandra West, Feb. 18, Myla to Pat, July 27, 29, Jeff to Pat, May 9—all 2010, all courtesy Pat West. Also, Hilde Hein to me, Sept. 14, 2010, in my possession; HZ and others, *Nation*, Feb. 1, 2010. For the details surrounding Howard's death, I'm grateful to Myla Kabat-Zinn (e-mail to me, Sept. 18, 2011).

23. My thanks to Anthony Arnove for underscoring Howard's multigenerational impact. I've deliberately omitted the names of the historians quoted, as well as the publications where their remarks were printed. I justify this on the selfish grounds of wanting to avoid a series of contentious dust-ups. But I assure the reader that the quotations are accurate.

24. Howard's legacy continues through the work of the Zinn Education Project (http://zinnedproject.org/). Working in collaboration with Teaching for Change and Rethinking Schools, ZEP creates free alternative curricula for teachers.

Index